T0342351

THE ANTITRUST PARADIGM

The Antitrust Paradigm

Restoring a Competitive Economy

JONATHAN B. BAKER

 Harvard University Press

Cambridge, Massachusetts
London, England
2019

Second printing

Library of Congress Cataloging-in-Publication Data

Names: Baker, Jonathan B., author.
Title: The antitrust paradigm : restoring a competitive economy / Jonathan B. Baker.
Description: Cambridge, Massachusetts : Harvard University Press, 2019. | Includes
    bibliographical references and index.
Identifiers: LCCN 2018039448 | ISBN 9780674975781 (alk. paper)
Subjects: LCSH: Antitrust law—Economic aspects—United States. | Competition—United
    States. | United States—Economic policy. | United States—Economic conditions—1945–
Classification: LCC HD3616.U47 B33 2019 | DDC 338.8/20973—dc23
LC record available at https://lccn.loc.gov/2018039448

To Susan, Danny, and Alex

Contents

THE ANTITRUST PARADIGM

Introduction

IN THE LATE 1970s, Robert Bork and Richard Posner published two of the most influential books ever written about antitrust law and policy.[1] As with Posner's broader work in law and economics, they were especially concerned that law not get in the way of efficient business practices. They argued that the antitrust rules did just that, harming the economy by systematically discouraging firms from capturing efficiencies. They maintained that antitrust advocates overstated the dangers of market power and sacrificed too much to prevent it. The two Chicago school lawyers proposed eliminating some rules and modifying others to make them less restrictive.[2]

Bork and Posner wrote amid political conditions favorable to their deregulatory impulse. Ronald Reagan's popularity was rising, and he would, in short order, win the presidency by promising to rescue the U.S. economy from state strangulation. Voters, politicians, officials, and courts were increasingly receptive to Bork and Posner's efficiency arguments, both on their intrinsic merits and to reduce the scope of government. The two lawyers wrote to persuade judges, who make the antitrust rules, except on rare occasions when Congress steps in. And they wrote to persuade the Antitrust Division of the Justice Department and Federal Trade Commission, which make federal antitrust-enforcement decisions. In both aims, the authors were successful. Even before Reagan took office, the Chicago school was making inroads in the courts and enforcement agencies.

For Bork, the antitrust paradox (his title) was that antitrust enforcement had popular support even though, in his view, antitrust law was a policy at war with itself (his subtitle). Bork contended that the antitrust law then in force was based on an intellectually incoherent mix of procompetitive and protectionist premises. Its doctrines could not be other than contradictory—sometimes preserving competition and sometimes suppressing it.[3] His prescription was to eliminate the contradictions, and the inefficiencies they created, by relaxing antitrust rules and their enforcement.

Of course, Bork and the Chicagoans did not know if their agenda would have the intended effect. They expected that relaxing antitrust rules would enable firms to achieve greater efficiencies. Firms would lower costs, possibly passing some of the savings through to lower prices. They would also improve their products and services, and innovate more quickly and extensively, boosting economic growth. But the Chicagoans were making a wager. The bet was that these efficiencies would more than compensate for any increased risk of firms exercising market power. If it worked, consumers would obtain long-term welfare benefits over and above any losses associated with anticompetitive practices.

We now know that the Chicagoans lost their bet. Since the implementation of antitrust deregulation, market power has widened, without accompanying long-term gains in consumer welfare. Instead, economic dynamism and the rate of productivity growth have been declining. The harms from the exercise of market power have extended beyond the buyers and suppliers directly affected to include slowed economic growth and a skewed distribution of wealth. Whatever efficiency gains the Chicago-inspired changes may have achieved have not compensated for the market-power effects of the antitrust deregulation they sought.

Market power has widened for multiple reasons. One is the Chicago school reforms to the antitrust laws themselves. Another has been the changing technological landscape of the economy. The information technology (IT) giants that now top the financial markets' valuation charts did not exist when Bork and Posner wrote their books. And firms in all sectors are investing in IT. As it grows, the IT economy raises a host of novel and challenging competitive issues, particularly with respect to innovation. Resolving these issues appropriately takes on an out-of-size importance: the information technology sector continues to innovate while productivity growth has been slowing overall.

Information technology has transformed many industries for the better, but it also gives firms new ways to limit competition and exercise market power. Businesses can use computerized algorithms to set high prices in coordination with their rivals. Google and Facebook's dominance of Internet advertising and Amazon's leading share of online shopping, potentially protected from competition by network effects and economies of scale, could give those firms the power to extract excessive fees from manufacturers and service providers seeking to reach prospective customers. IT giants may be able to forestall challenges from new competitors by acquiring potential rivals before they become market adversaries, as perhaps happened with Facebook's acquisition of Instagram.

In response, the need for stronger antitrust enforcement has become more politically prominent. "In every corner of our economy, competition is increasingly choked off," Senator Elizabeth Warren stated in 2017. "Airlines, banking, health care, pharma, agriculture, telecom, tech—in industry after industry, a handful of giant corporations control more and more and compete less and less. . . . It is time to do what Teddy Roosevelt did: pick up the antitrust stick again."[4] The Obama White House pointed to indicators of declining competition.[5] During the 2016 campaign, candidates Hillary Clinton and Donald Trump both sounded antitrust themes.[6] Trump announced plans to block a large media merger, apparently on competition grounds, and suggested that Amazon has an antitrust problem.[7] It has been decades since competition policy has received this much public attention.

Today's antitrust paradox is not Bork's: it is the surprising conjunction of substantial market power with well-established and extensive antitrust institutions. Antitrust doctrines and enforcement actions once thought adequate to protect competition are proving insufficient. Fixing the problem is urgent. The longer that anticompetitive practices persist, the greater the harm to the economy. The more our antitrust institutions fall short, the more politically difficult it will become to fix them. Instead, the public will favor more draconian regulatory responses, such as treating businesses in more sectors of the economy as public utilities when effective competition would have been possible. These could cause dramatic efficiency declines that antitrust avoids.

The Chicago school's failures increasingly cast our antitrust institutions in a bad light. Bork, Posner, and their ilk sought to improve economic performance by reshaping antitrust, and their method for achieving that outcome—economic analysis—is appropriate. The problem is the particular medicine they prescribed.

This book explains how to foster economic competition by strengthening antitrust. I explain why antitrust law should and does embrace technical, economic-oriented analysis in the service of political as well as economic ends. I use an economic framework to identify potential competitive harms from dominant information technology platforms and other distinctive features of the modern economy. I show why we can expect antitrust, by deterring the exercise of market power, to produce the economic benefits that Chicagoans blamed it for stifling.

The five chapters in Part I frame the problem. Chapter 1 presents evidence of substantial and widening market power and identifies the economic harms resulting from its exercise. The chapter also explains how an effective antitrust-enforcement regime benefits the economy by channeling firms toward the pursuit of better and cheaper goods and services.

Economic analysis and history both suggest as much. As Chapter 2 shows, the antitrust regime prevailing at midcentury had solved a central political problem: how to deal with the effects of monopoly power that developed with industrialization. The resulting political consensus has endured for more than seven decades, even through the Chicago-inspired antitrust deregulation.

Yet, as Chapter 2 also explains, our contemporary antitrust paradox works to undermine that political consensus. The chapter shows how a conservative Supreme Court's lax antitrust enforcement threatens to reject the antitrust approach by stealth. We may soon reach a point where the political consensus breaks down, with antitrust effectively replaced by a laissez-faire approach allowing firms to operate with little or no governmental supervision, inviting even greater exercise of market power. Eventually this could create the conditions for a political backlash, resulting in extensive regulation of large firms rather than the restoration of antitrust.

At the moment, we cannot count on the political branches to stand in the way of the Supreme Court. The White House is controlled by the political party that tends to advocate a less interventionist approach to economic policy and Congress is closely divided. Noninterventionism will continue to win the lion's share of campaign-finance support, as large donors and their firms tend to benefit from hands-off market-power regulation.

Our current president seems to invite deal making between the government and individual firms.[8] Chapter 3 addresses three political threats to antitrust that could flow from such activity, regardless of the party in power: partisan misuse, special-interest protectionism, and the development of a vicious cycle of crony capitalism, in which firms with market power exploit it to secure the political power that helps protect or extend it. This further erodes antitrust, creating more market power and so forth. Maintaining norms against direct political influence in enforcement is therefore essential.

In Chapter 4, I explore how antitrust rules balance the costs of insufficiently deterring anticompetitive conduct against the costs of excessively chilling procompetitive conduct and the costs of administration. I argue that substantial and widening market power justifies more interventionist rules and judicial presumptions in the United States. With the growing importance of burden shifting in the formulation of antitrust rules, courts can be expected to rely increasingly on presumptions to structure antitrust analysis. The chapter illustrates how antitrust rules can be reformed to enhance deterrence of harmful conduct by identifying ways to strengthen and supplement the presumptions courts employ when reviewing horizontal mergers.

Chapter 5 takes on nine erroneous arguments against antitrust intervention, including the assumptions that markets self-correct, that the harms from unwise judicial precedents outweigh those of market power, and that antitrust institutions are subject to manipulation by complaining competitors. Such arguments do real damage when they find sympathetic ears at the Supreme Court and enforcement agencies and justify hands-off conduct by those who might otherwise bristle at the anticompetitive activities of large firms.

Part II examines how antitrust rules can address four competitive problems new to the information economy or exacerbated by it: algorithmic coordination; exclusionary conduct by dominant platforms; threats to innovation; and harms to users on all sides of platforms—suppliers as well as customers. Giant Internet enterprises have been charged with monopolizing a wide range of online markets,[9] and corporate investments in information technology, even by non-IT firms, may also be associated with the exercise of market power.[10] In light of these competitive concerns—but also keeping in mind the economic benefits flowing from the IT sector—the chapter suggests presumptions courts should adopt to more effectively deter exercises of market power.

Chapter 6 addresses one possible anticompetitive consequence of artificial-intelligence capabilities we already possess: the prospect that firms will coordinate through pricing algorithms. The chapter explains how that prospect should alter how antitrust laws infer agreement among rivals from circumstantial evidence when firms raise prices in parallel. The chapter also identifies implications of the algorithmic-coordination problem for horizontal-merger policy.

Chapter 7 is concerned with exclusionary conduct by information technology platforms. It surveys a range of mechanisms by which platforms can harm competition—some familiar and others newly enabled by big data. For example, access to detailed information about individual buyers and suppliers may permit exclusion through targeted discounts. The use of price as an exclusionary instrument is particularly worrisome because the Supreme Court has raised the bar for challenges to predatory pricing. The chapter suggests ways courts should employ or modify presumptions to push back.

The cutting-edge nature of the information economy calls for antitrust attention to competitive harms to innovation, not just harms on the more familiar competitive dimensions of price, output, and quality. Antitrust enforcement is called for when business conduct harms competition by suppressing new business models, technologies, or products, but antitrust enforcers must be wary because action against firms engaged in research and development also could chill innovation. Chapter 8 identifies ways that courts and enforcers can do more to deter competitive threats in innovative industries, while limiting the chill to procompetitive conduct. The chapter focuses on threats to innovation competition and future product competition from mergers and the exclusionary conduct of dominant firms.

Chapter 9 considers circumstances in which antitrust law should allow benefits to some economic actors to offset harms to others. This question is becoming increasingly important with the growing prominence of information technology platforms. The question is whether competitive harms to one group of economic actors—which could be suppliers or workers paid prices below competitive levels as well as buyers charged prices above competitive levels—can be offset by linked benefits to other end users. The chapter explains that antitrust law allows benefits to offset harms within markets but not across markets, except as a matter of prosecutorial discretion in merger reviews. Accordingly, platforms cannot justify anticompetitive conduct that harms users on one side by showing benefits to users on another side. That rule sensibly prevents courts from having to engage in impossibly complex analyses and helps protect political support for the antitrust laws. To prevent the rule from discouraging economic growth, occasional exceptions could be made where the benefits are greatly disproportionate to the harms.

Notwithstanding substantial and widening market power, the threatened stealth rejection of antitrust, and novel competitive challenges raised by the IT-infused economy, all is not lost. Chapter 10, the sole chapter in Part III, offers a guide for restoring the antitrust enterprise in the shadow of a Chicago school–inspired Supreme Court majority unsympathetic to changing course.

Doing so will not be easy. It will require progress on many fronts: increased awareness that market power is substantial, widening, and harmful; political mobilization to restore antitrust; leadership from the antitrust enforcement agencies; litigation to exploit the space created by lower courts willing to question the Chicago school; and reliance on economic arguments. The Supreme Court is committed to an economic approach and will only change its antitrust stance if the majority is convinced that doing so makes economic sense.

This book is written for readers with varying policy perspectives. One goal is to challenge the prevailing Chicago approach. Another goal is to show how antitrust can be reformed to improve economic outcomes. In addition, I seek to demonstrate that, even though antitrust law evolves as political priorities shift, antitrust disputes can and should be resolved on the basis of economic analysis. Finally, I hope that readers disposed against antitrust because they believe it does not do enough to curb the political influence of large corporations will come to see antitrust as a step in the right direction. It doesn't eliminate the potential political harms of concentrated economic power, but by enhancing competition, it reduces the threat.

For decades, competition has been on the wane—a trend exacerbated by the growth of information technology. With this trend has come slower overall economic growth and a gaping chasm of inequality. Antitrust can help reverse the trend. It can help our society secure the benefits of a changing economy by ensuring that, no matter what businesses do, they do it in the context of competitive markets.

PART I

The Market Power Paroxysm and the Antitrust Paradigm

Chapter One

Market Power in an Era of Antitrust

S TEP INTO A STORE'S beer aisle, and the choices may seem overwhelming. Yet the owners of Budweiser and Miller control many popular brands and sell nearly three-fourths of the beer purchased in the United States.[1] In part because of their industry dominance, these firms have been able to set prices above competitive levels, exercising market power.[2] A large number of craft brewers have entered in recent years, making the industry look dynamic and competitive. But expansion is expensive, so craft brewers remain too small to undermine the market power of large firms.[3]

Similar stories play out across other industries. Large firms exercise market power unilaterally and collectively. They obtain, entrench, and extend market power through coordination, exclusion, merger, and other means. Firms exercising market power raise prices, slow the rate of innovation and quality improvements, and cut what they pay their workers and suppliers.

These expressions of market power occur in an economy where competition is supposed to be protected by strong and extensive antitrust institutions. In later chapters I look closely at how this strange circumstance came about. First, let us consider the current state of competition in the United States and the reasons why we should conclude that market power is on the rise. All the while, we must keep in mind that, while market power is good for the firms possessing it, its social impact is detrimental. Market power makes money for a few, at the expense of the social good.

A MARKET POWER PAROXYSM IN AN ERA OF ANTITRUST

An Era of Antitrust

The United States is institutionally committed to antitrust. Our business norms support competition and view anticompetitive conduct as generally bad for the economy and the nation. Courts have implemented those norms by developing a rich body of judicial precedents construing the antitrust laws. The two federal enforcement agencies, the Justice Department's Antitrust Division and the Federal Trade Commission (FTC), each have large professional staffs. Since the 1940s, their budgets have generally increased, consistent with the growth of the economy.[4] The major exception, a retrenchment during the 1980s, was followed by a restoration during the next decade. Further, regulatory agencies with authority over the communications, transportation, energy, and financial sectors often seek to foster competition and rely on antitrust principles and authorities when doing so.

This substantial antitrust capability does not lie dormant; enforcement can be vigorous. For instance, the lysine cartel litigation of the 1990s extracted a $100 million criminal fine from Archers-Daniels-Midland. Senior executives served prison time.[5] The government's monopolization case against Microsoft was the most prominent antitrust dispute in recent decades.[6] Some observers credit the government's high-profile case against Microsoft with protecting the emerging Internet from monopoly power,[7] creating space for Amazon, eBay, Google, Yahoo, and others to flourish.[8] The government's successful effort to block AT&T's acquisition of T-Mobile,[9] which protected competition in mobile wireless communications,[10] is yet another important recent example.

These were all federal cases, but antitrust enforcement happens at the state level as well, where officials implement both federal and state competition statutes. Consumers and firms victimized by anticompetitive conduct also can bring suit privately, benefiting from the expertise of an active plaintiff's antitrust bar. Although the number of private cases declined steeply during the 1980s, it has been growing since.[11]

Antitrust norms, especially the objection to collusive conduct, are consistently endorsed and upheld by enforcers and courts, regardless of political affiliation.[12] These norms have spread throughout the world, particularly since the 1990s, with the aid of a growing global antitrust community. Annual attendance at the spring meeting of the American Bar Association's Section of Antitrust Law—the premier gathering in the field—now exceeds 3,000, a threefold increase over the low ebb in the late 1980s. Several new academic journals dedicated to antitrust law, economics, and policy were launched in the last decade.

Antitrust enforcement has undoubtedly discouraged a great deal of anti-competitive conduct by businesses.[13] By contrast, when enforcement is lax, the substantial and long-lasting exercise of market power follows.[14] The most telling example was the period of ineffectual federal antitrust enforcement during the late nineteenth and early twentieth century. In 1895 the Supreme Court carved a loophole into the Sherman Act, then only five years old, triggering a huge wave of industrial consolidation. Rival manu-facturers across numerous industries combined into dominant firms that ex-ercised monopoly power.[15] Studies demonstrate successful, if imperfect, coor-dination in the steel, bromine, railroad, and petroleum-refining industries, as well as harmful exclusionary behavior by Standard Oil and American Tobacco.[16]

Something similar happened during the Great Depression, when Congress effectively suspended the antitrust laws. The National Industrial Recovery Act, which was in force from mid-1933 to mid-1935, allowed industries to develop "Codes of Fair Competition." In practice, these codes freed busi-ness from antitrust prohibitions.[17] A number of industries, including steel and brewing, engaged in collusive conduct. Firms fixed prices by setting mini-mums, prohibiting sales below average cost, prohibiting capacity expansion, or outlawing secret and selective price cutting.[18] Coordination persisted long after the statute was declared unconstitutional.[19]

Substantial and Widening Market Power

In spite of the scope and depth of antitrust norms, precedents, and institu-tions, there are many reasons to think that sellers now exercise substantial market power and that the exercise of market power has been widening for decades—extending to more markets, increasing in importance within mar-kets, or both.[20]

As sellers, firms exercise market power in output markets by raising prices or altering other terms of trade adversely to buyers (their customers), rela-tive to what would prevail in a competitive market.[21] Seller market power is called monopoly power.[22] Monopoly power may be exercised on a range of competitive dimensions—most obviously by raising prices, but also, for example, by reducing quality or convenience, modifying product features, and altering the geographic locations and product niches served.

The definition of buyer market power is analogous. Firms exercise market power in their input markets when they lower prices or alter terms of trade adversely to sellers relative to what would prevail with competition. Buyer market power is called monopsony power. While seller market power has been more extensively studied, many of the reasons for concern about its exercise also apply to buyers. I discuss the problem of monopsony more extensively in Chapter 9.[23]

Below, I offer nine reasons to believe that market power is on the rise in the United States and that it is a problem for the national economy. None are decisive individually, but their potential infirmities are not the same. So collectively, they make a compelling case.

Insufficient Deterrence of Anticompetitive Coordinated Conduct

The Department of Justice uncovers criminal price-fixing and market-division cartels at a steady rate, year after year.[24] On the one hand, this demonstrates successful enforcement. On the other, it shows that cartels continue forming in spite of substantial enforcement effort. Which is it? Evidence suggests that penalties for collusion, including treble damage awards to victims, are systematically low.[25] At the same time, there is little evidence suggesting that enforcement systematically chills procompetitive conduct or induces excessive expenditures on antitrust compliance. Hence, we should conclude that the stable rate of cartel prosecutions indicates insufficient deterrence.[26] Enforcement actions are happening, which is all to the good, but their impact is too little to discourage as much collusion as we should deter.

Cartels should be subject to greater scrutiny because they are indefensible from a competitive standpoint. They have little or no procompetitive justification. A recent survey concludes that the total overcharge to U.S. buyers from seventy-five cartels sanctioned between 1990 and 2010 was $182 billion, for an annual overcharge of $8.7 billion.[27] Because cartels last 8.1 years on average,[28] these figures imply that if the sample is representative, cartels are formed at a stable rate, and the annual probability of cartel detection is stable, then 28.9 cartels are active at any one time; the average cartel overcharges U.S. buyers by about $300 million annually; 3.6 cartels are detected each year; and the $8.7 billion annual overcharge will continue as existing cartels are sanctioned and new cartels are formed.[29]

Even more troubling, cartels prosecuted by the Justice Department are probably only the tip of a large market-power iceberg arising from coordinated conduct among oligopolists. It is probably substantially easier to deter express price fixing and market division, which are subject to criminal prosecution, than it is to deter tacit collusion that leads to higher prices. Hence it is reasonable to infer from the steady stream of cartel prosecutions that the exercise of market power arising from anticompetitive coordinated conduct is common in oligopoly markets generally. One case in point: a recent study finds that coordination between the brewing behemoths MillerCoors (now owned by Molson Coors Brewing Co.) and Anheuser-Busch InBev SA/NV raised beer prices by at least 6 percent after Miller and Coors joined forces in 2008.[30]

Insufficient Deterrence of Anticompetitive Mergers

A recent study of mergers carried out between rival manufacturing firms between 1998 and 2006 finds that those deals systematically increased price-cost margins at acquired plants without reducing costs. This suggests that the lost competition from horizontal mergers—the acquisition of one firm by another in the same market—generally resulted in higher prices.[31] That conclusion is supported by another recent study of horizontal mergers involving nearby plants producing ready-to-mix concrete, which finds that the harm from higher prices was not offset by higher productivity at acquired plants.[32] Other studies show that those horizontal mergers that were deemed close calls by the two federal antitrust-enforcement agencies turned out to harm competition on average.[33]

Acquiring firms systematically exaggerate the efficiencies from their deals,[34] which may explain why many harmful mergers between rivals are proposed. For example, a book-length analysis finds that media moguls "relentlessly undertake inherently foolish deals or overpay for ones that might have made sense at a different price."[35] This tendency also suggests that the enforcement agencies are, on average, giving too much credit to merging firms' procompetitive justifications.

Insufficient Deterrence of Anticompetitive Exclusion

Antitrust rules today insufficiently deter exclusionary practices that harm competition by raising rivals' costs or limiting rivals' access to customers.

These practices include destroying rivals' distribution facilities, fraudulently acquiring patents, redesigning upstream products to create incompatibilities with those of downstream rivals, engaging in sham litigation or manipulation of regulatory schemes, refusing to sell key inputs to downstream rivals or to distribute rivals' products, contracting with key sellers and distributors of inputs to prevent them from dealing with rivals, refusing to deal with firms that supply rivals or distribute rivals' products, acquiring suppliers or distributors to foreclose rivals' access to inputs, tying complementary products together while rivals' products are unintegrated, contracting with suppliers to obtain the benefits of any discounts they offer rivals (which prevents competitors from gaining a competitive advantage), and responding aggressively to entry in one market in order to deter entry in other markets.[36]

Many exclusionary practices are implemented through vertical agreements, also known as vertical restraints. (Agreements between rivals are horizontal, while those between firms and their suppliers, distributors, or customers are vertical.[37]) Indeed, most antitrust cases alleging anticompetitive exclusion are framed as challenges to vertical agreements or as monopolization, which is often achieved through vertical conduct. Thus antitrust rules governing vertical practices and monopolization reflect judicial attitudes toward exclusion.

In the late 1970s through the early 1990s, the Supreme Court targeted exclusionary-conduct rules for relaxation. Court decisions loosened the rule governing nonprice vertical restraints, raised barriers to plaintiffs seeking to prove predatory pricing, made it harder to challenge resale price maintenance, and made it more difficult for rivals to bring antitrust suits.[38] Taking these cues, lower courts modified the rule governing exclusive dealing.[39] Most of these changes remain in force today. Whether or not the prior rules were too strict, decisions from the late 1970s onward likely went too far toward relaxation,[40] at times conferring de facto legality on exclusionary conduct.[41]

The conclusion that exclusionary practices are insufficiently deterred is supported by evidence showing that prices were higher and output lower in U.S. states that allow resale price maintenance.[42] In states where this vertical practice is allowable subject to rule-of-reason review, which evaluates the actual or likely competitive effects of given instances of the challenged conduct, consumers were worse off relative to those in states where resale price maintenance is banned outright.[43] Some interpret prior systematic empirical studies of vertical practices as counseling against enforcement, but, as I detail in Chapter 5, this interpretation is flawed. It is based in part on studies of nonoligopoly markets, which are not where antitrust enforcement is concentrated. And importantly, these studies do not account for the possibility that anticompetitive uses of vertical agreements were deterred by past antitrust rules. Unlike the prior analyses, the resale price maintenance study convincingly rules out the deterrence explanation. In addition, the conclusion that exclusionary practices are insufficiently deterred is consistent with evidence showing that more than one-quarter of international cartels have used vertical restraints to support collusion: the restraints helped the cartelists discourage cheating or entry while keeping their collusive horizontal agreement secret.[44]

Market Power Is Durable

Market power is a concern because it is durable, not just because it is common. The average cartel terminated by antitrust enforcement lasts more than eight years before disruption.[45] A number have survived longer than forty years.[46] Similarly, monopolies and near-monopolies often persist for decades. Well-known twentieth century examples include General Motors, IBM, Eastman Kodak, RCA, U.S. Steel, and Xerox. Dominant firms and colluding firms frequently maintain their positions by erecting entry barriers to exclude new rivals. Collectively, this evidence shows that firms can sustain anticompetitive conduct—overcoming the incentives of cartel members to cheat and the incentives of entrants and other rivals to compete away monopoly profits—for long periods of time.

Increased Equity Ownership of Rival Firms by Diversified Financial Investors

Large institutional investors such as BlackRock, Fidelity, State Street, and Vanguard now collectively own roughly two-thirds of shares in publicly traded U.S. firms, up from about one-third in 1980.[47] If the top three financial investors were a single entity, they would be the largest shareholder in nearly 90 percent of firms in the S&P 500 and in more than 40 percent of all publicly traded firms, which account for nearly 80 percent of stock-market capitalization.[48] As a result, it is now typical for rival firms to have common financial-investor ownership. This may be bad for competition.

Recent studies of the airline and banking industries suggest that when rival firms have the same large shareholders, they may refrain from aggressive competition, leading to higher prices.[49] These studies are carefully conducted, and their results suggest a pervasive and serious problem. That conclusion must be considered tentative, though,[50] because the economic literature has not established the magnitude and scope of the problem in the economy as a whole. We also lack clarity on which of several plausible mechanisms leads firms with common ownership to raise product prices in the industries studied. And the studies do not account for the potentially countervailing impact of financial-investor ownership of complementary products. Still, this evidence, combined with the growth and widespread nature of common ownership of rival firms, raises the troubling possibility that financial investors are creating a pervasive source of market power.

The Rise of Dominant Information Technology Platforms

Many information technology (IT) firms that have taken off in the past few decades—such as Amazon, Apple, Bloomberg, Facebook, Alphabet (Google's parent company), Microsoft, and Oracle—have likely achieved their positions,[51] at least in part, through combinations of network effects, intellectual-property protections, endogenous sunk costs, and the absence of divided technical leadership. (Under divided technical leadership, different firms take the lead in supplying and improving key complementary platform components.) These features probably insulate many platforms from competition in some of their major markets, allowing them to exercise market power against buyers and suppliers.

Network effects may discourage entry when incumbent firms benefit from higher customer switching costs or other sources of customer captivity. The need to invent around rivals' intellectual property protections may also discourage entry. When incumbents have made substantial sunk expenditures, the market may not support additional firms at a viable scale, and the absence of divided technical leadership tends to slow technological progress by limiting the incentive of a firm that controls key platform components to allow those components to work with complements developed by other firms.[52] In the face of these difficulties, entrants may succeed by targeting newly developed niches, and some may seek to build on that success by adding capabilities similar to those of incumbents. But, even then, incumbent advantages may enable long-term exercise of market power regardless of whether incumbents also engage in exclusionary conduct or preemptive acquisitions of nascent rivals.

Mordecai Kurz documents that surplus wealth—the difference between firms' financial-market values and the value of their capital assets—has grown hugely economy-wide since the 1970s, probably owing to the growth of market power among firms investing heavily in information technology.[53] Among the seven firms that account for the most surplus wealth are Apple, Alphabet, Amazon, Facebook, and Microsoft. The other two are large telecom suppliers: AT&T and Verizon.[54]

An important study by Jan De Loecker and Jan Eeckhout of all publicly traded companies also speaks to the connection between IT investments and growing market power. The authors created the most sophisticated empirical industrial-organization analysis of market power across the U.S. economy to date. And the findings are striking: the average price-cost margin in the U.S. economy increased substantially after 1990.[55] In the preceding four decades, the mean markup of price over average variable cost (interpreted as a measure of marginal cost and weighted by sales) was usually between 1.2 and 1.3. Except during a decline amid the 2008 recession, the average markup has risen sharply since 1990, reaching 1.67 in 2014. De Loecker and Eeckhout infer a firm's markup trend from the ratio of its output elasticity of supply to the fraction of the firm's sales revenues accounted for by variable costs of production.[56] They find that the mean output elasticity held largely constant over their half-century long sample period, so their inference that markups rose sharply derives primarily from a steep decline in ratio of cost of goods sold to sales revenues.[57]

The study's broad conclusion that average margins have increased since 1990 is persuasive. But there are three reasons to question the precision with which the increase in margins is measured.[58] First, the industry definitions are highly aggregated from an antitrust point of view.[59] Hence, the production function estimates do not account for differences across firms, particularly across firms within industries, including in the way that information technology investments affect how firms produce.[60] Second, other researchers using different methods find smaller average markup increases.[61] Third, the study may overstate markups if low-margin firms systematically exited the sample of publicly traded companies, as through acquisitions by private equity buyers.[62]

The most plausible interpretation of De Loecker and Eeckhout's results is that market power has increased among firms that have made substantial fixed investments in IT.[63] Throughout the economy, firms have made such investments. For example, a wholesaler may invest heavily in IT to support its logistics and make ancillary investments to use that technology effectively. It might tag and track products to better manage orders, use customer-demand information to reduce inventories, integrate its IT system with those of its customers to facilitate ordering, install picking and packing equipment in warehouses, and reconfigure its warehouse space to facilitate the efficient use of that new equipment.

The inference that margins rose sharply is tied particularly to the growth of firms that control large IT and Internet platforms. Such firms tend to have relatively low cost of goods sold relative to revenues. Many of their platforms were created since 1990, so their fraction of the sales-weighted average markup has grown over time. But average margins rose in other industries too, suggesting that IT investments are associated with higher margins beyond the IT sector.[64]

Large IT and Internet platforms have delivered substantial consumer benefits. They have lowered search costs, made communication with friends easier, and improved shopper access to niche products. Their conduct does not necessarily violate the antitrust laws, even when they exercise market power. And the firms controlling these platforms are not insulated from all rivalry. They compete with each other in some product areas, including cloud-computing services, intelligent assistants, and smartphone platforms.

Yet consumers and the U.S. economy as a whole would likely benefit even more if these platforms faced greater competition. In general, for reasons discussed below, greater competition would be expected to increase the rate of innovation, increase the rate at which firms lower quality-adjusted prices, and reduce the potential for harm from anticompetitive exclusionary conduct in markets dominated by large IT and Internet platforms.

Oligopolies Are Common and Concentration Is Increasing in Many Industries

Many industries are oligopolies, in which a small number of firms account for most sales. For instance, airlines and hospitals have become substantially more concentrated in recent decades. In 2005, the United States had nine major airlines, including regional and low-cost carriers; today, after multiple mergers, there are four. A number of studies show that hospital consolidation has led to higher prices.[65] Casual empiricism suggests concentration is also increasing in other industries important to consumers.[66]

Concentration may have risen generally in U.S. manufacturing,[67] though the increases are modest and many industries in which concentration is rising remain relatively unconcentrated. But evidence about trends in concentration in the economy as a whole is less reliable than the evidence tied to specific industries. Studies of economy-wide concentration often use product definitions and nationwide aggregates that do not necessarily correspond to antitrust markets. If geographic markets are regional or local, and many firms do not sell nationwide, the concentration figures relevant for evaluating market power could be substantially higher or lower than the nationwide figures reported.[68] Other evidence involving broad national aggregates is also consistent with rising concentration,[69] but it may actually reflect that large firms increasingly compete with the same large rivals across multiple product lines or regions. Either interpretation would raise competitive concerns: as with increased concentration, growing multimarket contact could facilitate coordination among rivals.

Coordinated conduct is a serious threat in oligopolies for several reasons. First, oligopolists, acting in their individual interest, may have incentive not to compete aggressively. Repeated interaction may help firms reach consensus on the terms of a coordinated arrangement and discourage firms from cheating by exacerbating the punishment that coordinating rivals can inflict. Even if firms do not secure higher-than-competitive prices by identifying consensus terms and committing to punish rival cheating, they may achieve a similar anticompetitive outcome through parallel-accommodating conduct not pursuant to a prior understanding. For example, even without repeated interaction, competition may be dampened when firms find it costly or time-consuming to change their output levels under quantity competition or price competition when production capacity is fixed.[70]

Second, businesses are taught to exploit gaps in antitrust rules to deter entry and engage in coordinated conduct without running afoul of those rules.[71]

Third, empirical economics literature finds that greater market concentration is associated with an increased risk of anticompetitive conduct. This literature relates within-industry concentration to prices—not to profits, the concern of an older and more controversial literature.[72] This risk may arise in oligopoly markets regardless of whether concentration is the product of anticompetitive exclusion, scale economies, shifts in demand, or other factors.

Concentration and the associated threat of market power is not limited to product markets. While product market concentration is associated with the exercise of monopoly power, concentration among firms hiring workers is associated with the exercise of monopsony power, whether unilaterally or through coordination. Labor markets may be concentrated regardless of whether firms sell in concentrated product markets.[73] Recent evidence suggests that many workers are hired in concentrated labor markets and that labor market concentration in manufacturing may be increasing.[74] This evidence raises the possibility that firms exercise monopsony power in many labor markets, depressing wages.[75]

Increased Governmental Restraints on Competition

Another source of market power is increasing governmental restraint on competition. Such restraints include more extensive occupational licensing,[76] the widening scope of what may be patented, and excessive granting of patents owing to inadequate review of patent applications.[77] To similar effect, the competitive harm from "pay-for-delay" settlements—high drug prices arising from the settlement of patent disputes under an industry-specific regulatory framework that delays the entry of generic pharmaceuticals—has increased over time.[78] This trend was halted in 2013, when the Supreme Court made it easier to bring antitrust challenges against pay-for-delay settlements.[79] But the impact has already been felt and will continue to be, albeit to lesser degree.

Lobbying and other political rent-seeking activity by firms to limit competition and boost supracompetitive profits—a possible precursor to governmental restraints—may also be on the rise.[80] One example is the use by drug companies of citizen petitions before the U.S. Food and Drug Administration, in an effort to delay entry by rivals. The number of petitions has "essentially doubled" since 2003.[81]

The Decline in Economic Dynamism

Widening market power is a leading explanation for two troubling economy-wide trends over recent decades: the secular slowdown in business investment[82] and the rising profit share of U.S. gross domestic product.[83] Widening market power also plausibly contributes to the slowed rate at which firms and plants expand when they become more productive,[84] the four-decade long decline in the rate of startups,[85] and the growing gap in accounting profitability between the most and least profitable firms.[86]

These trends are connected to market power because productive firms have less incentive to expand, invest, and innovate when insulated from competition. They can instead maintain their edge by discouraging rivals' expansion, entry, investment, and innovation.[87] Unsurprisingly, economic growth increasingly comes from improvements to existing products by incumbent firms rather than the displacement of existing products by better ones or the creation of new product varieties.[88]

Market Power versus Alternative Explanations

Could these nine factors, interpreted here as suggesting substantial and widening market power, instead have a benign interpretation? The most plausible alternative points to a combination of growing scale economies and rewards to the first firms to adopt new information technologies. But these are unlikely to account fully for the market power evidence.

It is true that technological change has likely increased the importance of scale economies in various sectors of the economy. The efficient size of firms has plausibly grown over time in many industries as a result of the high fixed costs of investments in IT,[89] network effects, and an increased scope of geographic markets attributable to improvements in communications and transportation technologies, superior logistics, and reductions in barriers to international trade.

In addition, the first firms to invest in new information technologies may indeed earn substantial rents.[90] For instance, it took decades for factories to switch from water and steam power to electric power, and, during that transition, firms within the same industry differed in the extent to which they could profitably take advantage of the new technology.[91] Some were locked in to prior technologies by the age of their existing equipment, factory-floor layout, building design, and their success in learning how to use older technologies efficiently. As a result, there were first movers and laggards, and the former were in a position to offer better products or the same ones more cheaply, creating profit opportunities. More recently, IT investments have not taken place simultaneously across industries or the firms within them, creating new profit opportunities.[92] If IT investments do not confer market power, these rents should be temporary. In a dynamically competitive market, they would dissipate as other firms in the same market follow suit, technologically.[93]

As firms experiment with business strategies involving substantial sunk expenditures, that may increase demand—in this case, through IT investments[94]—so scale economies may grow, even in competitive markets.[95] In markets where scale economies are substantial and marginal cost does not increase with output, margins will be high. Under such circumstances, it will be necessary for competing firms to price in excess of their marginal cost in order to cover fixed costs.[96] Where unable to do so, they exit, increasing concentration even in competitive markets.

We probably are not actually observing only growing scale economies and temporary returns to early adoption within otherwise competitive sectors. Such an interpretation supposes that robust competition among large IT platforms, the constant threat of upstarts, the geographic expansion of firms, and the easy availability of financial capital to entrants have combined to limit the exercise of market power throughout the economy. Yet this benign interpretation cannot be reconciled with six of the nine categories of evidence of substantial and widening market power. Anticompetitive coordination, mergers, and exclusion have not been deterred; market power is durable; the marked increase in equity ownership of rival firms by financial investors has softened competition; and government restraints on competition are on the rise.

Nor is the benign interpretation persuasive with respect to the three other factors. Are we to attribute the rise of dominant IT platforms entirely to scale economies and first mover advantages? Doing so fails to recognize those platforms' ability to protect their position by excluding rivals. Is growing concentration entirely benign? Saying so requires ignoring empirical evidence showing that firms in industries such as brewing, airlines, and hospitals exercise market power. We would also have to discount the possibility that fixed expenditures on IT and other inputs, which can increase scale economies and concentration, have also deterred entry and softened competition.[97] Scale economies and rewards to firms successfully adopting new technologies likely contributed to the growth of dominant IT platforms and industry concentration—and to the formation of market structures in which firms exercise market power.

Some evidence for the final factor, the loss of economic dynamism, is consistent with growing scale economies and returns to the early adoption of new technologies in competitive markets as well as with increasing market power. This includes the rising profit share of GDP and the growing gap in accounting profitability between the most and least profitable firms. But other aspects of declining dynamism cannot be reconciled with the benign interpretation.

The issue is that the benign interpretation assumes that profits rise because markets are increasingly dynamic, with higher rates of entry, investment, and business failure. Scale economies yield higher profits because entrants have a greater risk of failure when fewer firms can succeed, and the profits to early adopters in IT are temporary, competed away by new or expanding rivals making their own investments. But evidence shows the reverse: a slowing rate of new entry, declining rate of expansion when firms and plants grow more productive, and secular slowdown in business investment.[98] Moreover, the combination of high stock-market valuations and low interest rates on corporate bonds in recent years suggests that the financial markets view corporate profit streams as less risky than in the past. Yet if markets were increasingly dynamic, as the benign interpretation supposes, those streams would be viewed as riskier. Thus, taking all the evidence into account, growing market power is a better explanation of current economy-wide trends than the alternatives of scale economies and early adopter rents.[99]

Growing market power is also consistent with the appearance of competition. Even firms that exercise substantial market power typically compete for some business.[100] For example, when basic cable-television rates were partially deregulated, cable providers increased rates substantially, most likely to the point where competition from satellite providers constrained further increases.[101] Notwithstanding the appearance of competition among cable and satellite providers, cable providers likely exercised market power. To similar effect, the observation that large IT and Internet firms compete in some lines of business—intelligent assistants, cloud-computing services, video programming, development of self-driving cars, search engines—does not preclude their exercise of market power in other sectors or even some of these lines of business.

The nine categories of evidence presented above show that market power has probably been growing for decades. But many of the reasons to think so became apparent only during the past few years.[102] For the most part, it is recent economic literature that shows insufficient deterrence of anticompetitive horizontal mergers and exclusionary conduct, competitive problems from common financial-investor ownership, rising concentration in major sectors of the economy, and declining economic dynamism. The paradox of substantial market power alongside robust antitrust may not have been evident in the past, but it can no longer be ignored.

WHAT'S WRONG WITH MARKET POWER

Some of the adverse effects of substantial and widening market power appear primarily in the markets affected directly. Others may extend to the economy as a whole in the form of slowed productivity and economic growth, as well as increased inequality.

Harms within Affected Markets

For the most part, antitrust analysis adopts what economists refer to as a partial-equilibrium framework, looking at competitive harms solely within the markets potentially affected by the exercise of market power. From that perspective, the exercise of market power by sellers is harmful in several ways. It transfers wealth from buyers to sellers and creates an allocative efficiency loss. Market power also can lead to wasteful rent seeking along with lessening the rate of innovation and slowing productivity improvements.

Wealth Transfer and Allocative Efficiency Loss

The exercise of market power in output markets leads to wealth transfer from buyers to sellers:[103] when prices rise, buyers are overcharged, and sellers earn supracompetitive profits. Market power also creates an allocative efficiency, or deadweight, loss, because some transactions that would occur in a competitive market are foregone. Though buyers value the product or service more than it costs sellers to make or provide it, no transaction is made. Hence the economy sacrifices wealth—gains from trade—that would have been created had buyers and sellers been able to transact.

The harms from wealth transfer and allocative efficiency loss are most easily described in a market for a homogenous product sold at a single price—perhaps grains, crude oil, raw metals, or industrial gases. But similar harms arise when products or services are differentiated, sold at diverse prices, or when competition is primarily in quality, convenience, or features rather than price, as with branded consumer products, professional services, and transportation. Victimized buyers may experience reductions in service quality and convenience as exploitative: firms competing for business may work to persuade potential buyers, but when it is not easy for a buyer to take its business elsewhere, customer service may suffer.

The exercise of market power by buyers (in input markets, including labor markets) leads to harms analogous to those arising from seller market power.[104]

When buyers exercise market power, suppliers (sellers) are paid too little, so wealth is transferred to buyers. In addition, allocative efficiency losses can arise because resources (inputs) may not be employed in the markets where they are most valued. If the hospitals in a city collude to depress the wages paid to nurses below competitive levels—as has been alleged across the United States[105]—then nurses will be underpaid, fewer will be hired than otherwise would be, some nurses will leave the profession, and others will invest less in improving their skills. Reduced input purchases may restrict downstream production, generating additional allocative efficiency losses. In this example, patient care may suffer.

Wasteful Rent Seeking

An efficiency loss to society from wasteful rent seeking arises when firms compete for the opportunity to profit from exercising market power.[106] That may happen when sellers spend resources lobbying to secure or protect anticompetitive privileges afforded by law. For example, such a privilege might be conferred through certificate-of-need laws, which can enable hospitals to serve a community free of competition. Patents offer another vehicle.

There are also nongovernmental means of rent seeking. For instance, sellers may spend resources to erect barriers to entry. Such expenditures are wasteful: they go to securing a firm against competition, not to developing better, cheaper, or more convenient products and services.

Slowed Innovation and Productivity Improvements

The exercise of market power may have adverse dynamic consequences for productivity and innovation.[107] First, the exercise of market power slows the rate at which firms improve products and production processes and the rate at which they lower costs. The loss of competition reduces firms' incentives to expand markets and take business from their rivals, which they might do by cutting costs and prices, improving quality and features, developing new and better products and production processes, or enhancing the value they offer customers by providing increased variety and better services.

The loss of competition also inhibits productivity-enhancing selection—the tendency of the best products and most efficient producers to win out as products, technologies,[108] business models, plants, and firms unable to price competitively or attract enough customers are forced from the marketplace. Not surprisingly, the modern economic and business literatures consistently and convincingly demonstrate that enhanced competition leads to greater productivity and that the exercise of market power reduces it.[109]

Second, because firms have an incentive to innovate to escape competitive pressures, firms protected from entry and exercising durable market power tend to innovate less. This incentive is important notwithstanding a theoretical qualification emphasized by the Schumpeterian side of a long-standing controversy about the relationship between competition and innovation.[110] That side points out that the exercise of market power could enhance innovation incentives if a firm's preexisting market power reduces the likelihood that its rivals will quickly copy its new products or processes. On this account, a firm lacking market power would not innovate for fear that rivals mimicking its advances would compete so aggressively as to prevent the firm from earning a profit sufficient to justify its investments in research and development (R&D). Some economists suggest that this danger is greater for product innovation than production-process innovation because new products can be more easily copied.

However, this theoretical qualification is unlikely to be important in most markets where antitrust issues arise, because firms making major R&D investments usually have many reasons other than preexisting market power for expecting to appropriate sufficient returns, even with some imitation. The reasons may include protections afforded by intellectual property rights, rapid market growth, scale economies, network effects, the sale of complementary products, and customer-switching costs.

Moreover, even if the prospect of greater post-innovation competition means a dominant firm would expect to earn less by innovating, the firm may still be led to keep investing in R&D for fear of losing out to its rivals, many of which have a strong incentive to pursue new products and production processes in order to steal business from the dominant firm.[111] At one time empirical economists thought that a degree of market power might foster innovation; after all, cross-industry studies found an "inverted-U" relationship between innovation and market concentration. But those studies were not reliable because they did not successfully control for differences in technological opportunity across industries.[112]

Given the unpersuasiveness of arguments for the innovation benefits of market power and the strong arguments for the innovation benefits of competition, we should feel safe concluding that greater competition generally enhances the prospects for innovation,[113] while the exercise of market power tends to slow innovation and productivity improvements.

Buyers, too, can exercise market power in ways that undermine supplier investments in innovation and improved production processes, creating dynamic harms. For example, if cable providers are able to depress the prices they pay for video programming through the exercise of market power in purchasing content, content providers may invest less in developing new programming.

Some might push back on the ground that lost competition is not necessarily a bad thing. True, competition can be wasteful. Competing firms typically make duplicative fixed expenditures. R&D competition often leads to duplication of effort. Excessive entry can occur when incumbents respond to entry by reducing output,[114] when financial markets are subject to "advantageous" selection,[115] and when firms can externalize social costs such as air pollution. If industry output would exceed the efficient level in a competitive market for any of these reasons, then it is possible that the output reduction associated with the exercise of market power would mitigate the efficiency loss to some extent. But there is no reason to expect a perfect offset. Aggregate welfare may end up lower than it would absent the exercise of market power, and even if aggregate welfare increases, consumer welfare may still be reduced.

These qualifications do not shake the overall conclusion. Taken as a whole, the economics literature strongly supports the view that market competition is beneficial and market power is harmful within affected markets, accounting for both static and dynamic effects.

Economy-Wide Harms

Looking beyond the individual markets affected by market power, the exercise of market power is harmful to the U.S. economy as a whole. Although competition operates market-by-market and industry-by-industry, the scope of market power can affect the overall economy. The harms are not limited to the participants in the particular markets in which competition has declined. The exercise of market power may also result in slowed economic growth and increasing economic inequality.[116]

Slowed Economic Growth

The McKinsey Global Institute has undertaken revealing cross-national and cross-industry studies. They demonstrate that differences in competition in product markets across nations are likely as important in explaining variation in productivity and economic performance as are cross-national differences in macroeconomic policies. Differences in competition are probably more important to productivity and economic performance than are cross-national differences in labor and capital markets.[117] National economies do better when competition is both "intense" and "fair," which means that it is not distorted by governmental subsidies to less productive firms.[118] Harvard Business School's Michael Porter, a leading expert on business strategy, reached a similar conclusion from a large cross-national study. Porter found that "vigorous domestic rivalry" in an industry helps make that national industry "gain and sustain competitive advantage internationally."[119] In addition, economists seeking to understand why some nations have grown wealthy consistently find that impediments to competition hinder innovation, growth, and prosperity.[120]

Firms with market power can also slow economic growth by using the political system to protect and enhance their economic advantages, in ways that may not benefit the national economy. This happens when firms and industries secure long-lasting political power through their size and lobbying influence, as discussed more fully in Chapter 3. Their economic and political power then reinforce each other in a vicious circle. Market power gives firms the resources to create and exploit political power, which they use to protect or extend their economic advantages. They then invest some of the resulting rents in maintaining and extending their political power.[121] Conceivably, they could use that political power to induce productive change, but they have a strong incentive to prioritize their own gains, whatever the wider effects.

Increased Inequality

The exercise of market power likely contributes to economy-wide inequality because the returns from market power go disproportionately to the wealthy.[122] Increases in producer surplus from the exercise of market power—that is, wealth transfers—accrue primarily to firms' shareholders and top executives, who are wealthier on average than the median consumer. In a recent year, the top 1 percent of the population categorized by wealth held half of the stock and mutual fund assets, and the top 10 percent held more than 90 percent of those assets. (That figure remains high—80 percent—after accounting for indirect ownership through retirement plans and similar accounts.[123]) In the past, unionized workers may have been able to appropriate some of the profits from the exercise of market power, but with the decline of private-sector unionization, that ability is of limited practical importance. Rather, the exercise of monopsony power in labor markets could further contribute to increased inequality.[124]

A Serious Problem

The harms from market power in affected markets can be substantial. In some antitrust cases, the overcharge to buyers or profits lost by excluded sellers amount to hundreds of millions of dollars—before trebling. These figures do not account for allocative efficiency losses, wasteful rent-seeking expenditures, or harms from slowed productivity improvements or innovation.

The adverse consequences of market power for the economy as a whole are less easily identified and measured. But the economy-wide harms from market power—slowed productivity and economic growth and increased inequality—are at least comparable in magnitude to the costs of business-cycle downturns and conceivably much larger.

Substantial and widening market power creates a serious public policy problem not adequately deterred by our extensive antitrust institutions.[125] This surprising conjunction of widening market power with well-developed judicial norms against anticompetitive conduct and well-established antitrust enforcement institutions challenges us to identify ways that courts, antitrust enforcers, and policy makers can better deter anticompetitive conduct. Later chapters take up that challenge. A range of other public policies— including efforts to improve new and small firms' access to finance, support competition through public procurement, tailor the scope of intellectual property rights to competition concerns, and rethink regulatory frameworks that entrench large incumbent firms at the expense of fringe rivals and entrants—might help to foster competition and undermine growing market power. I do not discount these, but I also do not focus on them. While others pursue these worthy goals, mine is to counter and discourage market power with antitrust enforcement.

Chapter Two

The Faltering Political Consensus Supporting Antitrust

IN 1796 A GROUP of private investors built the Charles River Bridge, a toll bridge, to connect Boston with Charlestown.[1] Thirty-two years later, the Massachusetts state legislature granted a charter to another group of investors to build the Warren Bridge, a nearly identical span adjacent to the first. The Warren, too, was initially a toll bridge and, for a time, the Charles River Bridge was able to compete and remain profitable. But the charter for the new bridge required that toll collection eventually come to an end. When the Warren became free, the Charles River Bridge could no longer cover its maintenance costs.

The Charles River Bridge challenged the chartering of the Warren Bridge in state court. Nearly a decade later, in 1837, after multiple appeals and substantial public controversy, the case rose to the U.S. Supreme Court, which decided in favor of the Warren Bridge.

The Charles River Bridge claimed that its charter,[2] awarded by the legislature in 1786, gave its owners the exclusive right to operate a bridge between Boston and Charlestown for seventy years. By chartering a second bridge in 1828, the legislature had, the plaintiff bridge argued, violated the agreement and so breached the constitutional obligation of states to refrain from impairing contract rights.

The constitutional question turned on an issue of statutory construction: Did Charles River's original charter grant that company the exclusive right claimed? But the legal issues were intertwined with the important public policy question of whether promoting competition among firms would lead to economic progress. The policy issue was critical to the majority and dissenting opinions. One key figure, Justice Joseph Story, defended the Charles River Bridge and its monopoly. Another, Chief Justice Roger Taney, took the side of the Warren Bridge. The Supreme Court held that the legislature had not unambiguously granted Charles River Bridge a right to avoid competition.

Story worried that unrestrained competition would impede economic progress. Who would invest in infrastructure if the state could undermine their profits by allowing others to compete? "If the government means to invite its citizens to . . . establish bridges, or turnpikes, or canals, or railroads," Story wrote, "there must be some pledge that the property will be safe." In particular Story noted that states could effectively punish success by allowing competitors to duplicate any investment that proved its worth. A useful product might become "the signal of a general combination to overthrow [a firm's] rights and to take away its profits."[3] Story undoubtedly also worried that if property rights were not protected in the bridge dispute, the door would be opened to broader mischief when other supplicants, such as hard-pressed debtors, sought legislative relief.[4]

By contrast, Taney embraced competition. If the Charles River Bridge were allowed to collect compensation from the Warren Bridge, Taney pointed out, then incumbents would block the development of innovative rivals. This was particularly an issue for railroads, which often had to follow the same line of travel as preexisting canals and turnpikes. "You will soon find old turnpike corporations awakening from their sleep, and calling up this Court to put down the improvements which have taken their place," the chief justice predicted.[5] In theory, if markets worked well, this shouldn't have mattered. The railroads could simply bargain with their turnpike predecessors, paying them for rights of way. But in practice, bargaining would not be so simple: it would be fraught with delay, impasses, and litigation. Demanding that railroads acquire rights of way from predecessors could be a recipe for seriously slowed economic development.

Taney was right on the policy dispute in *Charles River Bridge v. Warren Bridge,* and for the right reason. New investment, new products, economic growth, and technological development were spurred by competition. Story's fear that investors would be kept away by the threat of a lower return did not materialize. The Court's decision did not stymie investment, increase interest rates demanded by lenders, or impede economic development. On the contrary, the decision promoted growth by reducing entry costs for new firms and those seeking to deploy next-generation technologies in markets already served by others. This is certainly to the good. Over the course of human history, economic growth has substantially improved the well-being of all, including the poor.[6] The poor were perhaps six times better off at the end of the twentieth century than their counterparts at the start, and the middle class did even better.[7] Today, most Americans have access to valuable goods and services that their counterparts in 1900 could not buy at any price, including modern medicine and the health and lifespan it brings, computers and smartphones, washing machines, air conditioners, automobiles, rural electrification, and much more. The Court's procompetition decision undoubtedly helped to ensure the economic dynamism and growth that the United States historically has enjoyed.

The policy argument in *Charles River Bridge* has echoes in contemporary debates over the scope of antitrust enforcement. Following a logic much like Taney's, antitrust laws have long been relied on to prevent conduct that would suppress new technologies, products, and business models.[8] By the mid-twentieth century, courts had largely accepted Judge Learned Hand's view, expressed in the famous *Alcoa* decision, "that immunity from competition is a narcotic, and rivalry is a stimulant, to industrial progress."[9] But Story's vision never died and has lately been resurrected in the Supreme Court's 2004 *Trinko* decision.[10] The opinion defended the opportunity to charge monopoly prices as a free-market incentive to innovate. The temptations of market power, the Court asserted, would motivate the sort of risk taking that produces economic growth. This argument favored noninterventionist antitrust enforcement, not to mention broader intellectual property rights. Implicitly, the court was saying that it trusted private enterprise to generate socially useful outcomes regardless of market structure.

A third perspective on markets holds that they often perform poorly without extensive government supervision. This perspective was advocated in neither *Charles River Bridge* nor *Trinko,* but it has both deep roots and contemporary defenders in the United States. One early American advocate was Alexander Hamilton, who called for a substantial federal role in developing the economy, and particularly the growth of manufacturing in what was at the time largely an agricultural nation.[11] Hamilton's support for assertive industrial policy has parallels in today's progressive arguments for regulating dominant IT firms rather than relying on antitrust enforcement to discourage their exercise of market power.[12]

These three broad approaches—protecting and fostering competition (antitrust), business self-regulation (laissez-faire), and regulation via industrial policy—have been the recurring stars in policy debate ensuing at least since the passage of the Sherman Antitrust Act in 1890. The statute was written in broad and general terms, leaving it to the courts to work out just what sort of business conduct was to be prohibited. It is no wonder that political struggle over these fundamental questions persisted for decades to come.

Only in the 1940s did the U.S. political system resolve the bitter three-sided dispute by adopting the competition approach, implemented through antitrust enforcement. In multiple decisions, the Court has acclaimed antitrust as a steward of the most hallowed American values. The Court celebrated "the Magna Carta of free enterprise" and characterized the Sherman Act as a "comprehensive charter of economic liberty aimed at preserving free and unfettered competition as the rule of trade."[13] "The heart of our national economic policy," the Court observed, "long has been faith in the value of competition."[14]

When the Court began reframing antitrust law along Chicago school lines in the late 1970s, it did so without overturning the political consensus underlying the competition approach. If antitrust law is not strengthened now, though, the same legal rules will result in stealth implementation of laissez-faire policy. That predictable outcome threatens considerable political blowback, with the pendulum potentially swinging toward the other extreme—not antitrust but instead the sort of extensive governmental supervision that stirs the progressive imagination. We should be wary. Neither substantial market power nor unnecessary regulation is beneficial to society as a whole. To steer between Scylla and Charybdis, we must act now to reform our antitrust rules.

This chapter takes a closer look at the way decades of political controversy were resolved by consensus adoption of the antitrust approach. Lately, though, growing market power is reviving the once-prominent political dispute. To see how to respond to substantial and widening market power without overcorrecting, we will look first to the reasons our political system adopted antitrust.

ANTITRUST SOLVES A POLITICAL PROBLEM

During the late nineteenth and early twentieth centuries, the U.S. political system began to confront the large firms spawned by industrialization. New production and transportation technologies required substantial fixed expenditures and enabled firms to serve broad geographic markets, increasing the benefits of scale. But while the advantages were obvious, the downsides were also considerable. Old ways of life were swept aside. Many farmers, workers, families, and small businesses felt powerless to fend off exploitation by seemingly artificial concentrations of economic power. In response, Congress passed the Sherman Antitrust Act. In 1895, the Supreme Court amplified the natural tendency for firms to grow in size by creating a giant loophole in antitrust law for manufacturing firms to merge, setting the stage for an unprecedented wave of industrial consolidation. The Court closed the loophole in 1904, but not before rival manufacturing firms in numerous industries had combined into dominant enterprises exercising market power.[15]

Standard Oil and the Controversy over Market Power

Concern to foster competition in the United States traces back at least to the Boston bridges, but, as a matter of widespread political dispute, it took off in the late nineteenth century, amid industrialization.

An illustrative company, whose anticompetitive practices would eventually inspire significant legal change, was Standard Oil, the dominant firm in oil refining during the late nineteenth and early twentieth centuries.[16] It profited handsomely by combining economies of scale and scope with market power. By 1872 Standard Oil had acquired virtually all the oil refineries in Cleveland, which accounted for one-quarter of U.S. capacity. From this position, the company was able to secure an advantage in shipping costs. Standard Oil became a "cartel manager," working with three railroads to fix petroleum-transport prices. By shifting its oil shipment away from railroads that cut prices, Standard Oil dissuaded the railroads from offering discounts, which kept shipment prices relatively high. But the railroads only charged the higher price to their other customers. Standard Oil got discounted rates for its own oil shipments. The railroads also discouraged price cutting by paying Standard Oil penalties whenever they upped their shipping commitments with other refiners, as would be necessary to make discounting profitable. All told, the railroads got to extract larger payments from firms other than Standard, and Standard was compensated for discouraging the railroads from cheating on their petroleum-transport cartel by gaining an edge over rivals in shipment costs. The company then exploited that advantage to acquire its rivals inexpensively. By 1879 Standard Oil controlled more than 90 percent of U.S. refining capacity.

During the 1880s, Standard Oil gained bargaining leverage with the railroads. It built pipelines that provided an alternative to rail transportation and controlled a greater share of petroleum shipments and the railroad cars used to carry oil products. Standard Oil exploited this leverage to prevent entry of new refineries, thereby protecting its monopoly power.

These business methods won Standard Oil high profits but also harsh criticism. The muckraker journalist Ida Tarbell reported that the firm achieved its dominant position by using secret discriminatory railroad shipment rates and other unfair practices to crush competitors.[17] Her charges were confirmed by a government agency, the Bureau of Corporations.[18] In 1906 the Theodore Roosevelt administration responded with legal action, challenging Standard Oil's conduct under the Sherman Act. The government prevailed after a fifteen-month trial, and a federal district court ordered that Standard Oil be broken up. In 1911 the Supreme Court upheld that decision.

Standard Oil Co. v. United States[19] thereafter took on outsize importance in antitrust law. In its opinion, the Supreme Court majority established the "rule of reason," the framework for interpreting the Sherman Act that is still employed today. The decision also stoked a political debate that had been simmering for decades. Justice John Marshall Harlan's partial concurrence testifies to strong feelings underlying the Sherman Act, which he described as the product of a popular effort to prevent a "kind of slavery" that would result from "aggregations of capital" controlling "the entire business of the country."[20] In 1890, when the Act was passed, anti-monopoly sentiment had been widespread among farmers,[21] small-business owners, and others whose communities and ways of life were undermined by industrialization generally and the growth of large firms in particular.[22] But there were certainly differing views at the time, and twenty-one years later, the political questions surrounding policy toward competition and markets were not yet resolved. In 1912 they came to fore in the presidential election.

That contest was to a considerable degree fought over the role of large firms in the economy.[23] The candidates—President William Howard Taft, a Republican; Roosevelt, running on a third-party ticket; Democrat Woodrow Wilson; and socialist Eugene Debs—had sharply differing views on competition. Roosevelt was hostile to concentrated economic power, but he also thought that large firms were essential for industrial productivity and efficiency. He therefore advocated tolerating size but also regulating large corporations administratively through a national industrial commission.[24] Wilson criticized Roosevelt for welcoming monopolies, which he saw as illegitimate.[25] He called for aggressive use of antitrust laws to restore competition.[26] According to Wilson's closest adviser on antitrust issues, future

Supreme Court Justice Louis Brandeis, this meant dismembering the trusts.[27] Debs promoted nationalization, demanding that the federal government take ownership of the trusts.[28] Taft, finally, was by default the candidate most congenial to laissez-faire business interests.[29] Taft strongly supported antitrust enforcement in the courts under the Sherman Act,[30] but he stopped well short of embracing industrial policy, nationalization, or systematic deconcentration.

Wilson won the election, but his victory did not close the debate. In 1914, amid continuing political ferment, Congress passed a new antitrust statute, the Clayton Act, and created the Federal Trade Commission with the goal of preventing unfair competition. But even then antitrust was hardly entrenched as national economic policy. Bitter dispute continued for a quarter century,[31] reaching fever pitch during the 1930s.[32] The New Deal took something of a schizophrenic approach to competition, experimenting with seemingly contradictory policies. It began by allowing major industries to form self-regulated cartels under the auspices of the National Recovery Administration and ended with the formation of the Temporary National Economic Committee, a blue-ribbon panel that investigated the lack of competition in many of the very industries that had been allowed to cartelize. Various New Deal laws expanded direct federal regulation beyond railroads and electric power to include aviation, financial services, and communications.

A Political Bargain Emerges

By the end of the 1930s, the three major policy alternatives were still in play, with their outlines largely unchanged since the Sherman Act was passed. Under the antitrust approach, large firms would be given the freedom to pursue profits subject to legal review when they acted to harm competition. Under the laissez-faire approach, private enterprise would organize production and trade with little or no governmental interference. Under a more interventionist regulatory approach, large firms would be subject to direct regulation of prices and entry, constrained to follow broad industrial planning mandates, or broken up to deconcentrate the economy.

The basic question was how to organize markets to prevent exploitation while fostering the efficiencies that generate economic growth.[33] Each approach came with potential benefits and downsides. Laissez-faire would assure scale economies and benefit big business, but at the cost of permitting the exercise of market power, which would reduce output, investment, and innovation and victimize buyers, suppliers, and excluded rivals. Direct regulation would protect small business, farmers, and consumers from the distributional consequences of market power, but at the cost of distorting prices, impeding flexible business decision making, and forgoing scale economies.[34] By contrast, the antitrust approach promised to foster a dynamic, competitive economy in which sellers would pursue efficiencies and share the gains from economic growth with buyers, to the benefit of all. This position finally won out in the 1940s, when the political system reached an informal understanding, a kind of political bargain, whereby competition policy would be the primary approach to economic regulation.[35]

Thurman Arnold, who led the Justice Department's Antitrust Division from 1938 to 1943, had an important role in brokering and shaping this bargain. He ramped up enforcement by closely scrutinizing firm conduct in concentrated markets. This would, he hoped, prevent the exercise of market power without necessitating extensive and ongoing supervision by a regulatory agency or systematically sacrificing the efficiencies generated by large enterprises. His method incorporated elements of industrial planning and industry self-regulation consistent with a primary reliance on law enforcement under the antitrust laws. On the one hand, the Department of Justice (DOJ) would target specific industries by simultaneously bringing multiple enforcement actions aimed at their competitive bottlenecks. On the other hand, cases were often resolved by consent decree, allowing industry to participate in developing relief.[36]

Arnold's strategy was all the more enticing after the unhappy experience of the National Recovery Administration. In its wake, advocates of industrial self-regulation and of broad governmental planning were on the defensive, freeing political oxygen for Arnold's antitrust approach. Other branches of government soon ratified the strategy. In 1940 the Supreme Court established the per se rule against horizontal price fixing, which prohibited such agreements without need to prove that the firms exercised market power.[37] Five years later, a specially created appellate panel reinvigorated the Sherman Act's prohibition against monopolization.[38] In 1950 Congress toughened the antitrust statute governing mergers.[39]

I refer to this period, in which legal doctrines and antitrust enforcement were reorganized around hostility to market concentration, as antitrust's "structural era." The norms established then—particularly the uncompromising objection to pure horizontal price fixing and skepticism toward mergers between rivals in concentrated markets—remain central to antitrust today.[40] Amid the strengthened political consensus of the structural era, the debate came to a close. By 1964, historian Richard Hofstadter could write that antitrust had become "one of the faded passions of American reform."[41] With the bargain in place, antitrust was left to the ministrations of technocrats and courts.[42]

The bargain should be understood metaphorically, not literally.[43] It does not have clearly specified terms. It reflects an informal political understanding between groups that continued to understand their interests as distinct but that were capable of reaching a compromise that would conceivably benefit both.

Specifically, the bargaining frame interprets the competition-policy consensus as a coordinated arrangement between consumers—a group that historically also included farmers and small business—and producers, conceived as large firms.[44] This is, of course, a very rough division. Many individuals see themselves as consumers at home and producers at work. Meanwhile, the interests of shoppers, farmers, and small business operators frequently diverge. In the course of the competition debate, some consumers favored breaking up large firms and others, their domestication through governmental planning. The political interests of producers probably are less diffuse than those of consumers, further complicating the sense in which these form two distinct camps.[45]

In spite of all these caveats, the bargaining frame reasonably describes the consensus political understanding surrounding antitrust. Populist and progressive accounts of domestic politics as a struggle between "the people" and "the interests" capture an important aspect of the debates that occurred. The producer and consumer groups must mobilize their members politically in order to achieve their goals. It is reasonable to expect them to do so more effectively when they are out of power, as collective action problems can be overcome more easily under conditions of adversity than success.[46] This is thanks in part to political entrepreneurs who encourage diffuse group members to identify and act on a common interest[47] and also to the features of our political system that make it hard for winning coalitions to change the rules of political competition and lock in their success by making it difficult for losing groups to mobilize politically to unseat them.[48]

What happened in the case of competition policy is that the two aggregated actors—consumers and producers—reached a political equilibrium that increased their joint surplus. A tug-of-war between laissez-faire and regulation could have continued without end, with either outcome preventing firms from capturing efficiencies and limiting economic growth. The battle lines of ideology and interest would not change, such that if either group won the upper hand, the other would inevitably mobilize in opposition to dislodge them.[49] Under such conditions, institutions enhancing the overall welfare are of obvious appeal, though not the inevitable outcome of political competition.[50]

By the 1940s, the two groups at last accepted that they would do better in the long run by sharing a growing pie than by grabbing a larger slice of a smaller pie from a counterparty capable of mobilizing politically to take it back.[51] Each interest group in effect gave up its preferred policy while reaching a political accommodation that allowed the groups to share the efficiency gains from competition.[52] Some partisans in each group would not compromise, but the centrist antitrust approach prevailed.[53]

Shared welfare gains may have been sufficient to win the bargain political acceptance on its own terms.[54] But it is also reasonable to assess that "side payments" helped. Two features accompanying the bargain sweetened the deal for members of the more diffuse consumer group—particularly for small businesses, their workers, and their communities.[55]

The primary side payment was the contemporaneous development and later expansion of a more substantial social safety net.[56] Social insurance limits a market economy's downside risk to consumers, workers, and their families. This makes antitrust policy more attractive because it provides assurances that, even if businesses rise and fall in a competitive environment, individuals won't be ruined in the process. This heads off some of the political pressure to regulate large-firm conduct directly.[57]

Another less significant side payment was the appeal to social and political goals along with economic goals as a basis for antitrust rules. I discuss these in detail in Chapter 3. In addition, as Chapter 9 explains, antitrust's prohibition on cross-market welfare trade-offs operates as a side payment to consumers, workers, farmers, and small businesses.

Because the bargain was reached informally, "competition" was not defined with precision. Accordingly, antitrust rules and institutions aim not at particular economic outcomes but instead at the implementation, elaboration, protection, and enforcement of the political bargain. The political consensus means that antitrust rules pursue a generalized economic goal of facilitating economic growth by allowing firms substantial freedom to cut costs and develop new products and business models and by fostering rivalry among them. It does not tie down the specific welfare standard antitrust should apply. Nor does it determine the specifics of the doctrinal rules. The bargain constrains the antitrust rules as a whole, but it does not constrain each rule individually or mandate the outcome of individual cases.

In general, the courts have been assigned the institutional role of specifying the details. They have substantial room to maneuver, which allows the rules to change while preserving the bargain. As long as courts can maintain the efficiency gains that flow from competition, the antitrust approach could be expected to endure. Only if courts push too far in either direction— toward laissez-faire or regulation—would we anticipate political mobilization undermining the bargain. The losers would seek to overturn the rules and the winners to secure them.

The courts enforce the bargain in two senses—narrow and broad. First, they apply antitrust rules to resolve disputes among private parties and among government agencies and firms. Second, courts interpret and adjust antitrust rules. When doing so, they ensure that their modifications to antitrust policy, taken as a whole, do not stray too far toward business self-regulation or extensive government oversight. Some change is inevitable as we modify our understanding of the economic consequences of business practices, scrutinize new forms of business conduct, and alter our evaluation of the suitability of existing rules. But when rules change, courts ensure that antitrust policy remains consistent with the overall goal of preserving a legal framework sufficient to ensure that competition governs firm conduct.[58]

The antitrust rules employed from the 1940s through 1970s were, on the whole, consistent with the political bargain. As I detail below, the Chicago-oriented reforms were also consistent at the time. They did not fundamentally discard competition in favor of laissez-faire.[59] But they pushed the rules so that they approached the noninterventionist edge of the permissible spectrum.[60] In retrospect, that is why we have seen the development of substantial and widening market power. Accordingly, we must now strengthen the rules to preserve the political bargain. That does not necessitate returning to the rules that prevailed during antitrust's structural era, though, as later chapters make clear.

ANTITRUST REFRAMED

Chicago School Antitrust

From its inception in 1958, the *Journal of Law and Economics*, edited by pioneering Chicago school economists Aaron Director and Ronald Coase, solicited and featured conservative critiques of antitrust cases.[61] The editors chose articles with the aim of "skewering liberal belief in the importance of antitrust intervention."[62] Over the next twenty years, advocacy by business facilitated the judiciary's acceptance of Chicago school views. During the early 1970s, Henry Manne, who has been described as the first "organizational entrepreneur" of the law and economics movement in legal academia,[63] financed his educational program through contributions from major corporations such as U.S. Steel, which saw Chicago economics as "the only thing that could possibly save them from an antitrust debacle."[64] Justice Lewis Powell, the author of a famous 1971 memorandum for the U.S. Chamber of Commerce outlining a political strategy to defend big business and free enterprise,[65] became the first major advocate for this view on the Supreme Court. He was looking for an opportunity to change antitrust law and got it in 1977, with the case of *Continental Television v. GTE Sylvania*. In the majority opinion, written by Powell, the Chicagoans' criticism made its Supreme Court debut.[66]

In essence, the Chicago school argued that the rules established during the structural era had struck the wrong balance between deterring harmful conduct and chilling efficiencies.[67] Per Chicago, exclusive vertical distribution territories are not considered harmful market allocations or anticompetitive restrictions on interbrand competition; they are instead efficiency-enhancing means of preventing dealer free-riding on manufacturers' marketing investments.[68] Price cutting is not considered a dangerous monopolization tactic, but instead the essence of competition.[69] Most mergers and agreements among firms, even rivals, are described as mechanisms for lowering costs or improving products—two ways in which firms compete.[70] Antitrust concerns should be raised, according to the Chicago view, only when a firm has a dominant share of a market protected by entry barriers or when the government shields businesses from competition. Otherwise, when markets lack competition, entry solves the problem.[71]

In *The Antitrust Paradox*, Bork detailed precisely how antitrust law should be minimized. He argued that it should guard against only three classes of conduct: "naked" horizontal agreements to fix prices or divide markets,[72] horizontal mergers creating duopolies or monopolies, and an extremely limited set of exclusionary behaviors consisting primarily of predation through abuse of governmental processes.[73] A reformed and refocused antitrust would "abandon its concern with such beneficial practices as small horizontal mergers, all vertical and conglomerate mergers, vertical price maintenance and market division, tying arrangements, exclusive dealing and requirement contracts, 'predatory' price-cutting, price 'discrimination,' and the like."[74] Overall, this agenda circumscribed collusive offenses and virtually jettisoned exclusionary-conduct offenses.[75]

Some judges were swayed by Chicago arguments, and politicians amenable to Chicago critique appointed other judges, so the courts soon took up the incremental modification of structural-era antitrust rules.[76] Supreme Court decisions relaxed the rule governing nonprice vertical restraints,[77] raised barriers to plaintiffs seeking to prove predatory pricing,[78] overrode the nearly century-old rule declaring resale price maintenance illegal per se,[79] limited access to the courts for rivals seeking to challenge harmful conduct,[80] and narrowed the per se prohibition against horizontal restraints, which would now apply only when an agreement lacked a facially plausible efficiency justification.[81] Taking their cue from decisions such as these, the lower courts interpreted prior Supreme Court decisions as allowing a reasonableness analysis of exclusive dealing instead of focusing only on the magnitude of foreclosure.[82] Courts also permitted a wider range of factors to rebut the presumption of harm due to concentration from horizontal mergers and, over time, raised the level of concentration at which the presumption kicked in.[83] The Federal Trade Commission made clear that some conduct that had been previously considered as grounds for a finding of monopolization would no longer be considered sufficient to sustain charges.[84]

Although the Court did not declare any of Bork's "beneficial practices" legal per se, its decisions substantially narrowed the scope of potential liability for such conduct. Plaintiffs today rarely succeed when attacking nonprice vertical restraints; alleging predatory pricing; or, absent a prior voluntary course of dealing, challenging dominant firms' unilateral refusals to deal. Vertical mergers are almost never challenged in court, although the government's unsuccessful attempt to block AT&T's acquisition of Time Warner, now under appeal, is an exception. The government largely avoids price-discrimination lawsuits under the Robinson-Patman Act, though private enforcement remains active.[85]

The Chicago-oriented Supreme Court focused antitrust on economic concerns, discarding social and political goals formerly thought important.[86] The debate over the "welfare standard" that courts should apply when framing rules has largely been narrowed to a choice between two economic goals: consumer welfare and aggregate welfare.[87] The former is achieved by preventing reductions in consumer surplus, the latter by preventing reductions in aggregate surplus. These tests are routinely employed to analyze business conduct in the partial equilibrium (single market) context within which most antitrust cases are viewed, even though they do not map neatly to other common approaches in welfare economics and can be difficult to implement when accounting for enforcement institutions.[88]

Consumer surplus refers to the benefits that the buyers in a market collectively receive, measured by buyer willingness to pay less expenditures.[89] If I am willing to pay as much as $5 for a cup of coffee and the seller charges $2, I gain the equivalent of $3 from a purchase. The consumer surplus in the market sums these gains across all buyers. The producer surplus equals the contribution to profit that all sellers collectively receive from the market or, equivalently, the total payments sellers receive from buyers less the total variable costs of production.[90] If a coffee shop spends $1 on the incremental inputs required to make the coffee cup it sells to me for $2, my purchase adds $1 to its producer surplus. The aggregate surplus equals the benefits buyers collectively receive less the variable costs of production expended by all sellers. Aggregate surplus therefore is the sum of consumer and producer surplus. These welfare standards are well defined when the buyers are not consumers. When the product is an intermediate good, sold to producers of final goods, the direct purchasers are viewed as though they are consumers. In principle, these welfare standards can account for the complexity of real-world markets, including variation in product features, service quality, convenience, or other aspects of product differentiation valued by buyers and including efficiencies to producers that take the form of improved product quality or prospects for innovation as well as cost savings.[91] The welfare standards are analogously defined when evaluating harms from the exercise of market power by buyers. "Consumer welfare" means "supplier welfare" in such cases.

In practice, courts and enforcers are generally wary of tolerating conduct that harms or appears likely to harm a class of consumers. They tend to act consistently with the consumer welfare standard,[92] even though many Chicagoans, including Robert Bork, recommended aggregate welfare.[93] This approach makes sense as a way of implementing the political bargain in the current environment of substantial and widening market power. Pursuing a consumer welfare goal tends to lead to rules that favor deterrence of anticompetitive harms over rules that emphasize avoiding chilling business pursuit of efficiencies.[94] It would not undermine that end, though, if firms were permitted to capture increased producer surplus in exceptional cases where those gains are large and the lost consumer surplus small, so long as those cases are understood to be rare exceptions that account for unusual circumstances.

The Chicago school's success in focusing antitrust on economics is illustrated by the limited range of the welfare standard debate today between consumer welfare and aggregate welfare. The Chicagoans properly saw economic analysis as central to developing antitrust rules and identifying enforcement targets. Under their influence, supported by the administrability concerns of the contemporaneous Harvard school,[95] the Supreme Court rejected noneconomic goals and adopted modifications to antitrust rules to reduce the risk of false convictions. Those modifications were intended to address a concern that the earlier rules were chilling production efficiencies. This concern was not fanciful. At the time, even Robert Pitofsky, a leading liberal antitrust voice, accepted the need for reform.[96]

The Changing Political Context

Policy outcomes achieved within the political bargain—including antitrust's shift from a structural to a Chicago school approach—are best understood as the product of an interest group competition mediated by ideology. Mid-twentieth century economic regulatory policy emerged from a political competition among centrists, noninterventionists (on their right), and interventionists (on their left).[97] In this conceptual scheme, the centrists support competition policy and social insurance to provide a safety net, conservatives prefer self-regulation and private insurance, and progressives prefer direct regulation and direct provision of social services such as health care.

To the extent that centrists have held sway in economic policy, they have done so by partnering with members of the other camps. For the first few decades after the New Deal, centrists partnered mainly with progressives. For instance, centrists joined progressives to pass Medicare, a key safety net expansion, over the opposition of conservatives who viewed it as inappropriate government intervention in the marketplace.[98] During the Carter administration, Senator Edward Kennedy and his counsel on the Judiciary Committee, future Justice Stephen Breyer, brought conservatives into the tent. The right found common ground with the center-left coalition in enacting airline deregulation.[99] But the centrists switched dancing partners later, when the left grew disenchanted with regulatory reform.

Since the Reagan administration, centrists have gotten their way on regulatory policy by collaborating with conservatives rather than progressives.[100] These reforms were still centrist rather than conservative because they preserved regulation where competition would be insufficient to prevent the harms of market power.[101] Thus, while some deregulation occurred, the transmission and retail distribution of electricity remained subject to rate regulation.[102] Communications deregulation did not allow local phone companies to provide long-distance service until the long-distance market became competitive.[103] Congress reversed cable deregulation in 1992 after eight years in which hoped-for competition did not appear, then refined its regulatory scheme four years later.[104] Airline deregulation left safety regulation in the hands of the Federal Aviation Administration rather than relying solely on marketplace incentives to keep planes from falling out of the sky.[105]

Two factors were largely responsible for the shift from a center-left to a center-right coalition in regulatory policy. First, there was the difficult economic environment of the 1970s. For some three decades after World War II, the political bargain had delivered the American Dream of greater economic opportunity and better living standards for most people. But its ability to continue doing so was called into question by the decade of economic stagnation that began during the 1970s. Two oil shocks, high inflation, three recessions, a productivity slowdown, sluggish income growth for workers, and increased foreign competition had undermined public confidence in the midcentury consensus.[106] Second, the shift in the governing political coalition was also a reaction to the increased federal role in economic life, which resulted particularly from the implementation of legislation protecting civil rights, the environment, and worker safety.[107]

Although the Chicago-oriented reforms were carried out by a center-right coalition, they were substantially bipartisan, and they did not reject the political bargain.[108] In the 1970s and 1980s, Congress and the states balked at efforts to go farther with regulation, but any suggestion that the antitrust laws should be repealed remained outside the mainstream. Leading business consultants taking a broad, cross-industry perspective continue to support competition policy,[109] and state antitrust enforcement has grown in importance.

As described in Chapter 10, the D.C. Circuit, sitting en banc, unanimously rejected Microsoft's strongly pressed legal and public challenge to the legitimacy of antitrust and its application to high-tech markets. Since the 1980s, the federal antitrust agencies have enforced antitrust laws similarly in many respects across Republican and Democratic administrations,[110] particularly in attacking cartels. Merger enforcement was indeed unusually lax during the second Reagan and George W. Bush terms,[111] and Democratic administrations recognized a wider range of exclusion problems than their Republican counterparts.[112] But these differences in priority did not vitiate the antitrust bargain, ratified again in 2007 by the bipartisan Antitrust Modernization Commission, which endorsed the general state of enforcement.[113]

In short, the center-right antitrust and regulatory agenda was implemented within the political bargain, not by rejecting it. The Chicago-oriented reforms to the antitrust laws changed the antitrust landscape dramatically but not fundamentally.

APPROACHING A POLITICAL TIPPING POINT

Today, however, the political bargain is threatened by the results of these antitrust reforms. As we saw in Chapter 1, the Chicago-oriented revisions have abetted the widening exercise of market power, with deleterious consequences. In retrospect, the antitrust status quo moved too far toward nonintervention. Under current antitrust rules, in consequence, the problem of substantial and widening market power will continue to grow.

The Supreme Court has not questioned the current approach, even though the enforcement agencies have modified the way they evaluate some types of business conduct in response to new economic learning.[114] Antitrust conservatives continue to advocate erroneous assumptions about markets and antitrust institutions, which support the litigation positions of large-firm defendants. (I discuss these in Chapter 5.) Those positions would push the courts toward even less interventionist antitrust rules and the agencies toward even less enforcement.

It is no longer credible to defend circumscribing antitrust along the lines of Bork's minimalist approach. Looked at purely as a matter of decision theory,[115] without regard to political consequences, the growth of market power means that the concern with insufficient deterrence (false negatives) has grown, calling for a more restrictive antitrust policy.

In addition, the side payments that have supported antitrust politically are under attack. The conservative wing of the Republican Party, a prominent force in its congressional caucus, has exhibited a consistent and thorough-going hostility to social insurance.[116] With Republican control of the White House and a closely divided Congress, the social safety net may fray, exposing more workers and small-business owners to the threat of financial ruin when their firms lose out in the marketplace.

For a generation, the economy has not delivered sustained and shared economic growth and prosperity.[117] With the American Dream an increasingly hollow promise, it is not surprising to see contemporary echoes of the three-sided political debate resolved during the 1940s. The centrist approach to economic regulation—combining antitrust with a robust social safety net—is coming under pressure.

That much was clear well before the 2016 election, whose surprising success stories—Trump and Bernie Sanders—speak to discontents long brewing on both sides of the regulatory divide. During the Obama years, conservatives repeatedly fought against regulatory empowerment. Republican senators held up confirmation of the director of the new Consumer Financial Protection Bureau in a bid to water down the agency's powers and independence.[118] The House of Representatives, under the sway of conservatives, sought to overrule the Federal Communications Commission's open Internet rules on net neutrality.[119] The Affordable Care Act, a set of market-based reforms that Republicans had once endorsed,[120] was passed in 2010 without a single GOP vote. In 2012 and 2016, the entire Republican presidential fields called for the act's repeal.[121]

On the left, the Occupy Wall Street movement criticized the Dodd-Frank financial reforms as too little, too late.[122] Progressives rejected the 2003 prescription-drug benefit on the grounds that it was an expensive handout to pharmaceutical manufacturers and that its reliance on insurance companies was the first step toward privatizing Medicare.[123] Progressive support for the 2010 health-care law was muted, just sufficient for congressional enactment, because progressives preferred a government-run system such as Medicare to the Affordable Care Act's competition-based approach.[124]

Every regulation has its critics, but the turmoil of the Obama years was surprising because the administration followed the same centrist playbook for economic regulation that had won support since the Reagan administration. The standard playbook was failing because the center-right coalition

.had broken down, and no new coalition replaced it. Conservative opponents of "big government" ceased compromising with centrists, and the left did not pick up the baton, even with a Democrat in the White House.

The 2016 election exacerbated the discord. The central economic regulatory initiative that followed—the failed 2017 attempt to repeal and replace the Affordable Care Act—was a strictly partisan effort shaped largely by conservatives, with little deference to centrist concerns to protect competition and the social safety net. While a number of Democratic leaders have recognized a growing market power problem, the leadership of the Republican party has not.

The center-right coalition has arguably run its natural course, as its core program has become largely obsolete. After decades of regulatory reform, additional deregulation risks enabling the exercise of market power, creating other market failures, and undermining the safety net that enables the avoidance of competition-killing regulation in the first place. In other words, there is no space left for deregulation to achieve centrist goals because further deregulation would enhance neither competition nor social insurance.[125]

What this means is that the Chicago school's project, like deregulation generally, is basically complete.[126] Thus, in the early twenty-first century, some antitrust conservatives seemed to go it alone, advancing a noninterventionist agenda that shuns compromise with centrists. During the George W. Bush administration, the Justice Department issued a report on Sherman Act § 2 taking a hands-off approach, which the more centrist Federal Trade Commission pointedly refused to join and from which the Obama administration subsequently withdrew.[127] In *Trinko,* Justice Scalia's rhetoric rejected antirust outright, defending monopoly as "an important element of the free-market system."[128] Scalia went out of his way to say that: in the context of the decision, the discussion was dicta.[129] It also wasn't necessary to his economic argument, which could have recognized appropriability as a spur to innovation without seeming to welcome monopolies. Along with *Trinko,*[130] other recent Supreme Court decisions—*Credit Suisse,*[131] *Twombly,*[132] *Comcast,*[133] and *Italian Colors*[134]—evidence an interest in chipping away at private antitrust enforcement.[135] While these and other conservative initiatives have been wrapped in the language of antitrust, suggesting continuity with the past, they threaten to undermine and ultimately overturn the political bargain.

The Trump administration, for all its perceived radicalism in reducing economic regulation,[136] does not yet appear interested in discarding the political bargain. At the same time, it evinces no recognition of substantial and widening market power. The Trump electoral coalition can be thought of as combining traditional conservatives skeptical of government and sympathetic to laissez-faire with nonurban, less educated, and white voters with status anxiety who favor a small federal government in order to prevent social change. Voters in the latter group would not necessarily oppose antitrust. They could support intervention to protect local firms or U.S. firms generally from competition with global businesses or to protect small business. But these voters may not care strongly about regulatory policy.

Although some of President Trump's campaign rhetoric suggested that his administration would use antitrust aggressively to fix a rigged system,[137] and scattered conservative voices argue for stronger antitrust enforcement against large technology firms,[138] President Trump's antitrust appointees are similar to those of the George W. Bush administration in which many of them served, suggesting continuity with the past approach of Republican administrations. Working in the shadow of a conservative Supreme Court, those appointees would generally be expected to enforce antitrust as reframed by the Chicagoans, with some adjustments to account for economic learning postdating the 1980s. Although that course will result in stealth rejection of the political bargain in favor of laissez-faire, there is little prospect that either the administration or Congress will soon address the problem of substantial and widening market power.

Since the 2016 election, criticism of the current antitrust rules from the left has become increasingly prominent.[139] Progressive voices are concerned about adverse political and social consequences of growing market power,[140] not just with economic harms. With respect to the latter, they have called attention to harms to suppliers and workers as well as to buyers and consumers.[141] Many are uneasy about the growth of large information-technology platforms.[142] When they propose modifications to antitrust rules, they favor strong presumptions of anticompetitive effects from horizontal mergers, vertical mergers, exclusive dealing, and below-cost pricing.[143] Some recommend extending public utility regulation to dominant information technology platforms.[144]

Victims of market power could very well mobilize today.[145] William Kovacic anticipated as much in 1989. He predicted that political interest in deconcentration would revive in response to three conditions: adoption of a permissive approach toward evaluating alleged anticompetitive conduct, a major resurgence of popular sentiment against large corporations as might follow business scandal or economic crisis, and the emergence of scholarship rebutting prevailing conservative intellectual orthodoxy.[146] These prerequisites have been met. It remains to be seen whether the predicted mobilization will in fact occur,[147] but, if it does, centrists may find they have a progressive partner for a renewed antitrust coalition—or the mobilization may be sufficiently extreme in its goals that no partnership is possible.

The latter result grows more likely with each doubling down on the completed Chicago program and every new push away from antitrust intervention. The stronger the conservative ideological commitment to laissez-faire and to ignoring the harms of market power, the farther the pendulum will swing in response. A successful leftist political mobilization untethered from centrists cannot be expected to restore antitrust; anticorporate populists will seek extensive governmental supervision.[148] This possibility has long been feared. That fear underlay the antitrust bargain in the first place. Future Supreme Court Justice Robert Jackson understood this, writing in 1937, "Every step to weaken antitrust laws or to suspend them in any field, or to permit price fixing, is a certain, if unknowing, step to government control."[149] His successors on the Court should take heed.

Chapter Three

Preventing the Political
Misuse of Antitrust

A NTITRUST ENFORCEMENT is a powerful machine—
both for maintaining competition and for advancing the interests of politicians who wrest control of its operation. From his seat in the
Oval Office, Lyndon Johnson held up the antitrust review of a bank acquisition until a newspaper publisher, who also ran one of the merging banks,
agreed to reverse the paper's editorial position against him.[1] President Nixon
ordered the Justice Department not to appeal a lost court challenge to a
merger by International Telephone & Telegraph, allegedly in exchange for
a substantial contribution by ITT to the Republican National Convention.[2]
Nixon also threatened three major television networks with antitrust lawsuits in an effort to extract better news coverage[3] and allegedly accepted a
campaign contribution from Howard Hughes in exchange for withholding
an antitrust challenge to a planned Las Vegas hotel acquisition.[4]

Like law enforcement generally, antitrust can be corrupted by firms seeking
economic advantage, as with Nixon's alleged deals with ITT and Hughes.
It can be misused by politicians for partisan purposes, as with Johnson's and
Nixon's manipulations of journalists.

These examples provoke outrage because they violate a norm intended to
insulate antitrust enforcement from direct political influence. That norm
helps prevent firms from manipulating the political system to exercise market
power through special-interest protectionism and crony capitalism. It also
discourages politicians from exploiting enforcement decisions to further their
own interests without regard to the public good.[5]

These concerns reinforce the importance of insulating antitrust from politics, which holds no matter who is in power.[6] Antitrust law and enforcement should be apolitical, but they necessarily operate in a political context. Antitrust law once explicitly pursued social and political goals in addition to the economic goals that are central today. Moreover, progressives have grown more concerned about market power precisely because of its adverse political consequences. These critics seek to use antitrust systematically to attack corporate concentration in order to redistribute political power away from concentrated centers of wealth and thereby, progressives hope, increase economic opportunity.[7] Today's antitrust institutions face many political threats, not least of which is the stealth rejection of antitrust in favor of laissez-faire.

Yet, even though concerns about the politicization of antitrust are justified, a political mobilization to take on growing market power could strengthen the political bargain. For reasons I discuss below, this mobilization ought not promote the formula of midcentury antitrust, which explicitly, albeit secondarily, pursued political ends. These methods were of limited success, and pressing for their return would divert effort away from more promising reforms.

A movement focused on attacking market power would strengthen the political bargain, first and foremost, because market power has become a serious problem. And second, antitrust enforcement, as currently practiced, discourages the sort of political shenanigans exemplified by the Johnson and Nixon cases. These are rare exceptions in the modern era. For the most part, antitrust is successfully divorced from abuse by special interests and crony capitalists, and undermining market power would make such abuse even less likely.

In this chapter, I elaborate on the threats of politicization antitrust faces and explain how the legal system has developed in response. Many obstacles, including the norm against direct political influence and rules that limit judicial discretion, stand in the way of political abuse. Yet, even as antitrust shuns politics, it retains a connection to the popular will. This reflects an important distinction between politics and ideology, on which I elaborate below. Enforcement is, properly, responsive to ideological shifts, and enforcement would be stronger if the public were to mobilize against market power. But that doesn't mean antitrust enforcement would be subject as well to the sort of abuse that undermines trust in the fairness of the legal process.

SPECIAL-INTEREST PROTECTIONISM
AND CRONY CAPITALISM

Special-interest protectionism and crony capitalism are related ways of manipulating the political system to exercise market power. Special-interest protectionism refers to the ability of firms or other narrow interest groups to establish or entrench protected positions through government action. A particular firm or industry may influence the government to act in its favor, without regard to the public interest, in order to create or protect market power. Congress and the courts have created exemptions from the antitrust laws over time to benefit particular industries, perhaps for this reason.[8] Special-interest protectionism was a prominent concern of nineteenth-century constitutional interpretation and twentieth-century public-choice scholars. It is closely related to regulatory capture: the manipulation of a regulatory agency by a firm it supervises.[9]

The incentive underlying manipulation is obvious. Profit-maximizing firms, individually or along with their major rivals, can gain market power by investing in lobbying. Compliant government officials, elected or otherwise, may create entry barriers or foreclose fringe competitors' access to customers or low-cost inputs. Even Chicago school–oriented antitrust commentators, who question antitrust's concern with exclusionary marketplace conduct, acknowledge that predation through use of governmental processes could be a serious problem.[10]

While special-interest protectionism is transactional and episodic, "crony capitalism" is systemic and entrenched. Firms secure lasting political power through their individual or collective size and lobbying influence and use that power to obtain and protect market power. They may create entry barriers or, more corruptly, obtain other forms of enrichment for themselves or their political allies (that is, their cronies).[11] Crony capitalism becomes ingrained when firms with market power invest some of the resulting rents to secure the political power that helps protect or extend it.[12] This erodes antitrust constraints still further, creating more market power, and so forth, in a vicious cycle.

Crony capitalism differs from oligarchy, though they can be related. An oligarchy is a political system in which a small number of political actors control vast resources, which they deploy to enhance or defend their personal wealth and social position. In the U.S. political system, the threat of oligarchy comes from the ability of the wealthy to capture political institutions, change those institutions to lock in their political positions, and use their control of institutions to, among other things, lower their taxes.[13] Lock in might be facilitated by restricting the franchise, eviscerating constraints on corporate political contributions, or undermining institutions such as unions that could supply political opposition to large firms. This threat is not merely speculative: the disproportionate influence of the wealthiest on public policy is well documented,[14] and successful political coalitions may attempt to change the rules to protect their positions.[15] This combination is equally dangerous for political and economic competition. To the extent that large firms are owned by wealthy families, the political system could tend toward crony capitalism and oligarchy simultaneously. Political institutions could then both protect large firms from competition and systematically enrich the wealthy.

Trump's election has made concerns about special-interest protectionism, crony capitalism, and oligarchy more salient.[16] The norm against direct political influence is endangered by the combination of Trump's campaign statements threatening antitrust challenges for political ends,[17] his post-election meetings with executives from firms pursuing acquisitions under review at the enforcement agencies,[18] his agreements with certain firms to keep jobs from moving abroad,[19] his frequent criticism of law enforcement decisions with which he disagrees,[20] and his extensive personal and familial financial interests. These encourage firms to lobby the president directly in order to influence enforcement actions. They also raise the possibility that the president would base decisions on his political or financial interests. Trump's signals have been recognized by the business community: the chief executive officer (CEO) of AT&T said he was flabbergasted by the administration's decision to challenge his firm's proposed acquisition of Time Warner, in part because he has been one of Trump's "biggest defenders on public policy."[21]

Even where Trump's goals plausibly relate to public interests, they may not be acceptable under antitrust law. For example, boosting domestic employment is not cognizable under the Clayton Act as currently interpreted. Beyond flouting a norm or violating the Clayton Act, presidential involvement in antitrust enforcement decisions could contravene the Constitution. If a president instructs the Justice Department on the resolution of merger reviews or other antitrust investigations—particularly without hearing from agency staff and other interested parties and without reviewing the detailed factual record developed by an agency investigation—it is hard to be confident that agency enforcement decisions appropriately apply the law to the facts, uninfluenced by the political or financial interests of the president. That scenario would call into question whether the president has met his constitutional obligation to "take care that the laws be faithfully executed."[22] Even if agency decisions are free from direct presidential influence, the concern that they might not be undermines confidence that enforcement actions serve the public interest and undercuts political support for antitrust institutions and norms.[23] It also harms enforcement by diminishing the credibility of agency officials with courts and firms.

A prudent administration would insulate antitrust enforcement from direct presidential influence, as has been routine in the modern era and formalized institutionally since Watergate.[24] Trump's senior antitrust enforcers agree. During his hearing for confirmation as attorney general, Jeff Sessions said, "There will not be political interference" in the merger review process.[25] The assistant attorney general for antitrust, Makan Delrahim, agreed that political considerations should not influence the handling of antitrust cases.[26] But it remains to be seen whether the Trump administration will adhere to the norm. It is not always clear that Trump's senior appointees speak for him, and the Trump administration has put pressure on many other deeply entrenched political and institutional norms.

If we are concerned about the corruption of antitrust enforcement, we might seek in response to reintroduce the explicit social and political goals of the structural era. Doing so might, in theory, enable more effective constraint against the accretion of political power in firms, sapping their capacity to influence politicians and antitrust decision makers. But this approach comes with disadvantages, too.

LESSONS FROM ANTITRUST'S MID-TWENTIETH CENTURY PURSUIT OF NONECONOMIC GOALS

In 1979 Robert Pitofsky offered a full-throated defense of antitrust law's political values. A leading academic commentator on antitrust and a future chairman of the Federal Trade Commission, Pitofsky explained that antitrust emerged from "a fear that excessive concentration of economic power will breed antidemocratic political pressures," from "a desire to enhance individual and business freedom by reducing the range within which private discretion by a few in the economic sphere controls the welfare of all," and from an "overriding political concern . . . that if the free-market sector of the economy is allowed to develop under antitrust rules that are blind to all but economic concerns, the likely result will be an economy so dominated by a few corporate giants that it will be impossible for the state not to play a more intrusive role in economic affairs."[27]

Mid-twentieth century courts acknowledged these political values. Pitofsky felt the need to reassert them amid the Chicago school's assault, the power of which was becoming obvious when he wrote. Pitofsky worried that noneconomic goals would be lost if the Chicagoans had their way.

The other major midcentury noneconomic goal of antitrust was to provide small businesses a realistic chance to compete. Judge Learned Hand, in his seminal 1945 *Alcoa* opinion, derived this goal from the legislative history of the Sherman Act and subsequent court decisions.[28] In *Brown Shoe*, decided in 1962, the Supreme Court observed that Hand's conclusion had subsequently been reinforced through the legislative history of the 1950 amendments to the Clayton Act.[29] The Court observed that the Sherman Act "guaranteed each and every business, no matter how small . . . the freedom to compete."[30]

The goal of guaranteeing small business the freedom to compete was, however, in tension with another theme in *Brown Shoe:* that the legislative history of the 1950 amendments, taken as a whole, "illuminates congressional concern with the protection of competition, not competitors, and its desire to restrain mergers only to the extent that such combinations may tend to lessen competition."[31] In 1964, Bork and fellow Chicagoan Ward Bowman seized on this tension to argue that a concern for the preservation of small business was "questionable as a description of congressional intent, dubious as social policy, and impossible as antitrust doctrine."[32]

Commentators sympathetic to noneconomic goals responded to Bork and Bowman's hostility by arguing that these goals were pursued indirectly. For instance, Harlan Blake and William Jones noted that antitrust protected small business through the prevention of exclusionary practices.[33] On this view, antitrust was, foremost, a set of rules conditioning liability on market shares and market concentration and preventing exclusionary conduct that harmed competition. As Pitofsky explained, antitrust's political concerns were "clearly and expressly secondary."[34] Nonetheless vigorous antitrust enforcement would, without offering any such guarantee, "protect small business against the use of unfair tactics by larger companies to gain advantages unrelated to superior skill or efficiency of those larger units."[35]

The Supreme Court blessed this indirect interpretation in *Brown Shoe.* That decision looked to market concentration and an industry trend toward concentration in evaluating the horizontal aspect of a proposed merger under the newly revised Clayton Act. The Court looked to the foreclosure consequences of a trend toward vertical integration in evaluating the vertical aspect of the proposed merger. The Court did not assess directly the political power of the merging firms or the extent to which individual small businesses would be injured. It did, however, accept that its approach could prevent firms from achieving some efficiencies, suggesting that it had more than just economic concerns in mind.[36] And the Court offered its sense of the Sherman Act's beneficence toward small businesses, even though its decision was not predicated on that perspective.[37]

The Court's willingness to condemn horizontal mergers when a trend toward concentration was in its incipiency, Pitofsky argued, demonstrated its interest in preventing the political problems resulting from concentrated economic power.[38] The courts tilted the design of antitrust rules to limit the behavior of dominant firms and to limit concentration by merger, even though affected firms would be unable to take advantage of the benefits of scale. This was achieved through the Supreme Court's elaboration of horizontal merger law, which set minimum concentration levels at which harm would be presumed from acquisitions between rivals. The Court also expressed skepticism when firms defended mergers on the basis of efficiencies.[39]

The question today is whether, when strengthening antitrust, we ought to return to this vision. Outrage on the left focuses substantially on the desire to deconcentrate firms in an effort to reduce their political power. Doing so would revive the midcentury approach, allowing political and social considerations indirectly to influence the development of rules of general applicability.

But experience cautions against any expectation antitrust enforcement alone will transform society and politics. The social and political goals recognized at midcentury were not used to justify a direct attack on concentrated political power, as distinct from concentrated economic power, or to insulate small businesses from hardship—only to ensure them opportunities to compete. When government monopolization cases arose,[40] litigation properly focused on economic harms, not on the political power of defendants. Systematic deconcentration efforts between the 1940s and 1970s were spurred by political as well as economic concerns,[41] but they had little success.[42]

The midcentury merger rules presumably deterred many anticompetitive combinations, but they did not prevent the growth of large conglomerates.

The rules likely led some firms to expand through internal growth rather than merger, while discouraging other firms from undertaking procompetitive expansion when internal investment was risker or costlier than merger or would take much longer. The net result of these conflicting merger incentives is unclear. The benefits to small businesses were likely temporary, slowing but not preventing the demise of inefficient firms.

The primary benefit of the articulation of noneconomic goals may have been in helping to protect popular support for antitrust laws. But this effect is less important today. Social insurance was more limited at midcentury, necessitating more side payments to those who might have preferred regulation. These included not just consumers, farmers, small business, and workers but also politicians representing them in a center-left coalition whose more regulatory-minded members needed to be mollified. Today, though, with the growth of social insurance and with the primary threat to the political bargain coming from those seeking less intervention, investing in the political and social role of antitrust won't do much to save competition law.

Doing so would not only be unproductive, it could well be counterproductive. Against potential benefits of pursuing social and political goals, there are substantial costs. To the extent that noneconomic goals mattered to mid-twentieth century antitrust, they likely led the courts to adopt rules that chilled efficient conduct to a greater extent than would have been the case were economic goals the sole consideration. That outcome, real or perceived, strengthened the hand of Chicago critics, leading to an unwinding of the structural era's achievements in constraining the exercise of market power.

It is possible to imagine reincorporating social and political goals as a basis for developing antitrust rules of general applicability, as was done during the mid-twentieth century.[43] But we don't need to replay this scene. The evidence presented in Chapter 1 demonstrates the need for stronger antitrust rules on economic grounds: the social benefits of increased deterrence of anticompetitive conduct almost surely exceed—and by a wide margin—the social costs of any resulting chill to procompetitive conduct. These benefits can be realized with rules whose goals are solely economic. Nor should we incorporate social and political goals when determining the outcome of individual cases. It is hard to see how an explicitly politicized antitrust would work in practice.[44] By what metric do we identify firms with too much political power, as distinct from economic power? Is political power indicated by aggregate revenue? Employment? Investment? Must an offender's political power be national in scope, or could it operate at the level of states or smaller jurisdictions? These are thorny questions more likely to inspire rancor and division than reform.

None of this is to suggest that market power is devoid of adverse social and political consequences. The point is that these problems can be addressed more effectively by complementing economically focused antitrust law with non-antitrust approaches such as campaign finance reform, legislation limiting employee noncompete clauses, net neutrality regulation,[45] rules or laws assuring personal control of data, and legislative and regulatory support for unions. These approaches pair nicely with economic-minded antitrust by offering side payments suited to the new economy: protecting personal autonomy when firms trade on information, assuring entrepreneurs access to digital markets on nondiscriminatory terms, and hedging against job loss from automation by sharing the benefits of technological changes with workers.

Separating out these goals will also help to protect antitrust from its ideological opponents. There is some risk that politics, once acknowledged as a relevant judicial consideration, would be allowed to influence the outcome of individual case decisions directly.[46] Though that did not happen in the mid-twentieth century, even the possibility will raise concerns. And antitrust's critics will be that much more vociferous if they see that competition policy is being used for explicitly political purposes.

Accordingly, though antitrust needs to be reframed to combat market power, emulating the structural era's noneconomic goals is probably not the best way to achieve this end.

THE DISTINCTION BETWEEN POLITICS AND IDEOLOGY

The Nixon and Johnson examples illustrate inappropriate political influence on antitrust enforcement. Antitrust's mid-twentieth century social and political goals were appropriate, if not especially successful. Those goals were relied on to shape rules of general applicability, not to be used directly to resolve individual cases. The difference between acceptable and unacceptable roles for politics turns on a distinction between politics and ideology. Understanding the distinction between politics and ideology is necessary to policing the line between conduct that violates the norm against direct political influence and conduct that does not. The role of politics in antitrust is appropriate, we will see, only when mediated by ideology.

Politics

For our purposes politics can be defined as the influence of interest groups on decisions with the aim of securing outcomes favored by those groups. Crucially, these groups are concerned with outcomes, not with legal and policy arguments other than as vehicles for securing outcomes. This definition is implicit in the perspective on democratic politics sketched below.[47]

In a democratic polity with majoritarian political institutions, self-interested actors seek to assemble coalitions of voters or interest groups to achieve a majority in order to implement their views. A coalition develops a program—a collection of positions—consistent with those views. The program need not reflect intellectually coherent or consistent preferences.[48] Every voter and interest group pursues its self-interest—whether based on personal gain, group gain, or compassion for others—in deciding whether to stay in a coalition and in deciding what to insist on when negotiating a coalition's program.[49] The work of politicians is to assemble and preserve coalitions and implement their programs, in a world in which the self-interest of voters and groups keeps changing.

Coalition leaders usually give reasons for their positions, particularly in advocacy before an agency or court but also in legislative advocacy. Those reasons are typically crafted to appeal to the decision maker without inducing any coalition members to leave. For example, in arguing for a particular policy, coalition leaders may also acknowledge limiting principles that protect the interests of those members who fear the policy's potential reach.

If an agency or court bases its decision on these reasons, regardless of the identity of those presenting them, the decision would not be political in the terms developed here. The decision might instead be based on law, ideology, or cost-benefit analysis. The agency or court would be expected to pay attention to the identity of those presenting the reasons in order to gauge bias but not in order to determine what political coalition is advantaged by their desired outcome. (The latter is what a legislator does in implementing an interest group bargain.)[50] In other words, a decision is political when based on the identity of the interest groups advocating, not on the reasons proffered.

Politics in this sense is largely foreign to the courts, including in the interpretation of antitrust statutes.[51] At the federal antitrust enforcement agencies, politics almost never matters directly in case selection and evaluation,[52] though it occasionally influences the choice of industries or conduct to investigate.[53] With rare exceptions mainly involving the Johnson and Nixon administrations, U.S. antitrust enforcement since the mid-twentieth century has been almost entirely insulated from direct political influence.[54] The enforcement agencies occasionally testify before members of Congress or brief their staffs on completed matters and topical issues, but these are largely benign means of assuring agency accountability.[55] There also is little reason to credit "revolving door" concerns—the suggestion that senior antitrust officials take positions to benefit their former private sector employers or clients or to enhance their future employment prospects.[56]

The judgment that modern U.S. antitrust enforcement has been largely free from direct political influence is not inconsistent with anecdotal evidence of corporate lobbying on antitrust matters.[57] In most recent examples, the primary target is Congress or sector regulators such as the Federal Communications Commission (FCC),[58] not antitrust enforcement agencies or the courts. Occasionally, firms do undertake a substantial and expensive lobbying effort aimed solely at influencing the Justice Department or the Federal Trade Commission (FTC).[59] It may be rational for businesses to do so even though political pressure is unlikely to affect enforcement outcomes. So long as the firm's lawyers do not think that the lobbying will be counterproductive, and the costs of lobbying are small relative to potential benefits of avoiding enforcement, the businesses may be willing to invest in a long-shot effort to persuade. For similar reasons, the relevant firm's opponents may undertake counter-lobbying.[60] It is important to keep in mind that the occurrence of lobbying does not imply its effectiveness. Firms may lobby other government agencies successfully, which might lead executives to suspect incorrectly that antitrust lobbying efforts will pay off too.

Relatedly, we need not be concerned that the stock market responds positively when firms announcing potentially questionable mergers also increase lobbying expenditures.[61] That firms lobby harder when attempting to merge does not show that antitrust lobbying affects enforcement outcomes. At most it suggests that investors think this. Alternatively, and perhaps more likely, investors may view lobbying expenditures as a signal that a firm has also invested substantially in antitrust counseling, and thus that the firm has reasons to think that the transaction will survive antitrust review based on information known to it but unavailable publicly.

Based on my own experience, and the experience of colleagues who have served in senior federal enforcement agency positions, antitrust enforcement decisions at the Justice Department and FTC are invariably based on legal and policy arguments, the strength of the evidence, and institutional factors such as resource constraints—not on the identity of the interest groups or politicians favoring various outcomes. Political interest has led the agencies to open investigations, but it does not affect the resolution of individual law enforcement matters.

It may be that my judgment is too uncompromising—that one could produce an example or two of lobbying's effects on decision making by federal antitrust agencies. If so, agency decision makers are highly circumspect when discussing the possibility, indicating that the norm against political influence is strong.

Ideology

When politics matters in antitrust enforcement and policy decisions, it is mediated through ideology.[62] Here ideology refers to a perspective based on a coherent set of abstract principles that leads to policy preferences.[63] Ideology helps solve an agency problem governing the relationship between interest group members and the political leaders who act as their representatives. By making an ideology public, a political leader can signal to interest group members that when circumstances change or unanticipated issues arise after election, the leader will behave in ways consistent with the group's interests.[64] In consequence, interest group members select leaders, at least in part, on the basis of their ideological commitments. Doing so also facilitates monitoring of the leader's decisions by interest group members. It is often easier to determine whether elected officials' decisions are consistent with an ideological perspective than to determine whether those decisions benefit the interest group's members.

Within the bounds of the antitrust political bargain, an enforcer's or judge's ideology usually takes the form of a judgment about how to balance deterrence of anticompetitive conduct against the risk of chilling procompetitive conduct. Another way to frame the issue is to ask which imposes greater social cost: more enforcement or less? Favoring deterrence leads to greater antitrust intervention.[65] Favoring the avoidance of chilling effects leads to greater restraint.[66] Ideological differences may affect how courts balance competing concerns when formulating and applying judicial rules as well as how enforcement agencies make decisions in close cases.[67]

Even if public enforcement decisions are insulated from direct political influence and the substantive rules of antitrust law are appropriately crafted to deter the exercise of market power, district court judges of unimpeachable integrity but strong ideological perspectives bring those perspectives to bear when resolving the issues before them. Those perspectives affect the resolution of cases, particularly in bench trials where judges find facts as well as reach conclusions of law. The same point could be made about enforcement agencies when exercising their discretion to file complaints.

This outcome is legitimate in a system of representative government.[68] If the political system, through presidential appointment and Senate confirmation, appoints federal judges with a particular ideological perspective, and those elected officials themselves represent the popular will, one would expect judges to share the popular perspective, at least on average. If the popular perspective shifts, new judicial appointees over time would tend to reflect the newly popular view. Government enforcers and private plaintiffs would reinforce that outcome through case selection and the arguments they make.

In a legal field such as antitrust, in which courts establish most legal rules through the interpretation of broad and general statutory language, a new ideological perspective would do more than influence how judges resolve cases under existing rules. As the number of judicial appointees sympathetic to the new perspective grows, courts would be expected to modify legal rules, both substantive and procedural, to reflect the new ideological framework. The resulting modifications and their effects on resolution of individual disputes would be legitimate because the political process underlying judicial selection reflects the popular will.

Even though day-to-day antitrust enforcement is technocratic[69]—relying heavily on economic analysis in order to identify relevant facts and interpreting those facts through an economic lens[70]—over time, antitrust rules and enforcement are responsive to ideological shifts, along with new economic learning and changes in the way markets perform and firms behave.[71] Technocracy is neither a substitute for ideology nor the endorsement of a particular school of economic thought.[72] Rather, it is the means by which antitrust enforcers and courts implement the political bargain. If the ideology prevailing among judges and antitrust officials becomes sufficiently extreme—potentially, a legitimate outcome in a democratic system—technocratic enforcement would become insufficient to maintain that bargain.

Politics, Ideology, and the Abuse or Erosion of Antitrust Institutions

A strong norm against direct political influence on antitrust enforcement means that politics matters only through its influence on ideology. That limits special-interest protectionism and discourages crony capitalism, but it does not offer an insurmountable barrier to political abuse.[73]

Firms seeking to bring political influence to bear on antitrust enforcement decisions, notwithstanding the norm against doing so directly, can also lobby for the appointment of ideological sympathizers to senior positions in the enforcement agencies and on the bench. Sympathizers, though acting with personal integrity, may be less likely on average to evaluate critically arguments against antitrust intervention and the assumptions on which they are based. That tendency may be exacerbated by the credibility conferred on erroneous arguments when promoted by think tanks and other institutions supported by large firms exercising market power. This indirect lobbying effort would work primarily through selection, not incentives: it would be enough for large firms to support scholars with a sympathetic point of view, without the need to suppose that individual researchers are paid to alter their positions.

The more that Congress and the president favor the interests of firms exercising market power, the more likely it is that they will appoint judges who take, from the standpoint of the political bargain, what is an excessively noninterventionist perspective when deciding future antitrust cases, even when applying existing laws.[74] The more judges do so, the less successful antitrust enforcement will become in deterring the exercise of market power. The courts would be expected to develop antitrust rules that reflect the interests of large firms, so the rules could no longer be defended as implementing the bargain. The political branches would also lessen their support for antitrust enforcement institutions.

INSTITUTIONAL OBSTACLES TO POLITICAL MISUSE

Rules Limiting Judicial Discretion

Rules limiting judicial discretion reinforce the norm against direct political influence. The norm reduces judges' and enforcers' incentive to respond to political considerations in making decisions; the rules limit their ability to do so.[75] These are not long-run constraints; they do not inhibit political influence that operates through the appointment of ideologically sympathetic judges, which allows the rules to evolve over time. Even a short-run constraint can be valuable, however, in discouraging special-interest protectionism, partisan misuse, and crony capitalism.

Such constraints have grown that much more important as economic evidence in antitrust litigation has grown more complex. Even with the benefit of cross-examination, judicial education (within the confines of a trial or more generally), and neutral experts, who are sometimes employed, judges may have trouble evaluating economic testimony. Some trial lawyers have suggested that courts lack the ability to resolve disputes between economic experts and therefore tend to decide cases on other grounds.[76]

A comparison of two Seventh Circuit hospital-merger decisions, one from 1986 and the other from 2016, offers a sense of how much more sophisticated the evidence has grown.[77] The 1986 case looked to the number of competitors and their market shares and to features of the market, such as the role of doctors in choosing hospitals, the role of insurance companies in paying hospital bills, the implications of state certificate-of-need laws, the routine sharing of information on prices and costs among hospitals, the complexity of hospital services, and the speed of technological and economic change in the industry. Three decades later, the same court was concerned with more than shares and market features.[78] The testimony also included a model based on modern bargaining theory that incorporated econometric estimates of key parameters. The FTC's expert used the model to predict the merger's adverse price consequences.

Faced with such testimony, a judge might not know what to credit. He or she probably cannot independently evaluate the witness's statements or those of a countervailing witness. This creates space for an ideologically driven judge to essentially discard the merits of a case and proceed however the judge would otherwise prefer. But antitrust law limits such discretion by employing truncated approaches to condemnation. At one time this was done primarily by developing and enforcing per se rules. Today truncated condemnation is more often implemented through reliance on burden-shifting frameworks to structure litigation, use of sliding scales in weighing evidence, and adoption of presumptions.

Truncated Condemnation

During the structural era, many antitrust rules took one of two forms: unstructured reasonableness analyses or per se prohibitions. Per se rules constrain judicial discretion by conditioning liability on highly limited factual showings, as with the traditional rules against price fixing and market division among horizontal rivals. During the 1980s the courts generally shifted from per se rules to reasonableness review. The latter approach served Chicago school–policy ends by giving courts more discretion to consider efficiencies.

Antitrust decision rules have continued to evolve and today typically adopt a burden-shifting approach that structures the rule of reason and harmonizes it with per se analysis. Under this approach a plaintiff meets a burden of production—it sets forth its prima facie case—by presenting evidence of anticompetitive harm. The burden of production then shifts to the defendant, who must justify the conduct as by showing a legitimate business reason for it—that is, by demonstrating the conduct's efficiencies. If the defendant does so, the burden of production shifts back to the plaintiff, which has the ultimate burden of persuasion. In this final round, the plaintiff must show that harms to competition outweigh benefits or, in some cases, that the defendant could have achieved its legitimate goals in a manner less restrictive of competition. This structure increasingly applies to the analysis of claims decided under Sherman Act § 1, to the bad-act inquiry in cases decided under Sherman Act § 2, to mergers reviewed under Clayton Act § 7, and to tying arrangements and exclusive-dealing allegations evaluated under Clayton Act § 3.[79]

The burden-shifting structure has been augmented in many applications by judicial reliance on sliding scales to weigh evidence. Doing so is closely tied to the adoption of presumptions, which are discussed further in Chapter 4. Courts may harmonize reliance on presumptions with the burden-shifting framework by evaluating evidence on a sliding scale once the plaintiff and defendant each satisfy their initial burdens of production.[80] Under a sliding-scale approach, the stronger the plaintiff's case, the more that the defendant must show to overcome it—and vice versa.

A sliding scale permits condemnation without extensive analysis when a plaintiff's prima facie case is strong. Persuasive evidence of actual and substantial anticompetitive effects—or a strong case of probable anticompetitive effects based on the market context, judicial learning, and economic reasoning—typically win the day even if enough facts point in a different direction to allow the defendant to satisfy its initial burden. In addition, when a plaintiff shows that competitive harm is probable based on the nature of the conduct and the market power of the firms and demonstrates substantial market power, courts are similarly likely to side with the plaintiff. Courts are unlikely to be convinced by defendant's efforts to show that the conduct is justified based on efficiencies or that market structure—such as low market shares, evidence that coordination is difficult, or evidence that entry is easy—

makes competitive harm unlikely.[81] When the plaintiff's prima facie case is strong, a court may conduct searching judicial review of proffered efficiency justifications before accepting them.[82] By contrast, when the plaintiff's prima facie case is weak, courts are more likely to credit defendant's arguments, potentially allowing for exculpation without extensive analysis.

The combination of burden shifting and sliding scales has the practical effect of enforcing a strong norm against conduct that creates a strong prima facie case, such as horizontal price fixing and market division. This is not a formal limit on judicial discretion, but it can be a practical one.

Through judicial application of a sliding-scale approach, most horizontal agreement cases turn on the strength and weight of the evidence of adverse effects. When both parties satisfy their initial burdens, courts almost never decide cases by weighing harms against benefits in a quantifiable sense.[83] The structural presumption in horizontal-merger analysis can be understood similarly. In a case involving a merger creating duopoly, in which the defendants argued that coordination was difficult, the D.C. Circuit indicated that the merging firms must show that such difficulties are "so much greater" than in other industries that they rebut the normal presumption of coordinated effects in concentrated markets.[84]

As Chapter 4 explains in more detail, antitrust's reliance on burden shifting, presumptions, and sliding scales offers a reasonable resolution to the error cost trade-off at issue in formulating decision rules. These tools, and the truncated resolution of cases they facilitate, also reinforce the norm against direct political influence by constraining judicial discretion.

The structure of legal rules does not, however, form an impermeable bulwark against special-interest protectionism, partisan misuse, and crony capitalism.[85] A creative trial judge with a strong ideological perspective and familiarity with antitrust may be able to find facts and synthesize legal rules from prior cases in ways that lead to a decision not defensible on competition grounds.[86] Still, burden shifting, sliding scales, and reliance on presumptions of competitive harm reduce the likelihood of that outcome, particularly to the extent that substantive antitrust rules are regarded as consensus norms.

Private Enforcement Constrains Political Abuse

If, through the political influence of large firms, federal enforcers become excessively defendant-friendly, and state enforcers do not step up their efforts in response, robust private enforcement will continue to vindicate the competition laws. Outside of mergers and criminal-cartel enforcement, most antitrust cases are brought by private plaintiffs. That activity limits to some extent the potential adverse consequences of political influence in antitrust. Private enforcement is not a perfect substitute for public enforcement, however. Private parties have different information and incentives than government agencies, so they would not be expected to challenge the same conduct or pursue the same remedies. Private enforcement may also have less deterrent effect than public enforcement.[87]

Notwithstanding these qualifications, it is reasonable to believe that private antitrust enforcement, as with public enforcement, plays a substantial role in deterring anticompetitive conduct. Against this background, the recent trend at the Supreme Court to raise procedural hurdles to private enforcement, based on erroneous arguments about institutions discussed in Chapter 5, threatens to eviscerate this institutional protection against special-interest protectionism and crony capitalism.

CONCLUSION

The longstanding norm against direct political influence in antitrust enforcement, reinforced by legal rules that reduce judicial discretion, discourages the corruption of enforcement. There is no inconsistency between protecting that norm and welcoming a political mobilization for government action against substantial and widening market power, which works against the threatened stealth rejection of the antitrust approach to economic regulatory policy.

Chapter Four

Recalibrating Error Costs
and Presumptions

ANTITRUST ENFORCEMENT TODAY is at times stricter in the European Union (EU) than in the United States, particularly with respect to exclusionary conduct.[1] Google's differential treatment is the best-known example.[2] Whereas the European Commission has brought multiple unfair-competition cases against the tech giant and levied hefty fines, the Federal Trade Commission (FTC) in 2013 closed its investigation without charges.

This divergence might seem surprising. Both jurisdictions have sophisticated antitrust institutions and employ similar economics-based approaches to evaluate business practices. The enforcement agencies on both sides of the Atlantic work to harmonize their analyses, so that companies can expect similar results in Europe and the United States. Statutes and, in the case of European merger control, implementing regulations are comparable. There are some structural differences. The U.S. system is built on an adversarial model while the European system is built on an administrative model.[3] Less significantly, the Europeans use antitrust law to integrate national economies as well as protect competition,[4] and European enforcement has been shaped by distinctive Ordoliberal ideas.[5] But the effect of these differences has generally been minimal.[6] Few cases reviewed by enforcers in the United States and Europe come out differently, though the ones that do are often high profile.

When European enforcement is more restrictive, that result can typically be attributed to a difference in the evaluation of error costs. U.S. officials have recently criticized the Europeans for being insufficiently attentive to the costs of chilling procompetitive firm conduct, particularly when evaluating exclusionary conduct.[7] There is good reason, though, to believe that the opposite is true: widening market power suggests that U.S. authorities are too solicitous of large firms and fail to take seriously enough the costs of harmful conduct.[8]

With respect to exclusionary conduct in particular, the United States can learn from Europe. Indeed, the global spread of antitrust institutions—from a handful of jurisdictions after World War II to more than a hundred today, many with sophisticated enforcement operations—offers U.S. enforcers and courts many opportunities to gain insights from abroad.[9] Global influence in the development of enforcement approaches and practices no longer comes predominantly from U.S. antitrust institutions.[10]

In comparison to their U.S. counterparts, EU enforcers have struck a better error-cost balance. This issue is critically important because courts' views about error costs inform the presumptions they invoke—or forgo—when applying antitrust rules and may lead them to alter the rules themselves. The Chicago-influenced reforms described in Chapter 2 were predicated in part on elevated concern that enforcement errors will chill procompetitive conduct. But those reforms, whatever their merits when implemented, are no longer appropriate in an environment of substantial and widening market power. U.S. rules and presumptions now allow firms to get away with too much anticompetitive conduct.

This chapter explains the connection between error costs and enforcement presumptions and discusses how courts should employ these presumptions in light of growing market power. I focus on the role of presumptions in an area where they take on special importance: horizontal-merger policy. Merger review plays an essential prophylactic role by interdicting competitive problems that would be difficult to identify, challenge, or remedy after a merger is consummated.[11] It is therefore important that jurisdictions facing market-power problems adopt best practices in this enforcement area. I conclude that the long-standing structural presumption in horizontal merger-enforcement should be both strengthened and supplemented with two additional presumptions. This book addresses other aspects of merger analysis elsewhere, including coordinated effects in Chapter 6, vertical mergers in Chapter 7, innovation harms from merger in Chapter 8, and mergers that increase bargaining leverage in Chapter 9.

ERROR COSTS AND PRESUMPTIONS

Error-Cost Analysis

Error-cost analysis is another term for what economists call a decision-theoretic framework. This approach was first employed in the law and economics literature by Richard Posner during the 1970s[12] and introduced into mainstream antitrust scholarship by Paul Joskow and Alvin Klevorick in 1979.[13] Frank Easterbrook's widely cited 1984 article, "The Limits of Antitrust," more famously adopts the error-cost framework.[14]

The error-cost perspective evaluates antitrust rules—individually and as a whole—on the basis of whether they minimize total social costs.[15] The relevant costs include those of false positives (finding violations when conduct did not in fact harm competition), false negatives (failure to find violations when conduct harmed competition), and transactions associated with use of the legal process. Transaction costs include those of litigation and, for example, those associated with information-gathering by potential litigants and the institution specifying decision rules.[16] Transaction costs are not literally error costs, but they are social costs that must also be accounted for in a decision-theoretic analysis of rules.

Error costs track the overall adverse consequences of mistaken implementation of rules—consequences that may be borne by firms involved in litigation, by their competitors, customers, and suppliers, and by firms in unrelated markets that look to those rules for guidance on how to behave.[17] Accordingly, the evaluation of error costs must look to the consequences for firms throughout the economy, not just to effects on the parties to the case.[18] Error costs can also arise without errors in implementation. For instance, per se prohibitions, applied as intended, may lead to over- or underdeterrence.[19] Finally, to the extent that uncertainty about legal rules chills beneficial conduct, or means that the rules fail to deter harmful conduct, the error-cost analysis should account for those consequences.[20]

One technical caveat: false positives and false negatives may not neatly map to over- and underdeterrence, respectively, because the deterrence consequences of legal errors depend in part on the ways those errors affect marginal costs and benefits of conduct undertaken in the shadow of the law.[21] For example, and perhaps counterintuitively, false positives may create underdeterrence by reducing the value of complying with the rules.[22] However, in general, this caveat does not qualify the error-cost analyses of rules in this book.

Although the error-cost framework is a neutral economic tool, contemporary antitrust conservatives have relied on it to advocate rules that weigh against antitrust intervention. Their position is based on a series of erroneous assumptions about markets and institutions, which systematically overstate the incidence and significance of false positives and understate the incidence and significance of false negatives. In totality, the conservative critics understate the net benefits of various rules by overstating their costs. I discuss this further in Chapter 5, which identifies those assumptions and explains why they are faulty.

Presumptions

Many of the rules that courts have developed for deciding antitrust cases can be interpreted as presumptions. Some concern the ultimate determination as to whether competition is harmed by the conduct under review. These include the structural presumption in horizontal-merger analysis, which infers harm to competition from high and increasing market concentration; the presumption that naked price fixing harms competition, which infers competitive harm from an agreement concerning price in the absence of a plausible efficiency justification; and the safe harbor for above-cost pricing in predatory-pricing cases, which infers that price cutting does not harm competition when the discount price remains above a level determined by defendant's cost. Other presumptions concern intermediate elements of the alleged offense. In monopolization cases, for example, courts often presume that defendants with high market share have monopoly power, which is one predicate for a violation.

Presumptions can be rebutted with evidence undermining their factual predicates. For example, merging firms may rebut the structural presumption by showing that concentration, properly measured, will not increase nontrivially. Presumptions can also be rebutted with evidence challenging a court's inference. For instance, the structural presumption connecting high and increasing market concentration with the exercise of market power can be rebutted with evidence that entry would counteract or deter any competitive harms.

The decision rules that courts have created to implement the broad reasonableness requirements of antitrust statutes, presumptions included, can be pictured as lying on a continuum between unstructured standards, such as the comprehensive rule of reason adopted in *Chicago Board of Trade*,[23] and bright-line rules, such as the per se prohibition on price fixing adopted by *Socony-Vacuum*.[24] Relative to unstructured standards, bright-line rules constrain the evidence courts consider and the weight it is given.[25] The burden-shifting framework increasingly employed to evaluate both collusive and exclusionary conduct allows for hybrid rules that lie in between these poles.[26]

Unstructured standards and bright-line rules each can reduce error costs in different ways. Unstructured standards allow the court to consider all relevant information and decide how to weigh it. Doing so tends to reduce error costs by lessening the likelihood of false positives and false negatives, though unstructured standards also can increase error costs if a decision maker becomes confused by the range of evidence presented in a case. For their part, bright-line rules reduce error costs by lessening the transaction costs of litigation, unless the classification decision about whether to apply a bright-line rule is itself costly. Bright-line rules can also reduce firms' compliance costs by giving them guidance, thereby alleviating uncertainty about the likely judicial treatment of their conduct. The latter error-cost considerations justify reliance on presumptions too, though they do not indicate what particular presumptions courts should invoke.[27]

Because a presumption is a legal conclusion based on a limited and specified factual showing, its attractiveness is closely tied to qualities of the relevant factual predicates. The facts should be inexpensive to observe and the conclusion strongly correlated with them. It should also be expensive for firms to manipulate the factual predicates to improperly invoke or avoid the presumption.[28] The weaker the relationship between the factual predicates and the legal conclusion, the greater the likelihood that application of the presumption will generate an erroneous judicial decision and resulting costs.

It is therefore fitting that courts consider error costs in deciding whether to use, modify, or abandon presumptions—or craft new ones. When presumptions are applied, error costs are also essential in determining their strength, which is measured by the persuasiveness required of rebutting evidence. Their strength varies on a continuum: some presumptions are weak, others are strong, and still others are irrebuttable.

Courts are concerned with two ways of reducing error costs when they frame presumptions: deterrence policy and inferred effects.[29] For example, the safe harbor for above-cost pricing could have been defended solely on the basis of a plausible empirical regularity (inferred effects): that discounts rarely exclude rivals when prices remain above the dominant firm's costs. Above-cost predation is a genuine possibility, however, limiting the strength of the inference. The judicial choice to adopt that presumption and make it irrebuttable (as a safe harbor) turned instead mainly on deterrence considerations (a judicial view as to the error-cost balance), not on the strength of the underlying factual inference. The deterrence argument was that the safe harbor prevents the prohibition on predatory pricing from chilling competitive price cutting, and that this consideration is primary given skepticism about the need to deter competitive harm.[30] As explained in Chapter 7, though, what we now know about the error-cost balance justifies abandoning or at least modifying this presumption.

In some situations, a presumption could be invoked against a better-informed party to give that party an incentive to divulge what it knows. This reduces error costs by making more information available to the decision maker. In antitrust, this deterrence consideration has been used to allocate burdens of production—for example, by requiring merging firms to proffer an efficiencies defense.[31] This approach works well. In theory, though, a strong presumption that efficiencies do not justify mergers in concentrated markets could instead have been employed for this purpose.

Recall that some presumptions address the ultimate resolution of the competitive analysis—that is, whether competition is harmed by the conduct under review. In litigation, presumptions of this type matter in two ways. First, they may be the basis for shifting burdens of production. The structural presumption in horizontal-merger analysis provides an example: a plaintiff may satisfy its prima facie case by showing that market concentration is high and will increase as a result of the proposed merger.[32] If the defendant undermines the factual basis for a presumption by showing that concentration does not increase with merger, then the inference of competitive harm does not follow, so the presumption cannot be relied upon to make a prima facie case.[33]

Second, presumptions about the ultimate resolution of the competitive analysis affect the practical evidentiary burden placed on the party seeking to rebut the inference. Preponderance of the evidence—the usual evidentiary standard in civil litigation—can be thought of as competitively neutral. A party's practical burden under this standard can be modified by invoking a presumption about the ultimate resolution of the competitive analysis.

While the nature and strength of presumptions usually derives from two considerations related to error costs, deterrence policy, and inferred effects, it may also depend on overarching policy goals.[34] Recall from Chapter 3 that mid-twentieth-century courts justified antitrust rules limiting concentration by merger on political grounds. These courts argued that concentrated economic power produced political problems. Judges in these cases could be understood as incorporating overarching policy goals into the development and application of presumptions.

Because the structure of presumptions depends on error-cost analysis and overarching policy goals, when views about either change, courts may modify or abandon existing presumptions and develop new ones. As courts come to recognize the problem of substantial and widening market power, therefore, they may revise presumptions currently employed in antitrust analysis. In later chapters, I suggest and question several presumptions on this basis, considering how we can better use presumptions to curb market power. Now, I turn to the erosion of the structural presumption in horizontal merger analysis and suggest ways to restore it.

THE ERODING STRUCTURAL PRESUMPTION

Over the past several decades, legal doctrine surrounding the structural presumption has changed in ways that reduce defendants' practical rebuttal burden. During the 1960s the Supreme Court stated that the inference of competitive harm could be rebutted only by "evidence clearly showing that the merger is not likely to have . . . anticompetitive effects."[35] In practice, that high burden meant that "the Government always wins."[36] By 1990 the strength of the presumption had eroded to the point where the D.C. Circuit, in its influential *Baker Hughes* decision, described concentration as simply "a convenient starting point" for a "totality-of-the-circumstances" analysis and explicitly disclaimed a requirement that defendants make a "clear showing" to rebut the inference of competitive harm.[37]

At the same time, that court indicated that the strength of defendants' practical burden varies on a sliding scale: "The more compelling the prima facie case," which could be satisfied by relying on a presumption of competitive harm inferred from market concentration, "the more evidence the defendant must present to rebut it successfully."[38] Eleven years later, in *Heinz*, the D.C. Circuit reaffirmed the sliding-scale approach in concluding that the government was entitled to a preliminary injunction.[39] This means that the greater the increase in concentration from merger, and the greater the absolute level of postmerger concentration, the stronger the showing merging firms must make to rebut the inference of competitive harm. But the strength of the rebuttal evidence required to overcome the inference may vary with shifting judicial views. Such shifts played a role in the erosion of the structural presumption in horizontal merger litigation between the 1960s and 1990. According to the framework I use here, there are three factors potentially underwriting the erosion: a weakened economic basis for the factual inference of competitive harm from high and increasing concentration, a change in judicial views about the error-cost balance at stake, and a change in judicial views about overarching policy goals. Movement on all these fronts contributed to the wilting of the structural presumption.

The weakened economic basis is widely understood. During the mid-twentieth century, markets that were more concentrated were thought likely to perform less competitively on both theoretical and empirical grounds. As a matter of theory, the dominant and largely unquestioned view among economists and antitrust commentators was that when only a few firms competed in an industry, they readily would find a way to reduce rivalry, collude tacitly, and raise prices above the competitive level.[40] An empirical literature of that era supported the theory by finding a relationship between concentration and firm profits.

By 1990 the theoretical and empirical relationships were understood to have weakened. On the theoretical side, George Stigler showed that even when only a small number of firms participate in a market, oligopolists may have difficulty reaching a consensus on terms of coordination, and each may have strong incentives to compete by cheating on those terms.[41] Thus, supracompetitive prices are not inevitable in concentrated markets. Economists also questioned the empirical relationship between concentration and profits[42] and whether any such relationship, if observed, would reflect market power or efficiencies.[43]

Error-cost balance and overarching policy concerns also were understood differently in 1990 than during the 1960s. The Chicago school conviction that markets generally self-correct counsels that costs of failing to deter anticompetitive mergers are low. This shifted the error-cost balance in favor of mergers, because the perceived costs of chilling procompetitive conduct increased relative to those of stifling anticompetitive conduct. And, as we saw in Chapter 3, the Supreme Court discarded social and political goals to focus antitrust law on economic goals, undermining the policy concerns that once met concentrated economic power. Both of these shifts weakened the structural presumption.[44]

Today the justifications for the structural presumption look stronger than they did in 1990. The contemporary theoretical literature shows that greater market concentration leads to price elevation in noncooperative oligopolies and finds that greater concentration makes coordination more likely to persist. Moreover, in markets conducive to coordination, the fewer the number of significant firms, the greater the likelihood that a merger will harm competition by making coordination more effective.[45] For its part, the current empirical literature, referenced in the next chapter, finds a relationship between concentrated market structure and the exercise of market power.

Adopting a view based on the modern economic literature—a view under which greater likelihood of competitive harm should be inferred from higher market concentration—does not entail a return to the older idea that coordination is nearly inevitable in oligopolies. For one thing, the contemporary research finds that a range of industry- and market-specific factors beyond concentration are also important in determining the competitive effects of mergers. So recalibrating the strength of the inference does not mean that concentration will inevitably be seen as anticompetitive. For another, the empirical research does not reliably identify a "critical" concentration level across industries at which concentration raises particular competitive concern.

Notwithstanding these qualifications, the structural presumption is today better grounded in economics than the Chicagoans supposed.[46] Error-cost considerations weigh in favor of the structural presumption today because the concern to deter anticompetitive conduct is acute.[47] At the same time, the fear that blocking mergers will chill procompetitive acquisitions should be assuaged in light of merging firms' systematically excessive optimism concerning the efficiencies their acquisitions will generate.

Happily, courts have the tool they need to recalibrate the structural presumption: the sliding-scale formulation of *Heinz*. Courts already invoke a stronger presumption when concentration levels are high and will increase nontrivially due to a proposed merger. The modern economic view about the factual inference connecting higher concentration with competitive harm, combined with today's error-cost balance, supports requiring even stronger rebuttal evidence for any given concentration level and increase.[48]

Modern economic learning also suggests that courts analyzing horizontal mergers supplement the structural presumption with two additional presumptions.[49] First, courts should presume adverse unilateral effects of mergers between sellers of differentiated products when their products are close substitutes, i.e., when diversion ratios or demand cross-elasticities between the firms' products are sufficiently high.[50] Consistent with this view, the 2010

Horizontal Merger Guidelines recommend evaluating unilateral effects using an indicator of upward pricing pressure based on diversion ratios.[51] Second, courts should presume adverse coordinated effects from the acquisition of a maverick—a firm whose characteristics or conduct suggest that it constrains more effective coordination among market participants.[52] The 2010 *Horizontal Merger Guidelines* explicitly adopt this presumption as well.[53] I discuss its role in litigation in Chapter 6.

CONCLUSION

The problem of substantial and widening market power, recently recognized but growing for decades, changes the balance of error costs that courts should consider when formulating or modifying presumptions and rules. Today's antitrust presumptions are, in general, insufficiently attentive to the need to deter anticompetitive conduct and overly deferential to fears of chilling procompetitive behavior. To redress that balance, antitrust's rules and presumptions need to be strengthened. This chapter examined ways to do so in horizontal merger analysis. Later chapters broaden the lens to areas of antitrust analysis related to the growing economic significance of information technology and the Internet.

Chapter Five

Erroneous Arguments against Enforcement

A NTITRUST DECISION MAKERS properly pay attention to arguments framed around error costs. These are the right kinds of arguments to put forward: they focus decision makers on the benefits and costs of antitrust rules. The trouble is that antitrust conservatives have proffered error-cost arguments justified on the basis of erroneous assumptions about markets and institutions. Noninterventionists are ideologically disposed to ignore the mistakes, which have brought us to the precipice of antitrust's stealth rejection.[1]

Of course, not all antitrust conservatives think alike. Some would not subscribe to each of the assumptions criticized here. Some would push back at these criticisms selectively, accepting a handful and rejecting others as caricatures of their views or as the beating of dead horses.[2] Some noninterventionist arguments have changed over the years, so cutting-edge scholars may reject some of the views associated with their forebears. In addition, some of those cited as supporting an erroneous argument might resist the conservative label or take noninterventionist positions only with respect to some issues.[3]

But all nine of the assumptions discussed here have formed the basis of arguments dear to members of the antitrust right. That some members of that group dismiss one assumption or another, and that some of these assumptions have also been propounded outside the antitrust right, is not especially important. My aim is to discourage any erroneous assumption that might sustain the current paradigm of lax enforcement. Enforcers and courts should question these assumptions, no matter who relies on them.[4]

ERRONEOUS ASSUMPTIONS ABOUT MARKETS

Markets Self-Correct through Entry

Antitrust conservatives often presume that markets are self-correcting. The idea is that in the event firms exercise market power, entry by new firms or expansion by existing firms will tend to restore competition quickly and automatically, even in the oligopoly settings characteristic of antitrust cases. On this view, the social costs of market power are limited, so error-cost analysis will generally favor permissive antitrust rules.[5] Faith in market self-correction is a core component of foundational works of conservative antitrust scholarship, such as the writings of Easterbrook and Bork.[6]

The claim that markets self-correct through entry rests in part on an unobjectionable economic premise.[7] If entry is easy,[8] then the supracompetitive prices associated with the exercise of market power will prompt new rivals to enter the fray. That development would be expected to counteract any exercise of market power, and its prospect may deter the exercise of market power in the first place.[9]

However, there is a disconnect between, on the one hand, the empirical claim that, as anticompetitive conduct causes prices to rise, "new entrants will emerge to alleviate, or even eradicate, the problem," and, on the other, the conclusion that "[l]etting the guilty go free in antitrust is generally a self-correcting problem."[10] They are linked by the unstated premise that such entry is likely to succeed in policing market power under the oligopoly conditions of greatest concern in antitrust. Put another way, antitrust conservatives assume that entry will dull market power with sufficient frequency, to sufficient extent, and with sufficient speed that false positives are systematically less costly than false negatives.

Yet there is little reason to believe that entry addresses the problem of market power so frequently, effectively, and quickly as to warrant dismissal of concerns regarding false negatives. For example, the claim that airline markets are "contestable" by entrants,[11] once pressed in support of limiting antitrust intervention in that industry, is no longer seriously maintained.[12]

David Evans and Jorge Padilla support the self-correction claim with examples of near-monopolies that have eroded over time, "such as General Motors (automobiles), IBM (computers), RCA (television sets), Kodak (photographic film), Xerox (photocopiers), U.S. Steel (finished steel), and Harley-Davidson (motorcycles)."[13] It is noteworthy, however, that these firms'

dominant positions, while not permanent, persisted for decades. The antitrust case law supplies other examples of dominant firms that possessed durable market power, including Microsoft (operating systems) and Standard
Oil (oil refining).[14]

The case law also provides examples of dominant and colluding firms that
harmed competition by erecting entry barriers and excluding new rivals, including entrants that sought to introduce new technologies.[15] Microsoft, for
example, maintained the market power of its Windows operating systems
by excluding from the platform rival Internet browsers and the Java programming language, which threatened to erode the "applications barrier to
entry."[16] Another example is the *Lorain Journal* newspaper, which protected
its monopoly power by impeding the entry of a rival using a new technology—
radio.[17] Mastercard and Visa likewise adopted rules that prohibited banks
from issuing rival cards with innovative features.[18]

It is also clear that entry routinely fails to solve market-power problems
quickly. A study of eighty-one international cartels convicted in the United
States or European Union since 1990—most of which were terminated by
antitrust cases—found they had an average duration of more than eight
years.[19] Indeed, many cartels have lasted for decades.[20] Theoretical literature
agrees that the exercise of monopoly power need not be transitory or corrected by new rivals attracted by supracompetitive prices.[21]

The self-correction assumption is demonstrably faulty; one cannot simply
presume that entry by new competitors will correct instances of market
power.

Markets Self-Correct Because Oligopolies Compete and Cartels Are Unstable

Markets could be self-correcting even absent the threat of entry if those with
only a few participants—even just two or three—typically perform competitively. Bork considered this likely. "Oligopolistic structures probably do not
lead to significant restrictions of output," he writes.[22] This claim would be
defensible if firms in oligopoly settings typically respond to efforts by other
participants to exercise market power by expanding output or otherwise competing more aggressively—with sufficient speed and to a sufficient extent to
counteract or deter the exercise of market power. In that case, coordinated
arrangements such as cartels would break down quickly or never form in the
first place.[23]

But contemporary economic scholarship does not support this contention. Static, noncooperative oligopoly models show a connection between market concentration and price elevation.[24] Other theoretical literature relates concentration to cartel stability.[25] Empirically, market structure is related to the exercise of market power, demonstrating that markets do not inevitably self-correct.[26] Likewise, if Bork were right, cartels would not last so long. Neither the experience of antitrust agencies engaged in cartel prosecution[27] nor economic learning supports the assertion that the presence of two or three firms in a market is sufficient to ensure competition.[28]

Monopolies Innovate

Oligopoly and monopoly markets could perform well if markets with dominant firms were typically more innovative than markets with more competitive structures. Justice Scalia endorsed this defense of monopoly in dicta in the 2004 case of *Verizon Communications Inc. v. Law Offices of Curtis V. Trinko, LLP*.[29] Scalia's opinion suggested that monopolies are temporary and hence self-correcting, and that monopolies are not troublesome because they foster market growth.[30] He took a Schumpeterian perspective on competition, depicting firms with dominant positions, able to exercise market power, as routinely supplanted by innovative firms that enter by offering superior products or services. He also supposed that monopolies are innovative, not just rivals seeking to supplant them.[31] To similar effect, David Evans and Keith Hylton view antitrust's prohibition against monopolization as trading off the consumer harm from prices hikes against the benefits monopoly confers in enhancing incentives to innovate.[32]

This dynamic-competition defense of concentrated markets and market power is unconvincing. The defense ignores several important ways that greater competition enhances incentives to innovate, some of which I identify in Chapter 1. The defense does not account for the incentives of firms facing product-market competition to escape that rivalry through innovation. Nor does it account for the converse: the Arrovian point that firms have less incentive to innovate when doing so would cannibalize rents on current products. The defense also fails to account for the role that competition in innovation itself plays in fostering the development of new, better, or lower-cost products and services. The defense focuses exclusively on the incentive of firms to invest in research and development (R&D) arising from their ability to appropriate the gains from innovation, while ignoring the incentive of firms to increase R&D investment in response to greater investment by their rivals.[33] Nor does the defense account for empirical evidence showing that greater competition is commonly more important for enhancing innovation incentives than is the greater appropriability that a monopoly could confer.[34] The defense also ignores the ability of firms exercising market power to restrict, deter, or eliminate new forms of competition through exclusionary conduct.[35] To relax antitrust rules on the rationale that one firm is enough for markets to perform well would undermine innovation incentives under the guise of protecting them.

Monopolists Cannot Obtain More than a Single Monopoly Profit

Bork argued that antitrust should not automatically prohibit certain exclusionary business practices—including vertical mergers, exclusive-dealing contracts, and other restrictions on vertically related firms[36]—in part because doing so would make "the simple arithmetical error of counting the same market power twice."[37] He made a similar argument in advocating per se legality for tying (requiring that buyers of one product also purchase another product).[38]

This basis for declining to challenge dominant-firm behavior is commonly referred to as the theory that there is a "single monopoly profit." The theory inverts the claim that markets self-correct by taking the view that there is no middle ground: if a single firm somehow manages to exercise monopoly power, notwithstanding the tendency of markets to self-correct, the firm extracts all possible monopoly profits and cannot harm competition further through the exclusionary conduct under review. The claim is that monopoly markets cannot perform worse, so the monopolists should be allowed to do as they please.

Some U.S. courts have cited the single monopoly–profit theory as a basis for allowing monopolists to make exclusive vertical agreements.[39] The same argument has also been aimed at monopoly-leveraging claims, under which a monopolist would be found liable if it used its monopoly in one market to gain a competitive advantage in a second market, adjacent or complementary to the first.[40] Contemporary conservatives recognize that exceptions to the theory exist; however, they regard these exceptions as rare and implausible[41] and so effectively accept the single monopoly–profit theory in practice.

However, the single monopoly–profit theory is logically valid only in one extreme case. If the monopolist (or coordinating firms acting like a monopolist) has literally no rivals and faces no potential entrants, and if buyers have literally no alternative to the monopolist's products, then the monopolist may indeed be unable to increase the rents it derives from exercising market power through (further) exclusionary conduct. Outside such an exceptional circumstance, though, firms can obtain, extend, or maintain market power through exclusionary conduct that suppresses the alternatives that were just assumed away: fringe rivalry, potential entry, or buyer ability to substitute other products.[42] Thus a dominant firm or group of firms coordinating their strategies can exercise additional market power by excluding actual or potential rivals, leveraging market power in a complementary market, or preventing buyers from economizing on products they can use in variable proportions.[43]

Contrary to the implicit presumption of the single monopoly–profit theory, poorly performing markets can grow worse. We should, in general, be wary of appeals to economic theory that rule out the potential for competitive harm from exclusionary conduct by dominant firms.

Business Practices Prevalent in Competitive Markets Cannot Harm Competition

The conservative literature evaluating antitrust rules often relies on biased evidence when assessing the likely competitive effects of business practices, particularly exclusionary conduct. The problematic chain of logic begins with the observation, whether derived from casual empiricism or from systematic empirical studies, that some forms of business conduct—such as tying, exclusive dealing, and other vertical restraints—are prevalent in competitive markets.[44] This literature mistakenly infers that firms cannot readily use these practices to harm competition, either at all or on balance after accounting for efficiencies. The literature then concludes that antitrust rules should not prohibit such practices.[45]

However, the use of such practices in competitive markets does not preclude the possibility that firms also use those practices to obtain or maintain market power. Nor should we assume that those practices cannot harm competition when employed by firms exercising market power.[46] Indeed, a recent study of a sample of convicted contemporary international cartels concludes that at least one-quarter of them used vertical restraints to support collusion.[47]

Furthermore, the prevalence of certain practices, including exclusionary practices, in competitive markets does not support an inference that the same practices typically have an efficiency motive when used in oligopoly markets, which antitrust enforcement would chill. For example, the parallel adoption of simplified and common product definitions, price lists, and guarantees to buyers that they will get the seller's best price are each practices that firms can use to achieve efficiencies and to facilitate coordination.[48] It would be inappropriate to infer that, just because competition is sometimes compatible with these practices, that rivals cannot also use them to fix prices or divide markets or that they necessarily do so with such infrequency as to justify relaxing antitrust's concern with collusion.

Even if most instances of a practice benefit competition or are competitively neutral, that does not mean that the subset of instances challenged in court—by virtue of facts suggesting the possibility of competitive harm—typically benefit competition on balance or at all. Because today's antitrust enforcement makes it difficult for plaintiffs to prevail in exclusionary conduct cases, only plaintiffs bringing unusually strong cases are likely to succeed. Defendants' claims about the efficiencies arising from their conduct may also be overstated, particularly when the information needed to verify those claims is largely in defendants' hands.[49] All of this suggests that we should not infer from a lack of successful challenges that one or another practice is procompetitive.[50]

In addition, the empirical evidence underlying the assertion that practices prevalent in competitive markets do not harm competition is often misinterpreted. Much of this evidence comes from settings in which legal rules—including substantive antitrust rules prohibiting anticompetitive instances of the practices at issue—shape firm conduct.[51] Evidence that certain practices often promote competition in these settings provides little information as to whether the same practices would have harmful consequences if antitrust rules constraining their use were relaxed.

To illustrate these points, consider the enforcement and policy implications of studies showing a low incidence of competitive harm arising from vertical restraints. Assuming that the studies correctly measure incidence,[52] their findings might justify an enforcer declining to target for investigation an instance of vertical restraint that the enforcer selected at random. The low overall incidence, however, would not justify declining to target instances of vertical restraint selected on the basis of additional information suggesting competitive harm.

Furthermore, a low incidence of competitive harm in the sample would not supply a basis for presuming that vertical restraints benefit competition or adopting a rule of per se legality. To do so assumes that harmful conduct is rare because firms cannot readily use vertical restraints to harm competition. But it may be that harmful conduct is rare precisely because antitrust rules deter firms from using vertical restraints to harm competition.

Unless an empirical study compares settings with and without antitrust rules, or provides some other basis for ruling out the deterrence explanation, the study cannot demonstrate (*identify*, in the econometric sense) the competitive impact of the business practices that conservatives have targeted for antitrust abandonment. Studies in which all observations of the competitive effects of a practice come from settings in which antitrust rules constrain the ways in which firms employ that practice supply no information about the ways that firms would employ that practice in the absence of those rules. Hence such studies cannot support proposals that antitrust discard rules prohibiting that practice.

A recent, unpublished study addresses this methodological issue and highlights the role that antitrust rules play in deterring firms from using vertical restraints to harm competition.[53] The study, which uses Nielsen consumer-panel data to analyze changes in the prices and quantities sold for over a thousand categories of branded consumer products,[54] follows on the *Leegin* case. There, the Supreme Court ruled that resale price maintenance was no longer illegal per se but should instead be reviewed under the rule of reason. However, some states retain per se illegality. Thus the study is able to compare effects of per se illegality versus rule-of-reason review.[55] The authors find that in the fifteen states in which the rule-of-reason standard is most likely to apply, when prices changed, they were usually higher, and output lower, than in the nine states in which the per se standard was most likely to apply.[56] The greater reduction in output observed in the rule-of-reason states indicates that resale price maintenance typically harmed competition in the products studied. Industry output is a better indicator of the competitive consequences of minimum resale price maintenance than are industry prices because the practice would likely lead to higher prices regardless of whether it promoted or harmed competition.[57]

This study suggests that the rule of reason did not deter anticompetitive uses of resale price maintenance that the per se rule deterred. The study does not determine systematically whether manufacturers of branded consumer products employed resale price maintenance in the states where they were not necessarily prevented from doing so. Some likely did, however: the study reports anecdotal evidence to that effect and notes that a number of products in the sample were sold by manufacturers that had allegedly used resale price maintenance in the past.[58] The findings are consistent with the view that anticompetitive explanations for resale price maintenance tend to predominate over procompetitive explanations.[59] This conclusion is at odds with the views of conservative commentators about the likely competitive effects of vertical practices, including resale price maintenance.[60] To similar effect, empirical studies of the effects of exclusive dealing in beer distribution do not uniformly favor procompetitive explanations over anticompetitive ones.[61]

The problematic inference that practices prevalent in competitive markets do not harm competition has been deployed to various effects. Conservative critics use it to oppose an "aggressive enforcement policy" attacking vertical restraints (both nonprice restraints and resale price maintenance);[62] to support a rule-of-reason analysis that evaluates tying "in a manner that puts a high burden of proof on the plaintiff";[63] to support antitrust's use of a "hard to satisfy" test for plaintiffs in predatory pricing cases;[64] and to support per se legality for new-product introductions and unconditional refusals to share intellectual property.[65] These analyses together make a flawed case for downplaying the anticompetitive potential of exclusionary conduct, thereby undermining a core concern of antitrust.[66]

ERRONEOUS ASSUMPTIONS ABOUT INSTITUTIONS

Erroneous Judicial Precedents Are More Durable than the Exercise of Market Power

In arguing that the costs of false positives outweigh those of false negatives, antitrust conservatives often highlight the supposed durability of erroneous judicial precedents. "If the court errs by condemning a beneficial practice," Easterbrook writes, "the benefits may be lost for good" through the precedential effect of the judicial decision.[67] Easterbrook expresses particular concern with erroneous Supreme Court decisions,[68] presumably because lower courts' errors of law are frequently corrected on appeal.[69]

It is hard to credit the claim that bad precedents systematically outlive market power.[70] Erroneous precedents may not disappear overnight, but neither do cartels nor single-firm dominance. It took seven years for the Supreme Court implicitly to overrule the erroneous precedent of *Appalachian Coals*,[71] which had allowed coal producers to cartelize during the Great

Depression, and ten years explicitly to overrule *Schwinn*,[72] which had made vertical intrabrand nonprice agreements illegal per se. Yet these lengths of time are comparable to the typical duration of cartels cut short by antitrust enforcement and, in consequence, less than the cartels' likely duration if market forces were the sole mechanism for correction.[73]

Furthermore, even before the Court overrules an erroneous precedent, a number of circumstances may limit its practical effect. Precedents may be undermined by lower courts,[74] abrogated by legislative action,[75] or narrowed, procedurally or substantively, by the Court itself.[76] The instances in which the Supreme Court has overruled its own antitrust decisions, the range of mechanisms available for correcting bad court decisions, and the Supreme Court's thoroughgoing adoption of the Chicago school's critique all call into question Easterbrook's claim that erroneous judicial precedents, even from the Supreme Court, are more durable than monopolies and cartels.[77]

Antitrust Institutions Are Manipulated by Complaining Competitors

Antitrust conservatives also claim that antitrust-enforcement institutions make false positives too likely and too expensive, at least with respect to exclusionary-conduct violations and cases brought on behalf of classes of consumers. Supposedly, one source of this problem is the ease with which complaining firms manipulate antitrust institutions by alleging anticompetitive exclusion.

According to Easterbrook, "The books are full of suits by rivals for the purpose, or with the effect, of reducing competition and increasing price."[78] Such suits, on this view, impose unnecessary costs and, "given the unavoidable number of erroneous decisions in antitrust cases, the suits bring condemnation on useful conduct."[79] To address the problem, he recommends treating lawsuits brought by horizontal competitors "with the utmost suspicion"[80] and "generaliz[ing]" the antitrust injury doctrine[81] to curtail litigation by plaintiffs who would be harmed if the conduct they challenged promoted competition.[82]

Following the latter prescription, the antitrust injury doctrine has expanded over time, providing courts with a basis for dismissing much of the sort of litigation that troubled Easterbrook. Suits by terminated dealers, a particular concern for Easterbrook,[83] have also been limited by Supreme Court decisions circumscribing the ability of terminated dealers to challenge resale price maintenance.[84] In the judgment of Herbert Hovenkamp, author of the leading antitrust treatise, "While anticompetitive decisions were once relatively common, they are much less frequent today."[85]

Antitrust conservatives nevertheless continue to suggest that a disproportionate number of cases alleging exclusion, particularly those against dominant firms, lack merit. The claim is that these cases are often brought by inefficient and unsuccessful rivals or, when brought by the enforcement agencies, instigated by such rivals.[86] The main concern is with false positives: if such suits are in fact common,[87] and if complaining rivals bringing bad cases tend to have more influence over enforcement and judicial processes than do wrongly accused defendants, then enforcers will bring unwarranted cases, and courts will systematically find violations when they should not. The effect would be to chill procompetitive conduct by dominant firms. In addition, conservatives could then say, if the courts do not stop such cases, even efficient rivals would have an incentive to commence baseless actions alleging exclusion to discourage vigorous competition from the firms they name as defendants.

This concern seeks to remedy what is at best an implausible hypothetical. There is no reason to suspect that unsuccessful rivals enjoy systematically better access to the enforcement agencies or exert systematically greater influence on them or on the courts than do large-firm defendants. Large-firm defendants in exclusion cases tend to have the resources needed to present an effective courtroom case, make an effective public-relations appeal, and mobilize political support. The assertion that the enforcement agencies are systematically manipulated by complaining rivals also inappropriately discounts or ignores internal institutional checks within agencies, including layers of internal review and the independent institutional roles of agency economists and lawyers. Also discounted is the external constraint imposed on agencies by the prospect of judicial review.

Moreover, there is no reason to suspect that the agencies and courts are unable to understand the possible biases of rivals and to discount their testimony appropriately. Enforcers account for the biases of all interested parties, including those of the alleged excluding firms themselves.[88] Under these circumstances, a low probability of success should deter unsuccessful rivals from bringing speculative or unfounded antitrust complaints. In addition, we should keep in mind that competitor lawsuits offer benefits by enhancing deterrence of anticompetitive conduct. Rivals "often . . . are in the best position to detect and prosecute many antitrust violations early, before they cause significant consumer harm."[89]

If the courts were subject to systematic manipulation by complaining competitors, one would not expect to see them adopting legal rules that underdeter harmful practices. Yet they have done so. For example, until the Supreme Court stepped in,[90] the lower courts consistently ruled in favor of pharmaceutical-firm defendants that employed "pay for delay" settlements to prevent the entry of rivals producing generic drugs and adopted legal standards that largely insulated such settlements from antitrust lawsuits.[91] In addition, some appellate courts have viewed exclusive dealing as presumptively lawful when contracts have short terms[92] and perhaps when excluded firms retain alternative, albeit less efficient, means of reaching customers.[93] To the extent that courts and prospective litigants understand these presumptions as nearly impossible to rebut in practice,[94] and thus as tantamount to conclusions of law, anticompetitive conduct would again be underdeterred. This dangerous possibility appears to be receding, however, with recent appellate decisions finding that plaintiffs have established anticompetitive harm from exclusive-dealing arrangements.[95]

Courts Cannot Tell Whether Exclusionary Conduct Harms Competition or Promotes It

Some antitrust conservatives question enforcement against anticompetitive conduct on the ground that courts are often unable to make the detailed factual assessments required under the Sherman Act to determine whether conduct harms or benefits competition.[96] Yet conservatives deploy their skepticism selectively, primarily to question judicial competence in resolving monopolization claims and other exclusionary-conduct allegations.[97] If courts could not reliably determine whether exclusionary conduct is procompetitive or anticompetitive, they would have similar difficulty in assessing the competitive effects of allegedly collusive conduct such as horizontal price fixing and market division, which also can have efficiency justifications.[98] The selective conservative skepticism about the competence of courts to make factual assessments appears to reflect a reflexive hostility to exclusion cases rather than a sober response to limits on courts' institutional competence.[99]

Perhaps conservative skepticism about the ability of courts to apply the rule of reason should be understood instead as an argument for limiting antitrust enforcement across the board, constraining it to conduct that lacks any plausible efficiency justification or creates little or no procompetitive benefit. If that is the point, conservative scholars need to explain why they believe that a generation of doctrinal reform along Chicago school lines has been a failure[100] and why a radical retrenchment of today's reformed anti-trust rules—to the point of effectively abandoning antitrust altogether in an era of substantial and widening market power—is necessary. Although such an approach might seem to preserve the antitrust prohibition on naked car-tels, it would effectively exempt mergers from antitrust scrutiny and there-fore permit firms to collude through merger, as they did around the start of the twentieth century.

Some conservatives argue that firms subject to antitrust claims need broad safe harbors to limit uncertainty about the scope of antitrust rules, as might arise from the difficulty of distinguishing harmful from beneficial or neu-tral conduct. Conservatives suggest that this uncertainty imposes substan-tial additional compliance costs, foments fear of false positives, and chills efficiency-enhancing firm conduct.[101] To be sure, as discussed in Chapter 4, antitrust must routinely balance the advantages and drawbacks of bright-line rules against those of less structured standards.[102] But if some rules provide insufficient guidance and predictability, adopting broad safe harbors, which amounts to abandoning antitrust enforcement, is not an appropriate response. After all, restoring per se illegality would provide equally clear guidance.[103] Instead, an appropriate response might be to impart more structure to the rules in question by, for example, adopting presumptions.[104]

Courts Cannot Control the Costs of Private Litigation

Private antitrust enforcement in the United States allows successful plain-tiffs to recover treble damages, thereby augmenting the deterrent effect of public enforcement and providing compensation to victims.[105] Sometimes this enforcement occurs through class actions, which also come with many advantages. They avoid the high social costs of relitigating common issues in many individual actions, give plaintiffs economies of scale in pursuing their claims when collective action would otherwise be impractical, and confer deterrence benefits by making private enforcement feasible when in-dividual damages are small relative to the transaction costs of litigation.[106]

Notwithstanding these well-known social benefits of private enforcement, the Supreme Court has questioned the efficiency of private antitrust rights of action. Several recent Court antitrust decisions evince a concern with the transaction costs of private antitrust litigation, particularly class actions.[107] These decisions have circumscribed private antitrust plaintiffs' access to the courts. Some have even required that antitrust disputes be resolved outside the courts, by regulators or arbitrators.[108] Yet the Court adopted these measures with little evidence that lower courts are unable to manage private litigation[109] and without attempting to show that the benefits, if any, that society derives from reduced transaction costs exceed the social costs of restricting both private and public (federal and state) antitrust enforcement.

In the Chicago school era, the Court has taken several steps to limit access to judicial proceedings.[110] They include introducing the antitrust injury requirement, raising the standard that a dealer must satisfy to prove that its termination was pursuant to a resale price–maintenance agreement between a manufacturer and other dealers,[111] restricting damages claims by indirect purchasers,[112] and elevating the burden that plaintiffs must meet to survive a motion for summary judgment.[113] *Trinko* and *Credit Suisse* shift antitrust disputes from courts to administrative agencies.

These initiatives raise several concerns. Decisions limiting private plaintiffs' access to the courts necessarily discourage some meritorious lawsuits and reduce antitrust's deterrent effect. Decisions shifting competition enforcement from the courts to regulatory agencies will likely lead to outcomes that prioritize regulatory objectives at antitrust's expense. Both types of decisions create hurdles for government enforcers seeking to vindicate antitrust principles in the courts,[114] notwithstanding the trust that antitrust conservatives place in the ability of courts and government enforcement agencies to perform effectively when attacking cartels.[115]

Some recent Court decisions, particularly *Twombly*, cite the social costs of private litigation. The majority in that case views private antitrust enforcement, particularly consumer class action lawsuits, as an invitation for plaintiffs with meritless claims to use the threat of expensive litigation to extract wasteful settlements.[116] In addition, the majority in *Credit Suisse* views private antitrust litigation as imposing added social costs by bringing confusion to the law.[117] Daniel Crane sees the Court, influenced heavily by Justice Stephen Breyer, responding to institutional concerns about the competence of generalist judges and juries to evaluate complex antitrust cases and about the potential for private litigation to go awry.[118]

Though the Court has been eager to cut back on the litigation of private antitrust claims, it has done little analysis of the magnitude of these costs.[119] There has been scant comparison of these costs to the social benefits of private antitrust litigation and paltry acknowledgment that private antitrust litigation can serve the aims of competition policy by increasing deterrence.

The argument between the majority and dissent in *Twombly* was over the extent to which case-management tools allow judges to control discovery costs. In other words, the only matter of debate was the magnitude of the costs of private litigation, not the balance of its costs and benefits.[120]

The benefits of antitrust enforcement as a whole almost surely exceed the costs by a wide margin,[121] creating a strong presumption in favor of robust enforcement. To justify retrenchment of private antitrust enforcement, the Court must make one of two showings. First, it could show that private enforcement as a whole is radically less effective than public enforcement—so much less effective at deterring anticompetitive conduct, so much more harmful in chilling beneficial conduct, and so much more costly than public enforcement as to rebut the presumption in favor of strong enforcement. Second, and in the alternative, the Court could show that the specific ways in which it would curtail private enforcement would reduce social costs by an amount greater than the reduction in social benefits. The Court has not even attempted to make either showing.

CONCLUSION

Given the Supreme Court majority's conservative perspective on antitrust issues, arguments based on erroneous assumptions about markets and institutions enhance the threat that antitrust will be rejected by stealth. These bad arguments may encourage the Court to push today's already lax antitrust rules in an even less interventionist direction. Today's rules are likely the most favorable antitrust defendants have seen in at least seven decades,[122] but they could be relaxed even further. To protect a robust, effective, and socially beneficial antitrust, enforcers and courts must learn to recognize and question these arguments and the loose enforcement approach they help sustain.

PART II

Antitrust Rules and the Information Economy

Chapter Six

Inferring Agreement and Algorithmic Coordination

INFORMATION TECHNOLOGY (IT) has a significant impact on how prices are formulated. Two decades ago, soft drink producers experimented with vending machines that automatically increase prices as temperatures rise outdoors.[1] Computers and artificial intelligence have made even more ingenious pricing methods possible today. Future chapters will delve into the antitrust concerns raised by a particular region of online commerce—technology platforms. But I begin our tour of IT's antitrust challenges with a concern that applies to all dimensions of the Internet-enabled economy: the use of computer algorithms to coordinate prices.

The efficiency benefits of sophisticated, computer-controlled price shifting are obvious. But there are potential downsides as well. With firms increasingly setting prices by algorithm,[2] and algorithms learning to negotiate with each other,[3] the possibility of coordination by algorithm is an emerging antitrust enforcement issue. Indeed, such coordination may already be happening. In 2015 the Justice Department charged that sellers of posters on Amazon Marketplace had adopted computerized algorithms to set prices according to a prior agreement.[4] Firms need not employ complex algorithms in order to realize higher prices; experimental evidence shows that higher prices result even from simple algorithms that monitor and match rival prices.[5]

In addition to creating opportunities for coordination, algorithms raise novel antitrust enforcement challenges because they reduce the need for communication among firm executives, who may not even understand the reasons for price changes. As this chapter explains, under these conditions it will become more difficult to infer an agreement to fix prices under Sherman Act § 1. In consequence, antitrust laws will do even less to deter coordination than is currently the case.

We should therefore anticipate more coordination ahead. Firms still have an incentive to cheat on an arrangement coordinated by algorithm, but increased ease of coordination combined with increased impediments to enforcement would be expected to make coordination more likely on the margin. The likelihood and success of oligopolistic price elevation would grow economy-wide.

This would foster anticompetitive outcomes and excessive prices. The error-cost balance would shift toward insufficient deterrence of anticompetitive conduct. No one, regardless of ideology, wants to see these results. Rather than accept them, this chapter proposes that the courts adopt a new presumption that will curtail algorithmic price coordination. I argue that under certain conditions, courts should presume that rival firms have reached an agreement on price when they use algorithms in setting prices. Specifically, the presumption would apply to firms that compete with the same rivals in multiple markets, where cheating on a coordinated consensus on price in any individual market would likely be deterred by rapid price matching and where entry would not be expected to undermine a coordinated outcome. The presumption would be grounded in an economic analysis of error costs set forth below.

The presumption I describe would be rebuttable. A defendant could respond with evidence that prices respond to shifts in cost and demand, in ways consistent with what would be expected of firms engaged in one-shot pricing interactions.[6] A firm could also rebut by showing that its algorithm selects prices for each market without regard to prices in other markets. However, one would not expect to see the latter rebuttal routinely, because the products or services firms sell in various markets are often substitutes or complements, in terms of either supply or demand.

The presumption would not bar firms from using pricing algorithms, but it likely would impose certain requirements on them. To meet their rebuttal burden, firms probably would need to design their algorithms to create audit trails and to make transparent the factors that led the algorithm to change prices. This approach promises to deter pricing coordination by algorithm while still allowing firms to take advantage of algorithms in order to price competitively.

For conceptual clarity, this chapter focuses on the ability of competing sellers to exercise market power through the use of algorithms in price setting. However, the analysis would be similar if rival buyers used purchasing algorithms to exercise monopsony power. In addition, the legal analysis in this chapter concerns possible violations of the Sherman Act when pricing algorithms are used, by agreement, for purposes of coordination. It does not consider whether adoption of pricing algorithms, on its own, would violate the statute, though it might.[7]

I will argue that, beyond adopting the above presumption, antitrust agencies can discourage algorithmic coordination by relying more on horizontal-merger enforcement. Merger enforcement can prevent changes in market structure that would make coordination more likely or more effective. To redress the shift in the error-cost balance toward insufficient deterrence, more energetic merger enforcement to deter coordinated conduct would not specifically target markets susceptible to algorithmic coordination because many markets are susceptible. Accordingly, this chapter explains why the enforcement agencies should pay more attention to the potential coordinated effects of horizontal merger in all markets, in particular by identifying and challenging acquisitions between rivals in which one of the merger partners is a maverick.

ALGORITHMIC PRICING

In principle, any pricing rule employed by human decision makers could be codified into an algorithm. Consequently, algorithmic pricing could promote competition in some cases and harm it in others. But algorithms also can alter decision making in several ways. They may increase the decision maker's span of control, broadening the scope of markets one decision maker can reasonably understand and review closely. Algorithms may also increase the range of factors that a decision maker can consider. Algorithms may increase the speed with which a decision maker can observe and respond to rival decisions and changing market conditions. Indeed, the speed and complexity of algorithms are such that people may not even be able to grasp the reasoning underlying their output, effectively removing decision making from human hands.

Below, I illustrate these possibilities by comparing two hypothetical pricing algorithms, one more sophisticated than the other. The illustration suggests that the competitive danger from algorithmic coordination is greatest when coordinating firms sell in multiple markets (i.e., they sell the same product in more than one location, more than one product in the same location, or both). When firms sell a single product in a single location, algorithms may not provide much advantage over humans in reaching a coordinated consensus. The algorithmic advantage is greater when reaching consensus across multiple markets, a task whose complexity can be more daunting to humans.[8]

The examples are not meant to suggest all the ways that algorithms can coordinate.[9] It may turn out that, through experimentation and learning, price-setting algorithms end up applying different decision rules than those embodied in the two hypothetical algorithms.[10] But the hypotheticals do speak to algorithm's advantage over humans in reaching coordinated outcomes across multiple markets, as well as the increased harm from price coordination when it encompasses multiple markets. On the plus side, these models also suggest that we can fashion a remedy for cross-market coordination that does not chill procompetitive conduct.

A Leader-Follower Pricing Algorithm

In the first example, rival firms (or their vending machines) employ algorithms that mimic leader-follower pricing for each specific market. No other markets bear on the pricing decision, and it is assumed that customers pay the posted price. The example also supposes that the firms are oligopolists: they compete while recognizing their interdependence.

Assume further that firms would be deterred from cheating in any individual market if they expect their price cuts to be matched quickly by rivals. This is often a plausible outcome in, for example, markets where buyers are numerous, make small purchases, and cannot easily store inventories. In such cases, a firm that cuts prices may not be able to increase its sales substantially if its rivals match its price cut(s) quickly.[11] Assume also that entry is not a threat, regardless of whether it is prevented by natural barriers, discouraged by the expectation that discount prices would be matched quickly, or impeded by the exclusionary conduct of incumbents.[12]

In this sort of market, the primary impediment to successful coordination among rivals would be the difficulty of identifying a coordinated consensus as to the (supracompetitive) price the firms would charge. Sellers may solve this problem through leader-follower conduct.

Each firm's leader-follower pricing algorithm has four properties: (1) rapid matching of price increases up to some predetermined level, which is the maximum price the firm would like the industry to set and is presumably above the competitive price; (2) occasional trial price increases if prices are lower than a predetermined level, with those increases quickly reversed if not matched by all rivals; (3) rapid matching when a rival reduces price;[13] and (4) adjustments to price in response to new (exogenous) information about costs or demand.

The algorithm's rules could readily be adapted to deal with differentiation across products and regions. If prices are not initially identical, the price increases might preserve prior price differentials (either in dollar or percentage terms). Prior price differences might be thought of as compensating marginal customers for the valuation of differences in product attributes or seller locations.

The algorithm could be complicated further. For example, because rapid matching of rival price reductions discourages rival cheating on a coordinated price consensus, the algorithm might time those reductions more quickly than it does for matched price increases.[14] However, this discussion will ignore such adaptations and complications in order to highlight the central analytical issues that would confront a court considering whether to infer an agreement among firms employing leader-follower price-setting algorithms.[15]

For purposes of this exercise, assume that every firm adopts the identical leader-follower pricing algorithm. Each firm makes that adoption choice individually, aware that its rivals will adopt pricing algorithms of their own.[16] The common adoption of such algorithms is plausibly an equilibrium within a class of algorithms looking solely to pricing within a particular market (that is, among algorithms that ignore the cross-product or cross-region interactions relevant for pricing by multiproduct producers).[17]

When firms employ leader-follower algorithms, the price would be expected to end up at the lowest predetermined maximum established by any of the competing firms. If there are three soft drink producers, for example, and their predetermined maximum prices for vending machines in a particular location are $1.00, $1.10, and $1.20, respectively, the algorithms would eventually lead all three to select a price of $1.00. Suppose all firms initially charged $0.80. One firm might try raising price to $0.90 (property 2), which the others would quickly match (property 1). Once the price hit $1.00, one firm would stop matching, so trial price increases would quickly be reversed, leaving the price at $1.00. If the predetermined maximum prices are set above the competitive price, the firms would exercise market power.

A More Sophisticated Pricing Algorithm

Firms can coordinate in ways that go beyond what market-by-market leader-follower pricing permits. In the hypothetical case below, the firms coordinate across multiple markets.

Let's say Coca-Cola (or Coke) and Pepsi have vending machines in multiple cities, each a separate market, and the competitive price for soft drinks is $0.75. To keep the story simple, assume also that these are the only two soft drink firms, and there are just two cities—Atlanta and Boston. The firms are strong in different cities: Coke has greater market share and brand loyalty in Atlanta, and Pepsi in Boston. In Atlanta, Coke's predetermined maximum price is $1.20, while Pepsi's is $1.00. In Boston, Pepsi's predetermined maximum price is $1.20, while Coke's is $1.00.

The simple market-by-market price-leadership algorithm would lead the firms to charge $1.00 in each city. But coordination could be improved through more sophisticated algorithms that can optimize across markets, allowing the firms to exercise even more market power. Optimizing across markets could allow both firms to charge more, because it is plausible that they would do better if they raised the market price to $1.20 in each city. Coke would do worse than before in Boston but more than make up for it by doing better than before in Atlanta. Pepsi would enjoy a similar outcome, losing in Atlanta but gaining even more in Boston.

The algorithms could arrive at a price of $1.20 in both cities if they recognize or learn through trial and error that the firms can increase profits by connecting the two markets. Say Coke's algorithm raises price simultaneously in a strong city (Atlanta) and a strong city for its rival (Boston). Now suppose Pepsi's algorithm responds with its own simultaneous and identical action: it would either raise price to match in both cities or leave price unchanged in both, but it would not selectively match. If Pepsi's algorithm concludes that Pepsi would do better by increasing price in both locations, then Pepsi would match prices in both cities. The two firms would eventually land on $1.20 in Atlanta and Boston. This outcome can be described as a cross-market bargain.

When firms set prices at levels above their rivals' predetermined maximum prices, they need to deter cheating. The algorithms can do this through means similar to those they employ to reach prices exceeding those achieved by leader-follower algorithms. To see how, suppose that Pepsi and Coke charge $1.20 in both cities. Suppose further that Pepsi's algorithm then experiments by reducing the price in Atlanta to $1.00. Doing so would be profitable for Pepsi, even recognizing that Coke would lower its Atlanta price to match, so long as Coke maintained the price in Boston at $1.20. If the price becomes $1.00 in Atlanta, Coke would profit by lowering the price in Boston to $1.00, even recognizing that Pepsi would match in that city. If the pricing algorithms follow this logic, one might expect the coordinated prices of $1.20 in both cities to unravel, and prices to end up at $1.00 in both locations.

Coke would profit more if it could prevent that outcome and instead convince Pepsi to restore the price of $1.20 in Atlanta. A sophisticated Coke algorithm might engineer a restoration of the $1.20 price by matching Pepsi's price reduction to $1.00 in Atlanta and simultaneously reducing the price identically in Boston. Perhaps Pepsi's algorithm would kick back in and raise prices across multiple markets, after which Coke would match Pepsi's prices in both locations. Or perhaps Pepsi's algorithm would learn that after Coke simultaneously reduces its price across two cities unrelated in cost and demand, Coke will match a simultaneous price increase across the two cities.[18] Either way, the price would return to $1.20 in both Atlanta and Boston.

One might say Coke retaliated when Pepsi cheated, and that response led to the restoration of the original coordinated consensus.[19] Or one might think of the interaction between firms as beginning after Coke matched Pepsi's price reduction in Atlanta and simultaneously lowered its price in Boston. When Pepsi raised prices in both cities to $1.20 and Coke matched, those events could be seen as reaching a cross-market bargain much like the one the firms originally reached when raising prices to $1.20. Over time, Pepsi's pricing algorithm may come to anticipate Coke's response, and vice versa. The algorithm may conclude that it would not be profitable to cut price in Atlanta in the first place. Then, one might say that Pepsi's fear of Coke's retaliation deterred Pepsi from cheating.[20]

If the firms compete in multiple product markets (different soft drink flavors, perhaps, or soft drinks and snacks), analogous algorithms could allow them to exercise more market power than the single-market leader-follower algorithm achieves. Imperfect information about rival valuations—here uncertainty about the rival's predetermined maximum prices—would not necessarily impede this outcome. Suppose there are ten cities. Suppose further that Coke raises its price in a mix of five of its own strong and weak cities. If Pepsi does not find it profitable to match the higher price across the board,

Coke would quickly revert to prior pricing levels. But Coke's pricing algorithm could use that information to update its inference of Pepsi's valuations and try again with a different mix of cities. Or Pepsi could use Coke's choice of five cites to update its own inference of Coke's valuations and initiate an effort to raise its price on a different mix.

Through trial and error, the firms could find a more profitable outcome than they would achieve by employing simple leader-follower algorithms in each city and in consequence exercise greater market power. If markets are similarly sized, the greatest price increases beyond what leader-follower algorithms would yield would likely result from coordinating price increases across products such as soft drinks and snacks or across cities located far apart—that is, across markets that were unlikely to be subject to common shifts in cost or demand at the time the prices rose. The gains to the firms from employing sophisticated algorithms rather than leader-follower algorithms would tend to grow as the number of products and the number of firms selling them increases.

Through these more sophisticated pricing algorithms, the firms can be understood as reaching cross-market bargains. Coke in effect proposed quid pro quo conduct ("if you raise price in your strong city, then, and only then, will I raise it in mine"), and Pepsi accepted the deal. This is a constructive conclusion; it does not suppose that pricing algorithms make proposals and engage in negotiations, only that they reached an outcome that human actors would reasonably describe that way.

Buyers might attempt to defeat seller coordination using algorithms of their own, but success is not assured.[21] Such algorithms could speed buyer responses to changes in relative prices charged by sellers, but not necessarily enough to make firm cheating profitable. If cheating would not have been profitable absent pricing algorithms, it is unlikely that the introduction of algorithms on both sides of the market would alter the sellers' calculus with respect to cheating. Moreover, even rapid buyer response may not be a powerful force for competition where only a small fraction of customers make purchases at any given time. In such markets, buyer coordination may be insufficient to frustrate seller coordination.

In some cases, group-purchasing algorithms could discourage seller coordination by aggregating buyers. That could make seller cheating profitable when it was not previously. Overall, though, it is implausible to expect that countervailing use of purchasing algorithms will substantially lessen the problem of seller coordination by algorithm.

WHEN SHOULD A COURT FIND THAT ALGORITHMS AGREED?

Suppose firms using pricing algorithms achieve supracompetitive prices through coordination. Assume further that a court has no direct evidence—such as a written memorialization or an admission by a remorseful coconspirator—from which to identify an agreement on price and that the firms did not agree to adopt the pricing algorithms. The court must determine whether to infer an agreement on price from circumstantial evidence.

As in other antitrust circumstances, the legal standards underlying the court's determination seek to balance the benefits of deterring anticompetitive conduct against the costs of chilling procompetitive conduct and the costs of administration. Courts have historically resolved this trade-off by declining to infer an agreement when oligopolists act in parallel, except in the presence of certain "plus factors."[22] Algorithmic pricing raises the risk of inefficient deterrence, thereby altering the trade-off. The presumption advocated below strikes a better balance.

Human Decision Makers

If human decision makers engaged in conduct similar to that of the leader-follower algorithms, a court would be unlikely to infer that they had agreed on price. In 1954 the Supreme Court made clear that agreement would not be inferred when high prices result from mere "conscious parallelism," as when firms raise price or reduce output while recognizing that their rivals are paying attention and will react the same way.[23] That decision's practical effect has been to insulate supracompetitive prices reached through leader-follower behavior, absent additional evidence of agreement.

If human decision makers instead engaged in conduct similar to that of the more sophisticated pricing algorithm described above, a court would likely infer that the firms reached agreements on price in multiple markets. The hypothesized conduct resembles the airline behavior challenged by the Justice Department as price fixing during the early 1990s, though that conduct also involved features of airline fares other than pricing.[24]

This difference in the likely outcome of litigation in the two cases reflects the way courts have resolved the underlying policy tradeoff. On the one hand, if the courts make it relatively easy to infer an agreement from circumstantial evidence, then coordinated oligopoly conduct will more likely be challenged.

This strengthens deterrence of oligopolistic price elevation.[25] On the other hand, the more difficult it is to infer an agreement, the less likely that doing so will chill procompetitive behavior or, depending on the remedy, enmesh the courts in ongoing judicial supervision of market participants—a task for which courts, unlike regulatory agencies, are ill-suited.

Donald Turner highlighted the latter problems decades ago.[26] Turner argued on administrability grounds against finding a Sherman Act violation when oligopolists achieve a coordinated outcome and charge supracompetitive prices merely through watching each other's market behavior and responding to it independently, as leaders and followers. Turner questioned whether firms could behave differently—that is, whether the prohibited conduct was actually avoidable. Turner also wondered how courts could be expected to devise viable remedies that avoid chilling beneficial conduct.

These are important concerns. In oligopoly settings, firms cannot be expected to avoid learning about rivals' prices and responding to the information those prices convey about shifts in market demand and costs. Nor can firms be expected to avoid following rivals' price increases that reflect higher industry costs or greater industry demand. If a Sherman Act agreement to fix prices were inferred solely from the fact that one firm raised its price and a rival followed, the rival would be exposed to antitrust liability unless it could prove that its follow-on price increase was justified, or that its new price was no higher than would be obtained in a competitive market. But courts, unlike industry-specific regulatory agencies, are not well equipped to make such determinations.

Perhaps the rival could seek to show that that its costs had gone up by an amount commensurate with the price rise.[27] Yet proving the magnitude of a cost increase may be challenging when higher costs are associated with factors such as changes to the scale of firm operations, the difficulty and expense of meeting unexpectedly high demand, greater opportunity costs, or increases in the common costs of producing multiple products. Providing such proof may also be challenging when the cost increase results from higher input prices, and the firm would be expected to alter its input mix or change its production technology in response. The rival could avoid liability by choosing not to raise its price, but that would be harmful if the competitive price had actually increased. A firm forced to charge below the competitive price could even be forced out of the market.

Furthermore, if price-fixing agreements were inferred solely from evidence that prices rose in parallel, courts would often lack realistic remedies. Fines are unattractive because the prospect of them confronts firms with a perverse choice between risking liability by raising prices and avoiding liability by setting lower-than-competitive prices. In theory, a damages remedy set appropriately would deter anticompetitive conduct.[28] But neither damages nor any other remedy would successfully do so when oligopolists are uncertain as to what behavior is cause for liability. That uncertainty could also lead oligopolists conspicuously to refrain from matching price increases or price cuts. Even when a firm that is not coordinating would alter prices, oligopolists might refrain for fear that such conduct would be misinterpreted as coordinated. Cautious firms may thereby avoid justified price changes, forgoing efficient or procompetitive responses to what they have learned about cost or demand. Or they might otherwise distort their behavior relative to what they would do in a repeated one-shot interaction, in order to demonstrate that they are not responding to rivals' strategic decisions even when they learn about cost or demand from rivals' price changes.

To avoid these outcomes, courts could instead seek to determine the competitive price and enjoin prices set above that level.[29] But it will often be difficult to determine the competitive price,[30] and enjoining firms to charge it would require essentially permanent regulatory supervision by courts illsuited to the task. If courts infer an agreement to fix prices, they could also seek to prevent future coordination by breaking up the firms into smaller entities.[31] This remedial option would require the wholesale restructuring of multiple industries, which would again be impractical for courts to administer. Moreover, if the restructuring initially pushed firms below an efficient scale, the remedy could be ineffective in lowering prices or avoiding an oligopolistic market structure in the long run.

Finally, Turner's problem of avoiding liability may be equally troublesome if the parallel conduct involves allocating customers according to, say, geographic regions or historical relationships. Suppose a Sherman Act agreement to divide markets can be inferred solely from the fact that each firm focuses its marketing efforts on potential customers or regions not currently served by any firm. That is, the firms do not compete for rivals' customers or regions; they seek only new markets. In that case a firm would be exposed to antitrust liability unless it could justify its marketing choice before a court poorly suited to determine what a firm would do were it behaving competitively. The firm could avoid liability by marketing to its rivals' customers or in its rivals' territories, but the firm would need to show that its efforts were more than half-hearted. That could be wasteful if even aggressive marketing efforts prove insufficient to overcome customer-switching costs or the rivals' reputational advantages. Nor can a court easily devise a reasonable remedy. It would be difficult, for example, for a court to determine the competitive level of marketing effort in order to enjoin firms from doing less.

In light of the sorts of problems Turner identifies, economists have been tempted to discard inferences of agreement and seek instead to ground the agreement requirement in an economic model of coordination. For instance, some have argued that the legal idea of agreement should be equated with oligopolistic price elevation, either relative to marginal cost[32] or relative to a price that would result in an oligopoly without repeated interaction.[33]

Relying on an economic model of coordination to infer agreement is, in theory, a commendable idea. But, in practice, it is probably unworkable. Identifying agreement by simply comparing the oligopoly price with marginal cost is unappealing because of the difficulty of administering relief. Even if industry marginal cost can be identified with confidence, which may not be an easy task, this approach requires ongoing judicial supervision of the market participants. When marginal cost is difficult to identify, this approach also threatens to chill beneficial conduct by discouraging justified price hikes by cautious firms. The social costs of chilling procompetitive behavior could be substantial even when oligopolistic price elevation is substantial, so the deterrence benefits of enforcement would also be consequential. This approach also risks forcing firms to price below a competitive level in markets in which fixed costs are substantial, the competitive price is best understood as entrant average cost (the price an efficient entrant would set), and entrant average cost exceeds incumbent marginal cost. The comparison of oligopoly conduct (including price) with what an oligopoly would do in a one-shot game is unappealing for similar reasons.[34]

Plus Factors

Without an objective economic measure to turn to, but also wary of inferring agreement from circumstantial evidence alone, the courts have developed "plus factors" to help establish conditions under which firms are liable for parallel conduct.[35] These plus factors are features of markets or firm conduct beyond parallelism sufficient to sustain a conclusion that the exercise of market power is the product of an unlawful agreement. The plus factors were devised to uncover covert conspiracies such as unwritten price-setting agreements arrived at via secret verbal communications. In general, the plus factors constitute evidence that alleged conspirators reached a coordinated outcome through what I term a "forbidden process" of negotiation and exchange of assurances,[36] rather than through the sort of leader-follower behavior that firms cannot be expected to forswear and that courts cannot be expected to remedy.

The approach of inferring agreement through plus factors has clear advantages. Plus factors reduce uncertainty, guiding firms on how to avoid liability and damages by abstaining from the forbidden process. Relief is also practical because the forbidden process can be enjoined.

The inference of agreement is most convincing when courts synthesize the plus factors to explain how engaging in the forbidden process helps the coordinating firms improve their ability to solve one or more of the their "cartel problems": reaching consensus on terms of coordination, deterring cheating, and preventing destabilizing new competition.[37] For example in *In re Text Messaging Antitrust Litigation* (2010),[38] the Seventh Circuit implicitly saw the plus factors as suggesting that an agreement was needed to permit the rivals to reach a coordinated price consensus.[39] In another case, the dissenting appellate judges in an en banc decision of the Eighth Circuit implicitly interpreted the plus factors as showing that the defendant firms had used interfirm price-verification communications to deter cheating.[40]

The plus factors can be divided into two groups.[41] The group more important for the analysis here comprises factors that seek to distinguish agreement from conscious parallelism directly—that is, to determine whether it is more reasonable to view firm conduct as the outcome of the forbidden process of negotiation and exchange of assurances than as the result of conscious parallelism. These plus factors include, first, communication between rivals—or, more weakly, the opportunity to communicate—about competitively sensitive information.[42] A second plus factor in this group is conduct too complicated to be explained by mere parallel behavior, which would therefore be irrational absent an agreement. Finally, conduct lacking an evident efficiency explanation may serve as a plus factor.[43]

The second group of plus factors seeks to identify whether the industry is conducive to coordination, and hence whether it would be rational for firms to engage in the forbidden process. The logic of these plus factors is that if successful coordination is unlikely, reaching an agreement would not have made "economic sense," so the plaintiff must proffer "more persuasive evidence" to persuade the court to infer an agreement.[44]

Many of the plus factors in the second group look to whether the firms appear able to reach consensus on terms of coordination, deter cheating, and prevent new competition.[45] These plus factors also include indicators that the leading firms in an industry are exercising market power.[46] But the many cases finding express collusion in markets that appear to include a large number of firms show that firms may coordinate even absent features thought to facilitate it.[47] Hence, the absence of plus factors in the second group should not be a bar to inferring agreement when plus factors in the first group are persuasive on their own.

Indeed, the plus factors in the second group, while probative, probably are not sufficient to infer agreement without additional plus factors from the first group. One reason is that industry features that tend to suggest that firms are exercising market power do not necessarily mean the firms are coordinating. For example, these features may not distinguish coordination from the behavior of a dominant firm. Another reason second-group factors are not enough is that even if the firms are coordinating, they may be doing so without engaging in the forbidden process—negotiation and exchange of assurances.[48]

By relying on plus factors, courts tend to reach the right outcome when human decision makers set prices. In these cases the plus factors draw a sensible line by distinguishing mere leader-follower conduct, which would not be deemed an agreement, from cross-market coordination, which likely would.

What distinguishes cross-market coordination from leader-follower behavior is the complexity of the conduct and the absence of an efficiency justification for various price changes—two plus factors from the first group. (In both cases, all exchange of information takes place through pricing, not conversations, and the executives do not have an opportunity to meet or talk, so communication factors are not implicated.) In the cross-market case, the firms raise price across multiple cities unrelated in cost or demand and repeatedly assemble different groups of cities for trial price increases until one of those efforts is matched by all. It is reasonable to describe their behavior as negotiating cross-market bargains, practical for a court to enjoin that conduct, and reasonable to expect that firms in similar settings will be able to avoid liability. Thus, with plus factors at the ready, coordinated conduct across multiple markets by human decision makers would likely be deterred, with limited risk of chilling procompetitive conduct or creating excessive administrative costs.

Algorithmic Decision Makers

In theory, there need be no difference between the antitrust analysis of price coordination effected by humans and by algorithms. In both cases, leader-follower conduct and cross-market bargains could be distinguished. Courts could plausibly characterize firm conduct when coordinating algorithmically across markets as they do when humans make the pricing decisions: as negotiating outcomes that the firms could not reach through leader-follower conduct.

Yet there are also two reasons the antitrust analysis of firm conduct in reaching cross-market bargains could change when decision making shifts from humans to algorithms. First, the plus factors may be harder to apply when humans are not involved. Price changes could occur rapidly, and outside observers may not be able to identify which markets experienced parallel changes in price. Such markets could presumably be identified through computerized analysis of detailed market information, but outsiders would need to have thought to do the analysis and found it worthwhile to make that investment in order to uncover cross-market bargaining. One can imagine a large business customer doing so and either bringing a private damages suit or, more likely, sharing what it learned with an antitrust-enforcement agency to encourage an investigation. But outsiders are less likely to undertake that effort for consumer products such as soft drinks and air travel.

Second, conduct that seems complex when undertaken by human decision makers may no longer seem that way when undertaken by computerized decision makers. This hamstrings one of the plus factors because, when the issue is possible human coordination, the complexity of the outcome is a signal of agreement—the more firms engage in what look like trial-and-error efforts to identify a package of cross-market bargains, the more the ultimate pattern of price changes appears too complex to be interpreted as the product of leader-follower conduct. But in the algorithmic case, large numbers of prices and markets may be involved, and prices may change constantly, making it hard for industry observers, enforcers, and courts to recognize complex patterns.[49]

In consequence, the case for inferring an agreement among algorithms may turn most heavily on a different plus factor in the first group: the absence of an efficiency justification for connecting cities unrelated in cost or demand when changing prices. If the algorithms connect markets that would otherwise have no relationship, the resulting price increases are unlikely to have a legitimate business justification. In some cases, the firms may be able to show that their pricing algorithms allow them to learn (from rival prices) and account for (in their own prices) shocks to industry-wide cost or demand more quickly or less expensively than other means of gaining that information, and that such shocks are sufficiently frequent and substantial as to make doing so important to efficient market functioning. But legitimate justifications like these would be unlikely to apply when prices rise simultaneously and identically in unrelated markets.[50]

In short, two of the three types of plus factors in the first group—communication and complexity—may not strongly differentiate the use of sophisticated algorithms from the use of leader-follower algorithms. The absence of an efficiency justification, combined with the obvious anticompetitive motive to enhance coordination through cross-market bargains, would provide that differentiation. But when algorithms are involved, it could be more difficult to infer a pricing agreement on this basis. When humans set prices, they can be asked to explain the relationship between markets that called for common price changes, and that explanation can be evaluated. When algorithms set price, they cannot be interrogated similarly.

For these reasons, it may be more difficult to attack coordination through pricing algorithm using traditional Sherman Act § 1 approaches than to challenge the analogous pricing coordination among human decision makers.

In addition, the use of pricing algorithms may make coordination easier to achieve. Future pricing algorithms that augment our hypothetical sophisticated algorithm with artificial intelligence could plausibly identify ways of coordinating across multiple markets that humans could not and reach terms of coordination far more quickly than can human decision makers. Hence a trend toward routine business reliance on pricing algorithms would be expected to exacerbate the underdeterrence of coordinated conduct under current antitrust rules.

To recalibrate the error-cost balance, courts should presume that in an industry in which single-market cheating would likely be deterred by rapid price matching,[51] and entry would not be expected to undermine a coordinated outcome, firms competing in multiple markets and setting prices by algorithm have reached an agreement on price for the purpose of enforcing Sherman Act § 1. That presumption would place a burden of production on defendant firms. They would need to demonstrate that their algorithms' pricing decisions respond to shifts in cost or demand consistent with what would be expected by firms engaged in one-time pricing interactions.[52] Courts applying this presumption may make mistakes in evaluating firm conduct, but judicial errors would be no more likely than they are now.

This approach promises to increase deterrence in two ways. First, it directs attention to the potentially decisive aspects of firm conduct. It looks primarily to a single plus factor in the first group—the absence of an efficiency justification—in a setting in which the presence or absence of the other plus factors in that group is unlikely to be telling. Second, it induces firms to create and make available information that would help enforcers and courts identify algorithmic conduct that would violate the Sherman Act if engaged in by human decision makers. To meet their burden as defendants, firms using pricing algorithms would most likely be led to design the algorithms to create audit trails and to make transparent the factors that caused the algorithm to make price changes. The firms may not object because explanations may help human researchers make algorithms more effective.[53] In the alternative, these forms of transparency could be mandated by statute or by a competition rule promulgated by the Federal Trade Commission.

This approach to inferring an agreement when firms use pricing algorithms is unlikely to chill procompetitive conduct when some firms use sophisticated algorithms while others do not. To see why, suppose that all but one of the firms competing in multiple markets employs the sophisticated algorithm described above. The idiosyncratic or less sophisticated firm—call it the simple firm—engages in leader-follower conduct, market by market. In that setting, the firms may be able to coordinate across markets, though not quite as effectively as they would if the simple firm also used a sophisticated algorithm. The simple firm would not stand in the way of all cross-market bargains. If the simple firm could demonstrate that its algorithm makes simultaneous pricing decisions across markets only in response to common shifts in cost and demand, as by matching rivals,[54] that should satisfy its burden to rebut the presumption that it has participated in an agreement. In this hypothetical setting, only the firms employing more sophisticated algorithms should be found to have agreed on price.

One might contend that no such presumption is needed, because coordinated conduct should be directly identifiable by applying a straightforward implication of an economic definition of coordination. Narrowly defined, coordination can be said to occur whenever firms in equilibrium adopt strategies that depend on history, with or without discussion or communication among rivals.[55] More broadly, outcomes are coordinated if the firms take actions that anticipate accommodating actions by their rivals.[56] In principle, then, coordinated conduct could be identified by examining firm strategies, and oligopolistic price elevation deterred by prohibiting strategies that satisfy either the narrow or broad definition.[57] Joseph Harrington suggests that this approach may actually be more practical if prices are set by algorithm than by humans, because the algorithm's strategies are incorporated in computer code that could be studied.[58]

In practice, however, this approach appears likely to founder on the difficulty of discriminating between conduct that, on the one hand, carries out a previously developed strategy in which a firm's behavior depends on history (which, under this approach, would be the basis for inferring an agreement on price) and, on the other, conduct that is the product of adopting single-period strategies while responding to what the firm learned from the past, including from prices previously charged by rivals and information about cost and demand. Firms would be expected to do the latter with or without engaging in coordination.[59] Absent progress in distinguishing these behaviors empirically, it would be more practical to discourage algorithmic coordination through application of the presumption suggested here.

IMPLICATIONS FOR HORIZONTAL-MERGER ANALYSIS

As algorithmic pricing grows, antitrust enforcement will become less effective in deterring coordination among rivals in oligopoly markets, particularly markets where rapid price matching would likely discourage cheating and entry would not undermine a coordinated consensus. The harder it becomes to deter coordination, the more important it becomes to prevent mergers that would facilitate coordinated effects in susceptible markets. Yet in recent years, antitrust enforcers appear to have shied away from challenging horizontal mergers on a coordination theory.[60] One case was tried largely on a unilateral-effects theory (by which competition would be harmed even if other firms do not change their behavior).[61] Ultimately, coordinated effects were successful in sustaining the challenge, but this theory was raised as an afterthought.[62]

The Justice Department's airline-merger cases over the past two decades illustrate the government's preference for unilateral effects.[63] Although the major airlines have historically exercised market power through coordinated conduct across multiple routes,[64] the Justice Department's airline merger challenges have usually avoided alleging coordinated effects. Instead, merger reviews focused on trading off the danger of unilateral effects from the loss of head-to-head competition on individual routes against the potential for efficiency benefits, such as passenger convenience from increasing flight frequencies and extending route networks or cost reductions from operating at greater scale at individual hubs and nationwide.[65] The Justice Department pointed solely to efficiencies when explaining two decisions to allow major airline mergers to proceed,[66] declined to challenge a third on efficiency grounds (notwithstanding overlaps on some nonstop routes),[67] and justified a fourth merger on efficiency grounds after the government's unilateral-effects concerns were addressed by a divestiture of takeoff and landing slots at a hub airport.[68] When the Justice Department and a dozen states announced they would sue to block a fifth, the government's detailed press release identified unilateral effects only.[69]

Since 1989, when jurisdiction over airline mergers shifted from the Department of Transportation to the Department of Justice, coordinated effects have been alleged only twice in government-initiated merger cases: in 2000, when the Justice Department went to court to unwind Northwest's ownership of a controlling equity interest in rival Continental[70] and thirteen years later when the government challenged US Airways' acquisition of American Airlines.[71] A common thread connects the two: in each case the government alleged that one of the merging firms was a maverick constraining premerger coordination. The government did not rely solely on the structural presumption and the identification of factors suggesting the industry was conducive to coordination in its complaints. Instead it explained why the acquisition would attenuate the competitive influence of a rival that constrained industry coordination. In the Northwest/Continental litigation, the Justice Department identified Northwest as a maverick and explained how the challenged transaction affected its incentive to constrain coordinated conduct. In the more recent coordinated-effects merger case, the government alleged that coordination would be enhanced by the US Airways/American merger on two different dimensions, with US Airways a maverick on one dimension (involving discounted connecting fares) and American a maverick on the other (involving aggregate capacity).[72]

As the airline experience suggests, and other government coordinated-effects cases further illustrate,[73] the government is on its firmest ground in demonstrating coordinated effects when it can show that one of the merging firms is a maverick—a firm with the ability and incentive to prevent coordination from becoming more effective.[74] This is for good reason: by showing that one of the merging firms is a maverick, the government can explain why the merger matters.[75] As mentioned in Chapter 4, when a merger in an industry conducive to coordination involves a maverick, it is appropriate to presume that the transaction harms competition by making coordination more effective.

To build on recent judicial successes in blocking horizontal mergers on coordinated-effects grounds, the enforcement agencies should place more emphasis on identifying and challenging acquisitions between rivals in which one of the merger partners is a maverick. That effort is particularly important in industries in which firms employ algorithms for price setting or seem likely to do so.[76]

CONCLUSION

Courts should address the threat of algorithmic coordination by presuming that rival firms have reached an agreement on price when they set prices across multiple markets through algorithms in industries in which coordinating firms are concerned more about reaching consensus than deterring single-market cheating or preventing entry. Doing so would increase deterrence of anticompetitive conduct in an environment in which antitrust law has been systematically underdeterring oligopolistic price elevation and in which algorithmic coordination is hard to detect without markedly chilling procompetitive conduct or increasing the administrative burden on courts.

The presumption would be rebuttable, so it would not prevent firms from using pricing algorithms for competitive decision making. Firms will understand that they cannot engage in cross-market pricing interactions unless those interactions respond to factors that would influence pricing similarly across those markets, were prices in those markets set individually. In addition, the enforcement agencies should seek to lessen the threat of algorithmic coordination by increasing their attention to the possibility of coordinated effects when evaluating horizontal mergers in susceptible markets and by relying on the presumption that an acquisition involving a maverick in an industry conducive to coordination will harm competition.

Chapter Seven

Exclusionary Conduct
by Dominant Platforms

I N A 2016 speech on competition policy, Senator Elizabeth Warren singled out threats to competition from Google, Amazon, and Apple. While their platforms "deliver enormously valuable products," and the firms deserve their success, she stated, they can "snuff out competition" from small rivals that depend on their platforms to compete.[1] Warren's comments reflect an increasing anxiety about large information technology platforms—anxiety particularly acute among political progressives[2] but also felt by conservatives.[3]

Dominant information technology and Internet platforms have drawn some enforcement attention, though more in Europe than in the United States. A potentially far-reaching single-firm conduct case in the United States, the Federal Trade Commission's (FTC's) investigation of Google's search business, resulted in no enforcement action.[4] The federal antitrust agencies have investigated a number of acquisitions by such platforms but have often closed their investigations without a challenge.[5] By contrast, European enforcers have brought cases against Google's conduct[6] and platform most-favored nation (MFN) provisions.[7] That said, the Justice Department has pursued two high-profile litigated challenges to anticompetitive conduct by leading payment-systems platforms.[8]

When dominant platforms receive antitrust scrutiny, the competition issues frequently involve exclusionary conduct.[9] Here and throughout this book, "exclusion" is used broadly to encompass conduct that raises rivals' costs, limits rivals' access to customers, or prevents potential rivals from competing at all.

Exclusionary conduct harms competition by creating what can be thought of as an involuntary or coerced cartel, thereby allowing the excluding firms to exercise market power.[10] Rivals that could or would have undermined the exercise of market power are discouraged or prevented from doing so. The involuntary-cartel terminology is least natural as a description of the adverse competitive effect of exclusion when a dominant firm forces its rivals to exit, making the dominant firm a literal monopolist. Even in this limiting case, though, the term appropriately captures the way a firm forces its excluded rivals to do what a cartel participant does voluntarily: avoid aggressive competition. The involuntary-cartel formulation also emphasizes the source of harm in exclusionary conduct: competition is undercut through horizontal effects, even if these are accomplished through vertical practices or acquisitions.

It is not surprising to see dominant firms choosing exclusionary tactics to maintain or extend their market power. They may gain more by excluding entrants and discouraging expansion by competitors than by coordinating with fringe rivals, or find the former task easier. But what may be surprising are the particular exclusion issues raised by dominant information technology platforms. Today's platforms can exploit detailed information about individual buyers and suppliers, leading to novel problems of exclusion, discussed below.[11]

Recall that, decades ago, antitrust commentators associated with the Chicago school expressed deep skepticism about enforcing the antitrust laws against competitive threats from exclusionary conduct.[12] Although we saw in Chapter 5 that many of the arguments against enforcement, on which the Chicago school relied, are erroneous, norms against exclusionary harms remain contested in antitrust discourse.[13] Too often, courts and commentators describe collusion as antitrust's "core" concern, implicitly and improperly relegating exclusion to the periphery of antitrust enforcement.[14] The involuntary-cartel perspective on exclusion explains why that distinction cannot be defended: collusion and exclusion are two sides of the same market-power coin.

While the economic distinction between exclusion and coordination does not map neatly to familiar categories in antitrust law, enforcement actions involving exclusionary conduct are more likely to be brought as monopolization or vertical-restraints cases than as horizontal agreements.[15] Not surprisingly, given the Chicago school's views on exclusion, conservatives argue most strongly for presumptions against enforcement in vertical-restraints and monopolization cases.

The courts, acting properly, have not backed away from treating exclusion as a serious competitive problem, even while following Chicago-oriented rules that relaxed scrutiny of vertical conduct and monopolization.[16] The antitrust rules governing all categories of exclusionary conduct appear to be converging toward a common burden-shifting reasonableness framework.[17] However, rules governing predatory pricing—the legal category where the courts have gone the farthest toward institutionalizing Chicago school skepticism of exclusionary conduct allegations—may be an exception, particularly because they establish a safe harbor for above-cost pricing.

This chapter examines ways that dominant platforms can harm competition by excluding rivals, through the lens of insufficient deterrence of exclusionary conduct overall. I begin with an overview of platform economics, then turn to ways that dominant information technology and Internet platforms can exclude. These include vertical integration, exclusive dealing, exclusionary conduct involving big data, conduct that increases customer switching costs, the use of platform MFNs, and predatory pricing. Although these categories are broad, they do not encompass all the ways platforms can harm competition by excluding competitors.

The chapter goes on to explain how the modern burden-shifting framework for evaluating the reasonableness of exclusionary conduct permits truncated condemnation under certain circumstances. Application of that framework, while rejecting presumptions of efficiencies advocated by conservatives, will enhance the deterrence of harmful exclusionary conduct. Other chapters address related issues. Harms to innovation competition and competition in future products from exclusionary conduct are discussed in Chapter 8. Market definition, including the complications posed by seemingly "free" goods on one side of a platform, is taken up in Chapter 9.

Platforms are not identical. As discussed below, they vary in the nature and strength of the network-effect benefits they confer on their users, in the magnitude of user switching costs and user willingness to multi-home (patronize competing platforms), and in the efficiencies they can obtain through exclusionary conduct. The modern framework for antitrust analysis allows for careful evaluation of the implications of those differences under comprehensive reasonableness review and truncated condemnation when it is appropriate to presume anticompetitive effect.

A PRIMER ON PLATFORM ECONOMICS

Platforms facilitate transactions or economic interactions among parties known as end users.[18] Each type of end user corresponds to one "side" of a platform.

A shopping platform differs from a traditional vendor in that it allows end users to interact directly. A retailer that purchases goods at wholesale and re-sells them to the public is not a platform; it simply has upstream suppliers and downstream customers. By contrast, a consignment shop is a platform: it al-lows sellers and buyers to find each other and takes a commission on the sale. Amazon's experience with e-books crystallizes the distinction. Initially it had a supply relationship with publishers selling e-books, but when it switched from wholesale distribution to agency distribution (by which the publisher sets the retail price and splits the revenues with Amazon), its e-book business operated as a platform with publishers and readers as two types of end users.[19]

As the consignment-shop example demonstrates, platforms are not new. Long-lived platforms include shopping malls, which connect shoppers with retailers, and newspapers, which connect advertisers with readers. But as Senator Warren emphasized, the concern today is increasingly with exam-ples from the information technology sector. Amazon's Marketplace con-nects shoppers with sellers. The Apple and Google Android app stores connect smartphone users with application providers. Facebook and search providers such as Google and Microsoft (Bing) allow advertisers to interact directly with consumers using social media or searching the Internet. Pay-ment systems such as Visa connect shoppers and their banks with merchants. Restaurant reservation services such as OpenTable connect restaurants with diners. Cable and broadband providers connect content providers and their advertisers with viewers and connect consumers with online providers of con-tent, applications, and services.

Some platforms are owned by a single firm, while others are shared among firms. Visa and Mastercard originally were owned and operated by the banks that issued their cards, while American Express is a single firm. Facebook operates a platform. It also participates on two mobile communications plat-forms. On the iPhone platform, Facebook and other application providers share technical leadership with Apple, which contributes the iOS operating system, iPhone devices, and its app store. On the Android platform, Face-book and other application providers share technical leadership with Google and device manufacturers such as Samsung.

This chapter is concerned primarily with platforms owned by a single firm, not platforms where technical leadership is divided.[20] It is also concerned primarily with markets dominated by a single platform. In such markets, smaller-platform rivals are often the primary competitive constraint limiting the dominant platform's exercise of market power.

Platforms and their users may benefit from network effects. Network effects, also referred to as buyer or demand-side scale economies, arise when the value of a product to buyers depends on the number of other users.[21] Network effects may be direct, as in communications networks. They may also be indirect: a high-circulation newspaper may be more valuable to its readers because it generates more advertising revenues, allowing the newspaper to include more content, which readers value directly.

Network effects are often the reason for the success of a platform's business model,[22] particularly for the large information technology platforms that are the primary concern of this chapter.[23] When network effects are substantial, one platform tends to achieve dominance. Markets in which network effects are important are prone to tipping, so even a small competitive disadvantage can snowball into a major disability.[24] If a platform loses users as a result of dominant-firm exclusionary conduct, it may become less attractive to other users, potentially further diverting demand to the dominant platform and enhancing the dominant firm's ability to exercise market power.

However, a platform with a dominant position in its markets need not be a natural monopoly or even exercise market power.[25] One way smaller platforms can still succeed is by sharing the advantages of network effects. That might happen if platforms are interoperable or end users use multiple platforms—the multi-home scenario.[26] For example, advertisers that purchase space in competing newspapers multi-home, while readers who subscribe to only one paper single-home.

Conduct by a dominant platform that prevents interoperability or impedes multi-homing can exclude smaller rivals and harm competition.[27] When a dominant platform insists on single-homing, some users who might otherwise have multi-homed will pick the dominant platform in order to benefit from network effects and for fear that nondominant platforms will not be able to attract enough users to succeed. By contrast, when users have the option to multi-home, an entrant may be able to gain a toehold and then build network effects. This will allow it to attract additional users and potentially enhance demand by creating optimistic user expectations of its prospects for success.[28]

Smaller platforms may also succeed by providing differentiated or niche products or services that make them particularly valuable to some end users, even when network effects benefiting a dominant platform are strong. Consider that, in the second half of the twentieth century (but before the growth of the Internet), most large U.S. cities had one or two dominant daily newspapers with distribution throughout the metropolitan area. These newspapers likely obtained substantial demand-side scale economies on both sides of their platforms. But these cities often also supported other newspapers with more limited circulation: weekly papers that focused on specialized local audiences of, for example, suburban residents, African Americans, and participants in the counterculture. National papers with specialized audiences, such as the *Wall Street Journal*, also flourished in this way.

A platform may benefit from economies of scale in supply.[29] It experiences scale economies if its average cost decreases when its output grows. The fixed costs of operating the platform alone may confer substantial scale economies on a large platform.

Platforms may charge end users by setting a fee for platform access, as with newspapers' annual subscription price to readers, or by charging for platform usage, as with newspapers' advertising rates. Regardless of the way prices are specified, a platform may have an incentive to keep the price to end users on one side low, or even subsidize those end users. If one kind of end user is especially responsive to price (more price elastic) or if attracting more of one kind of end user (e.g., readers) would make a larger difference in attracting the other kind (e.g., advertisers), then the case for subsidizing a particular kind of end user is strong.[30] As a result, the price to end users on one side may be high relative to the marginal cost of serving them, while the price to the end users on another side may be low relative to the marginal cost of serving them or even below marginal cost.[31]

Platforms may compete with other platforms on multiple sides, as with the Amazon and Walmart shopping platforms. As discussed in Chapter 8, this competition could go beyond current products and services to include future products and services, including the development of future platforms.[32] Platforms may also compete with nonplatform rivals on one side, as with the competition between online shopping platforms and brick-and-mortar retail stores. In addition, platforms may facilitate competition among their users, as with competition among book publishers selling through Amazon's shopping site, apps sold on the Android store, or the banks issuing Visa cards.

WAYS PLATFORMS CAN EXCLUDE

There are several exclusionary mechanisms dominant platforms may employ to harm competition. I do not claim to exhaust every possibility here. Familiar methods include exclusivity through vertical merger and through exclusive dealing. But dominant information technology and Internet platforms also have new techniques, based on access to individualized customer or supplier information. They can also engage in predatory pricing and conduct that increases customer switching costs, and they can take advantage of platform MFNs. In some examples below, the exclusionary conduct harms competition among platforms. In others, it harms competition among users on one side of a platform, some of which could be other platforms but need not.[33]

For expositional convenience, many of the examples, often hypothetical, involve Amazon's shopping platform. Amazon's shopping platform is a convenient source of illustrations because examples involving retail products tend to be easy to grasp. There is no need to explain technical details about the way a retail platform works. While search and social media end users may not be charged directly for the products and services on one side of the platform, no such complications arise with Amazon.[34] Amazon also presents an attractive subject because prominent critics of dominant information technology platforms have argued that the company's leading position in online shopping and cloud computing raises serious competitive concerns.[35] Although the examples here do suggest ways in which Amazon's conduct could harm competition, I do not argue that Amazon has engaged in any of the hypothesized behavior, nor do I endorse the broad charges raised by critics.

Exclusivity through Vertical Merger or Exclusive Dealing

Dominant firms—platforms included—can employ exclusivity arrangements with suppliers or distributors to foreclose rivals from access to key inputs or distribution channels and thereby harm competition. They can achieve exclusivity by merger or by contract. These methods of anticompetitive exclusion are well understood, so I sketch them here without extensive discussion, emphasizing ways that vertical merger or exclusive dealing can raise rivals' costs or otherwise foreclose competitors without necessarily affecting scale economies. Later sections will highlight anticompetitive mechanisms that raise rivals' costs by forcing those competitors to operate at a lower scale.

Hypothetical examples illustrate four ways that vertical merger or contract can lead to anticompetitive exclusion.[36] First, the platform could foreclose users competing on one of its sides. For example, if Amazon acquired a manufacturer of a particular product such as diapers—as the company has in fact done—it would gain the incentive to exclude from its platform other producers of the product in order to reduce competition. Amazon might exclude rivals by charging them a higher commission for listing on its marketplace or by reducing rivals' prominence in search results on the Amazon platform. If rivals do not have good alternatives for reaching consumers (e.g., through Walmart's online shopping site), their distribution costs could rise, leading them to compete less aggressively. In consequence, product prices could rise, harming consumers.

Amazon could do the same thing through contract. Instead of acquiring the diaper manufacturer, it could enter into an exclusive-dealing arrangement. Then Amazon might find it profitable to exclude product rivals, particularly if the exclusivity agreement gives Amazon a greater share of product revenues.

Second, if a platform had previously been seen as a potential entrant into the end-users' market, the platform could harm competition among end users through vertical integration or exclusive dealing. Suppose Amazon did not sell shoes on its shopping platform, but shoe manufacturers sold their products through other distribution channels at competitive prices for fear that, if they charged more, Amazon would see that as a competitive opportunity and enter shoe retailing. Or suppose Amazon sold shoes on its shopping platform but did not make them, and the shoe manufacturers charged competitive prices for fear that if they charged more, Amazon would enter shoe manufacturing. Either way, if Amazon acquired a shoe manufacturer[37] or entered into an exclusive dealing arrangement with it, its incentives would become mixed: its shoe-manufacturing business would benefit from higher retail prices even though its shoe-retailing business would benefit from lower shoe prices. The merger or exclusive-dealing arrangement would lessen the competitive constraint Amazon's potential entry had previously placed on retail shoe prices, potentially leading those prices to rise.

Third, the platform could exclude its platform rivals. Suppose Amazon acquired or introduced major retail brands in a number of product categories—a baby-products brand, a clothing brand, a consumer-electronics brand, and more. If many consumers would not shop on sites that do not offer those brands, Amazon may be able to exercise market power as a shopping platform by withholding its branded products from rival shopping platforms or threatening to do so in order to negotiate a higher wholesale price from those platforms. Either way Amazon could potentially disadvantage its platform rivals, leading them to compete less aggressively and potentially allowing Amazon to raise prices on all products sold by rival platforms, even in product categories where Amazon does not own a brand. Again, Amazon could accomplish the same end through a series of exclusive-dealing contracts.

Fourth, a platform could lessen the constraint that large sellers of complementary products place on each other through vertical acquisition or exclusive dealing, harming competition. Suppose that Amazon is the dominant e-book retailer and—hypothetically and counter to fact—that Simon & Schuster is the dominant firm in e-book publishing. Neither firm is a literal monopolist: Simon & Schuster competes with Macmillan, Hachette, and other publishers, while Amazon competes in e-book retailing with Barnes & Noble and Apple's iBookstore. Premerger, Simon & Schuster has an incentive to foster competition among e-book retailers in order to reduce Amazon's bargaining power when negotiating the wholesale price of books. As a result, it might promote more heavily on Barnes & Noble's and Apple's platforms to help those firms gain share. For the same reason, Amazon has an incentive to foster competition among publishers or to enter e-book publishing.

If Amazon and Simon & Schuster merge, those incentives may change. The merged firm may instead find it profitable to exclude rival publishers or retailers. Amazon might make Simon & Schuster books available exclusively through its Kindle system and demand that Macmillan and Hachette do the same in order to have access to Kindle customers. Or Amazon might decline to offer Macmillan and Hachette books on the Kindle and demand that Barnes & Noble and Apple do the same in order to be able to sell Simon & Schuster books. The foreclosed rivals may lose scale economies, and, in consequence, compete less aggressively. With less competition in publishing, author royalties could fall. With less competition in retailing, consumers could face higher book prices.

Amazon and Simon & Schuster would not need to merge to accomplish these ends. They could deny to rival publishers distribution on Amazon's shopping platform or deny to rival e-book retailers access to Simon & Schuster e-books through exclusivity agreements.

Neither vertical merger nor exclusive dealing necessarily harms competition. If, for example, enough customers respond to foreclosure of product rivals by shopping on other platforms, Amazon may find that it profits more by allowing product rivals to sell on its platform than by excluding them.[38] Moreover, both forms of exclusivity may benefit competition by allowing firms to obtain efficiencies.[39]

Exclusionary Conduct Involving Big Data

Big Data

The term "big data" refers here to detailed information about individual buyers or suppliers, including the information a dominant platform can often obtain from end users that interact on its platform.[40] A shopping platform's data on buyers typically includes, but is not limited to, information about what they searched for or purchased in the past.[41] A social network may know its users' social connections and tastes.[42] Although I focus on personalized information about consumers, suppliers using platforms are similarly situated, and access to supplier information may raise analogous competitive issues.[43]

Many firms, not just platforms, collect such data in the course of doing business.[44] Some personalized consumer information is also available for purchase from third parties.[45] While detailed customer information is available to many firms, apparently allowing some online sellers to discriminate in price,[46] firms may differ in their access to inexpensive customer data of the type most valuable in their industry.[47]

The two exclusionary mechanisms discussed in this section turn on the possibility that a dominant platform would have greater access to big data than its rivals do. First, the dominant platform may be able to disadvantage rival platforms by denying them scale economies derived from customer or supplier data. Second, a dominant platform may be able to exclude rival platforms by exploiting its information advantage to target rivals' customers for discounts.

These two possibilities do not encompass the full range of benefits and costs of big data. Big data may benefit competition by allowing firms to provide consumers with products and services that more closely fit their preferences; identify desirable product improvements; improve marketing effectiveness; or lower distribution costs, as by improving retailers' product-stocking decisions. The availability of big data also raises concerns not discussed here:

some not involving competition, about the nonexclusionary consequences of price discrimination, the creation of entry barriers, and privacy.

Denial of Scale Economies

Dominant firms can deny rivals access to the customer data they need to achieve promotional scale economies by obtaining the exclusive rights to that data from third parties that own it. One way is through merger,[48] regardless of whether the acquisition is horizontal, vertical, or conglomerate. For example, if Amazon were to acquire a large cable and broadband provider such as Comcast, an antitrust enforcer might ask whether the transaction would harm competition by denying rival shopping sites such as Walmart the ability to lower promotional costs by contracting with Comcast for access to its detailed customer information. Amazon could achieve the same potentially anticompetitive end without merger by contracting with Comcast for access to its customer data with the stipulation that Comcast not sell customer information to any other shopping platform.

These forms of conduct may harm competition because a dominant firm's access to detailed and individualized information about customers may confer a form of scale economies. Those economies derive from the ability of firms with access to individualized buyer data to identify potential customers. Doing so could allow such firms to meet the needs and interests of potential customers by customizing products and promotions, including by offering individuated discounts on price if customer arbitrage is difficult. In this way, customer data may allow sellers to reduce their quality-adjusted promotional costs, thereby achieving scale economies. Alternatively, and equivalently, the customer data could be said to confer a quality advantage in promotion.

It is reasonable to suppose decreasing returns to scale: at some point, more data does not substantially improve a firm's ability to attract customers through targeted promotion or customized product design, or else the marginal cost of acquiring the additional customer data needed to continue promotion and product-design efforts increases. If so, large firms—which, in this case, means firms that have on average more or better individualized customer data than their rivals—would have a competitive advantage over smaller firms that is equivalent to lower distribution costs.

Competition is generally benefited when firms, including dominant platforms, pursue scale economies by lowering prices, improving products, and exploiting network effects. But competitive problems may arise when firms exclude rivals through conduct that denies those rivals scale economies. By placing rivals at a cost disadvantage, or forcing them to exit, a dominant platform can lessen the constraint those rivals place on its exercise of market power. A rival forced below an efficient scale may remain in the market, but with higher costs. As a result, it may compete less aggressively. A rival forced below minimum viable scale would exit. Either way, if the constraint on dominant-firm pricing imposed by rivals is relaxed, market prices may exceed competitive levels.

The competitive threat from exclusionary conduct generally, and perhaps particularly from conduct that denies rivals scale economies, is a concern in markets in which few firms can achieve an efficient scale. That will often include markets in which a dominant platform benefits from scale economies in demand (network effects) on any side of its platform, or in which the platform benefits from scale economies in supply. When a platform can achieve scale economies that are large relative to the size of the market and can thereby obtain a substantial advantage over smaller platform rivals or prospective entrants, only a handful of platforms may be able to achieve sufficient scale to compete on relatively even terms. Or, a single platform may become dominant.[49] When few platforms compete at scale to begin with, exclusionary conduct that pushes a formerly efficient platform below efficient scale or stops a smaller platform from reaching an efficient scale can be particularly dangerous to competition.

Targeted Discounting

A potentially important exclusionary mechanism involving a dominant firm's access to big data has not been considered in the case law: a platform's ability to exploit its access to customer (or supplier) information to exclude platform rivals through targeted price cutting (price discrimination).[50] Selective discounting may be an attractive strategy for a potential predator because it is less costly than across-the-board price cutting. Two hypothetical examples illustrate this exclusionary approach.

The first example assumes that Amazon knows more about the preferences of many or even most households than other online shopping sites know.[51] Suppose, in particular, that Amazon can identify occasional Amazon shoppers who are the best online customers of Best Buy, Macy's, Staples, or Walmart and can target those shoppers with low prices.[52] Amazon would have no trouble cutting prices: it could obviously reduce prices for those products for which it has price-setting authority (i.e., products on wholesale distribution), and apparently it can also lower the price targeted customers pay for products sold on its site by third-party vendors, so long as it pays those vendors the price they sought to charge.[53]

While selective and targeted price cuts to potential customers may seem like a pure benefit to competition, and in some cases would be, the practice could harm competition when employed by a dominant platform to exclude. If Amazon can take away from its rivals a substantial group of their most frequent customers, it can raise its rivals' marginal cost of attracting additional sales. The rivals could be led to raise prices in order to avoid losses. Or, regardless of whether the rivals had been charging prices that exceed their now-higher costs, the rivals may choose to compete less aggressively with Amazon to induce it to back off. Either way, Amazon may be able to obtain, maintain, or enhance market power in online shopping, and all online shoppers may end up paying more. Amazon may not even need to implement targeted price cuts to induce its rivals to back off competitively—at least, not often. Once Amazon has the ability to selectively target the customers of a rival that lacks a comparable ability to target Amazon's customers, and its rivals recognize that ability, the threat of selective discounting may be enough to induce the rival to avoid provoking Amazon by undercutting Amazon's prices.[54]

Just as Amazon could exploit its superior data access to lessen competition among platforms, it could harm competition among firms participating just on one side of its platform. This possibility is illustrated with a second hypothetical example involving Amazon's private-label diaper business.[55]

Suppose, possibly counter to fact, that Amazon would be able to exercise market power in the sale of diapers by discouraging competition from rival sellers of diapers on its retail shopping platform, notwithstanding the potential ability of diaper customers to purchase diapers through other shopping platforms or physical retail channels. If Amazon can use its superior access to customer data to identify consumers likely to buy diaper brands that compete with Amazon's private label, it could offer discounts on its private label diapers to those customers. Again, Amazon's discounting would be selective. It would not make those offers available to customers that it expects would purchase the private-label diapers without additional inducement. If Amazon, with superior access to data, is better able than its rivals to identify customers likely to buy from others and target them with discounts, it can raise the marginal cost to those rivals of attracting new customers. That could make the rivals less aggressive competitors. If so, diaper prices would rise.

To similar effect, Amazon may be able to exploit its information about product sales to identify rapidly features of rival diaper brands that customers find attractive. Amazon could quickly add those features to its own private-label products, limiting the profits its rivals earn from their product improvements.[56] If Amazon does so systematically, its diaper rivals may become less willing to innovate and experiment. As a result, rival diaper producers would be less likely to compete away any market power Amazon may exercise in the sale of private-label products.[57] Amazon also could bias the search results it reports to selected customers in favor of its private-label products.[58]

The shopping-platform example and the diaper example are based on a common assumption: the dominant firm is better able to target its rivals' customers for discount prices than vice versa. Doing so can be understood as price discrimination. Price discrimination is ubiquitous in the economy and is particularly prevalent in industries such as Internet platforms where marginal-cost pricing is unlikely to cover fixed costs. Price discrimination and related practices such as producing multiple versions of products, which also allows sellers to charge prices that vary with buyer willingness to pay, are often a natural way to recover the high fixed costs of information technology.[59]

Firms discriminate in price when they charge different prices to different buyers or groups of buyers, or when they charge different price-cost margins if the cost of serving those buyers or buyer groups differs. Suppose, for example, that delivery costs a restaurant $5. A restaurant that adds a $10 delivery charge relative to the price it would charge to a customer that picked up the order could be said to discriminate in price. Or if a gallon of premium gasoline costs one cent more to produce and distribute than regular gasoline, a gas station that charges ten cents more for the premium product could be said to discriminate in price. (Alternatively, one could view the products as different and describe the gas station and restaurant as selling differentiated products at different prices rather than as discriminating in price.) To discriminate in price, a seller must have the ability to sort customers or customer groups by their willingness to pay or price sensitivity. It must also prevent arbitrage; that is, it must ensure that buyers who are offered the product or service at a low price cannot buy it cheaply and resell it to buyers offered it at a high price.

As a matter of economic theory, the welfare consequences of price discrimination in monopoly markets are ambiguous.[60] The practice may allow sellers to charge higher prices to buyers that value the product highly, relative to the price the seller would set if constrained to charge all customers the same price. Higher prices reduce consumer surplus, harming buyers, and reduce aggregate surplus.[61] Price discrimination may instead, or also, benefit buyers and increase aggregate surplus. It may permit sellers to serve buyers that value the product at more than the product's cost but who would otherwise be priced out of the market. To similar effect, when consumer search is costly, targeted advertising can help buyers identify products that match their tastes more quickly and easily.[62] Empirical analysis would be required to determine whether price discrimination is more harmful or beneficial in any particular monopoly market.

In oligopoly markets, price discrimination has additional potentially harmful and beneficial consequences.[63] When sellers are equally vulnerable to targeted discounting, the opportunity for price discrimination can enhance competition but does not necessarily do so. The theoretical ambiguity as to the welfare effects of price discrimination in monopoly markets, and in oligopoly markets in which sellers are equally vulnerable to targeted discounting, cautions against presuming that price discrimination is beneficial in such settings, contrary to what some conservative commentators appear to believe.[64]

On the one hand, when sellers are equally vulnerable, their ability to target customers may induce greater competition for price-sensitive customers, leading to lower prices. Each oligopolist may target its rivals' less loyal (more price-sensitive) customer groups, leading to a more competitive outcome overall.[65] Moreover, the possibility of selective customer targeting may discourage or undermine coordination among rivals because targeting may make cheating more lucrative.

On the other hand, an increased threat of enhanced price competition may facilitate coordination, leading to higher prices. Coordination could take the form of mutual forbearance from head-to-head competition,[66] which could be understood as a form of parallel exclusion.[67] Or an increased threat of price competition in response to cheating could discourage price-cutting in much the same way that increased multimarket contact facilitates coordination.[68]

The hypothetical examples involving Amazon suppose that competing sellers are not equally vulnerable to targeted discounting. They suppose instead that a dominant firm is less vulnerable to targeted discounting than are its rivals. Then price discrimination among oligopolists would create both exclusionary and collusive threats.[69]

In a market with a dominant firm, the exclusionary threat may be the more plausible.[70] If one firm has superior access to personalized consumer information, it may be able to target selectively its rivals' most profitable customers with discounts, while its own customers remain largely insulated from a targeted response. Under such circumstances, selective customer targeting or its threat can discourage aggressive competition from rivals and potential entrants, allowing the firm with superior information to obtain, maintain, or enhance market power.[71] Moreover, selective customer targeting may be inexpensive: the dominant firm need not reduce prices to its existing customers—only to customers likely to purchase from its rivals.[72]

It is not surprising that a dominant firm's superior ability to engage in selective customer targeting can have adverse competitive consequences, because the competitive implications of the practice bear a family resemblance to the effects of price-matching guarantees (also termed meeting-competition clauses or meet-or-release clauses).[73] When firms institute such guarantees, rivals have less to gain from cutting their price: some customers the rival might otherwise attract would not end up switching. In consequence, rivals may be discouraged from competing aggressively, leading all firms to charge higher prices.[74] Similarly, when rivals to a dominant firm and prospective entrants know that price cutting will be met by targeted discounting, they have less to gain from lowering price. Rather, those rivals may avoid aggressive price competition.[75]

Increased Customer Switching Costs

In several well-known antitrust cases, a dominant platform foreclosed its rivals' access to end users by increasing the captivity of its own customers (i.e., making it more difficult or expensive for end users to multi-home or to switch). The *Lorain Journal* newspaper did so by refusing to accept advertisements from firms that advertised on a competing radio station.[76] FTD, the leading flower delivery network,[77] and Mastercard and Visa[78] excluded rivals by preventing their members from using rival platforms.

A 2000 FTC staff report identified a number of potentially exclusionary practices that one type of platform—a business-to-business (B2B) marketplace—could use to harm competition with its platform rivals.

B2Bs may use a variety of carrots (profit interests or rebates or revenue-sharing devices in return for commitments to achieve certain volume levels) or sticks (minimum volume or minimum percentage requirements, bans on investment in other B2Bs, up-front membership fees or required software investments, or pressure on suppliers and buyers) to capture business. These exclusivity practices impose switching costs in terms of benefits to forgo or penalties to pay if a participant chooses to support another B2B.[79]

For the most part, the practices cited by the FTC exclude by increasing customer captivity, thereby raising the costs to end users of switching platforms.[80] The list does not exhaust the ways dominant firms can harm competition by increasing customer captivity. For example, a firm could also increase customer captivity by making it costlier for customers to obtain accurate information about product features.[81]

A firm's customers may become its captives for many reasons, including buyer habit, customer search costs, or customer switching costs. Switching costs may arise from customer investments in learning to take advantage of a product or service or from customer preferences with respect to product features or locations or seller reputation. Customer captivity can create an important competitive advantage for a firm that controls a platform. The more end users that a platform captures on one side, the more difficult it may be for its rivals to attract end users on the same or other sides (given feedback effects). This dynamic enhances the exclusionary effect of conduct that directly harms competing platforms on any side.

In markets with a dominant platform, the extent of competition may turn primarily on the ability of smaller rivals or potential entrants to obtain scale economies by taking business away from the platform leader,[82] as by developing a better product or by cutting cost and price. Conduct that increases end-user (customer) captivity interdicts this competitive mechanism. Such conduct makes it more difficult for rival platforms or new platform entrants to compete successfully in a setting in which rivalry is already limited, by making it more costly or difficult for those competitors to achieve scale economies.[83] Even if rivals are not forced to exit, those firms may not be able to expand cheaply, particularly if they must go beyond serving a narrow product or geographic niche to do so or if they have unique cost advantages that dissipate with scale.[84] When dominant platforms increase end-user captivity, and those end users do not patronize multiple platforms, rivals may provide little constraint on dominant platforms' exercise of market power,[85] regardless of whether the rivals produce at an efficient scale.[86]

Various practices used by today's dominant information technology and Internet platforms potentially raise end-user switching costs. These may include Amazon Prime, a fee service that presumably encourages shopper loyalty by offering members rapid shipping at no charge, less fulfillment risk, and product discounts.[87] Another example may be the set of barriers Facebook creates for users wishing to transfer their posts and social connections to other social media platforms.[88] Finally, Google's control of data on past searches using rival search platforms means that those rivals cannot learn from as many past searches as Google can. That may lead rival search algorithms to be less precise than Google's, making it less attractive for some Google users to use rival search engines.

Of course, platform practices that might appear to raise end-user switching costs do not necessarily harm competition, even when employed by a dominant firm. Upon investigation, the conduct may turn out not to foreclose rival platforms, or its efficiency benefits may outweigh any competitive harm. But there is reason for antitrust concern when dominant platforms take steps to increase customer captivity.

Platform Most-Favored Nation Provisions

Amazon employs a platform most-favored nation (MFN) provision, also termed a price-parity provision, if it requires third-party vendors selling through its shopping platform to commit not to sell on other platforms at lower retail prices.[89] A platform MFN could be imposed whenever the online platform employs an agency distribution model, as is common with online platforms for hotel and transportation bookings, consumer goods, and digital products.

A platform MFN can be thought of as an exclusivity agreement for a business model: it excludes rival platforms or entrants that wish to adopt an alternative model predicated on discounting retail prices by obligating the third-party vendors not to deal with those platforms. Accordingly a platform MFN can make it impossible for a rival platform to adopt a strategy of charging a lower commission to vendors that agree to pass through their savings by reducing the price consumers would pay. By discouraging online platform rivals or entrants from competing on price, a dominant platform can protect its market power from erosion.[90] For example, in Europe, online hotel-reservation sites were found to have used platform MFNs to preclude the development of discount bookings sites. Some platform MFNs could be justified as protecting the platform's incentive to invest in improvements against the threat of customer free riding, but this efficiency claim will not be persuasive in many settings.

Predatory Pricing

A dominant platform can also exclude rivals by charging low prices, known as predatory prices. In one case, a newspaper that used targeted price cutting to attempt to exclude a rival paper was found to have violated the Sherman Act § 2 prohibition on attempts to monopolize.[91] In a recent attention-getting article, Lina Khan credits Amazon's success in achieving dominance as an online platform in part to its use of predatory pricing tactics that evade antitrust enforcement.[92]

Khan characterizes Amazon's business strategy as a combination of loss-leading prices (a "willingness to forgo profits in order to establish dominance"[93]) and expansion into multiple lines of business.[94] She argues that Amazon's investors are "willing to fund predatory growth" in a growing range of businesses in anticipation of recouping those losses at least a decade later,[95] presumably in many markets simultaneously, by raising the prices buyers pay, reducing payments to suppliers, or both.[96] Khan suggests that Wall Street's high valuation of Amazon, relative to the company's thin profit stream, supports this contention.

However, there may be other reasons investors are bullish on Amazon. The financial markets could be betting on the success of other Amazon businesses, including cloud computing, where Amazon is the profitable market leader, and the development of complementary services that exploit Amazon's investment in artificial intelligence.[97] Investors may also think Amazon is investing in its scale and scope by pricing low relative to current costs (but perhaps not relative to anticipated future costs) and by widening its product and service offerings. Such investors could be betting that Amazon would come to have lower costs than rival shopping platforms, potentially making Amazon's platform profitable even if its long-run prices are not above the level at which reasonably efficient rival platforms would cover their costs and earn their owners a competitive return on capital.

So we might look elsewhere for a successful predatory-pricing case against Amazon. Plausibly, this could involve an individual product.[98] Amazon might, for example and hypothetically, seek to discourage competition from physical book retailers by charging low prices for that product.[99] It is possible that low book prices could exclude competing retailers, whether online or brick-and-mortar, and that Amazon would have reasonable prospects for profiting through conduct that would harm competition. It might harm competition by raising physical book prices, expecting its remaining retail rivals not to compete aggressively in response. Or it might profit by negotiating lower wholesale prices from publishers. Recoupment could take place on any side of Amazon's platform or multiple sides simultaneously. These issues— exclusion of rivals, harm to competition, and expected profitability (when the harm is prospective)—arise in all exclusion cases.[100]

As with other forms of exclusionary conduct, Amazon may have procompetitive reasons for charging low book prices. Doing so may help Amazon sell other products at the same time.[101] Or low book prices, and the increased sales they generate, may pay off in increased future sales, for example by building Amazon's customer base,[102] supporting Amazon's reputation for discount pricing, or giving Amazon information about customer preferences that the company can use to recommend other products. It is nonetheless possible that the harm to competition from the exclusionary consequence of charging low prices would exceed these potential procompetitive benefits.

PRESUMPTIONS AND EXCLUSIONARY CONDUCT

Given the overarching concern to enhance deterrence of market power by dominant platforms and in general, there is good reason for enforcers to increase scrutiny of exclusionary conduct by large information technology and Internet platforms. This conduct should not be presumed legal, nor should there be a safe harbor for above-cost predatory pricing. At the same time, the range and plausibility of possible efficiency justifications for exclusionary behavior cautions against invoking an across-the-board presumption of competitive harm, as some progressives have suggested. In general, antitrust law should evaluate the reasonableness of exclusionary conduct without invoking across-the-board presumptions except in certain settings, noted below or in other chapters, where courts should presume competitive harm or condemn the relevant practice on a truncated factual showing.

This section begins by explaining when truncated condemnation is appropriate for conduct in legal categories associated with exclusion: vertical agreements reviewed under Clayton Act § 7, vertical restraints reviewed under the Sherman Act or Clayton Act § 3, and vertical conduct not involving allegations of predatory pricing in monopolization cases. The rest of this section takes up some distinctive legal issues that arise when the exclusionary conduct involves targeted discounting and predatory pricing.

Reasonableness Review of Exclusionary Conduct and Truncated Condemnation

Vertical-merger enforcement illustrates the legal landscape governing exclusionary conduct generally. It also shows the vast difference in the perspectives of Chicagoans and contemporary progressives. In general, courts should avoid both approaches and instead apply a reasonableness analysis without relying on general presumptions. Exceptions would arise when truncated condemnation is appropriate or when the reasons for invoking a specific presumption of competitive harm apply.

Chicagoans

According to Richard Posner, writing in 1979, the change in antitrust thinking brought about by the Chicago school was "nowhere more evident than in the area of vertical integration."[103] Twenty years before, he observed, the leading structural era commentators had recommended forbidding any vertical merger in which the acquiring firm enjoyed a market share of 20 percent or more.[104] That proposal was broadly consistent with the case law of the era.[105] By the time Posner wrote, in contrast, the leading antitrust treatise exhibited little concern about vertical integration, and, if forced to choose between per se illegality and per se legality, favored the latter.[106] The courts took note of this sea change in thinking. In 1989 a district court summarized the Chicago view: "vertical integration is not an unlawful or even a suspect category under the antitrust laws."[107]

Modern Enforcers

Notwithstanding this change of judicial emphasis, the enforcement agencies have continued to question some vertical mergers. Over time, the agencies assimilated the modern economic learning on exclusionary conduct, which postdates the literature on which Bork, Posner, and Easterbrook relied. The modern literature recognizes that vertical mergers and mergers among firms selling complementary products can harm competition through input foreclosure or customer foreclosure and other means.[108] In recent years the agencies have settled many vertical-merger challenges by consent, including a case against Google's acquisition of ITA, a travel-bookings engine.[109] Until 2018, when a district court rejected the Justice Department's challenge to AT&T's acquisition of Time Warner, the courts had not undertaken a substantive analysis of a vertical merger since the 1980s.[110]

Progressives

To update Posner, the difference between progressive and Chicago views on antitrust is nowhere more evident than in the presumptions they bring to evaluating vertical integration. Thus some contemporary progressives reject the agencies' middle ground in favor of reverting to the pre-Chicago norm. They advocate presuming competitive harm whenever a dominant information technology firm thought to provide a vital service to suppliers or customers—such as Amazon, Facebook, Google, or Comcast—buys or owns a firm that depends on its platform's services.[111] In the view of these commentators, a dominant platform almost invariably has both the incentive and ability to foreclose rivals to the vertically related firm it owns or acquires and thereby harm competition in its upstream or downstream market.

In its strongest form, a prohibition on vertical integration by dominant platforms, whether arising through merger or by internal expansion, could prevent Amazon from selling private-label products on its shopping platform or Comcast from owning programming networks or a film studio. It might stop Google from offering flight-booking information in response to search queries and bar Google and Apple from selling smartphones that run the Android and iPhone operating systems, respectively. (These conclusions turn on characterizing the various platforms as dominant, which the firms may contest.)

Applied just to mergers, a presumption of competitive harm due to vertical integration might have blocked a number of recent transactions by dominant platforms, at least in part. Among these are Amazon's purchase of Zappos, an online retailer of shoes;[112] Quisdi, a collection of online shopping sites including the baby-products site diapers.com;[113] and the grocer Whole Foods. Facebook acquired Instagram (a photo-sharing social media platform), WhatsApp (a mobile messaging service), Oculus (a virtual-reality entertainment firm), and Ozlo (an artificial-intelligence firm). Google has acquired YouTube (online videos), Motorola Mobility (smartphones), Waze (automobile-navigation software), Nest (home-automation devices), ITA (software powering travel-bookings sites), firms that manage online advertising (DoubleClick and AdMob), and artificial-intelligence firms (Deep Mind and Dark Blue Labs).[114] All of these acquisitions would have been suspect under the progressive presumption.

These transactions were not exclusively vertical (acquisitions of suppliers, distributors, or sellers of complementary products). Some can also or instead be seen as horizontal (acquisitions of rivals) or as acquisitions of potential competitors.[115] Amazon's acquisition of Quisdi, for example, had both horizontal elements (a merger of two shopping platforms) and vertical elements (a merger between a shopping platform and a manufacturer of private-label products). Facebook's Instagram acquisition could have been a potential-competition merger, to the extent Instagram could have evolved from a photo-sharing platform into a broader social-media platform. As a group, though, these acquisitions fairly represent the breadth of vertical-merger activity among dominant platforms.

The fact that the progressive-supported presumption against vertical mergers would have broad reach is not, of course, an argument against it. The concern is not the potential scope, but the extent to which such a prohibition would chill efficiencies. For example, vertical acquisitions may allow firms to use complementary assets to lower costs or improve products. Vertical acquisitions may allow firms to produce and distribute products and services more cheaply or more effectively by aligning the incentives of firms with those of their suppliers or distributors. After a merger, vertically related firms may have an incentive to lower prices and expand output by eliminating double marginalization (successive markups). In some cases, the claimed efficiencies from vertical merger will be small, speculative, or readily available through contract, internal expansion, or other means not requiring a merger. As with efficiencies claimed for horizontal mergers, these would be reasons to discount or reject the asserted competitive benefits of vertical integration. But in other cases, the efficiency gains will be substantial, not practically available through other means, and worth considering. A blanket ban on vertical integration would preclude doing so.

Reasonableness Review

Courts reviewing vertical mergers should generally evaluate potential benefit and threat to competition without invoking either a Chicago-oriented presumption that vertical integration is procompetitive, or a progressive-supported presumption that it is harmful.[116] (However, a presumption defended in Chapter 8—that innovation competition will be harmed when a dominant firm in an innovative sector acquires a firm it does not presently compete with but possesses capabilities that make it a threat for competition in future products—could apply to a vertical merger.) Similarly, courts also should refrain from invoking either presumption when evaluating vertical restraints, including exclusive dealing and platform MFNs,[117] or when evaluating other exclusionary practices.

Still, in recognition of the economy-wide market power problem and the recent history of underdeterring anticompetitive exclusion, enforcement agencies should give more attention to the potential competitive problems raised by exclusionary conduct, whether implemented through vertical agreements or otherwise. And in some cases, competitive harm should be presumed—as with application of the rules governing truncated condemnation.

Truncated Condemnation

The modern burden-shifting framework used to evaluate the reasonableness of firm conduct under antitrust laws allows for truncated condemnation of exclusionary conduct across legal categories when the excluding firms have foreclosed competition from all actual or potential rivals other than insignificant competitors[118] and when the exclusionary conduct lacks a plausible efficiency justification.[119] Condemnation is described as truncated because it does not require a comprehensive analysis of the nature, history, purpose, and actual or probable effect of the practice evaluated. Truncated condemnation may be invoked when exclusionary conduct is evaluated as an attempt to monopolize and in cases of actual monopolization, exclusionary group boycott, nonprice vertical restraint, and exclusive dealing.[120] Truncated condemnation also could apply to vertical mergers when the efficiencies identified by the merging firms are not substantial or merger-specific.

This approach can be understood as adopting a rebuttable presumption of competitive harm from foreclosure of all significant rivals and making that presumption conclusive when the conduct cannot plausibly be considered procompetitive. The involuntary-cartel intuition explains why a conclusive presumption is economically sensible. If a firm or firms exclude all significant rivals though conduct that would not benefit competition—that is, without lowering costs and prices or improving quality—their conduct creates the equivalent of a naked price-fixing cartel and would be expected to harm competition.

The Seventh Circuit has extended this economic logic. If the excluding firm or firms have market power and have demonstrated the ability to foreclose at least one significant rival, that court recognized, it is reasonable to presume that they have the ability and incentive to harm competition by foreclosing all significant rivals.[121] Accordingly, exclusionary conduct can also be condemned without full rule-of-reason review on a showing that one or more rivals were excluded, the excluding firms possess market power,[122] and the exclusionary conduct at issue had no plausible efficiency justification.

The market power predicate for truncated condemnation under the Seventh Circuit's approach may be understood in alternative ways: first, as a factor tending to suggest the ability to exclude other significant rivals; second, as a reason to expect that exclusion would confer the ability to raise price or otherwise harm competition. The interpretation affects whether market power would be evaluated from a pre-exclusion or postexclusion standpoint. (Postexclusion market power could be retrospective, if the plaintiff alleges competition has been harmed, or prospective, if the plaintiff alleges harm to competition going forward, or both.) Under the first interpretation, truncated condemnation could look to either, as pre- or postexclusion market power would each suggest an ability to exclude. Under the second interpretation, only postexclusion market power matters. For example, a firm clearly can exercise market power by excluding all its rivals no matter how small its prior share.

PRESUMPTIONS AND PRICING

Platforms may use price discounts to exclude, as with two of the exclusionary methods discussed above: targeted discounting and predatory pricing. While antitrust law has historically adopted special rules for evaluating predatory pricing, targeted discounting involves a new mechanism that should be analyzed differently. For reasons explained below, courts should assimilate the analysis of both forms of exclusionary conduct involving pricing into the burden-shifting framework for evaluating exclusionary conduct generally, without invoking special presumptions.

Targeted Discounting

Exclusion by dominant platforms with superior access to customer data through targeted price discounts resembles exclusion through predatory pricing insofar as both mechanisms involve pricing. But targeted discounting is far removed from the core idea of price predation: steep across-the-board price cutting within a market that the predator can maintain longer than the prey.[123] The focus of litigation over targeted discounting should be on whether rivals are targeted systematically, not on the level of prices. The general antitrust rules governing exclusionary conduct should apply, not the additional rules specific to predatory pricing.

When targeted discounting is evaluated within the general framework applied to exclusionary conduct, the dominant firm's business justification would be expected to take center stage because it determines whether the conduct can be condemned under Sherman Act § 2 through a truncated analysis. Assume that the plaintiff can show that a rival or rivals were excluded in the past or likely will be if the harm is prospective. Assume further that the plaintiff can show that all substantial rivals were excluded, or else that some were and the dominant platform has market power or a dangerous probability of achieving monopoly power.[124] Then the practice should be condemned without further analysis unless the platform defendant has a plausible business justification for targeting particular customers and products for discounts.

For example, if Amazon systematically targets rivals' customers with discounts, without offering comparable discounts to its own loyal customers or others, and if the other predicates for truncated condemnation are met, the platform would likely be found liable under the antitrust laws without further analysis. By contrast, if the platform instead, say, targets customers more likely than most to make additional purchases, some of whom happen to patronize rival platforms, then the conduct should be evaluated for its reasonableness to determine whether the competitive harm from targeting's exclusionary effect outweighs the procompetitive benefit.[125]

If a platform is systematically targeting rivals' customers, it might seek to wrap itself in conservative rhetoric skeptical of predatory pricing: it may argue that targeting discounts toward potential customers likely to buy from rivals is justified as the essence of competition. That argument should be rejected summarily. It is tantamount to saying that transactions between a willing buyer and willing seller are inherently procompetitive. The competitive issue is not whether the parties to the transaction are both made better off in the short run, as the argument supposes. Rather, the issue is whether the seller's conduct is likely to harm competition by excluding rivals.

Courts and enforcers can also address the threat of targeted discounting by dominant platforms with superior access to customer information prophylactically, by preventing agreements or mergers that give the dominant firm exclusive access to customer data useful for targeting.[126] Doing so would be particularly important if courts analyze targeted discounting as predatory pricing, because the Supreme Court has introduced special rules that raise hurdles for plaintiffs alleging that offense.

Predatory Pricing

Predatory-pricing cases are often difficult for plaintiffs to win, in part because the courts apply two rules in evaluating such claims to help structure the general-reasonableness analysis of predatory conduct (under Sherman Act § 2) or competitive harm (under Sherman Act § 1): a recoupment test and a safe harbor for prices above some measure of cost (often marginal cost or average incremental cost).[127] The recoupment test is appropriate for evaluating exclusionary conduct generally and does not invariably bar such claims when price discounts are used to exclude. The price-cost safe harbor strikes an inappropriate error-cost balance and should be abandoned or modified.

Recoupment

The recoupment test requires the plaintiff to explain why the predator would reasonably expect to profit in the long run from pricing below cost in the short run. The test is unobjectionable conceptually: a firm is unlikely to adopt any exclusionary strategy unless it sees an advantage from doing so.[128] The profitability issue in exclusion cases is not whether the firm expected to profit from the challenged conduct—if the firm is economically rational, that will always be the case—but whether the conduct would be profitable if the exclusionary interpretation is correct.[129]

In practice, expected profitability is a contested issue primarily when the competitive harm is prospective and the exclusionary strategy is costly, as with some forms of predatory pricing.[130] Even with respect to predation claims, the Supreme Court has invited "a flexible, context-specific approach to recoupment," sensitive to market structure, competitive conditions, and the predatory strategy employed.[131]

The recoupment test does not operate as a death sentence for all predatory-pricing claims, because the modern economic literature has identified a range of plausible mechanisms by which recoupment can occur. A multimarket monopolist may respond aggressively to single-market entry and profit from doing so mainly by discouraging entry in other markets, allowing the monopolist to protect its market power there (predation with multimarket recoupment).[132] A predator may also profit by convincing lenders or investors to discontinue supporting the prey ("deep pocket" predation), by convincing a prospective entrant that the predator's costs are too low to make entry profitable (predation by cost signaling), or by convincing a prospective entrant that its product will be unattractive to buyers (test-market predation).[133] Predatory pricing may also succeed by denying the prey economies of scale when the prey has fewer captive.buyers[134] or by denying the prey demand-side scale economies on the other side of a two-sided platform.[135]

It may be feasible to demonstrate the plausibility of recoupment in a hypothetical predatory-pricing case against Amazon that challenges its below-cost pricing in a narrow product category, such as best-selling e-books. Amazon might be expected to recoup by charging publishers higher fixed fees or paying them lower wholesale prices or by raising the retail price of e-books. Even if the recoupment test were satisfied, of course, Amazon could prevail on other grounds.[136]

If a dominant platform engaged in targeted discounting sets prices at levels below the platform's costs, and that conduct is evaluated as predatory pricing (contrary to what was recommended above), the recoupment test may not be difficult to satisfy. The platform would likely recoup by maintaining a supracompetitive price in its sales to the many customers not given selective discounts. The profits from discouraging aggressive competition by rival platforms would accrue immediately; they would not be delayed until the dominant platform stopped making selective price cuts.[137]

The recoupment test would probably be hard to satisfy in a case based on the firm-wide predatory-pricing theory Khan appears to have in mind, whereby Amazon has been keeping prices low for a wide and expanding range of online retail products, funded by investors who expect it to profit many years later by raising prices to buyers or bargaining down the wholesale prices paid suppliers. Even if the evidence showed that Amazon's low prices are exclusionary and not primarily investments in future competition—overcoming another hurdle to proving firm-wide predatory pricing—the prospects for profitability of the predatory pricing strategy Khan postulates will be challenging to demonstrate because of uncertainty about the timing and magnitude of future price increases to buyers or future reductions in the wholesale prices paid suppliers. This difficulty identifies an aspect of the economic logic of the exclusionary theory that a plaintiff should be asked to address with evidence and economic analysis, not an inappropriate legal hurdle that courts should be asked to remove.[138]

Safe Harbor for Above-Cost Pricing

By contrast, the second antitrust rule applied specifically in predatory pricing litigation, the safe harbor for above-cost pricing, should be revisited to account for changing views about the error-cost balance. Although the safe harbor derives from Areeda and Turner's influential article on predatory pricing, that article actually proposed that a dominant firm's below-cost pricing should create an irrebuttable presumption of monopolization.[139] The courts flipped the test from a screen to a safe harbor to avoid chilling procompetitive price cutting. In *Brooke Grp. Ltd. v. Brown & Williamson Tobacco Corp.* (1993), the leading modern decision on predatory pricing, the Supreme Court explained that, absent a safe harbor for prices above an appropriate measure of cost, the prohibition on predatory pricing could chill aggressive and legitimate price competition.[140] As the court recognized, firms may charge low prices, even prices below cost, for procompetitive reasons.[141]

More generally, the Court argued in 1993, error-cost considerations justify imposing a high hurdle for plaintiffs seeking to prove predatory pricing. On one side of the error-cost balance, the Court expressed serious concern that predatory-pricing litigation would chill procompetitive discounting. On the other side, the Court saw little anticompetitive threat: it cited "the general implausibility of predatory pricing."[142]

Yet experience applying the price-cost test and developments in economics since 1993 indicate that the safe harbor for above-cost pricing implements a mistaken view of the error-cost balance. Predatory pricing no longer appears implausible. Recent economic studies provide a number of examples of successful predatory pricing,[143] and the modern learning on the feasibility of recoupment helps explain why. Moreover, the safe harbor, as applied, is poorly targeted to deter anticompetitive conduct. It focuses attention on the wrong question—measuring the defendant's costs—when courts should focus on whether rivals were excluded and, if so, whether the defendant was able to obtain, maintain, or enhance its market power. When applied to multisided platforms, including many dominant technology platforms, a safe harbor for above-cost pricing will tend to channel scrutiny toward pricing behavior on the sides of platforms where end users are not charged or subsidized, as a potentially procompetitive means of stimulating usage in order to induce greater participation on other sides. Yet enforcers and courts should instead be looking for platforms that cut prices in order to deny platform rivals an efficient scale or otherwise exclude those rivals. The safe harbor also fails to recognize that predatory pricing can be effective as an exclusionary strategy even if the predator's price reductions leave its prices above cost.[144]

The underdeterrence problems involving predatory pricing and the need to increase deterrence of anticompetitive conduct more generally suggest reconsideration of the safe harbor for above-cost pricing. Rather than screen cases with a price-cost test, courts should demand what they ask for in evaluating predatory strategies generally: evidence that rivals are excluded; evidence that, by excluding, the predator will be able to obtain, maintain, or enhance market power; and, in a setting in which the costs of price cutting are already apparent but the harms from exercise of market power are forecasts, evidence that the defendant should reasonably expect to profit from the exclusionary strategy.[145] Demanding such evidence would prevent the underdeterrence that arises from relying on a safe harbor that insulates a wide range of potentially anticompetitive conduct from liability.

For similar reasons, if the below-cost pricing safe harbor is nonetheless maintained, it should be modified. The safe harbor should be interpreted as setting the cost level at which price cuts are tested against average total cost, thereby removing liability protection from a wider range of potentially anticompetitive conduct. Although the allocation of fixed and common costs is arbitrary,[146] any reasonable allocation would remove some harmful conduct from the overbroad safe harbor. In applying the screen, moreover, courts should not compare prices to costs averaged across a product line as a whole.[147] Any prices below cost should be sufficient for the case to proceed.

Looking beyond predatory pricing, some commentators and courts writing since *Brooke Group* have relied on an error-cost analysis similar to what the Court employed in that case to advocate subjecting alleged refusals to deal by dominant firms to an elevated standard of proof analogous to the standards used in predatory-pricing litigation.[148] As with the Court's defense of a safe harbor for above-cost pricing, the error-cost analysis they employ is overly solicitous of the concern to avoid chilling procompetitive conduct, in part for reasons discussed in Chapter 8 in connection with analyzing dominant firms' appropriability defense. This error-cost analysis also is insufficiently attentive to the administrative difficulties created by the tests they propose and insufficiently concerned with deterring anticompetitive conduct in an era of substantial and widening market power.

CONCLUSION

The products and services provided by large information technology and Internet platforms are wonders of the modern world. By any reasonable reckoning, our lives have been greatly enriched—perhaps immeasurably so—by online shopping, web search, social media, household broadband, smartphones, and so on. These platforms make it quick, simple, and convenient to obtain information and interact with friends, sellers, and others. The antitrust question is not whether these businesses benefit us; it is whether some aspects of their conduct limit competition, thereby preventing consumers, workers, and the economy as a whole from benefiting even more.

This chapter has identified a number of anticompetitive exclusionary practices that dominant information technology and Internet platforms may have the ability and incentive to employ. The modern framework for analyzing the reasonableness of exclusionary conduct permits courts to condemn some exclusionary conduct without a comprehensive reasonableness review when certain factual predicates are met, including the absence of a plausible procompetitive justification. That approach, combined with a reasonableness review when the conduct is plausibly justified; a rejection of noninterventionist presumptions in cases involving vertical conduct or the unilateral conduct of large firms; improved understanding of the mechanisms by which dominant platforms can harm competition through exclusion; and greater enforcement attention to exclusionary conduct generally promises to strike a better balance between deterring competitive harms and chilling beneficial conduct.

Chapter Eight

Threats to Innovation from Lessened Competition

ANTITRUST LAW SPEAKS about dominant firms and innovation with two voices, much as it does with respect to competition. One voice expresses concern that market power harms innovation, the other that antitrust enforcement does. On the one hand, evidence shows that competition promotes innovation and productivity.[1] On the other, there is worry about the appropriability effects of enforcement: if antitrust enforcement reduces the expected return to a dominant firm's investments in research and development (R&D), will that discourage R&D by current or would-be dominant firms, chilling innovation?

These voices on dominant firms and innovation appeal to the opposing sides of the more general error-cost balance that frames antitrust rules: one side concerned with deterring competitive harm and the other with chilling procompetitive conduct.[2] The two voices can be understood as the contemporary descendants of competing theoretical positions associated with Kenneth Arrow and Joseph Schumpeter, respectively.[3]

In striking a balance between these positions, antitrust law has long recognized the need to protect entry or expansion of rivals with lower costs, superior production technologies, or better products. In prominent cases, the courts prevented Microsoft from impeding the development of a new method by which software could access personal-computer operating systems;[4] the *Lorain Journal* newspaper from curbing the entry of a rival using a then-new technology, radio;[5] and the Visa and Mastercard networks from denying consumers access to products with new features and discouraging innovation in services.[6]

Innovation issues are important in merger review, too, but that is a recent development at the enforcement agencies. The *Horizontal Merger Guidelines* first made reference to innovation in 1992, but only in passing and in a footnote.[7] By contrast, the 2010 guidelines identify a way in which a horizontal merger can harm innovation rivalry consistent with economic theory and recent agency investigations: the merged firm has an incentive to cut back on R&D when either (or both) of the merging firms was aiming to develop a new product that would capture substantial revenues from its merger partner or has the capability to do so. A recent survey found that the enforcement agencies now identify innovation issues in one-third of their merger challenges, almost always along with other concerns not involving innovation. Mergers taking place in R&D-intensive industries are almost always flagged for innovation concerns.[8]

However, these statistics overstate the extent of enforcement attention. Half the time innovation comes up, the agencies simply mention innovation without elaboration.[9] And while the agencies have lately shown interest in innovation issues, the courts have not yet grappled with the mechanisms by which mergers can harm innovation.

In an environment of substantial and widening market power, and given the connection of that problem to a loss of dynamism in the economy as a whole, it is essential that antitrust law listen more to the first voice than it does now. This chapter explains why and identifies what enforcers should do to protect innovation from market power. I discuss ways to rebalance antitrust law to increase deterrence of anticompetitive conduct harming innovation, without ignoring the possibility that antitrust rules could chill firm incentives to develop new, better, or less expensive products and services or more cost-effective production processes. With the growth of dominant information technology and Internet platforms, which are often heavily reliant on R&D and able to exclude innovation rivals, deterring anticompetitive harms to innovation is an especially pressing issue.[10]

Innovation competition and future product-market competition are appropriate concerns under the antitrust laws. The D.C. Circuit, sitting en banc, unanimously rejected Microsoft's claim that nascent competition is too speculative to protect under the Sherman Act.[11] Merger enforcement under the Clayton Act "involves *probabilities,* not certainties or possibilities"[12] and so reaches threats to nascent competition too. Merger law's potential-competition jurisprudence does not indicate otherwise: those cases address the loss through merger of anticipated rivalry in current products,[13] not the loss of rivalry in innovation or future products.

Most of this chapter is concerned with the first voice. The first part surveys a range of ways in which reduced competition can harm innovation. The survey is framed around mergers, but the mechanisms discussed could also arise in non-merger enforcement. The major argument against antitrust intervention in innovative industries other than appropriability—the claim that it is too difficult to identify anticompetitive conduct when products and markets are changing rapidly—is addressed by describing the factual showings on the basis of which harm to innovation can be presumed.

The second part of the chapter looks at ways innovation can be harmed by the exclusionary conduct of dominant firms. At that point I consider the appropriate scope of the second voice by explaining when not to credit a defendant's appropriability defense. The chapter sets forth economic bases for antitrust liability when lessened competition threatens to harm innovation, largely putting aside the specification of appropriate remedies.[14]

INNOVATION HARMS FROM MERGER

Horizontal-merger law's structural presumption connects increased concentration with reduced competition. Some commentators who accept that presumption when the competitive concern involves prices or closely related competitive dimensions are agnostic about relying on it to evaluate competitive effects of mergers in innovative industries, when the primary concern is that the merger may discourage the development of new or better products and production processes.[15] Over time, the enforcement agencies have augmented the structural presumption with more detailed analytical approaches to evaluating horizontal mergers tied to specific theories of competitive effects. That approach, codified in the merger guidelines, allows courts and enforcers to understand, explain, and evaluate the economic mechanism by which the particular increase in concentration from merger may harm competition.[16] Doing so allows horizontal-merger enforcement to target competitive problems more closely, reducing enforcement errors in both directions, and has probably helped the enforcement agencies explain their merger challenges more convincingly in court.

This section adopts a similar strategy for addressing innovation harms from merger. I describe two mechanisms by which mergers of actual or potential rivals can lessen innovation competition and reduce future product-market competition: by allowing the merged firm to internalize future product-market competition (a unilateral-effects theory) or by deterring new product development by rivals (an exclusionary theory).[17] In Chapter 7 I described ways that acquisitions by dominant information technology platforms can harm competition by excluding rivals. Here I discuss the innovation consequences of such acquisitions, particularly acquisitions of potential platform rivals, in the context of internalizing future product-market competition.

I will argue that courts and enforcers should adopt two presumptions to govern their analysis of the harms from mergers that threaten innovation competition. First, courts and enforcers should presume that the merger of innovation rivals will harm competition when only a handful of firms participate in an innovation market. Second, courts and enforcers should presume that innovation competition would be harmed when a dominant firm in an innovative sector acquires a firm that possesses capabilities that make it a threat to compete in future products, even if the firms do not presently compete.

Internalizing Future Product-Market Competition

When merging firms are competing to develop products that are themselves likely to compete once introduced, or when these firms are developing ways of reducing the cost or improving the quality of products that now compete, the merged firm may have an incentive to lessen their head-to-head R&D competition.[18] Even if only one merger partner is developing new or cheaper products, the merged firm may have incentive to slow that R&D effort or channel it in a different direction, when R&D success would have led the successful innovator to divert substantial sales and profits away from the products of the other merger partner.

In these cases, the merged firm reduces its combined R&D effort because it recognizes that some of the benefit of one of the premerger firm's successful R&D would have come at the expense of the other premerger firm's business. In other words, the merged firm cuts back on R&D because it internalizes future product-market competition. As a result, expected competition in future products is lessened. In future product markets, prices would tend to be higher or quality reduced relative to what would otherwise have obtained.[19] The anticompetitive incentive may outweigh any competitive benefits from the merged firm's ability to develop new products or production processes more quickly, or improve their quality, by combining formerly independent research efforts with different strengths.[20]

The competitive concern can be understood in two complementary ways. First, it can be thought of as a potential-competition analogue to the adverse unilateral competitive effects that arise from merger between sellers of differentiated products: both theories suppose that one firm would capture substantial revenues from its merger partner. From this perspective, the competitive concern goes beyond the loss of potential competition from the acquisition of a rapid entrant into current product markets[21] to reach the loss of potential future product-market competition from the acquisition of an innovation rival. Second, the competitive concern can also be seen as one of exclusion: the merged firm has an incentive to suppress or cut back on what would otherwise have been a research program with prospects of creating future product-market competition.

The Merger Guidelines and Agency Cases

The *Horizontal Merger Guidelines* address two variants of the anticompetitive theory discussed above.[22] First, the *Guidelines* state that the theory applies when one (or both) of the merging firms works to develop a future product that would be expected to capture substantial revenues from the other firm. This version of the theory is routinely considered when the Federal Trade Commission (FTC) evaluates mergers among pharmaceutical firms with products in the Food and Drug Administration– (FDA-) approval pipeline, though it also comes up in other industry settings.[23]

Second, the theory applies when the merging firms are not presently developing next-generation products but have capabilities that make it likely they would each undertake R&D to do so, in the absence of merger. The relevant capabilities may include, for example, R&D assets and skills (including technological expertise), manufacturing assets and skills, and marketing or distribution assets and skills.

When the focus of antitrust analysis is on capabilities rather than ongoing R&D efforts, it may be difficult to describe with specificity the new products that the firms would seek to develop, particularly when firms have modified features of their products and services rapidly in the past and could do so in the future. If the firms now compete in the same product niche, it is plausible that one firm's new product would be expected to capture substantial revenues from the other in at least two settings: when competing today confers an advantage in developing next-generation products to serve the same niche, or if the merging firms have the general R&D capabilities needed to do so when few or no other firms have similar capabilities. In either situation, the merger would be expected to lessen competition in future products.

Three enforcement-agency examples illustrate the second variant. First, a proposed merger between firms that manufacture leading-edge semiconductor tools for high-volume manufacturing was abandoned when the Justice Department found that only a few firms had the capability to do so and that the merging firms were among the most able of this group—possibly the only viable options in some areas of tool specialization.[24] Second, the FTC prevented a pharmaceutical firm from acquiring the U.S. rights to develop a competing drug from a firm uniquely able to do so.[25] Third, the FTC blocked Nielsen's acquisition of Arbitron on the ground that these were the two firms best positioned to develop national, syndicated, cross-platform audience-measurement services, a next-generation product valuable to programming and advertising decision makers. While the agency described the competitive problem as involving lost future product-market competition,[26] it is also reasonable to conclude that the problem involves diminished incentives to innovate. Similarly, the European Commission portrayed its objection to the Dow/DuPont merger as a diminished-innovation problem.[27]

Relevant Factors and Presumptions

Although the *Guidelines* are concerned about the merged firm's unilateral incentive to cut back on its R&D effort, the *Guidelines* do not set forth the particular factors agencies should look at when evaluating whether this incentive is likely to produce anticompetitive harm.

A model developed by Richard Gilbert provides a useful starting point for identifying relevant factors.[28] In the base case, multiple firms are engaged in R&D efforts to produce a new product, all firms' research streams have an equal and moderate likelihood of success, and each new product takes away business from all other new products more or less equally. In this setting, a merger can lead to the loss of a research stream. Even though the lost research stream was profitable for the acquired firm premerger, the merged firm might find that, with multiple research streams to choose from, the incremental cost of retaining a given stream exceeds the incremental benefits.

Shutting down a research stream may harm competition by reducing the probability that at least one research stream succeeds and by lessening expected future price competition, both relative to what would obtain absent the merger. In addition, if firms would likely bring a research project to completion less expensively (in present-value terms) were they to work more slowly and systematically—saving money but delaying going to market—the merger may also harm competition by slowing the introduction of new products. When there are fewer research streams, coming in last matters less in terms of reducing prospective revenues. So the merged firm has incentive to progress more slowly if doing so can save money.

In Gilbert's model, R&D rivalry promotes innovation but with diminishing returns: moving from one to two rivals greatly increases the probability of discovery, but the effect of each incremental rival is less than the one before. The model's focus on research streams rather than firms allows for the possibility that the merged firm would continue both research streams. Gilbert finds that the loss of an R&D stream through merger generally has little effect on the aggregate likelihood of innovation success so long as at least five or six research streams remain, though the critical number could be reduced if a firm's innovation success benefits its complementary R&D efforts or complementary products. This result provides a benchmark for evaluating whether the R&D efforts of non-merging rivals are sufficient to prevent competitive harm.

But the benchmark case is not a good guide in all situations. Even if more than five or six research streams remain postmerger, a merger can harm innovation competition when successful new-product development would cannibalize profits from firms' existing products. (This economic incentive is known as Arrow's "replacement effect.") Gilbert's model also assumes symmetry among firms and that no firm currently produces a product. Both assumptions are important to determining the critical number of research streams in the benchmark case. These assumptions don't apply to every potential merger scenario.

Firms may be asymmetric in ways that increase the merged firm's incentive to cut back on its R&D effort and reduce the ability of non-merging firms to prevent competitive harm. For instance, firms may differ in their "R&D capital": prior investments by the firm that enhance the expected payoff for R&D success, considering both the eventual profits and the likelihood of earning them. A research stream may have greater expected payoff if conducted by a firm with related prior expertise, as by a pharmaceutical firm able to draw on its firm-wide experience when developing drug-delivery mechanisms. A research stream may also have greater expected payoff if conducted by a firm with expertise in regulatory approvals or marketing, when such expertise is difficult to obtain through contract. R&D may also have greater expected payoff if conducted by a firm with an installed base of customers who own products that would complement any new product developed. The expected payoff may be reduced if the new product would take business away from the firm's current products. In other words, Arrow's replacement effect can be thought of as reducing firms' R&D capital.

The last point means that a firm with a substantial business in current products may be a weaker innovation rival than otherwise. All else being equal, that firm counts for less in evaluating innovation competition. It also means that if a firm with a substantial business in current products acquires a potential rival, the merged firm may have a unilateral incentive to shut down the acquired firm's R&D effort, reducing the overall industry prospects for innovation success.[29]

Firms' R&D capital matters to merger analysis in two ways. First, a firm with a dominant share of the R&D capital relevant for a particular research effort may have an incentive and ability to deter innovation rivals from challenging its position.[30] If a merger of two firms with substantial R&D capital creates such a firm, or a merger enhances the position of a firm already dominant, the transaction can thus harm R&D competition and future product-market competition. When an acquired firm has a strong record of disruptive innovation, that history may augment this concern.

Second, firms relatively low in R&D capital would be expected to have lesser prospects for success in developing or marketing new products than innovation rivals with more R&D capital. Accordingly, the prospect of innovation competition from non-merging firms low in R&D capital may be unlikely to discourage a merged firm from cutting back its research effort. There may be many firms competing in R&D, but innovation rivalry from those with little R&D capital may be insufficient to prevent adverse effects on innovation incentive when firms with more R&D capital merge. Put differently, when firms participating in an innovation market vary substantially in the extent of their R&D capital, only those with relatively high R&D capital are likely to be effective innovation rivals, and only effective rivals should be counted in evaluating the number of postmerger innovation competitors.

R&D capital should be understood metaphorically, analogously to human capital. It is a conceptual device for distinguishing firms whose advantages make it more likely that their research efforts will succeed and be profitable. In some markets in which firms are competing to develop similar new products (innovation markets), it may be reasonable to suppose that a firm has substantial R&D capital if it has a high R&D budget or has introduced new products at a rapid rate in the past. Even absent plausible quantitative measures, it may be possible using qualitative information to distinguish high–R&D capital firms from those less endowed.

Independent of R&D capital, some firms' research efforts may be more similar than others in the sense of spatial differentiation, making it more likely that the new products the firms develop would take business away from each other. Firms may, for example, have similar types of R&D expertise, similar access to key inputs and distribution channels for new products, or a similar head start over other firms pursuing the same new product or production process. If firms with similar research efforts merge, the combined firm may have a greater incentive to cut back on its R&D effort than would arise from a hypothetical merger involving other pairs of innovation rivals. Accordingly, the similarity of merging-firm research efforts may provide a reason to challenge a merger even when multiple other firms are pursuing similar R&D activities.

To apply either the R&D capital or spatial differentiation variant of this theory in evaluating particular mergers, it is necessary to identify actual innovation rivals or potential innovation rivals (i.e., firms with the required capabilities). Those rivals are participants in an innovation market.[31] They may also be participants in a future-product market. The competitive effects of merger may be analyzed in either or both types of markets.

It may be feasible to define future-product markets. When applying the conceptual approach of the *Guidelines,* a court or enforcer could assume a set of product features and a plausible price-range conditional on innovation success and consider the extent to which buyers of such a product would be expected to substitute other products in the event the price rises by a small amount. That question would likely be easiest to answer if the future product is expected to be substantially improved vis-à-vis existing products. In that case buyers would be unlikely to treat existing products as alternatives unless, perhaps, the price differential were substantial. If the firms are instead competing to develop a cost-saving production technology, the future product market would often be the same as the current product market (though current market shares may not indicate firms' competitive significance in the future market).

In general, the closer firms are to introducing new products, the easier it will be to define future-product markets and evaluate the consequences of a merger for future product-market competition.[32] When successful new product development is far off, or the competitive concern results from the combination of R&D capabilities, the merger may instead (or in addition) be evaluated by defining an innovation market. Doing so requires an understanding of what the innovation would do, at least in a general way: an innovation market is defined in terms of R&D assets directed toward a particular goal—new or improved products or processes—or toward close substitutes.[33] Here, as always, market definition is concerned with one economic force: demand substitution. As a conceptual matter, the buyers are firms or consumers that would value the new or improved product or process, and the market participants are firms with research streams directed toward developing that product or process or a close substitute, or with assets that can potentially be used to do so. Geographic markets will often be global, though they may exclude foreign locations where foreign innovators cannot or would not compete with the merging firms in the United States, nor would license or sell their innovations to firms that would.

Evidence of firm innovation efforts and capabilities may be hard to come by.[34] Many of the case examples involve pharmaceutical R&D because firms are required to report their ongoing progress in new-drug development to the FDA. As with product markets, R&D markets can be nested or overlapping. If the same firms would have similar capabilities for developing a variety of future products, and the competitive analysis would be similar across each R&D market, one might reasonably define a "cluster market" in R&D for the purpose of analyzing innovation rivalry that encompasses all those products for analytical convenience.[35] The firms that participate in an R&D market need not match the set of firms that participate in a current-product market. Some firms now participating in any particular product market may lack the capabilities needed to develop next-generation products, and some firms not participating in that product market may have those capabilities.

It will not always be easy to establish various factors relevant to assessing competitive effects within an innovation market, such as the nature and amount of firms' R&D capital and the extent to which the merging firms' innovation efforts are similar. In analogous circumstances in evaluating coordinated effects, courts can rely on the structural presumption.[36] Similarly, it would be reasonable for enforcers and courts to presume that merger of innovation rivals will likely harm competition when only a handful of firms participate in the innovation market.[37]

Gilbert's study suggests invoking such a presumption when six firms participate premerger. The presumption would be modest with six firms but the likelihood of harm would increase as the number of (equally capable) firms with premerger R&D directed to similar ends decreases. At a minimum, competitive harm should be presumed when the merger would create a monopoly within the innovation market.[38] Alternatively, if R&D capital is thought to be correlated with firms' R&D budgets or the rate at which firms have produced new products in the past, those metrics could be used to create R&D capital shares for the market participants, allowing application of concentration standards such as those used in presuming product-market harms.[39] With any number of innovation rivals, the presumption of competitive harm would be stronger if one merger partner has a substantial business in current-generation products and the other does not. Under such circumstances, Arrow's replacement effect would further reduce the merged firm's incentive to support two ongoing or future R&D efforts. That said, innovation by one firm could make it easier for another firm to innovate too. Holding constant the number of firms engaged in R&D, substantial knowledge spillovers would enhance the likelihood of future product competition and weaken the inference of competitive harm.[40]

As with the structural presumption, this presumption would shift a burden of production to the merging firms to demonstrate that overall prospects for future product innovation and development would not decline. This presumption also would establish an inference of competitive harm that the plaintiff can rely on to satisfy its burden of persuasion in the event defendants satisfy their initial burden. And the presumption would impose on defendants a practical rebuttal burden using a sliding scale. Defendants might seek to rebut by, for example, showing that they would find it unprofitable to cut back on their R&D efforts, perhaps because they could take advantage of merger-related R&D efficiencies. Or the defendants might show that the remaining R&D rivals would be expected to respond to any R&D cutback by stepping up their R&D efforts, to the point where overall innovation prospects and the expected extent of future product-market completion are not diminished. But the fewer the capable innovation rivals there are, the greater the likelihood that competition will be harmed, so the more compelling the defendants' evidence questioning the inference of competitive harm must be to overcome the presumption of anticompetitive effect.

Acquisitions of Potential Competitors by Dominant Platforms

Future competition may be threatened when a dominant information technology platform (or other large firm) acquires a potential rival. When the potential rival would be expected to innovate were it to enter, possibly leading the dominant incumbent to upgrade its products or services in response, the competitive harms from merger may involve reduced innovation incentives, not just lessened future price competition.

Carl Shapiro describes two possibilities. In the first, a large incumbent firm acquires "a highly capable firm operating in an adjacent space."[41] He has in mind mergers such as the vertical acquisitions by dominant platforms discussed in Chapter 7, including Google's acquisition of YouTube and DoubleClick and Facebook's acquisition of Instagram and Oculus. In Shapiro's second possibility, a large incumbent firm merges with a large supplier, customer, or seller of complementary product or services, where the acquired firm is one able to enter in competition with the incumbent.[42] His example is the acquisition by Ticketmaster, which provides ticketing services to concert venues, of LiveNation, a concert promoter developing its own ticketing services.[43]

In these cases, the acquired firm has at least some capabilities that could be used to compete with the incumbent it merges with, so it is a possible future competitive threat. Sometimes no one, the firms included, knows whether the acquired firm will ever try to enter, or whether its attempt would succeed. In each case the acquired firm could have developed into a strong challenger to the incumbent. The merger forecloses that possibility, harming competition in an expected sense. Dominant firms have strong incentives to seek out and acquire smaller firms that, if left alone, would grow to become strong rivals. The more entrenched the incumbent, Shapiro observes, the greater its incentive and the higher the premium it will pay to acquire a potential future rival.[44]

A dominant firm that acquires a potential rival may have a unilateral incentive to cut back on the combined firm's R&D effort. Consider Facebook's acquisition of Instagram in 2012. This merger could have harmed future competition by reducing incentives to innovate. Yet the FTC allowed the acquisition to proceed without challenge or comment.[45] The UK's Office of Fair Trading (OFT) simultaneously cleared the transaction with an explanation.[46] The OFT's analysis provides a starting point for evaluating the acquisition's potential harms to innovation.[47]

At the time of the transaction, Instagram was an application allowing users to modify photos taken with smartphones and other cameras and to share those photos via its network, Facebook, and other social networks. While Facebook users shared their information primarily with friends, Instagram posts were generally available to all users of the service. OFT's analysis found that Instagram was only a distant potential rival to Facebook in the area of online display advertising. Facebook specialized in display advertising that promoted brands; the social-media giant could take advantage of its data on user demographics and behavior to target these ads. The OFT distinguished such brand advertising from transactional advertising designed to make a specific sale, as on eBay or Amazon, which was seen as Instagram's métier. Thus Instagram was seen as poorly suited to challenge Facebook in its primary advertising market, where, in any case, Facebook was already competing with Google, Yahoo, and Microsoft.[48]

The OFT did recognize that Instagram could have evolved into a social network that would rival Facebook, but the agency did not consider this a reason to challenge the acquisition. Yes, Instagram had a growing user base, including high-profile figures such as Barack Obama. And, yes, Instagram could easily have expanded its services to include functions similar to those of Facebook. OFT even noted that Facebook might have perceived Instagram as a possible future competitor in social networking.[49]

Still, the OFT gave two reasons to avoid analyzing this potential competitive threat to Facebook's social networking platform. First, it argued that, even with the acquisition, Facebook would face credible competition from Google—with its Google+ social network, strength in advertising, and access to valuable user information. Second, Instagram's rapid growth demonstrated that entry and expansion of new applications or social networks would be easy, so there was little concern that the acquisition would stymie potential upstarts by further empowering a major incumbent.[50] The OFT did not address an apparent inconsistency in these rationales: the first seemed to suggest that Google was the only significant actual or potential rival to Facebook; the second that any number of firms, including ones not presently competing, were in a position to constrain Facebook's possible exercise of market power in advertising.

The framework for analyzing a merged firm's unilateral incentive to cut back on its R&D effort, set forth above, provides a possible route through which the OFT or FTC could have found that the merger harmed innovation, depending on the facts that a more complete investigation may have uncovered. An enforcement agency could have reached that conclusion if it found that Instagram was one of a few significant potential rivals to Facebook with the capability of someday offering attractive advertising services on a social network.[51] If social networks were, or were likely to become, particularly good vehicles for some types of advertisers, and more attractive to those advertisers than advertising in response to user searches,[52] then Facebook and Instagram would have been close rivals in an innovation market and a future product market for advertising on social media platforms.[53] The agency could also have found an innovation harm if it concluded that Instagram was one of a small number of significant potential rivals with capabilities that could be used to create a social network with some prospect of successfully attracting users. Then the merged firms would have been close rivals in developing better user interfaces, improved privacy protections, and other quality improvements valued by social network users. Or the enforcement agencies could rely on a presumption, explained and defended below, that innovation competition would be harmed when a dominant firm in an innovative sector acquires a firm it does not presently compete with but which possesses capabilities that make it a threat to compete in future products. Relying on a presumption could also help the FTC demonstrate harm from lost competition in court.

Once the agency concluded that Facebook's acquisition of Instagram would harm innovation, it could reasonably have challenged the transaction on that ground unless the merging firms could show benefits to future advertising competition or service quality competition that would outweigh the threatened harm. The merging firms might also have claimed offsetting benefits in current product markets from integrating services that were complements at the time of the merger. Perhaps, for example, the merger allowed Facebook to incorporate Instagram's photo-related capabilities more quickly, more effectively, or less expensively than if Facebook tried to do so purely through internal growth or gave Instagram distribution advantages it could not easily obtain on its own that would make it easier for Instagram to market its application to a broader audience. Chapter 9 takes up a question the latter possibilities pose: whether efficiencies in one market (here for a current product) should be allowed to offset harms in another market (for innovation or a future product).

By focusing on the loss through merger of innovation rivalry among firms with the capability to develop future products, this example shows, enforcers and courts can do more to prevent and deter mergers that would harm innovation.

Mergers that Deter New Product Development

A merger between actual or potential innovation rivals could also harm innovation by discouraging R&D investment by non-merging rivals. The merged firm could do so through foreclosure of inputs or customers or by threatening rivals with the prospect of more aggressive competition in future products. These anticompetitive mechanisms are exclusionary. They do not depend on internalizing future product-market competition through merger. They may be important in evaluating both horizontal and vertical acquisitions.

Foreclosure of Inputs or Customers

Vertical mergers may harm innovation through the foreclosure of access to inputs or customers. The Justice Department and FCC challenged Comcast's acquisition of NBC Universal (NBCU) in part on such an exclusionary theory. Comcast was a cable distributor and NBCU a large supplier of programming. The agencies found that the merged firm would have the incentive and ability to exclude online video distributors (OVDs), which were potential future rivals to Comcast.[54] Without the prospect of access to NBCU programming, the agencies concluded, OVDs would invest less in improving and marketing their services, lessening future competition in video distribution. Both agencies allowed the transaction to proceed with conditions.

Similarly, a horizontal merger could harm innovation by excluding non-merging rivals. The merger may give the merged firm an incentive, when introducing next-generation products, to raise switching costs for its installed base, thereby making those customers more captive and potentially excluding rivals for reasons discussed in Chapter 7.[55] But the profitability of this strategy is not guaranteed: new customers and customers of rival firms may become more reluctant to choose a firm's product, even over a somewhat lower quality or more expensive alternative, for fear that the firm would exploit them later by raising prices or by delaying upgrades to save on R&D expenses. That prospect could sometimes prevent the merged firm from adopting this anticompetitive strategy.

A hypothetical example illustrates how a horizontal merger might foreclose innovation or future-product rivals, and thereby harm competition, by raising switching costs. The example supposes that smaller firms prefer to limit switching costs to attract new customers, while larger firms strike a different trade-off.[56]

Assume a market for gaming-system hardware; the games themselves are a complementary product purchased by the same customers. Suppose that the two largest hardware firms each account for 30 percent of both new hardware sales and the installed base and that they compete with several smaller rivals. If the largest hardware firms merge, the merged firm may have an incentive to upgrade its gaming system and games in ways that make it impossible for users to play its games on rival gaming systems. Doing so may make it harder for the merged firm to attract new customers, but it may do better overall, even in the short run, if it can keep a greater fraction of what has become a much larger installed base. In the long run, the large firm's increased customer captivity could make it harder for smaller rivals to increase sales through adoption of their own product upgrades. They will anticipate earning smaller profits from developing next-generation products, so they may reduce their own R&D efforts. Both innovation competition and future product competition could be lessened.[57]

Threatened Future Competition

Firms, especially dominant ones, can exclude rivals and harm competition by making commitments that convince rivals that aggressive conduct will be met with a strong response.[58] When this strategy works, rivals conclude that their best choice is to live and let live, avoiding competitive moves that would provoke the giant. One such commitment, involving predatory pricing, was discussed in Chapter 7.

Similar harms to competition may be achieved through a horizontal merger that commits the merged firm to more aggressive future product-market competition or to greater R&D competition. Increased competition on either dimension would reduce the expected payoff to rival R&D. Greater product-market competition means that the rival will earn less on its new products. Greater R&D competition also means the rival will earn less: the rival may not be first to market or it may compete with a better product when its product comes to market. Of course, we want rivals to compete aggressively to produce high-quality products. The trouble may come when a dominant firm's commitment to aggressive competition leads its rivals to back off from competing—in this case by reducing their own R&D investments. That could lead ultimately to reduced future product competition overall.

Four hypothetical scenarios illustrate this potential adverse competitive effect of merger for innovation competition and competition in future products. First, when a merger allows the resulting firm to spread fixed costs over a large sales base or otherwise confers substantial scale economies, the merged firm could exclude because non-merging rivals would then compete with a firm that has lowered its costs. The greater scale economies mean cost savings to the merging firm, so they may support an efficiency justification. But they also may harm future product competition by lessening rivals' innovation incentives. These incentives would be reduced if rivals recognize that their disadvantages in scale undermine the potential returns to their R&D investments.

Second, a merger that aggregates portfolios of patents related to the development of new products that would compete in a product market, or of new production processes that would lower the costs of competing in a product market, may deter rival R&D by expanding the effective scope of the merging firms' intellectual property rights.[59] Patent aggregation may make it more difficult for rivals to prove that the merged firm's patents are invalid or narrow in scope or make it more costly for a rival to analyze its likelihood of prevailing in infringement litigation brought by the patent portfolio owner. The merged firm may be more likely to have some patent that would be found valid and broad in scope, thereby adding complexity and difficulty to licensing negotiations and increasing the likelihood that the portfolio owner would assert infringement. Merger also may shift ownership of weak patents from the acquired firm to a firm more likely to enforce them against product-market rivals.

Third, a similar exclusionary effect could arise when one of the merging firms treats R&D as a strategic complement—that is, when the firm responds to greater R&D investment by its rivals by investing more as well.[60] The merger could lead the firm to treat R&D as more of a strategic complement than before, perhaps because the merged firm reasonably expects to account for a greater market share in next-generation products than either merging firm would anticipate achieving on its own.[61] When non-merging firms would anticipate that the merged firm would respond more aggressively to their R&D efforts than before, they would be expected to invest less in R&D or slow their new product development efforts. That would make it more likely that the merged firm would develop next-generation products well ahead of any rivals, and more likely that the merged firm would obtain a dominant position in next-generation products and exercise market power in selling them.

Fourth, and similarly, when a dominant firm in an innovative sector acquires a firm that possesses capabilities making it a threat to compete in future products, R&D rivalry will likely be reduced. The acquired firm may not be a rival in current products, only in innovation. It may also be a fringe rival with limited ability to expand—so not presently constraining the dominant firm significantly—but with capabilities that give it a leg up in devel-

oping future products.[62] Or the acquired firm might sell a demand complement, supply products or services to the dominant firm, use the dominant
firm's product as an input, or sell its product to customers that also purchase
from the dominant firm. Firms in the latter categories may have advantages
in developing future products if they know a great deal about the industry
and have a strong reputation in it already.

R&D rivalry will likely be reduced because the dominant firm would be
expected to treat R&D as a strategic complement. That is likely because, as
discussed more fully later in this chapter, the dominant firm would typically
anticipate that it would retain its leading position in the event it and rivals
both develop next-generation products (or neither does) but lose substantial
share if its rival innovates and it does not. When the dominant firm views
R&D rivalry as a strategic complement,[63] it will have a postmerger incentive
to channel the acquired firm's R&D capabilities into developing complementary products for those of the dominant firm rather than substitute
products. As a result, buyers will have fewer substitutes to choose from, and
the merged firm's products will face less competition.

In light of these plausible scenarios, enforcers and courts should presume
harm to innovation competition when a dominant firm in an innovative sector
acquires a rival with capabilities for developing next-generation products, as
when Facebook merged with Instagram. The presumption of competitive
harm from merger would be rebuttable. In its defense, the merging firm might
seek to show, for example, that many other firms have similar or better capabilities, so the merger would make little difference to the strength of R&D
competition; that the dominant firm does not treat rival R&D as a strategic
complement, perhaps because the dominant firm's business is heavily weighted
toward highly profitable complementary products and so would benefit regardless of whether it or a rival upgraded an existing product;[64] or that the
merging firm would be expected to improve its new products or make new
product introduction more likely because of efficiencies arising from merger,
and thereby enhance innovation prospects for the industry overall.

INNOVATION HARMS FROM EXCLUSIONARY
CONDUCT BY DOMINANT FIRMS

Outside of mergers, antitrust enforcement aimed at preventing the loss of
innovation competition has largely been concerned with the exclusionary
conduct of dominant firms.[65] Antitrust cases of this sort most commonly

arise in two ways: through challenges to foreclosure of access to inputs or customers or through challenges to licensing practices or other exclusionary conduct undertaken by patent holders. In this section, I will recommend that courts and enforcers presume that competition in innovation or future products is harmed when a dominant firm excludes all its actual and potential innovation rivals, apart from insignificant competitors, or when it excludes any rival in an innovation market in which only a handful of firms participate. I will also explain why the antitrust laws can help protect innovation incentives when patent holders contribute their intellectual property to an industry standard, and show how to evaluate a dominant firm's appropriability defense to exclusionary conduct allegations.

Foreclosure of Access to Inputs or Customers

The antitrust laws prevent firms from discouraging the introduction of new technologies, products, or business models by making it costlier or more difficult for innovation rivals to obtain key inputs or access to customers. The Justice Department's case against Microsoft is the most prominent recent example.

According to the D.C. Circuit, sitting en banc, Microsoft discouraged a "nascent" competitive threat to its Windows operating-system monopoly.[66] That threat was posed by new products under development in complementary markets: Netscape's web browser and Sun Microsystems' Java programming language. These new products had the potential to allow Windows software to run on rival operating systems, thereby making rival operating systems better substitutes for Windows. That would be expected to enhance operating-system competition.

The courts found that Microsoft impeded Netscape through conduct that limited the latter firm's access to key channels of product distribution. The conduct included exclusivity agreements with Internet-access providers and the physical integration of Microsoft's browser with Windows.[67] Microsoft was found to have impeded Sun by requiring software developers to make Java products compatible with Windows only, deceiving Java developers about the Windows-specific nature of the tools Microsoft distributed to them and coercing the chipmaker Intel to stop aiding Sun in improving Java technologies.[68]

If Sun and Netscape had not been impeded, their technologies would have eroded the applications barrier to entry that protected Windows from competition with rival operating systems.[69] By excluding Netscape's browser and Sun's Java, Microsoft discouraged the development of key building blocks that rival operating systems could use when developing next-generation operating systems. That reduced the prospects for future innovation and price competition in operating systems.[70]

As the *Microsoft* case illustrates, enforcement agencies and courts evaluate conduct that may harm innovation by foreclosing rivals from access to inputs or customers in the same way that they analyze exclusionary conduct alleged to harm competition on other dimensions.[71] The FTC and European enforcers most likely analyzed the competitive effects of Google's search practices according to a similar framework, though the two agencies reached different conclusions.[72]

The *Microsoft* case also shows that product-design decisions can be considered exclusionary. The appeals court that upheld the district court's conclusion expressed skepticism about claims that product design changes harm competition—a skepticism rooted in its desire to avoid chilling product innovation.[73] But the court also found that the government met its initial burden to show competitive harm and that Microsoft failed to meet its burden to proffer a justification.[74] To similar effect, other appellate decisions have indicated that a firm could harm competition through deliberate efforts to create incompatibility with a rival's products without improving quality or lowering costs.[75]

Enforcers and courts should presume that competition in innovation or future products is harmed when a dominant firm excludes all its actual and potential innovation rivals, other than insignificant competitors. Doing so would be consistent with the way exclusionary conduct generally is treated by the courts, as I discuss in Chapter 7, and with the way the D.C. Circuit analyzed innovation harms in *Microsoft*. Competitive harm should also be presumed when a dominant firm excludes even one innovation rival from an innovation market in which only a handful of firms participate. That presumption would be consistent with a presumption of harm from exclusionary conduct by a firm with market power described in Chapter 7 and with the presumption previously suggested for merger analysis when a dominant firm acquires a potential innovation rival. Both presumptions—with respect to a dominant firm's exclusion of all innovation rivals, or just one in a low-participation market—would shift a burden of production to the defendant to justify its conduct. When defendants cannot justify their conduct, they would be subject to truncated condemnation. When they can satisfy their burden of production, the court would undertake a comprehensive reasonableness analysis of harms and benefits.

Exclusionary Conduct Involving Patents

Patent owners often license their intellectual property rights to other firms, such as manufacturers of products that use patented technologies. Those licenses may include conditions of potential concern to antitrust enforcers. For example, a licensor may impose restrictions on the prices licensees charge, the output they produce, and the territories or customers they serve. Licensors may also restrict the uses to which a patent can be employed or the industries that can be served by licensed products. Licenses may require exclusive dealing, exclusive licensing, or tying arrangements involving patented technologies. Licensors may restrict how royalties are calculated and at what rates, limit the ownership or use of intellectual property created by the licensee that improves on the original patent (grant backs), restrain assertions of intellectual property rights against the patent owner or challenges to patent validity, or impose restrictions on contributors to patent pools.

During the 1960s and 1970s, the Justice Department viewed some patent-licensing practices—the so-called "Nine No-Nos"—as presumptively unlawful.[76] To similar effect, during antitrust law's structural era, courts frequently resolved government antitrust litigation against dominant firms by requiring that they license their patents, either royalty free or for a reasonable royalty.[77] In 1988 the Justice Department announced a new view: no patent licensing restrictions would be considered presumptively illegal. Even the nine no-nos could only be found to violate the antitrust laws if shown to be unreasonable.[78] The federal enforcement agencies adopted guidelines on intellectual property licensing in 1995 and revised them in 2017 to explain more fully how they would conduct such a reasonableness analysis.[79]

The 1988 change of course was predicated on two ideas. First, patent licenses were seen as vertical restraints. Beginning with the 1979 decision in *GTE Sylvania*, the Supreme Court became more hospitable to agreements between firms and their customers or suppliers. Some noninterventionist commentators, then and now, argued (wrongly) that vertical agreements should be virtually legal, per se. During the Reagan administration, the Justice Department came close to adopting that position with respect to patent licensing.[80]

Second, patent-license terms that increased the market value of intellectual property were seen as beneficial to innovation on the theory that raising the return to patents would enhance incentives to innovate.[81] This argument is highly problematic, though, because it could justify any conduct that increases the effective scope of intellectual property while ignoring the countervailing potential for exclusionary conduct to reduce innovation incentives. It is tantamount to endorsing an appropriability defense when patent licensing is challenged as anticompetitive, without requiring the defendant to show that innovation would be enhanced and without considering the limits to that defense that I discuss later in this section.

Contrary to the Reagan administration's laissez-faire view, patent licenses can harm competition when they increase the effective scope of patents by restricting rivalry.[82] The fraudulent assertion of patent claims can do the same.[83] Firms can also harm competition by in effect increasing patent scope through the manipulation of standards.[84] In some recent cases, firms contributing patents to industry standards have allegedly monopolized by evading commitments to license on reasonable terms.[85] Objections to these practices have primarily been concerned with anticompetitive conduct leading to higher prices, but innovation may be harmed as well.

In a common scenario, patent holders contribute their technology to an industry standard adopted by a standard setting organization (SSO). Standards are valuable to downstream producers because they make interoperability possible—for example, among components of a laptop or smartphone. Once the SSO promulgates a standard, downstream producers must pay royalties to the patent holders in order to utilize the standard in their products.

A competitive problem may arise after a standard has been promulgated and adopted in many products. At that time the product producers are locked in: they must rely on the standard to sell products that their buyers wish to purchase. When the SSO is choosing among competing technologies, the competition for inclusion in the standard often leads patent owners to agree to set fair, reasonable, and nondiscriminatory royalties. Sometimes, though, the SSO does not impose such requirements, or the owner of a patent essential to the standard finds a way to raise the royalty it charges licensees, notwithstanding its contract with the SSO.[86]

When patent owners act opportunistically this way, they can exercise market power. The immediate harm is in higher prices. Over a longer term, the inability of SSOs to prevent such conduct contractually will discourage standard setting generally. That will, in turn, make it more difficult and more costly for new products to assure interoperability, limiting their marketplace success and, in consequence, discouraging new product development. Innovation is thereby harmed indirectly. Under such circumstances, antitrust law can supplement contract and patent law to protect innovation incentives as well as to prevent patent holders from setting supracompetitive royalties.[87]

Appropriability Defenses in Exclusionary-Conduct Cases

In its defense a dominant firm charged with anticompetitive exclusion may try to convince enforcers that its conduct will enhance the prospects for innovation. The firm could make two arguments to this effect. First, the firm could say that its conduct would confer efficiencies that make its R&D effort less expensive or more effective. In the merger context, that might happen if, for example, a pharmaceutical firm with a lead in developing a therapeutic agent combines with a firm with a lead in developing a delivery mechanism or if a pharmaceutical firm strong in R&D combines with one strong in marketing.

Second, and of primary interest here, a dominant firm may argue that its exclusionary conduct gives it a greater incentive to invest in R&D by allowing it to appropriate more of the benefits if it successfully develops a new product or production process.[88] This argument is analogous to a familiar economic argument for patents: the ability of patent holders to exclude others allows them to earn a greater profit by appropriating a larger share of social gains from their innovations, a prospect that provides would-be innovators with incentives for R&D investment.

This appropriability defense of exclusionary conduct can be offered as an argument against liability, an argument for construing the antitrust laws narrowly to avoid proscribing the challenged conduct, or as an argument against a particular remedy.[89] In the *Microsoft* litigation, the defendant's economic expert argued on appropriability grounds against any relief that would reduce the profits to successful software development. Such relief, he contended, would harm competition and consumers by lessening Microsoft's and other firms' incentives to develop new and better software.[90] This type of argument has also been suggested in the merger context.[91]

The courts have given appropriability defenses a mixed reception. The Supreme Court explicitly rejected the defense when it was proffered by the dominant firm in *Kodak*.[92] An influential district court decision in *United Shoe Machinery* rejected the defense both on the law and the facts.[93] But in *Trinko* the Supreme Court encouraged the defense by citing appropriability as a basis for questioning whether a unilateral refusal to deal would satisfy the anticompetitive conduct element of the monopolization offense.[94] Moreover, in a notable monopolization decision addressing alleged predatory innovation, the Second Circuit in *Berkey Photo* expressed resistance to finding antitrust liability when doing so would force dominant firms to predisclose product improvements to rivals or otherwise share the financial rewards to innovation, in part based on the appropriability concern that such relief would undermine the dominant firm's incentives to invest in R&D and develop new products.[95]

Appropriability defenses are concerned with just one side of the error-cost balance: the possibility that antitrust enforcement will lessen incentives to innovate. Although couched in terms of the innovation incentives of the defendant firm, an appropriability defense makes an argument, implicitly or explicitly, about overall industry incentives to innovate, accounting for both the defendant and its potentially excluded rivals. The argument ignores the possibility that when antitrust enforcement reduces the reward to dominant-firm innovation, overall industry innovation incentives would nonetheless be enhanced by virtue of the increased competition that enforcement fosters. Accordingly, an appropriability defense should not succeed if the exclusionary conduct would harm overall industry incentives to innovate. Nor should the defense succeed if overall innovation incentives are enhanced but the resulting benefit is outweighed by the competitive harm from the exercise of market power on other dimensions such as price.[96]

A court could conclude that rejecting an appropriability defense would not reduce overall industry innovation incentives, or not reduce them much, for any of three reasons. First, a court could find that forbidding the exclusionary conduct would not make much practical difference to the dominant firm's incentive to innovate. That is, it could conclude that the dominant firm's expected payoff to successful innovation, and thus its incentives to invest in R&D, would remain high because of other market features. Those features may include rapid market growth, scale economies, network effects, sale of complementary products, and high customer switching costs. The reward to innovation success may be lower absent the exclusionary conduct, but features such as these would keep it high, so the dominant firm would not cut back its R&D effort much if at all.

Second, even if the reduction in the reward to innovation success would have some effect in discouraging innovative effort by the dominant firm, a court could identify another influence on the dominant firm's incentives: the possibility that greater rival investments in R&D would enhance the dominant firm's innovative effort. That innovation-enhancing incentive could counteract in whole or part the innovation-reducing incentive of a reduced reward for dominant-firm R&D success. If so, the dominant firm again may not cut back its R&D effort at all or not cut it greatly.

It is often reasonable to expect a dominant firm to increase its own R&D investment in response to greater R&D investment by its rivals (i.e., treat rival R&D investment as a strategic complement). Greater R&D investment by rivals increases the likelihood of rival innovation success. If the dominant firm's incremental gain from its own innovation success is greater when rivals successfully innovate than when rivals fail to do so, the dominant firm will seek to improve its own prospects for innovation success by investing more in innovation when rivals increase their R&D investments.[97]

The dominant firm is more likely to react this way when (1) it anticipates that it would have a high market share in the event both it and its rival successfully innovate; and (2) the dominant firm anticipates that it would lose a great deal of business to its rivals if the rivals innovate and it does not. Both factors increase the dominant firm's incremental gains from developing a next-generation product when its rivals introduce an upgrade—the first factor by raising the benefits of dominant-firm innovation when rivals also innovate, the second by raising the cost to the dominant firm of not matching rivals' innovation.[98] If the factors go the other way, however, the dominant firm would more likely reduce its own R&D effort in response to greater R&D investment by its rivals, potentially helping to support an appropriability defense.

Third, even if a prohibition on exclusionary conduct would be expected to reduce the dominant firm's incentive to innovate—notwithstanding the possibility that other market features would tend to preserve appropriability of the reward to dominant firm R&D success and the possibility that the dominant firm would respond to greater rival innovate effort by increasing its own investments in R&D—a court could find that the overall innovation consequences of that disincentive to dominant-firm innovation would be outweighed by the benefits of enhancing innovation incentives for the dominant firm's rivals. If so, the industry-wide prospects for innovation success in developing new, better, or less expensive products in the market would be enhanced, justifying rejection of a dominant firm's appropriability defense. Even if industry-wide prospects for innovation would be reduced, moreover, the court could find the exclusionary conduct harmful on balance and prohibit it, if the conduct leads to higher prices or other anticompetitive effects.

CONCLUSION

In an environment of substantial and widening market power, antitrust law needs to listen harder to the first voice with which it speaks about dominant firms and innovation: the voice expressing concern that competition-lessening conduct harms innovation and future product-market competition. To do so, enforcers and courts must evaluate the consequences of conduct that lessens competition for innovation and the development of new products. The anticompetitive effects and potential procompetitive benefits of reduced innovation competition, including the benefits assumed by a defendant's appropriability defense, are susceptible to analysis, and courts can reasonably invoke the suggested presumptions to foster industry-wide innovation by increasing deterrence of conduct that harms competition.

Chapter Nine

Harms to Suppliers, Workers, and Platform Users

IN 2017 the D.C. Circuit upheld a district court decision to block the merger of two large health insurers, Anthem and Cigna.[1] The merging firms acted as plan administrators for large, self-insured employers. They assembled provider networks, negotiated fees with providers, and handled claims from covered employees. The merger was stopped primarily on the ground that it would likely have increased costs to customers, who would be forced to pay higher fees for health-plan administration.[2]

The merging firms had disagreed. They argued that postmerger Anthem would negotiate lower prices from hospitals and doctors and pass those benefits on to the employers who signed up with them.[3] But neither the district court nor the appellate majority credited this defense. The district court rejected the claim on the facts. The appellate majority accepted that efficiencies evidence could be used to rebut a prima facie case but questioned on the law whether efficiencies could be proffered as a defense to an otherwise anticompetitive merger.[4]

So, concern for the customer won the day: both courts affirmed that reduced competition would likely result in higher prices. But there is another reason why the merger might have produced anticompetitive harm: the merger threatened competition in the purchase of health-care services from hospitals and doctors. Here the concern is not harm to customers from the exercise of a seller's market power but rather harm to suppliers—care providers—from the market power of a buyer, in this case an insurance administrator. Thus, there were potentially two classes of victims.

Although the decision did not turn on the suppression of supplier payments, the government did raise the issue, and it would have been able to make a credible case.[5] The defendants pointed to lower input prices as part of their efficiency defense, but the government charged that those lower input prices were independent sources of competitive harm to the suppliers. Even the dissenting appellate judge left open the possibility that the merger could harm competition in a market for the purchase of services from buyers, and he supported remanding the case to the district court to decide that question.[6]

The first section of this chapter—on anticompetitive conduct harming suppliers—addresses issues raised by the Anthem case. The section explains why conduct depressing prices paid to suppliers, including workers, is not insulated from antitrust review even when those low input prices remain above competitive levels. Efficiencies can be used to offset competitive harms, but only when both accrue within the same market. The courts do not permit benefits to downstream consumers to offset harms to upstream suppliers when the upstream and downstream markets differ.

That observation sets the stage for the analysis of competitive harms on one side of a multisided platform, discussed in the second section of the chapter. There I consider related issues raised by anticompetitive conduct on or by information technology and Internet platforms. Some platform end users can plausibly be characterized as suppliers. Even when that characterization seems a stretch, the relationship among end users on different platform sides raises issues about defining markets and trading off efficiencies in one market against harms in another that are analogous to those that arise when suppliers are harmed.

Cross-market welfare trade-offs would arise if benefits to customers in downstream markets were permitted to offset harms to suppliers in upstream markets, or if benefits to platform users in markets involving one side of a platform were permitted to offset harms to platform users in markets involving other sides. Although conservative commentators argue that antitrust law should routinely make such trade-offs,[7] the courts properly reject doing so. Were antitrust law to allow such trade-offs, reasonableness analysis would often become too complex for practical judicial administration. In addition, the prohibition on cross-market welfare trade-offs helps to protect the political support for antitrust and the political bargain described in Chapter 2. Harmed suppliers or platform participants will often be sympathetic groups such as workers, farmers, and small businesses. If cross-market welfare trade-offs were allowed under antitrust, these suppliers would tend to suffer, weakening support for the antitrust project as a whole. These justifications support a general rule against cross-market welfare trade-offs, but courts could reasonably choose not to apply the rule when it is evident from a qualitative comparison that the benefits to competition in one market greatly exceed the harms to competition in another and there is no practical way to obtain the benefits without accepting the harms.

ANTICOMPETITIVE CONDUCT THAT HARMS SUPPLIERS AND WORKERS

When a reduction in competition harms suppliers—firms upstream from the defendants—the conduct can violate the antitrust laws regardless of whether the reduction in competition also harms buyers downstream from the defendants.[8] The antitrust laws have long been understood to prohibit buyer cartels that depress the price paid to suppliers.[9] The antitrust laws also reach unilateral conduct and mergers that harm suppliers.[10] As in all antitrust cases, restrictions on competition are a predicate for finding harm; harm to suppliers matters only when it results from conduct limiting competition, not from any other sources.

These suppliers include workers, so antitrust laws may be used to vindicate their claims.[11] For example, the Justice Department issued a compliant, settled by consent, charging Adobe, Apple, Google, Intel, Intuit, and Pixar with an agreement not to solicit employees working for each other.[12] Private plaintiffs bring such challenges as well. One plaintiff class brought claims against agreements among various metropolitan hospitals to depress nurses' wages.[13] Another challenged an agreement among colleges to prevent payments to student athletes, who are like employees.[14] A merger that would reduce competition in labor markets, leading to a reduction in wages or salaries, could also be challenged.[15]

Monopsony as the Mirror Image of Monopoly

Antitrust law views market power harming sellers (monopsony power) and market power harming buyers (monopoly power) as "analytically similar."[16] That is not surprising: as a matter of economic analysis, monopsony is the mirror image of monopoly.[17]

Antitrust law's objection to anticompetitive conduct harming suppliers derives from the economic welfare standards commonly discussed by commentators and courts: consumer welfare and aggregate welfare.[18] These welfare concepts, defined in Chapter 2, are used to evaluate business conduct in the partial-equilibrium context in which antitrust cases are assessed.[19] A "partial equilibrium" is an outcome that arises in a single market, without reference to the production and consumption of other goods in the economy.

To the extent that the term "consumer welfare" suggests that harms to suppliers are ignored, the term is misleading. In a partial equilibrium welfare analysis, lost surplus to suppliers is a form of consumer surplus, just as lost surplus to intermediate buyers, not final consumers, is a form of consumer surplus. The term "consumer" surplus should be understood as meaning "counterparty" surplus (or "trading partner" surplus), thus including buyers and suppliers when they are the direct victims of anticompetitive conduct.

The means by which firms exercise market power, whether in purchasing from suppliers or selling to customers, may vary with industry features. In some markets, firms depress the prices paid to suppliers by reducing aggregate purchases. This method by which monopsony power is exercised is the mirror image of raising prices to buyers by reducing output. In other markets, firms depress the prices they pay for inputs by obtaining increased negotiating leverage over their suppliers. For example, a merger that reduces the number of purchasers of supplies acquired through bargaining may have this effect.[20] This means by which monopsony power is exercised is the mirror image of raising prices to buyers by increasing negotiating leverage, as may happen when the number of rival sellers is reduced through merger.[21]

The dissenting judge in *Anthem* sought to distinguish between the exercise of monopsony power, which he viewed as potentially anticompetitive, and ordinary bargaining leverage, which he viewed as legitimate.[22] But firms can exercise upstream market power by exploiting bargaining leverage as well as by reducing the cost of input purchases. Both forms of anticompetitive conduct harming suppliers are properly reached by the antitrust laws.

When firms exercise market power over suppliers, they may obtain more favorable nonprice terms as well as reduce the price they pay. In reviewing a recent cable merger, Charter's acquisition of Time Warner Cable, the government feared that the merged firm would protect high cable-television prices by inducing content providers—upstream firms supplying programming—to avoid dealing with rival online video distributors.[23] In the mirror image, firms may exploit downstream market power to obtain favorable nonprice terms, as by inducing distributors to accept contractual provisions that exclude potential entrants and thereby protect downstream prices from eroding.

Depressed Prices versus Subcompetitive Prices

The dissenting judge in *Anthem* argued that a plaintiff should be required to prove that a defendant's conduct depressed the price paid by suppliers to a subcompetitive level. I disagree.

To see why, begin by considering the mirror-image problem of showing that customers were harmed by conduct that allowed firms to raise prices to customers. If the price increase is the product of an agreement among sellers that is illegal per se (e.g., price fixing or market division), a defendant is not permitted to escape liability by showing that the price level was reasonable. When higher prices result from conduct reviewed under a reasonableness standard, liability turns on whether the price increased or likely will increase relative to a hypothetical counterfactual in which the conduct did not take place (the "but-for" world). Prices in the but-for world could be at competitive levels, but in the oligopoly markets typically addressed by antitrust enforcement they need not be and often are not. Whether the but-for prices are competitive is not part of the competitive-effects inquiry. If competition would be harmed on dimensions other than price, such as quality or innovation, it would also not matter whether the price (or the quality-adjusted price) exceeds a competitive level. The antitrust issue is whether the reduction in competition made the terms of trade adverse to buyers relative to the but-for world, regardless of the dimensions on which the firms compete or the absolute level of prices.

The transformation of these observations about the exercise of harm to buyers to the analysis of supplier harm should be evident. Liability for the exercise of buyer power turns on whether conduct lessening competition made the terms of trade adverse to suppliers relative to the but-for world, not on whether price is below a competitive level.[24]

Even if a court focuses on aggregate welfare and chooses to ignore transfers between firms and their suppliers when evaluating the competitive consequence of firm conduct, the exercise of market power upstream harms competition. Again, a mirror-image analysis of downstream market power helps make the point. When firms exercise market power in selling to buyers, leading those buyers to pay more, aggregate welfare is lessened. If market power is exercised through a reduction in industry output, the foregone gains from trade represent an allocative inefficiency. If sellers instead exercise market power by taking advantage of enhanced negotiating leverage over their buyers, the higher price may lead the buyers to reduce their aggregate purchases—either substituting other products or doing without—and thereby create an allocative efficiency loss. When the victims are buyers of an intermediate good, they may invest less in improving their products or in expanding their downstream output. In consequence, they may purchase fewer inputs in the long run regardless of whether they also reduce their purchases in the short run.[25] Doing so would generate an additional allocative inefficiency in the form of foregone gains from trade.

With respect to the exercise of market power over suppliers, the allocative inefficiencies are analogous. The quantity of the input supplied may be reduced, creating foregone gains from trade. Firms exercising market power may reduce their purchases, some suppliers may shift their production assets in order to supply goods and services in other markets, and some suppliers may exit. Whether or not input quantity falls in the short run, suppliers may invest less in product improvements or capacity expansion than they would have otherwise, again generating allocative inefficiencies.

In the context of a case, courts undertake welfare analysis solely in the market where the harm occurs, consistent with the partial-equilibrium framework employed in antitrust law, regardless of whether the concern is with consumer welfare or aggregate welfare. When seller market power is said to harm buyers and competition, welfare is evaluated in the relevant downstream market. When buyer market power is said to harm suppliers and competition, welfare is evaluated in the relevant upstream market.

Accordingly, when anticompetitive conduct allegedly harms suppliers, courts may consider efficiencies from that conduct when evaluating competitive effects to the extent that they accrue within the same market as the harm. That is the practical import of allowing defendants to proffer efficiencies to rebut a plaintiff's prima facie case.[26] But courts do not consider such efficiencies when they benefit buyers or sellers in other markets, including markets downstream,[27] unless the exercise of buyer power also harms competition in those markets.[28] Proof of harm to suppliers (after accounting for in-market efficiencies) is sufficient for antitrust liability from the exercise of buyer power; courts neither consider the impact on downstream customers nor presume they benefit.[29]

Upstream Harms versus Downstream Harms

Some commentators have suggested that courts evaluating conduct harming suppliers through the exercise of buyer power should also consider effects on prices and output in downstream markets.[30] To the extent the firms exercising market power over suppliers pass price reductions through to their own buyers, those effects may include lower prices to downstream buyers, potentially enhancing downstream competition.[31] The effects may also include reduced output downstream or lower-quality outputs, due to reduced input supply, potentially harming downstream competition.

These possibilities raise a more general question: Should harms to competition in one market be offset by benefits to competition in another? In the context of harms to suppliers, the two markets are an upstream one, in which goods are supplied, and a downstream one, in which firms exercising market power over their suppliers sell their own products and services. In the context of harms to platform users, the two markets may be on different sides of a platform.

As I discuss further in the next section, my answer to this question is ordinarily no. Antitrust law properly rejects cross-market welfare trade-offs. Courts should not allow benefits to downstream buyers to justify competitive harm to upstream suppliers except in unusual cases.

ANTICOMPETITIVE CONDUCT INVOLVING PLATFORMS

Antitrust cases involving multisided platforms may be concerned with harm to competition among platforms or with harm to competition among the users on one or more sides. The analysis of either possibility may consider feedback effects across the platform's sides. As explained in Chapter 7, a reduction in the number of end users on one platform side may reduce the platform's value to end users on other sides. Cross-platform feedback effects should be evaluated, but courts and commentators have debated when to do so: whether to consider them when defining markets or when evaluating competitive effects.

The choice of when in the analysis to consider feedback does not matter if the defendants argue that it would be unprofitable to engage in the alleged anticompetitive conduct in the alleged market because of feedback effects involving other platform sides.[32] That profitability assessment does not depend on whether different platform sides are in different markets or in the same market. But with different markets on different platform sides, defendants must overcome the judicial reluctance to make cross-market welfare trade-offs in order to use feedback effects to argue instead that benefits in one market should offset harms in another. Even if such trade-offs are permitted, defendants would have a burden of production to show the offsetting benefits.

If instead feedback analysis is incorporated into market definition, courts would be expected to balance in-market harms and benefits, so the plaintiff must disprove offsetting benefits as part of its prima facie case. That approach is friendlier to platform defendants. This section explains why courts should not indulge platform defendants in this way. I take up market definition first, then efficiencies and cross-market welfare trade-offs.

Market Definition

In antitrust analysis, a market is a collection of products and geographic locations used to help make inferences about market power and anticompetitive effects of business conduct. After markets relevant to the analysis are defined, the market participants are identified, market shares are often computed, and the competitive consequences of firm behavior are evaluated. When a plaintiff is required to define markets and identify market participants, it is led to state with reasonable specificity what competition will be harmed by the challenged conduct. Among other things, that allows the defendant to rebut a plaintiff's claim that competition is limited by arguing for a wider market that includes additional participants.

Under the standard approach employed by the courts and enforcement agencies,[33] market definition accounts for a single economic force: demand, or buyer, substitution. That is, a market includes products and geographic locations that would be acceptable alternatives to buyers (i.e., reasonably interchangeable in demand). The agency merger guidelines, and, increasingly, courts, look to the "hypothetical monopolist" test as a conceptual device for identifying substitutes to include in a market. Under that test, a set of products and locations is a market for antitrust purposes if a hypothetical monopolist would find it profitable to exercise market power, accounting for the incentive of buyers to respond by shifting to other products and locations or doing without. The hypothetical-monopolist test provides a metric for judging whether to accept a candidate market: if demand substitution would make it unprofitable for a hypothetical monopolist to increase price, the candidate market would be expanded.[34]

Application of the standard approach to market definition does not mean that antitrust analysis ignores economic forces other than demand substitution, such as supply substitution, entry, or rivalry among market participants. Other economic forces are accounted for, and market power assessed, when evaluating whether the challenged conduct harms competition, but these forces are not considered in market definition.[35] Nor does the standard approach mandate that courts evaluate market power by looking to market shares once a market is defined; market power may be evaluated in other ways, too.

The standard approach does not identify a single, best market for analyzing a competitive problem. Any collection of products and locations that would be profitable to monopolize, after accounting for likely buyer responses to supracompetitive prices, counts as a market. Almost invariably, a competitive-effects allegation can be analyzed in multiple markets, including overlapping or nested markets, each satisfying the hypothetical-monopolist test. In an appropriate case, soft drinks might be a product market, but so might all beverages—a larger product category—or cola-flavored soft drinks—a smaller category. Soft drink sales in a metropolitan area may be a market, and so may sales in the state or the country as a whole.[36]

When firms participate in multiple antitrust markets, whether or not the markets overlap or nest, firm conduct may permit the exercise of market power in some markets but not in others. In theory, if a firm's conduct harms competition in *any* market, it violates the antitrust laws. In practice, courts consider only a small number of possible markets because the plaintiff picks out one or more candidate markets for the court to use in evaluating competitive harms, and the defendant may contest the choice of markets. The defendant may argue, on the basis of buyer-substitution evidence, that one or more candidates is not in fact a market, or the defendant may dispute the inference that it enjoys market power or has harmed competition within the candidate markets. The court is not looking for the best or smallest market and does not need to. Rather, it is looking for a market or markets suggested by the plaintiff's allegations that appropriately account for demand substitution in order to conduct a competitive analysis.

Errors in defining markets can lead courts to find competitive harm when it does not exist and miss competitive harm when it does exist. But this is just a type of error that courts should try to avoid, not a fatal conceptual problem for an analytical approach that employs market definition. I disagree with Louis Kaplow's contention that the process of market definition is incoherent.[37]

While the standard approach to market definition is neither impervious to error nor always necessary, it is often useful.[38] It is often appropriate in the evaluation of competitive issues arising with multisided platforms. Markets can be defined even when the products or services provided on one side can be characterized as freely provided. For instance, shopping malls could be a product market for evaluating alleged harm to shoppers even though they do not charge shoppers for mall access, though the malls may be thought of as subsidizing shoppers by providing free parking. Social media and Internet search could be product markets for evaluating alleged harm to users even though they do not charge participants directly, though they collect data about participant behavior and arguably lessen the quality of the user experience by inserting ads or promoted search results. Newspapers and music streaming services could be product markets for evaluating alleged harm to readers and listeners, even though some newspapers are free to readers and some music streaming services offer advertising-supported music at no charge. In all of these cases, the conceptual experiment for market definition—the hypothetical-monopolist test—may be implemented for a candidate market on the "free" side of the platform by supposing that the hidden costs go up (e.g., the mall starts to charge for parking) or service-quality declines (e.g., the search engine makes promoted results more prominent).

In general, a platform competes in separate markets on each of its sides, and feedback across the sides is properly and fully accounted for when analyzing competitive effects, not when defining markets. Yet some commentators have proposed that, when harms to competition on one side of a platform are alleged, courts should throw out the standard approach to market definition in order to account for economic forces beyond buyer substitution. Instead, these commentators suggest that when defining markets, a court should account for effects on all sides of a multisided platform when evaluating the profitability of a hypothetical price increase experienced by end users on one side.[39]

The exclusive demand-substitution focus of market definition is well established in the case law, including when defining markets in which platforms participate,[40] other than one prominent but narrow exception involving transaction platforms.[41] This is appropriate; courts are right to reject the alternative approach to market definition, for four reasons.

First, it is confusing to account for feedback effects across the sides of platforms when defining markets. Consider, for example, product-market definition in a hypothetical case involving magazines in the pre-Internet era. Magazines are platforms with two types of end users: subscribers and advertisers. On the advertising side, a magazine might compete with other magazines, broadcast and cable television, newspapers, billboards, and direct mail, among other products. On the subscriber side, a magazine might compete with other magazines, cable television, newspapers, and books. Some potential rivals on each side—magazines, newspapers, and cable television—are also platforms; others—billboards, direct mail, broadcast television, and books—are not.

Suppose an advertiser charged that one or more magazines engaged in conduct that harmed competition for advertisers, and, in consequence, the magazines raised ad rates. Under the standard approach, the plaintiff might allege a product market in magazine advertising. The parties would argue about whether a hypothetical magazine monopolist could profitably raise advertising rates a small amount—holding constant the prices of other products, including magazine subscription rates—or whether that would be made unprofitable by some advertisers choosing instead to advertise more via other media including television, newspapers, and billboards. If magazine advertising were not a market, the candidate market would be expanded to include some or all of these substitutes.

Under the alternative approach that accounts for feedback across platform sides, the market definition exercise could proceed differently after the plaintiff alleges a magazine-advertising product market. The defendant might argue that it would not be profitable for magazines to raise advertising rates because of feedback involving subscribers. Higher ad rates would lead to less advertising, which would in turn lessen the attractiveness of certain magazines to subscribers, either because they enjoy the ads or because they interpret declining advertiser interest as a signal of reduced content quality now or in the future. A reduction in magazine subscriptions would lessen advertiser demand further through the operation of network effects. After accounting for the feedback from ad rates to subscriptions and back to advertising, and so on in further rounds, the defendant may contend that it would have been unprofitable for magazines to raise advertising rates and suggest that any observed rate rise must instead have had an innocent cause, thereby hoping to escape antitrust enforcement.

The defendant's cross-platform feedback argument unquestionably should be considered before concluding that its conduct harmed competition and led to an increase in advertising rates. The issue is merely at what point in the process it should be considered. Under the standard approach, that analysis is conducted after markets are defined, when evaluating competitive effects. Under the alternative approach, it would be conducted as part of market definition. This is the trouble spot. In order to conduct the feedback analysis in the course of market definition, a court would have to simultaneously consider the consequences of demand substitution—in this case, between magazines and other ways to advertise—and demand complementarity—in this case, between the products and services offered on different platform sides.[42] The alternative approach creates confusion by forcing courts to account for multiple economic forces in the same analytical step.[43]

A second disadvantage of the alternative approach to market definition is that, if nonplatform rivals constrain platform pricing on one or both sides, courts may be misled when they turn to competitive-effects analysis.[44] In the magazine example, a court that wishes to consider cross-platform feedback effects in market definition could end up with a market that includes magazine advertising and subscriptions, but which excludes billboards and direct mail. Suppose there are few magazines, a plausible assumption if the candidate market is genre-specific—say, sports magazines rather than all magazines. Then the sale of advertising space could appear concentrated even when advertising rates are constrained by the possibility that advertisers will substitute to other media. That fact could lead the court to find a violation when competition would not be harmed. A court could easily make this mistake when its attention is diverted from buyer substitution and toward cross-platform feedback when defining markets.

If the concern is with competition among platforms rather than with competition to serve advertisers or readers alone, it would still be necessary to evaluate constraints on platform pricing from nonplatform rivals in serving each user group, as well as competition from other platforms that may serve both groups (such as newspapers), in order to determine the consequences of the conduct for advertising rates and subscription rates. Again, focusing on the feedback among prices across platform sides may raise the likelihood of judicial error by diverting the court's attention away from buyer substitution.

In these examples, a court could potentially account for both buyer substitution and the consequences for feedback across the sides appropriately in a single analytical step. But doing so would require the same analysis of buyer substitution that would be required under the standard economic approach while adding another complex technical economic analysis. Feedback analysis would be particularly challenging when some firms participating in the candidate market are platforms (magazines in the example) and others are not (billboards or direct mail), when some platforms have different business models than others (advertising-supported magazines versus subscriber-supported magazines), or when some platforms compete with others (magazines and newspapers). By limiting market definition to evaluation of a single economic force—buyer substitution—and deferring the evaluation of feedback effects, courts lessen the potential for confusion.[45]

Third, the alternative approach to market definition can lead a court to adopt market-share measures that mislead or are difficult to interpret. Returning to the example, suppose the concern is that advertising rates would be elevated. Under the standard approach, the market participants would be assigned market shares based on their advertising revenues only (assuming, as is likely, that shares are measured by revenues). Under the alternative approach, in which the products or services on both sides of magazine platforms are included in the market, magazine revenues would include subscription revenues as well as advertising revenues. The resulting shares would likely understate the potential competitive constraint from billboards and mailers on magazine advertising rates. In addition, under the alternative approach, the market shares of subscription-supported magazines would be higher than under the standard approach. The resulting shares would likely overstate the significance of ad-light, subscription-supported magazines in constraining magazine advertising rates, again possibly leading a court to fail to recognize a competitive problem in advertising.

Finally, adopting the alternative approach to market definition will take courts a step down a slippery slope. If market definition accounts for feedback effects on other sides of a platform when evaluating the profitability of a price rise by a hypothetical monopolist on one side, why not also account for the consequences of the hypothetical price increase for the profitability of other products sold by multiproduct sellers participating in the candidate market, whether substitutes or complements? And why not also consider the constraint posed by supply substitution or entry? At the bottom of this slippery slope, nearly the entire competitive-effects analysis would be incorporated into market definition,[46] rendering market definition nearly useless except as a vehicle for an ex post rationalization of a wide-ranging evaluation of competitive effects.

Some of these difficulties are avoided entirely under the standard approach to market definition, which looks solely to demand substitution. Accounting for feedback effects continues to require a complex technical analysis, but deferring that analysis to the evaluation of competitive effects protects market definition from confusion, leads courts to account for nonplatform substitutes sensibly, makes market shares more meaningful guides to potential competitive issues, and avoids the slippery slope that would undermine the utility of market definition. Indeed, in some cases, deferring the consideration of feedback effects across platform sides will make any such consideration unnecessary, sparing the court a complex technical problem. If the defendant wins by showing low concentration in a market defined under the standard approach, or by showing that entry would counteract or deter the alleged competitive problem, a court would not need to spend time and effort evaluating the defendant's arguments about the competitive significance of feedback effects across platform sides.

Efficiencies and Cross-Market Welfare Trade-Offs

The argument about the role of market definition in antitrust cases involving platforms is in part a dispute over whether courts should allow harms to some platform users to be offset by benefits to users on other platform sides. Should a shopping platform, for example, be allowed to justify anticompetitive conduct that depresses the prices paid to suppliers by showing that the same conduct led the platform to compete more aggressively in selling products to shoppers, so shoppers paid less?

When the standard approach to market definition is employed, the products or services on different sides of platforms are typically not included in the same market. If in addition, only within-market efficiencies count, harm to the users on one side of a platform cannot be defended by showing benefits to users on another side. A prohibition on cross-market balancing does not foreclose a platform defendant from relying on feedback effects to attack the plaintiff's case, however. The defendant can still show that it would have no incentive to harm competition on the platform side where harm is alleged once the consequences of feedback with other sides are taken into account.[47]

When the defendant's argument about effects across platform sides turns on offsetting efficiencies across markets rather than on the unprofitability of the alleged conduct, though, the defendant cannot prevail unless a court is willing to undertake cross-market welfare trade-offs when evaluating the reasonableness of firm conduct. Even when the defendant also argues that feedback effects would make the alleged conduct unprofitable, the defendant may wish to put the courtroom focus on benefits to end users on the other side of the platform by framing its case in terms of offsetting efficiencies. Accordingly, cases in which the plaintiff alleges harm to end users on one side of a platform may raise the issue of whether antitrust law should incorporate cross-market welfare trade-offs when evaluating whether conduct harms competition.

Consistent with the case law involving harms to suppliers, antitrust law does not permit courts to offset competitive harms in one market with competitive benefits in another. Consider the Supreme Court's *Philadelphia National Bank* decision.[48] In that 1963 case the Court concluded that the merger of two large Philadelphia banks harmed competition in commercial banking in the Philadelphia area. The Court declined to consider the merging firms' proposal that the transaction be allowed because the merger would enhance competition in a different market, a national market for loans to large firms. As a matter of prosecutorial discretion in merger review, the antitrust enforcement agencies may permit benefits in one market to offset harms in another when the two are inextricably linked,[49] but under *Philadelphia National Bank*, which still controls, courts cannot follow suit.[50] The same rule applies in non-merger litigation.[51] Courts may look to both benefits and costs within the same market when evaluating the reasonableness of challenged conduct, but they may not count benefits in one market against harms in another.[52]

The main argument for overruling *Philadelphia National Bank* on this issue, and allowing benefits in one market to offset harms in other, is the contention, which has some force, that all buyers and suppliers in the economy should be treated identically in working out social gains and losses from firm conduct. If, for example, the users on one side of a platform lose $10 collectively from the challenged conduct while the users on another side gain $30, permitting the practice would create an aggregate benefit of $20. Put differently, allowing cross-market welfare tradeoffs facilitates economic development by helping to prevent the antitrust rules from conferring entitlements that could stifle economic growth—a danger similar to the one avoided by the Supreme Court in *Charles River Bridge*. Why not allow society to capture net benefits and grow overall by allowing a court to weigh the benefits in one market against the harms in another, at least when the benefits could not practically be obtained without also tolerating the harms?[53] There are several reasons.

The judicial prohibition against cross-market welfare trade-offs has an obvious administrability justification: the prohibition reduces the complexity of the reasonableness evaluation of the conduct under review.[54] If a court must also evaluate alleged benefits to competition in another market, the litigants must conduct discovery about that market too, and the court must conduct an additional competitive analysis. The additional discovery burden and analytical effort may be limited to the extent that some of the relevant information overlaps, competitive conditions are similar, and the markets are structured similarly, but in general, much of the required discovery and analysis will not be duplicative. To assess harms or benefits within the additional market, the litigants and court may consider, for example, evidence about buyer substitution among the products and services included in the market and substitution to outside products; the nature of rivalry among market participants; features of the market that affect that rivalry (such as factors that might facilitate or frustrate coordination); the likelihood of entry, expansion, and product repositioning sufficient to counteract or deter the alleged harm; and efficiencies. In addition, it will often be more difficult to compare harms and benefits across markets than within markets, because the beneficial or adverse consequences of the conduct under review are more likely to accrue to different market participants in the former case. This difficulty can arise when harms and benefits accrue in the same market, but it is more likely when making trade-offs across markets.

Even worse, if the court is allowed to consider benefits in the market that a defendant points to, why should the court not consider welfare consequences in other markets, too? If prices would increase in one market, they may also increase in markets for substitute products not included in the market. Or, if the market is for an intermediate good, prices may also rise in downstream product markets. These price changes will have ripple effects on prices and output in still other markets. We can see where this is going: it would be impractical to evaluate the consequences of harmful conduct in one market for all other markets potentially affected by the conduct under review. Yet once the analysis extends beyond the market in which harm is alleged, there may be no principled stopping point short of undertaking what is unrealistic if not impossible: a general equilibrium analysis of harms and benefits throughout the entire economy.

The problem of substantial and widening market power provides a reason beyond administrability to avoid undertaking cross-market welfare trade-offs. The reason stems from the observation that cross-market welfare trade-offs allow firms exercising market power in one market to avoid liability on the ground that participants in other markets would benefit more. If the direct victims in the markets where harm occurs are final consumers or suppliers (perhaps including workers, farmers, or small businesses),[55] then antitrust law will systematically and conspicuously fail to protect or compensate economic actors whose political support is essential for preserving antitrust institutions. Buyers or suppliers in other markets may benefit, and some of those benefits may ultimately accrue to final consumers, workers, farmers, or small businesses. But these benefits will rarely be obvious.[56] It is also reasonable to expect that allowing cross-market welfare trade-offs will tend to impose on these direct victims harms that exceed any benefits, even after accounting for benefits they might receive in other cases and other markets from cross-market trade-offs in their favor. Hence the legal prohibition on cross-market welfare trade-offs operates informally as a type of social insurance against the risks of losses from anticompetitive conduct to interest groups vulnerable to injury from the exercise of market power by large firms.

It is hard to tell consumers, farmers, workers, and suppliers—groups whose political support for antitrust is needed in order to prevent the stealth replacement of antitrust by laissez-faire—that they must experience competitive harms in order to permit large firms to lower costs or to allow buyers purchasing in other markets to pay less, without leading those victims of market power to question the benefits of the political bargain. Accordingly, the legal bar to cross-market welfare trade-offs operates as a side payment that helps preserve the political bargain. For reasons given in Chapter 3, this political-economy argument should be understood as a justification for barring cross-market trade-offs across the board, not as a principle to be applied through case-by-case analysis of the distributional consequences of the anticompetitive conduct.

The administrability and political-economy arguments against cross-market welfare trade-offs could reasonably be overcome in an unusual situation, however. In order to interdict the creation of entitlements that would discourage economic growth, a court should allow a cross-market welfare trade-off when it is evident from a qualitative comparison that the harm to competition in one market is small while the benefit to competition in another market is vastly greater and there is no practical way to obtain the benefit without accepting the harm.[57] This possibility does not justify altering the general rule against undertaking cross-market welfare trade-offs, but hugely disproportionate benefits could provide a reason to allow an exception in an unusual case, such as one in which the buyers of the products in a small market are adversely affected while much larger customer groups buying products in other markets benefit greatly.[58] In practice, this exception would be unlikely to justify anticompetitive conduct that lowers the prices paid to suppliers when the defendants pass through their cost savings to buyers. Nor would it be expected to justify, say, a merger that raises downstream prices when the firms distribute most of the resulting rents to workers as higher wages.

CONCLUSION

Courts sensibly allow efficiencies to offset competitive harms within markets. But they properly avoid undertaking cross-market welfare trade-offs when evaluating anticompetitive conduct that harms suppliers, including workers, or the users on one side of a multisided platform. Doing otherwise would create serious administrative difficulties. Perhaps for that reason, courts declined to modify the long-standing prohibition on balancing effects across markets during the 1980s, even as the Supreme Court otherwise undertook a thoroughgoing reformation of antitrust rules to reduce their chill to procompetitive conduct. Given that today's dominant error-cost problem is the reverse—insufficient deterrence of anticompetitive conduct—and given the need to protect political support for antitrust, there is now even less reason to revise antitrust law's general prohibition against cross-market welfare trade-offs.

PART III

Looking Forward

Chapter Ten

Restoring a Competitive Economy

IN 2001 the D.C. Circuit, sitting en banc, issued a unanimous decision affirming Microsoft's liability for monopolization.[1] The decision, its context, and its aftermath show how antitrust fended off a substantial noninterventionist challenge to the political bargain. This chapter begins by surveying that decision and its lessons for this moment, when the hazards of market power are serious and growing.

I then turn to the contemporary imperative of restoring a competitive economy by strengthening antitrust rules and enforcement, in particular the challenge of engineering change in a conservative legal environment. I have proposed a slate of new presumptions that would enable courts and enforcers to respond to contemporary market power problems made more complicated by the growth of sophisticated, information-technology powered firms. But the Supreme Court stands in the way. I have therefore emphasized the sort of arguments that can convince the Court: economic ones. This is not to suggest that the problems of market power are only economic; market power threatens the political bargain and fosters conditions in which crony capitalism thrives. Nor is it my contention that political mobilization is unimportant; quite the contrary. However, the justices will be most responsive to economic arguments and evidence concerning competition and welfare.

LEARNING FROM *MICROSOFT*

Microsoft was the most important U.S. antitrust decision of the past three decades. For one thing, it was the rare antitrust case that captured broad public attention.[2] The U.S. government was asking a court to break up a leading firm in a rapidly growing, cutting-edge industry—a firm whose owner was enormously famous and the wealthiest person in the world. The Justice Department's lawsuit was brought during the Clinton administration and settled shortly after the D.C. Circuit's 2001 decision with conduct relief, not divestitures, during the first year of the George W. Bush administration.

Microsoft helped to create a consequential legal precedent. Along with the Supreme Court's 1985 decision in *Aspen Skiing*,[3] *Microsoft* established a structured reasonableness framework for evaluating a dominant firm's conduct under Sherman Act § 2.[4] It also made clear that the antitrust laws reach nascent competitive harms or threats to potential competition, even in innovative industries where markets change rapidly.[5] Importantly too, the judges not only rejected but ridiculed Microsoft's claim that it had "an absolute and unfettered right to use its intellectual property as it wishes." Such a claim, if sustained, would have justified any anticompetitive exclusionary conduct that took the form of restrictions on software licensing.[6]

Microsoft's impact on antitrust enforcement and policy outside the four corners of the decision may have been more significant than the precedent. Through public-relations efforts while the litigation was underway, Microsoft issued a high-profile challenge to the legitimacy of antitrust and antitrust institutions. Microsoft contended that the litigation threatened the company's "freedom to innovate," as if to claim that it could do as it pleases in developing and distributing new technology, letting the competition chips fall where they may.[7] The company also depicted the Justice Department as the pawn of its rivals, which, it said, had turned to the government for help when they were unable to succeed in the market.[8] Microsoft even lobbied Congress to cut the Justice Department's antitrust-enforcement budget.[9] These moves added up to a wholesale indictment of antitrust, charging that enforcement undermines economic rights and facilitates inefficient rent seeking by rivals and that the antitrust laws are unsuited for governing firm behavior in high-tech markets.

Microsoft's public indictment gained political traction during the 2000 presidential election campaign between George W. Bush and Al Gore. Gore was the sitting vice president in the administration that brought the Microsoft case and sought to break up the firm. Bush signaled his opposition and perhaps his sympathy for Microsoft's freedom-to-innovate argument.[10] One

of his surrogates signaled that, if Bush were elected, the case would be resolved in Microsoft's favor.[11]

Meanwhile, the litigation proceeded. A lower court's breakup order was
placed on hold while the D.C. Circuit reviewed the case. In recognition of
the importance of the case, and to forestall a direct appeal to the Supreme
Court, the D.C. circuit made the unusual decision to hear arguments en
banc. The most important vote was likely that of Judge Douglas Ginsburg.[12]
Ginsburg is both an antitrust expert and a regulation skeptic.[13] If the courts
were going to mount a broad noninterventionist challenge to antitrust enforcement, Judge Ginsburg was the obvious intellectual leader to frame the
critique.

Judge Ginsburg and his colleagues instead reinforced the central role of
the antitrust laws. It is plausible that Ginsburg's decision to join the majority
convinced colleagues who might have joined him in dissent, resulting in a
unanimous decision rather than a narrow majority. Unanimity put an excla-
mation point on the court's approval of antitrust enforcement's legitimacy.

It is possible to imagine a counterfactual opinion, whether by the majority
or in dissent, sympathetic to Microsoft's freedom-to-innovate argument.
Such an opinion might have claimed that antitrust law is concerned to avoid
chilling innovation, particularly by exempting the application of antitrust
rules to the development of new products. For support, the hypothetical
opinion could have relied on a Supreme Court decision affirming a lower-
court decision that exempted developing industries from the traditional per
se prohibition against tying in order to allow new firms to develop a reputation for quality;[14] a Court decision holding that price fixing is not illegal per
se when the agreement allowed the firms to create a new product;[15] appellate decisions that could have been read to establish that the introduction of
a new product cannot be the basis for a Section 2 violation unless the new
product offers no benefit to buyers and instead operates purely to raise compatibility problems for rivals;[16] and the routine acceptance by the antitrust-
enforcement agencies of the development of better and cheaper products as
a justification for what might otherwise be an anticompetitive merger or joint
venture.[17]

Based on these observations, the hypothetical opinion would have concluded that antitrust law strongly presumes that competition and consumers
benefit from unilateral conduct or vertical agreements entered into by firms
in rapidly changing high-tech markets. The opinion would have found for

Microsoft by applying this presumption to evaluate the specific claims of anticompetitive tying, exclusive dealing, and monopolization at issue in the litigation.

If this analysis had been at the core of the majority opinion in the D.C. Circuit, the likely result would have been to establish the principle that antitrust laws do not apply in cutting-edge industries beyond the prohibition against horizontal collusion and perhaps the bar on anticompetitive horizontal mergers. Such an outcome would have been a large step toward abolishing concern with exclusionary conduct from antitrust laws altogether.

In the actual case, several features of the appellate decision helped insulate it from criticism by conservatives skeptical of antitrust intervention:[18] it was handed down without dissent, it was grounded in economics without any nod toward social or political goals, its holding was based upon the rich factual record assembled by the district court, and it reached its outcome without taking sides on what it described as a "significant debate amongst academics and practitioners over the extent to which 'old economy' §2 monopolization doctrines should apply to firms competing in dynamic technological markets characterized by network effects."[19] These factors helped to ensure that Microsoft's public relations attack on the legitimacy of antitrust did not gain traction.

The importance of the unanimous decision against Microsoft only increases when we consider what came later. In the context of a legal and political system increasingly disposed to favor laissez-faire and the resulting exercise of market power, a decision in Microsoft's favor, or even a divided decision against, could have served to aid the strong forces pressing against antitrust. For instance, a ruling favorable to Microsoft could well have been endorsed and amplified when the Supreme Court decided *Trinko* three years later.[20] *Trinko* should be read narrowly[21] as precluding monopolization liability in a setting in which a statute other than the Sherman Act provided for extensive regulation aimed at promoting competition. But the sweeping rhetoric of Justice Scalia's opinion allows for a broader reading that questions the application of antitrust laws to monopolization through nonprice exclusionary conduct, particularly in innovative industries.[22] Had *Microsoft* come out differently, *Trinko* might have gone farther to question the legitimacy of the antitrust prohibition against monopolization.

Microsoft's public attack on antitrust might also have influenced the subsequent deliberations of the Antitrust Modernization Commission (AMC). The legislation that led to the creation of the AMC was introduced the day before the D.C. Circuit released its en banc decision on liability against Microsoft. Its sponsor, House Judiciary Chairman James Sensenbrenner, promoted for AMC consideration several issues that arose in the *Microsoft* litigation.[23] One was suggestive of Microsoft's freedom-to-innovate argument: Sensenbrenner wanted the antitrust laws "calibrated" to reflect an "increasingly information-driven digital economy."[24] When the AMC asked for public comment on its agenda, a leading conservative activist responded that "the antitrust laws, if they ever served a useful purpose, now only exist to stifle productivity growth and development of new products and services."[25]

If the D.C. Circuit had split in the *Microsoft* case, with one opinion endorsing the freedom-to-innovate critique and the Bush Justice Department seemingly endorsing that critique through its settlement with Microsoft, it is easy to imagine the AMC recommending changes that would have limited scrutiny of high-tech firms. The Justice Department probably would have endorsed such recommendations. After all, the Justice Department did not bring any monopolization cases between 2001 and 2008, excepting three technical violations.[26] The Antitrust Division seemed hostile to monopolization claims in its 2004 amicus brief in *Trinko* and, in 2008, in its Section 2 report on "Competition and Monopoly."[27] The Congress that created the AMC would not have stood in the way of major reform. With all three branches of government flirting with a noninterventionist perspective on monopolization, a divide in the D.C. Circuit over *Microsoft* could have sparked a broad reworking of the antitrust laws that would ultimately have undermined the political bargain.[28]

But with the D.C. Circuit's unanimous decision, the AMC chose not to push for wholesale change.[29] As a result, the noninterventionist initiatives of the three branches—the *Trinko* decision at the Supreme Court, the DOJ's "Competition and Monopoly" report, and Congress's creation of the AMC— were uncoordinated. No major reforms resulted.

The *Microsoft* case, and the ensuing decade's dampened political response to the D.C. Circuit's decision, offer two important lessons for today. First, ideology may be influential, but it does not dictate judicial decisions. When strong facts support a sensible economic analysis, conservative judges can reach pro-enforcement decisions. (Liberal judges, similarly, can reach decisions counter to ideological expectations.) This suggests that, even when judges are conservative, litigants can push the courts to address substantial and widening market power through judicious case selection that emphasizes strong facts supported by modern economic analysis. Even cases involving seemingly small economic stakes can have long shadows if they establish valuable pro-enforcement precedents. Over time, in a target-rich environment created by growing market power, this process could move antitrust rules toward increasing deterrence of harmful conduct.

Second, antitrust policy is shaped over time by all three branches of government. The political bargain took hold when the enforcement approach advanced by Thurman Arnold, an executive branch official, was accepted by the courts and Congress. The bargain was preserved during the first decade of the twenty-first century because the three branches did not act in a coordinated way to undermine it. This suggests the importance of political mobilization to address market power for preserving the bargain today.

ENGINEERING LEGAL CHANGE TODAY

Today's noninterventionist challenge to the political bargain is, in an important respect, greater than that of the 2000s. Then the problem was to prevent the antitrust laws from being affirmatively undermined. Today growing market power threatens to overturn the political bargain by stealth. The problem now is not to hold fast against the actions of an easily definable opponent, but the more difficult task of changing the status quo—to reverse a trend toward nonenforcement by strengthening the antitrust laws.

We can be confident that such change is possible. After all, antitrust rules were substantially modified on two occasions in the twentieth century: during the 1940s, with the development of structural-era rules, and during the 1980s, when courts and politicians adopted Chicago school–oriented positions. These episodes suggest three factors that can lead to doctrinal change.[30]

First, antitrust law may adjust to major developments in business practices and economic activity. The structural-era rules were a response to the concentrating effects of industrialization. The changing form, size, and power of business led to decades of debate over how to treat large firms, which was resolved by the new rules of the 1940s.

Second, political realignments can create opportunities for antitrust reforms. For many, the Great Depression undermined faith in the *Lochner* worldview that underlay the classical era of antitrust enforcement. The electoral response cleared the field for the New Deal to experiment with regulation and eventually for Arnold's new course and the political bargain.

Later, amid the Reagan-era mobilization against government intervention, the Chicago school's antitrust views became ascendant.

Third, developments in economic analysis may alter the way business practices are understood for purposes of antitrust enforcement and adjudication. That can lead enforcers and judges to change how they apply individual antitrust rules and courts to adjust those rules.[31] For instance, the introduction of empirical tools for evaluating and simulating unilateral effects of merger led to the acceptance by enforcers and courts of unilateral-effects theories,[32] deterring anticompetitive mergers that might otherwise have escaped enforcement. Edward Chamberlin's work on monopolistic competition helped shape enforcement decisions in antitrust's structural era, while Chicago school economic thinking strongly influenced the way antitrust rules were formulated and applied beginning during the late 1970s.[33]

All three factors fostering legal change are at work today, and they point in the direction of strengthened antitrust. First, new business forms, driven by information technology, present the novel competitive challenges discussed throughout Part II.[34] Second, market power is increasingly a politically prominent issue. It is, for example, central to the Democratic Party's Better Deal program for domestic policy announced in mid-2017.[35] And advances in economics are forcing us to confront the market power in our midst. Industrial-organization economics has been thoroughly reconstructed using game-theoretic arguments, and new empirical tools allow more precise measurement of incentives, conduct, and effects. These developments, underway for a generation, often demonstrate that conduct thought benign actually harms competition. It is true that antitrust rules remain heavily influenced by Chicago school economic thinking, but that is in part because the rules have not fully assimilated the consequences of new theory and findings.

In a critical respect, however, the current environment is inhospitable to course correction. The overriding difficulty is a Supreme Court that largely accepts and protects the Chicago approach. The replacement of Justices Scalia and Kennedy appears unlikely to make much difference to the Court's antitrust jurisprudence.

The senior leadership at the Antitrust Division, and the Trump administration's Republican nominees to the Federal Trade Commission (FTC), are unlikely to lead a change of course. Many of them served in the George W. Bush administration and are comfortable with the contemporary approach to antitrust jurisprudence and enforcement.[36] Republicans under Trump have not suddenly begun confirming judges who would take a more interventionist approach. Nor is there any reason to expect congressional Republicans to encourage the agencies or courts to change course. Accordingly, it seems that Chicago-oriented antitrust may remain dominant for a long time, particularly at the Supreme Court, barring a 1932-style political realignment and its consequences for judicial appointments.

One wild card is populism, which has been bolstered as slowed productivity growth, globalization, and technological change have, on the whole, harmed the lower and middle classes. One the one hand, Walmart exploits its global supply chain to sell goods at low prices, e-commerce firms such as Amazon are creating jobs for less-educated workers,[37] and Uber gives new employment opportunities to part-time workers. On the other hand, and more importantly, the median income has stagnated, and gains from the post–Great Recession recovery have gone disproportionately to the top of the income and wealth distributions.[38] These developments undermine individual income stability and family self-sufficiency, making social insurance simultaneously more difficult to implement and more necessary. These trends also threaten the commitment of consumers, workers, and farmers to the political bargain because they suggest that—notwithstanding what the United States now provides in social insurance, an important side payment to those groups—future gains in economic efficiency from competitive markets will not be widely shared.

To date the populist political response has mainly been from the right. Trump mobilized working-class voters who resented foreigners and immigrants and viewed global trade skeptically, though analysts dispute the extent to which dimmed economic prospects, rather than concerns about social position, influenced by race, have shaped those voters' views.[39] Before the start of the Trump administration, the most sustained and influential recent political mobilization was conservative, from the Tea Party, which established its populist bona fides in opposition to bailouts of financial institutions during the recession.

That said, it is possible to imagine a competing populist mobilization from the left.[40] The Occupy Wall Street movement had some success from the progressive side of the spectrum, as did social-democratic Senator Bernie Sanders in his 2016 presidential primary campaign. Many supporters of these movements blame the wealthy and large firms for their inability to get ahead or escape their debts. It is surprising that the banks were not blamed more for the rash of mortgage foreclosures during the financial crisis; we may yet see those chickens come home to roost. It is also possible that workers will attribute low wages, and farmers low prices, to the conduct of the large firms they work for and sell to. And small businesses, which can mobilize strong political support, may come to see large platforms such as Amazon's and Google's more as threats than sources of opportunity.

Populist political pressures from the right might not favor more aggressive antitrust enforcement: Trump-style conservative populism—present more in rhetoric than policy, as of this writing—could support some combination of a stronger safety net, protectionist international trade policies, and domestic infrastructure spending without challenging firms' market power. Indeed, market power might even be enhanced through trade protection. By contrast, as Senator Warren's speeches suggest, political pressures from the left would likely encourage antitrust enforcement and regulatory policies reining in the exercise of market power.[41] In the current political environment, this position would serve to reinforce the political bargain.

Lest this left-right dichotomy strike readers as simplistic, it is noteworthy that, in the midst of Trumpian populism, the broad categories of socialism, liberalism, and fascism remain endemic both to political conversation and to the operation of states. China models a type of socialism featuring state-led growth in partnership with a private sector. Trump and the leaders of some Eastern European nations flirt with fascism, at least rhetorically. Western Europe and Canada model open, free societies with strong antitrust enforcement. This suggests that the left-right political categories that have structured domestic politics for decades remain appropriate for understanding economic policy making and the future of the political bargain.[42]

Within this framework, it is possible that Democratic gains in 2018 will signal a leftward movement in the electorate. But any supposition that the electorate will shift decisively to bring champions of stronger antitrust enforcement to power in the political branches, and thereby change the composition of the judicial branches over time, is highly speculative. Moreover, this possibility assumes that noninterventionist incumbents do not lock in their electoral success by, for example, limiting the franchise and gerrymandering voting districts.[43]

In short, efforts to protect the political bargain and restore a competitive economy must, for now and in the foreseeable future, take place within a conservative judicial environment. In the background, however, change in the economy, new economic thinking, and a political reaction to growing market power may encourage the courts to see the antitrust landscape differently as time goes by, creating more possibilities for legal change.

This does not mean that advocates should be idle, waiting for new economic and political conditions, and new economic scholarship, to sink into courts on their own. That is not how the Chicago school won the day: its supporters made concerted efforts to win over the legal intelligentsia, so that there would be likeminded jurists available for judicial nomination once the changing political environment supplied opportunities to break into the bench. Change, in other words, will not happen on its own. Restoring a competitive economy through more effective antitrust enforcement will require progress on five related tasks.

The first is to increase awareness of market power. Citizens need to understand that the exercise of market power in the U.S. economy is substantial, widening, and harmful. Although books such as this one sound the alarm, market power is not understood as widely as it needs to be. Part of the reason may be the complexity of the story. As demonstrated in Chapter 1, the growing exercise of market power has many roots, including factors outside antitrust law, such as the growth of large information technology platforms. Factors internal to antitrust law, such as the shortcomings of specific legal rules, are difficult to explain to a voting public that should not be expected to follow legal arcana. It therefore behooves politicians and public commentators to explain antitrust's many successes and to differentiate antitrust from the sort of thoroughgoing business regulation of which many Americans are wary.[44] Microsoft's story may be useful in this respect. Although the company complained that anything less than total latitude would kill off high-tech innovation, antitrust successfully attacked Microsoft's anticompetitive conduct even as high-tech business development flourished.

The second task, closely related to the first, is to nurture a political mobilization against the exercise of market power. To date, the concern about large-firm market power has been an elite issue, framed by think tanks and journalists and acknowledged by the Democratic Party leadership. It has yet to break into popular consciousness to the extent needed. This could change if elite attention attracts candidates for office running on progressive economics. Their candidacies will help to bend popular attention to antitrust. If they win office, these candidates would be in a position to shape directly the attitude of the political branches toward antitrust enforcement and indirectly (through approval of judicial nominees) that of the courts. In a changed political environment, an energized Congress also could push the courts toward more interventionist outcomes legislatively.[45] But direct political interference in antitrust enforcement must be avoided.

Third, the antitrust enforcement agencies must lead in pushing the courts to strengthen antitrust. With greater public support, and enforcement-agency leadership attuned to that political mood, the agencies would be able to count on more resources and take greater litigation risks. The agencies can also help focus public attention on market power through enforcement actions, research from staff economists, and FTC industry studies relying on that agency's power to compel firms to supply information.[46] These activities would also be expected to provide fodder for outside academic research. The agencies may be able to enhance deterrence by naming individuals as well as firms as defendants more often.[47]

The antitrust agencies also can continue to deploy competition advocacy to support efforts by other agencies and departments to attack the exercise of market power through nonantitrust levers such as procurement and regulation.[48] For example, in appropriate cases, the Defense Department can use its procurement authority to foster competition. The Departments of Agriculture and Transportation, the Federal Communications Commission, the Federal Energy Regulatory Commission, and the Federal Reserve all have regulatory authority that can be used to promote competition. Such advocacy may be hard to come by without buy in from the White House,[49] but state agencies can pick up some slack by taking procompetitive actions of their own.

Fourth, antitrust plaintiffs must exploit the space created by those lower courts that are willing to question the Chicago approach. Litigants might include the federal enforcement agencies. State antitrust enforcers and private plaintiffs will also need to press their cases.

Fifth and finally, with an eye to persuading the Supreme Court, plaintiffs should rely heavily on arguments rooted in modern economics. Economic arguments supported by economic evidence are the key to persuading a Court committed to understanding the antitrust laws as advancing economic goals. The analysis in Part II provides a playbook. Economic arguments support beneficial enforcement actions under the existing antitrust rules and encourage the development of more interventionist rules.[50] It will be up to plaintiffs to dissuade the courts from turning to faulty economics, such as the erroneous assumptions addressed in Chapter 5, to advance the stealth rejection of antitrust.

The work of antitrust reconstruction requires sensitivity to antitrust institutions as well as sound economic analysis. The growing complexity of economic arguments and the economic evidence relied on in antitrust enforcement and litigation means that antitrust rules must also pay attention to administrability. But while concern for administrability ties down the form that the rules take, it does not affect their substance. On substance, economic analysis provides the best guide. And antitrust institutions must continue to embrace the norm against direct political influence on enforcement.

To address substantial and widening market power, particularly in recognition of the distinctive competitive problems of the information economy, courts should be encouraged to adopt a number of rules and (rebuttable) presumptions defended in this book.

In analyzing horizontal mergers (Chapter 4), courts should require more evidence to rebut the inference of competitive harm from high and increasing market concentration, presume adverse unilateral effects of mergers between sellers of differentiated products when diversion ratios (or demand cross-elasticities) between the firms' products are sufficiently high, and presume adverse coordinated effects from the acquisition of a maverick.

To reduce the threat of coordination (Chapter 6), courts should presume that in an industry in which single-market cheating would likely be deterred by rapid price matching, and entry would not be expected to undermine a coordinated outcome, firms competing in multiple markets that set prices using algorithms have reached an agreement on price for the purpose of enforcing Sherman Act § 1.

To help address exclusion (Chapter 7), courts should presume that competition is harmed when all significant rivals are excluded, or when excluding firms with market power demonstrate the ability to foreclose at least one significant rival. Those presumptions should become conclusive when the exclusionary conduct lacks a plausible business justification. Courts also should eliminate the safe harbor for above-cost pricing, decline to presume that vertical integration is procompetitive, and consider seriously a broad range of exclusionary mechanisms.

Courts should adopt several presumptions with respect to innovation competition (Chapter 8): that the merger of innovation rivals will harm competition when only a handful of firms participate in an innovation market; that innovation competition would be harmed when a dominant firm in an innovative sector acquires a firm whose capabilities make it a threat to compete in future products, even if the firms do not presently compete; and that competition in innovation or future products is harmed when a dominant firm excludes all its actual and potential innovation rivals, other than insignificant competitors, or excludes any rival from an innovation market in which only a handful of firms participate.

Last, to preserve antitrust law's ability to deter harms to suppliers, as discussed in Chapter 9, courts should decline to undercut the long-standing prohibition on undertaking cross-market welfare trade-offs outside of occasional situations where the competitive benefits are greatly disproportionate to the competitive harms.

CONCLUSION

Three quarters of a century ago, the U.S. adopted antitrust enforcement as the best response to large-firm market power. Leading alternatives—on the one hand, laissez-faire notions of business self-regulation; on the other, regulation or deconcentration—were rejected in favor of fostering competition. And for good reason: competition leads firms to pursue new and better goods and services and to find cheaper ways of providing them.

Yet market power has returned, notwithstanding our extensive antitrust institutions. Market power harms buyers and suppliers, consumers and workers. It has accumulated to the point where it may be impeding growth economy-wide. Once again, the best answer is antitrust. But today's antitrust rules do not appropriately balance error costs and must be reworked to enhance deterrence.

Revising the status quo will be not be easy, because a changing economy adds complications and because the Supreme Court continues to hold on to Chicago school views that have proven inadequate. The Chicagoans succeeded in making economics the center of antitrust analysis, which is all to the good. But their goal of securing business dynamism has been thwarted. Maintaining the Court's posture will, over time, lead to the stealth rejection of antitrust enforcement, with laissez-faire policies and greater exercise of market power filling the vacuum.

In response, citizens concerned with ensuring business competition must increase awareness of the market-power problem and mobilize politically against it. Antitrust enforcers must push the courts to question the Chicago school approach. Plaintiffs must be strategic in bringing cases to lower courts willing to reject that approach. And scholars must press the courts to recognize that modern economics demonstrates the welfare benefits of stronger antitrust enforcement. By pushing back on all fronts, we can hope to renew the antitrust paradigm and restore a competitive economy.

Notes

Introduction

1. Bork 1978; Posner 1976.
2. The Chicago school of antitrust was an influential intellectual movement led by lawyers and economists loosely associated with the University of Chicago. Posner 1979.
3. Bork 1978, 7, 408.
4. Daniel Marans, "Elizabeth Warren Has a Real Plan to Drain the Swamp in Washington," *Huffington Post,* May 16, 2017.
5. Council of Economic Advisers 2016b.
6. Timothy B. Lee, "Hillary Clinton Just Took a Step toward Elizabeth Warren's View on Monopolies," *Vox,* October 4, 2016, https://www.vox.com /new-money/2016/10/4/13156432/hillary-clinton-antitrust-agenda; Kevin Drum, "Here's Hillary Clinton on Antitrust and Entrepreneurism," *Mother Jones,* October 4, 2016, http://www.motherjones.com/kevin-drum/2016/10 /heres-hillary-clinton-antitrust-and-entrepreneurism/.
7. Brian Fung, "Why Trump Might Not Block the AT&T-Time Warner Merger, After All," *Washington Post,* November 11, 2016; David Goldman, "Donald Trump's War on Jeff Bezos, Amazon and the Washington Post," *CNNTech,* May 13, 2016, http://money.cnn.com/2016/05/13/technology /donald-trump-jeff-bezos-amazon/.
8. David McLaughlin and Todd Shields, "Trump's Talks With Dealmaking CEOs Rattle Antitrust Lawyers," *Bloomberg,* January 13, 2017; Chris Sagers, "Buyer Beware," *Slate,* January 13, 2017.
9. Foer 2017; Taplin 2017. See also David Dayen, "Big Tech: The New Predatory Capitalism," *American Prospect,* December 26, 2017.
10. See the discussion of "The Rise of Dominant Information Technology Platforms" in Chapter 1.

1. Market Power in an Era of Antitrust

1. Complaint at 10, United States v. Anheuser-Busch InBEV SA/NV, No. 1:16-cv-01483 (D.D.C. July 20, 2016).
2. Miller and Weinberg 2017.
3. See Complaint at 12–13, United States v. Anheuser-Busch InBEV SA/NV, No. 1:16-cv-01483 (D.D.C. July 20, 2016). In 2015, the 21 largest breweries amounted to 0.4 percent of all U.S. breweries, while accounting for 84 percent of beer brewed. "Industry Facts," National Beer Wholesalers Association, https://www.nbwa.org/resources/industry-fast-facts.
4. Crane 2011, 31 (figure 2.1), 85 (figure 4.3).
5. Archers-Daniels-Midland (ADM) also paid hundreds of millions of dollars to settle private class action cases from victimized lysine buyers and antitrust complaints brought by foreign governments. United States v. Andreas, 2216 F.3d 645 (7th Cir. 2000). Senior ADM executives were prosecuted too and served prison sentences. See also Eichenwald 2001; Lieber 2000; Connor 2007.
6. United States v. Microsoft Corp., 253 F.3d 34 (D.C. Cir. 2001). Several books have been written about the case. Gavil and First 2014; Page and Lopatka 2007; Auletta 2001; Heilemann 2001; Brinkley and Lohr 2000.
7. For the most part, the Microsoft case was concerned with harm to operating system competition. But the government's complaint also included a claim that could be interpreted as concerned with browser competition: it charged that Microsoft had unlawfully tied its Internet Explorer web browser with its Windows operating system. The district court found Microsoft's tying conduct illegal per se, but the appeals court held that the claim should have been evaluated under the rule of reason. On remand, the government chose not to pursue it further.
8. Bresnahan 2010; Steven Pearlstein, "Is Amazon Getting Too Big?" *Washington Post,* July 28, 2017.
9. See Complaint, United States v. AT&T Inc., No. 1:11-cv-01560 (D.D.C. Aug. 31, 2011); Staff Analysis and Findings, Applications of AT&T Inc. and Deutsche Telekom AG for Consent to Assign or Transfer Control of Licenses and Authorizations, FCC WT Docket No. 11–65 (Nov. 29, 2011), http://hraunfoss.fcc.gov/edocs_public/attachmatch/DA-11-1955A2.pdf. See generally Bliss 2016; Andrew Ross Sorkin et al. 2011, "AT&T to Buy T-Mobile USA for $39 Billion," *New York Times,* March 20, 2011; Jenna Wortham, "For Consumers, Little to Cheer in AT&T Deal," *New York Times,* March 21, 2011; Ben Protess, "AT&T Deal Joins a History of Antitrust Fights," *New York Times,* March 21, 2011; Edward Wyatt and Jenna Wortham, "AT&T Merger with T-Mobile Faces Setbacks," *New York Times,* November 24, 2011; Michael de la Merced, "AT&T Ends $39 Billion Bid for T-Mobile," *New York Times,* December 19, 2011.
10. Six years later, the leading wireless providers continued to improve their networks, and price competition among them was a front-page story. Ryan

Knutson, "Era of Costly Cell Service is Ending," *Wall Street Journal,*
June 24, 2017, A1; see Jon Gold, "5G Wireless Behind AT&T, Verizon's
Big Buys," *Network World,* April 14, 2017, http://www.networkworld.com
/article/3190040/mobile-wireless/5g-wireless-behind-atandt-verizon-s-big
-buys.html; Jacob Kastrenakes, "T-Mobile just spent nearly $8 billion to
finally put its network on par with Verizon and AT&T," *The Verge,* April 13,
2017, https://www.theverge.com/2017/4/13/15291496/tmobile-fcc-incentive
-auction-results-8-billion-airwaves-lte; Jeff Hawn, "In-Depth: State of 5G
for the Big Four Carriers," *RCR Wireless News,* November 29, 2015,
http://www.rcrwireless.com/20151129/carriers/5g-efforts-for-the-big-four
-carriers-tag15.
11. Crane 2011, 53 (figure 3.1), 55 (figure 3.2).
12. Kovacic 2003, 477; Timothy Muris, Chairman, Fed. Trade Comm,
"Antitrust Enforcement at the Federal Trade Commission: In a Word—
Continuity" (speech), Remarks at the American Bar Association Antitrust
Section Annual Meeting, August 7, 2001, http://www.ftc.gov/speeches
/muris/murisaba.shtm.
13. Competition and Markets Authority 2017.
14. Beyond the examples referenced in this paragraph, two other examples of lax
enforcement, more limited in industry scope, further illustrate the exercise
market power in the absence of antitrust constraints. First, the United States
has permitted export cartels for a century. A study of these found many
examples of long-lived export agreements motivated by price fixing, as well
as examples of cartels undermined by price wars and fringe competition.
Dick 1996. Second, airline mergers were subject to an unusually permissive
enforcement regime during part of the 1980s, when they were reviewed by
the Department of Transportation (DOT). Retrospective studies of two
large acquisitions involving carriers with substantially overlapping route
networks during that period, which the DOT allowed to proceed over the
opposition of the antitrust enforcers at the Justice Department, found higher
fares and a reduction in flight frequencies (a reduction in quality of service).
See Peters 2003. Some of these studies suggest that fares fell in city pairs
where the merging firms had not previously competed, but these are markets
where antitrust enforcers would probably not have identified competitive
problems. The Justice Department's opposition to these transactions is a
strong signal of their competitive problems because federal antitrust
enforcement was relatively relaxed during the second term of the Reagan
administration.
15. The loophole was created by the Supreme Court's decision in United States
v. E.C. Knight Co., 156 U.S. 1 (1895), which allowed mergers to create a
monopoly in sugar refining on the ground that the Sherman Act's prohibitions on restraints or monopolization of "commerce" concerned the disposition
of manufactured goods, not the prior manufacturing step. The Court closed
the loophole nine years later. Northern Securities Co. v. United States, 193
U.S. 197 (1904); see also Addyston Pipe & Steel Co. v. United States, 175

U.S. 211 (1899). A wave of manufacturing mergers occurred after the Supreme Court's decision in *E.C. Knight*. Lamoreaux 1985.

16. Scherer 1996 (steel); Levenstein 1996 (bromine), 1997 (bromine); Ellison 1994 (railroads); Porter 1993 (railroads); Hudson 1890 (railroads); Granitz and Klein 1996 (petroleum refining and Standard Oil); Burns 1986 (American Tobacco).

17. Pub. L. No. 73–67, 48 Stat. 195 (1933). At about the same time as the passage of the National Industrial Recovery Act, the U.S. Supreme Court held that under the emergency conditions of the Great Depression a large group of distressed coal producers could form an exclusive, joint selling agent (effectively, a cartel), notwithstanding the antitrust laws. Appalachian Coals, Inc. v. United States, 288 U.S. 344 (1933). The Court repudiated this lax attitude toward price fixing in 1940. United States v. Socony-Vacuum Oil Co., 310 U.S. 150 (1940).

18. See generally Brand 1988; Irons 1982; Hawley 1966; Lyon et al. 1935.

19. Alexander 1997; McGahan 1995; Baker 1989. But other attempts at collusion were unsuccessful. Alexander 1994.

20. The antitrust laws prohibit conduct that allows firms to obtain, maintain, or enhance market power. In the United States, the mere exercise of market power, as with firms that set prices above competitive levels without engaging in anticompetitive conduct, is policed by regulatory agencies, not by courts enforcing the antitrust laws.

21. If entry is easy and price discrimination is feasible, then firms can exercise market power with respect to some customers without elevating their average prices above competitive (free entry) levels, and thus without harming competition overall. See Baker 2003b, 651.

22. In evaluating monopolization claims under Sherman Act § 2, courts use the term "monopoly power" to mean substantial market power, commonly inferred from a high market share.

23. Evidence on labor market monopsony power is surveyed briefly below in the section on "Oligopolies Are Common and Concentration Is Increasing in Many Industries."

24. See, e.g., Antitrust Division, "Criminal Enforcement Trends Charts," U.S. Dept. of Justice, 2018, https://www.justice.gov/atr/criminal -enforcement-fine-and-jail-charts; compare Ghosal and Sokol 2018. Cartel activity includes many large firms. Sertsios et al. 2016; Marshall 2017.

25. Connor and Lande 2012. Connor and Lande may overstate the extent to which private damages deter collusive behavior if, in some cases, cartels anticipate that they will be required to pay antitrust damages in the future. Under such circumstances, the firms may pass through the expected damages payment to buyers in advance, in the form of even higher prices. The frequency of serial collusion by large multi-product firms reinforces the concern that penalties are too low. Kovacic et al. 2018.

26. It once appeared possible that the 1990s cartel cases would turn out to be a one-time spike related to improved cartel detection, and the rate at which price-fixing and market division conspiracies were uncovered would decline as deterrence increased. Baker 2001, 825. But there is no indication that the overall rate of cartel enforcement has declined since the 1990s in the way this story would imply.

27. See Connor and Lande 2012, 468, 477n250.

28. Levenstein and Suslow 2011. Harrington and Wei (2017) found that the average cartel discovered by the Justice Department lasted 5.8 years and Hyytinen et al. (forthcoming) found that when cartels were legal in Finland, the average cartel lasted 8.5 years.

29. Annually, $75/21 = 3.6$ cartels are detected, and $8.1*75/21 = 28.9$ cartels are active. This calculation assumes no net effect from sample censoring (overcharges from before the sample period that were included, and overcharges from cartels that were sanctioned after the sample period that were excluded). The calculation is conservative because the sample excluded some cartels for which data was not available. The assumption that cartels are formed at a stable rate ignores the potential deterrent effect of changing enforcement techniques such as modifications to the leniency program. The inference that 12 percent of 29 active cartels are detected annually is roughly consistent with the results of a 1991 study of the distribution of the duration of cartels challenged by the Justice Department, which concluded that at least thirty-six to fifty cartels are active at any time, and that at most 13 percent to 17 percent are detected annually. Bryant and Eckard 1991. A more recent study found that a cartel has a 19 percent chance annually of either collapsing or being discovered. Harrington and Wei 2017.

30. Miller and Weinberg 2017.

31. Blonigen and Pierce 2016. The study reports estimates of the average percentage increase in the price-cost margin resulting from merger, but those estimates are imprecise because of uncertainty in measuring the increase in margins and the mean premerger margin. The study adopts several strategies to control for bias from the possibility that firms systematically acquired plants because they expected those plants to improve productivity or exercise market power, but it is hard to evaluate the success of those approaches. It does not control for the possibility that higher prices reflect improved product quality. (Methodological issues discussed below with respect to De Loecker and Eeckhout 2017 may also arise here, as the two studies employ similar empirical methods.)

32. Kulick 2017.

33. Ashenfelter and Hosken 2010; Kwoka 2015. For a critique and response to Kwoka's meta-analysis, see Vita and Osinski 2018; Kwoka 2017a, 8–12.

34. The event study evidence shows this, but the accounting evidence is mixed. Kaplow and Shapiro 2007, 1154–1155; Röller et al. 2006, chap. 3 § 2.1.3; Moeller et al. 2006, 759; Quantamental Research Group, "Mergers &

Acquisitions: The Good, the Bad, and the Ugly (And How to Tell Them Apart)," *S&P Global,* August 26, 2016, 3, https://www.spglobal.com/our -insights/Mergers—Acquisitions-The-Good-The-Bad-And-The-Ugly-And -How-To-Tell-Them-Apart.html; compare Malmendier Forthcoming.

35. Knee et al. 2009, 205. The deals reviewed included both horizontal and nonhorizontal acquisitions.
36. Baker 2013b, 539–543.
37. Agreements between firms that sell complementary products, like peanut butter and jelly, would also be vertical.
38. See generally Baker 2002b, 66–67.
39. Baker 2002a, 67.
40. Looking to the outcome, reasoning, and tone of judicial decisions since that time, the Supreme Court and the appellate courts have applied the more relaxed approach to address exclusionary conduct without consistently favoring either defendants or plaintiffs. Baker 2013b, 536–537.
41. Ginsburg 1991a.
42. A manufacturer or supplier engages in resale price maintenance when it specifies the price at which its product can be resold downstream by an independent dealer.
43. MacKay and Smith 2014.
44. Levenstein and Suslow 2014.
45. Levenstein and Suslow 2011, 463. See Harrington and Wei 2017; Hyytinen et al. Forthcoming. Measures of average duration have been found not to be biased markedly by the possibility that the distribution of discovered cartels may differ from the distribution of undiscovered cartels. Harrington and Wei 2017.
46. Levenstein and Suslow 2006, 53 (table 2).
47. Blume and Keim 2014, 5; see The Conference Board 2010, 22 (table 10) and 27 (table 13).
48. See Jan Fichtner et al. 2017.
49. Azar et al. 2016, 2018a. See generally Schmalz 2018. Common financial-investor ownership may also discourage competition between branded and generic drug manufacturers. Xie and Gerakos 2018; Newham et al. 2018.
50. In addition to the issues raised in the text, the identification strategies the studies employ to address the possible endogeneity of common ownership are sensible but may be questioned. Compare Gramlich and Grundl 2017. For other critiques, see, e.g., Hemphill and Kahan 2018; O'Brien and Waehrer 2017; Patel 2018.
51. When firms throughout the economy are ranked in terms of financial market capitalization (enterprise value)—a measure of firm size and expected future profitability—the top four are Apple, Alphabet, Microsoft, and Amazon; Facebook is sixth. Dogs of the Dow, "Largest Companies by Market Cap," April 8, 2017, http://dogsofthedow.com/largest-companies-by -market-cap.htm.

52. See Bresnahan and Greenstein 1999.
53. Kurz 2017.
54. Kurz 2017, § 1.1e (table 2).
55. De Loecker and Eeckhout 2017.
56. This comparison identifies firm markups conditional on the assumption that firms are minimizing their costs. To determine output elasticities of supply, De Loecker and Eeckhout estimate production functions. They use accounting data on cost of goods sold as a proxy for variable costs.
57. De Loecker and Eeckhout 2017, § 3.2 and table 1.
58. In addition, the reliability of the proxies the study employs to measure variable expenditures, and their decomposition into input quantities and prices, may be questioned. First, the proxies do not account for differences between accounting and economic concepts of marginal or variable costs. Second, in rapidly innovating industries, it may be appropriate to view expenditures on developing new and better products as variable costs, while De Loecker and Eeckhout treat them as fixed. Information technology expenditures are treated as fixed without considering, for example, how firms compete through incremental investments in content distribution networks (to deliver information services more quickly and reliably), or improved targeting of advertising by mining customer data. Hence their measure could overstate the decline in the fraction of sales revenues accounted for by variable costs of production, and their study may overstate the increase in estimated markups. Traina 2018. Third, the proxies do not account for the marginal costs firms bear when they adjust to new technologies. These costs may include expenses for worker retraining and the costs firms learn to avoid as they gain experience with new technologies. Firms' costs of adjusting to productivity shocks have increased markedly since the 1990s. Decker et al. 2018. As a result, an increase in estimated markups could in part actually reflect higher marginal adjustment costs. I am indebted to Dennis Carlton for a helpful discussion of these issues.
59. The data are for 2-, 3-, and 4-digit NAICS industries. Even the four-digit industries are broader than the product markets commonly defined in antitrust litigation. Werden 1988; Werden and Froeb 2018. In industries with local and regional markets, the data also aggregate across those regions.
60. This approach is at odds with the way empirical industrial organization economists have approached the estimation of market power since the 1980s, because it suppresses the idiosyncratic aspects of individual industries that affect firm conduct. See generally Bresnahan 1989. Here, aggregation across heterogeneous firms may introduce errors into the estimates of the output elasticity of industry supply. The direction of the bias will depend in part on whether the firms that invest the most in information technology (and hence experience the largest reduction in the fraction of sales revenues accounted for by cost of goods sold) have experienced the greatest or the

least increase in the responsiveness of output to changes in variable inputs such as labor.

61. Eggertsson et al. 2018, 26. A.21 (figures 6 and A.5); Hall 2018. See Díez et. al. 2018.

62. Traina 2018.

63. De Loecker and Eeckhout interpret the sharp increase in margins as an increase in the exercise of market power rather than what would happen to margins in competitive markets (a zero-profit equilibrium) when fixed costs increase and marginal costs fall. They accept this interpretation because expected profits rose: the sharp increase in margins took place at the same time that the average level of firm dividends and financial market capitalization (viewed as a discounted stream of future dividends) increased. Other reasons to reject an alternative explanation for higher margins are set forth later in this chapter. De Loecker and Eeckhout do not connect greater market power with increased IT investments.

64. See also Kurz 2017; Bessen 2017.

65. Cutler and Morton 2013; Gaynor and Town 2012; Dafny et al. 2016. The economic evidence on market concentration in the health-care industry, including hospitals, health insurers, and physician services, is surveyed in Martin Gaynor, "Examining the Impact of Health Care Consolidation," Statement before the Committee on Energy and Commerce Oversight and Investigations Subcommittee, U.S. House of Representatives, February 14, 2018.

66. Kevin Drum, "Oh Yes, American Industries Are Much More Concentrated than They Used to Be," *Mother Jones*, August 23, 2017, http://www.motherjones .com/kevin-drum/2017/08/oh-yes-american-industries-are-much-more -concentrated-than-they-used-to-be/. For other examples of market power in industries that have grown more concentrated see Miller and Weinberg 2017 (brewing), Cosman and Quintero 2018 (local residential construction), and the discussion of airline mergers in Chapter 6. Other industries have become less concentrated over time, however, or, to similar effect, some once-narrow markets may have broadened and, in consequence, now include more partici-pants. E.g., "Statement of the Federal Trade Commission Concerning the Proposed Merger of Office Depot, Inc. and OfficeMax, Inc., No. 131–0104," press release, November 1, 2013, https://www.ftc.gov/news-events/press -releases/2013/11/ftc-closes-seven-month-investigation-proposed-office. Compare *The Economist*, "Invasion of the Bottle Snatchers: Smaller Rivals Are Assaulting the World's Biggest Brands," July 9, 2016. Substantial horizontal merger activity, which increases concentration, occurs among firms below the size thresholds for premerger notification. Wollmann 2018.

67. Peltzman 2014; Ganapati 2017; "Corporate Concentration," *The Economist*, March 24, 2016; Autor et al. 2017.

68. In some industries, expansion by large firms may simultaneously increase national concentration and reduce local concentration. Rossi-Hansberg et al.

2018. The significance of those trends for inferences about market power turns on whether local regions are appropriate geographic markets for evaluating competition in those industries.

69. White and Yang 2017; Theo Francis and Ryan Knutson, "Wave of Mega-deals Tests Antitrust Limits in U.S," *Wall Street Journal,* October 18, 2015; Grullon 2016, figures 2-B, 2-C, and 2-D; but see Keil 2016, table 3.

70. Kreps and Scheinkman 1983. Competition is also dampened without repeated interaction in the Markov perfect equilibrium of a model with adjustment costs. Maskin and Tirole 1987, 956.

71. Greenwald and Kahn 2005, 230–232, 293–321; McAfee 2002, 11–16, 69–70, 138–146, 342–344, 379–380; Porter 1980, 93–95, 106.

72. Schmalensee 1989 (Stylized Fact 5.1); Bresnahan and Suslow 1989 (aluminum); Evans et al. 1993 (airlines); Singh and Zhu 2008 (auto-rental industry). Studies relating price to market concentration (or a firm's market share) typically face two important econometric challenges: addressing the possible endogeneity of concentration, and giving the relationship a causal interpretation. If the parameters of a demand function can be estimated separately, and the equation relating price to concentration is understood as a supply relation generated from a first-order condition, then excluded demand-shift variables may be available as instruments for addressing endogeneity in the supply relation. Even then, the estimated effect of concentration will commonly mix conduct and cost parameters. In economic terms, when higher prices arise in response to an increase in demand, and those higher prices are associated with greater concentration, the concentration effect on price could reflect a mix of higher costs and softened competition. To distinguish these interpretations and identify the causal effect of concentration on conduct, it would be necessary to estimate cost parameters separately. If the equation finding a positive relationship between price (or price-cost margins) and concentration is understood instead as a reduced form, it is hard to give the estimated relationship a causal interpretation without at least informally addressing alternative possibilities such as these: (a) a firm's lower costs gives it a greater share, increasing market concentration, while simultaneously leading that firm and the industry on average to charge higher prices relative to cost, even in a competitive market; or (b) a shift in demand to favor a particular firm in a differentiated product industry gives it a greater share, increasing market concentration, and, with rising marginal cost, simultaneously leads the firm and the industry on average to raise price, even in a competitive market. Doing so may be challenging because a reduced form equation does not have excluded exogenous variables to use as instruments. Empirical methods of identifying market power are discussed in Bresnahan 1989 and Baker and Bresnahan 1992.

73. It will often be appropriate to define "product" markets (here, labor markets) as limited to narrow job categories and geographic markets as limited to metropolitan areas. Those markets will tend to be narrow in job categories

where workers have developed skills tied to their employment function, so they are reluctant to switch job categories and are limited to what may be a handful of potential employers that value those skills. Labor markets will also be limited geographically when workers develop roots in a community or find it costly to search at a distance for better jobs. See Naidu et al. 2018. Market definition in cases alleging that firms exercise market power over their workers turns on the willingness of those workers to substitute to other occupations in response to a small reduction in the wage, analogous to the way market definition in cases alleging product market harms turns on the willingness of buyers to substitute other products in response to a small price increase.

74. Azar et al. 2017; Benmelech et al. 2018; Azar et al. 2018b; Council of Economic Advisers 2016a. See also Dube et al. 2018, but compare Bivens et al. 2018.

75. Azar et al. 2017; Benmelech et al. 2018. These studies relate the wage to a measure of market concentration, and therefore create similar econometric challenges as arise in studies relating price to concentration. For example, suppose wages are found to decline in response to an exogenous increase in concentration. Attributing that decline to greater employer market power would require ruling out, for example, the possibility that an increase in the size of the largest firms generated both higher concentration and reductions in the marginal revenue product of labor. See also Council of Economic Advisers 2016a; Webber 2015; Ashenfelter et al. 2010.

76. Edlin and Haw 2014; Kleiner and Krueger 2013. But compare Vaheesan and Pasquale Forthcoming.

77. Masur 2011. See Federal Trade Commission 2003; Jaffe and Lerner 2004, 34–35, 115–119. On the more recent response by Congress and the courts to concerns about patent scope and validity, see Anderson 2014a, 2014b.

78. Federal Trade Commission 2010.

79. Fed. Trade Comm'n v. Activis, Inc., 133 S. Ct. 2223 (2013). See Federal Trade Commission, Bureau of Competition 2017.

80. Groll and Ellis 2016, 1; de Figueiredo 2004; Bessen 2016.

81. Feldman et al. 2017, 104; see Feldman et al. 2018; Carrier and Minniti 2016 326 (table 1).

82. Gutiérrez and Philippon 2017a, 2017b. See Fahri and Gourio 2018.

83. Barkai 2016; Eggertsson et al. 2018. See also Shapiro 2018, § 3.B; Dobbs et al. 2015. But see Karabarbounis and Neiman 2018. Economic forces other than growing market power that potentially have contributed to the decline in the labor share of GDP are surveyed in Autor et al. 2017; Caballero 2017, n2 and accompanying text.

84. Decker et al. 2017. See also Decker et al. 2018, figure 10; 2016.

85. Decker et al. 2016; Hathaway and Litan 2014, 1, figure 1. See Guzma and Stern 2016.

86. Furman and Orszag 2015, 10 (figures 8 and 9).

87. Compare Jason Furman, Chairman, Council of Economic Advisers, "Beyond Antitrust: The Role of Competition Policy in Promoting Inclusive Growth," September 16, 2016, https://obamawhitehouse.archives.gov/sites /default/files/page/files/20160916_searle_conference_competition_furman _cea.pdf. On the other hand, De Loecker and Eeckhout find that after correcting aggregate productivity measurements for increased price-cost margins, productivity growth has not slowed since 1980. De Loecker and Eeckhout 2017 (Implication 7).

88. Incumbent firms increasingly account for productivity improvements relative to entrants and other rivals. Garcia-Macia et al. 2016.

89. See Walter Frick, "The Real Reason Superstar Firms Are Pulling Ahead," *Harvard Business Review,* October 5, 2017, https://hbr.org/2017/10/the-real -reason-superstar-firms-are-pulling-ahead; Bessen 2017; Andrew McAfee and Erik Brynjolfsson, "Investing in the IT That Makes a Competitive Difference," *Harvard Business Review,* July–August 2008, https://hbr.org /2008/07/investing-in-the-it-that-makes-a-competitive-difference. In some cases, information technology may instead reduce the fixed investments necessary to compete, as may happen if a startup Internet application substitutes cloud computing for the purchase of a server.

90. If a market is dynamically competitive, the rents required to induce the investment would not raise the long run expected return to capital, adjusted for risk, however.

91. David 1990. Electricity, like computers and the Internet, is a "general purpose technology" because it offers wide scope for technological improvement across a broad range of uses. The full effect of general purpose technologies on economic activity is not realized until waves of complementary innovations, organizational changes, and new skills are developed. Brynjolfsson et al. 2017.

92. Mark Muro et al., *Digitalization and the American Workforce,* Washington, D.C.: Brookings Institution, Metropolitan Policy Program, November 2017, 17, https://www.brookings.edu/wp-content/uploads/2017/11/mpp _2017nov15_digitalization_full_report.pdf.

93. When the new technologies potentially available to an industry are not developed all at once, the first movers in early rounds may or may not also be the first movers in later rounds. Laggards may even surpass current leaders through "leapfrog" innovation in product or processes based in part on technological improvements. If some firms are good at innovating, though, they could end up as successive leaders. See Autor et al. 2017. Persistent technological leadership could instead reflect the exercise of market power. Carlton and Waldman 2002.

94. In this story, information technology investments play the role that John Sutton attributes to advertising and R&D generally in his books on endogenous sunk costs. Sutton 1991, 1998. See generally Bresnahan 1992.

95. Shapiro 2018, §§ 3.A.3, 3.B. See Crouzet and Eberly 2018.

96. The competitive price would equal industry marginal cost properly understood as an efficient entrant's average cost, but incumbent firms would price above their own marginal costs.

97. When technological changes lead firms to make substantial sunk investments, the number of firms tends to shrink. See, e.g., Ellickson 2007. In consequence, competition tends to soften, allowing firms to exercise market power. One exception could involve markets in which demand is growing rapidly, perhaps stimulated by the new products made possible by successful R&D. Then the growth in demand could create a countervailing force that stimulates entry, and the number of firms may not shrink. Competition may also be softened by intellectual property protections for investments in intangible capital.

98. To similar effect, Jason Furman and Peter Orszag conclude that rising concentration and declining dynamism cannot be reconciled with slowing productivity growth. Furman and Orszag 2018, 10. See also Philippon 2018. For a defense of the benign interpretation, see Van Reenen 2018.

99. This conclusion does not, of course, mean that market power has grown in every market, nor that the benign alternative should never be credited as the primary explanation for changes in a market's structure and performance.

100. This is an implication of the well-known *Cellophane* fallacy (named after a Supreme Court case that failed to recognize this point). United States v. E. I. Du Pont De Nemours & Co., 351 U.S. 377 (1956) *(Cellophane)*.

101. See Rubinovitz 1993; Goolsbee and Petrin 2004; Crawford 2000.

102. Some authors addressed aspects of the contemporary market power problem earlier than that. E.g., Crawford 2013; Lynn 2010; Stiglitz 2012, 338; Zingales 2012. These works predate Piketty 2014, which has spawned a substantial literature on the connection between market power and inequality.

103. The long-standing debate about whether antitrust should aim to prevent wealth transfers or allocative efficiency losses is surveyed critically in Baker 2013a, 2176–2180.

104. Large buyers sometimes have the ability and incentive to undermine seller coordination, as by sponsoring entry, integrating upstream, or shifting purchases to sellers that discount. Large buyers that induce greater competition among sellers are not necessarily exercising buyer market power and do not necessarily prevent sellers from continuing to exercise market power against other buyers.

105. E.g., Final Order and Judgment as to VHS of Michigan, Inc., d/b/a/ Detroit Medical Center, Cason-Merenda v. VHS of Michigan, Inc., No. 06–15601 (E.D. Mich. January 27, 2016); Final Judgment, United States v. Arizona Hospital & Healthcare Ass'n, No. CV07-1030-PHX (September 12, 2007); Stephen Greenhouse, "Settlement in Nurses' Antitrust Suit," *New York Times*, March 9, 2009, A23.

106. Posner 1975b; Fisher 1985.

107. Slowed productivity growth and innovation are measured relative to what would be expected in a more competitive market. Thus, dominant firms with a strong record of innovation would likely have been more innovative had they faced greater competition. See, e.g., Baker 2016a, 453–454. The innovation harms from the exercise of market power may include discouraging both follow-on innovation and initial innovation. Compare Vickers 2010.

108. E.g., Mendonça 2013; Collard-Wexler and De Loecker 2015.

109. Holmes and Schmitz Jr. 2010; Bloom and Van Reenen 2010, 215; Lewis 2004. See Backus 2014, 1; Baker 2007a, 583–586; Shapiro 2012, 376–382.

110. See generally Baker 2007a. For the reasons given in this section, economic evidence generally favors the Arrovian side over the Schumpeterian position.

111. See Baker 2016a.

112. See Cohen 2010, 146–148, 154–155; Shapiro 2012, 380. In some studies, the technological opportunity problem is addressed by evaluating the innovation effects of competition within an industry over time. E.g., Zitzewitz 2003.

113. The modern Schumpeterian growth literature concludes that greater product-market competition fosters R&D investment by all firms in sectors where the firms operate at the same technological level and suggests that in the event that product markets were to grow more competitive, the innovation incentives of a dominant firm with a technological lead would remain high. This literature does not bear directly on the innovation consequences of greater antitrust enforcement against exclusionary conduct by dominant firms, however, because it models increased product market competition as arising from greater imitation (hence reduced appropriability for entrants) rather than as arising from increased contestability (hence increased appropriability for entrants). Shapiro 2012, 372–374.

114. Mankiw and Whinston 1986.

115. Mahoney et al. 2014. Market power can also limit the harmful consequences of adverse selection. Mahoney et al. 2014.

116. The economic literature has yet to measure successfully the magnitude with which increasing market power has contributed to the post-1970s slowdown in the rate of U.S. productivity growth or the rise in inequality relative to other causes. The likely timing of the productivity slowdown, the rise in inequality, and the growth of market power are not perfectly consistent, but none are measured well, so the timing is not decisive for evaluating whether they are related.

117. Lewis 2004.

118. Lewis 2004.

119. Michael E. Porter, "The Competitive Advantage of Nations," *Harvard Business Review*, March–April 1990, https://hbr.org/1990/03/the-competitive-advantage-of-nations.

120. Baumol 2002; Easterly 2001, chap. 9; Mokyr 2002; Parente and Prescott 2000; Rosenberg and Birdzell Jr. 1986; Shleifer and Vishny 1998.

121. Zingales 2012, 29; Acemoglu and Robinson 2012, 335–357.
122. Ennis et al. 2017; Ennis and Kim 2017, 133; Baker and Salop 2015.
123. Wolff 2014, 38 (table 7) (statistics for 2013).
124. Naidu et al. 2018.
125. Antitrust enforcement is not costless, and some steps taken to prevent anticompetitive conduct risk chilling beneficial conduct, so it is unreasonable to expect even the best antitrust institutions to deter market power completely. But it is unlikely that the market power now exercised is socially efficient. Baker 2003a, 42–45.

2. The Faltering Political Consensus Supporting Antitrust

1. Kutler 1971; Charles River Bridge v. Warren Bridge, 36 U.S. 420 (1837).
2. At the time, corporations were chartered individually by state legislatures for specified and limited purposes.
3. *Charles River Bridge,* 36 U.S. at 608.
4. McClellan 1971, 194–237.
5. *Charles River Bridge,* 36 U.S. at 552–553. This possibility was not, technically, at issue in the case itself. The Warren Bridge was not a railroad bridge. But Taney knew that turnpike owners were not building the railroads; the railroads were sponsored by new investors.
6. DeLong 2000, § B.1.
7. DeLong 2000, § A.4. Absent taxes, transfers, and Coasian bargaining, the pure pursuit of efficiencies leads to economic policies that strongly favor the wealthy. Liscow 2018, § V.
8. Baker 2013b, 559–562.
9. United States v. Aluminum Co. of America, 148 F.2d 416, 427 (2d Cir. 1945) *(Alcoa).*
10. Verizon Commc'ns Inc. v. Law Office of Curtis V. Trinko, LLP, 540 U.S. 398, 407 (2004) (dictum). As with the defendant in *Charles River Bridge,* the defendant in *Trinko* had been granted a government franchise, then subjected to competition by later government action. *Trinko*'s significance is discussed further in Chapter 10.
11. Hamilton 1824.
12. Barry C. Lynn and Phillip Longman, "Populism with a Brain," *Washington Monthly,* June / July / August 2016.
13. United States v. Topco Assocs., Inc., 405 U.S. 596, 610 (1972); N. Pac. Ry. Co. v. United States, 356 U.S. 1, 4 (1958). See also United States v. Socony-Vacuum Oil Co., 310 U.S. 150, 221 (1940); Appalachian Coals, Inc. v. United States, 288 U.S. 344, 359 (1933); *Trinko,* 540 U.S. at 415.
14. Nat'l Soc'y of Prof. Eng'rs v. United States, 435 U.S. 679, 695 (1978) (quoting *Standard Oil Co. v. FTC,* 340 U.S. 231, 248 [1951]).
15. See Chapter 1's section on "An Era of Antitrust."
16. Granitz and Klein 1996; May 2007.

17. Tarbell turned her influential magazine articles into a book. Tarbell 1904.
18. See Kearns Goodwin 2013, 440–445.
19. Standard Oil Co. v. United States, 221 U.S. 1 (1911).
20. *Standard Oil,* 221 U.S. at 83. The opinion of the Court makes a similar point less graphically. *Standard Oil,* 221 U.S. at 50. See also Lande 1982, 93–95, 99. The Sherman Act was understood by the courts at the time of enactment, during the *Lochner* era of constitutional interpretation, less tendentiously: as protecting natural rights to economic liberty, security of property, and the process of free and competitive exchange from artificial interference by private actors. May 1989. Compare Meese 2012.
21. Sanders 1999; Boudreaux et al. 1995.
22. See Hofstadter 1954; Weibe 1967, 45–46, 52–53.
23. Chace 2004, 7–8. See also Kolasky 2011a; Hawley 1966, 7–9; Sanders 1999, 280–282.
24. Kovacic 1989, 1129–1130. When Theodore Roosevelt served as president during the first decade of the twentieth century, his administration brought a number of high-profile antitrust cases against trusts, including the Standard Oil case. Although Roosevelt earned fairly his reputation as a trustbuster, his litigation program was rooted more in a desire to assert the power of government over big business than in a commitment to antitrust. See Wiebe 1959, 55; Winerman 2003, 17; Kolasky 2011b. In the 1912 campaign, Roosevelt attacked the Sherman Act as antiquated. Winerman 2003, 23.
25. Kovacic 1989, 1131. Wilson also questioned the administrative feasibility of industrial planning and expressed concern about regulatory capture. Kovacic 1989, 1130.
26. Hawley 1966, 49n7; Kolasky 2011a, 86.
27. Kolasky 2011a, 86; Chace 2004, 194–196; Kovacic 1989, 1130–1132. Notwithstanding Brandies' influence, Wilson may have hoped to address the trusts without dissolving them. Winerman 2003, 43–45.
28. Eugene V. Debs, "Capitalism and Socialism" (campaign speech), Lyceum Theatre, Fergus Falls, MN, August 27, 2012, https://www.marxists.org /archive/debs/works/1912/1912-capsoc.htm.
29. The Republican party, the party of business-friendly William McKinley, was the more natural home for business interests than the Democratic party, the party of McKinley's 1896 opponent, William Jennings Bryan. Sixteen years later, the Republicans had developed a cleavage between progressives, who preferred Roosevelt, and conservatives, who favored Taft. Winerman 2003, 22. Some progressives saw Taft's support for Sherman Act enforce- ment under the rule of reason as "an attempt to emasculate the statute in the interests of the trusts." Winerman 2003, 27 (quoting "Taft Will Enforce Law to the Letter," *New York Times,* October 28, 1911). But see Wiebe 1959, 58. To the extent business leaders expected that Roosevelt's program would evolve into business self-regulation, however, that approach would have

appealed to them more than Taft's antitrust approach. Compare Hawley 1966, 8–9.

30. Kolasky 2011a, 85.
31. Winerman 2003. Compare Eskridge Jr. and Ferejohn 2010, 135.
32. Hawley 1966.
33. In the long run, from the perspective of the economy as a whole, efficiencies are closely related to economic growth. Put more technically, this discussion equates long run "efficiencies" with potential Pareto improvements or, more loosely, increments to aggregate social surplus (i.e., aggregate willingness to pay for goods less their costs).
34. This discussion is focused on regulatory approaches to address the market power of large firms. Regulation may increase the total economic pie when used to address other market failures.
35. Baker 2006, 497–499.
36. Waller 2004; Wells 2002, 82; Kovacic 1982, 610; Eskridge Jr. and Ferejohn 2010, 137–138. Arnold's approach was foreshadowed by his predecessor, future Justice Robert H. Jackson. See Jackson 1937a, 1937b.
37. United States v. Socony-Vacuum Oil Co., 310 U.S. 150 (1940).
38. United States v. Aluminum Co. of Am., 148 F.2d 416 (2d. Cir. 1945) *(Alcoa)*.
39. Cellar-Kefauver amendments, Pub. L. No. 81–899, 64 Stat. 1125 (1950), to the Clayton Antitrust Act, 47 Pub. L. No. 63–212, 38 Stat. 730 (1914). See Brown Shoe Co. v. United States, 370 U.S. 294 (1962). See also Baker 2016b, 220–222.
40. Kovacic, 2003; Leary 2002.
41. Hofstadter 1964. Similarly, antitrust had first appeared in political party platforms in 1888 and was routinely endorsed every four years thereafter for a century. But it largely disappeared from those platforms after 1988, until it returned in the Democratic platform in 2016. William Page instead implicitly sees political passions as episodic: he describes antitrust law as oscillating since 1890 between two ideological visions of the market and the state. Page 2008.
42. Hovenkamp 2018c.
43. Baker 2010b.
44. Baker 2006, 495–498.
45. Compare Wilson 1980, 367.
46. Baker 2006, 487–489.
47. For examples of contemporary politicians seeking to organize a consumer interest group to oppose large firms exercising market power, see David Dayen, "Anti-Monopoly Candidates Are Testing a New Politics in the Midterms," *The Intercept*, October 1, 2017, https://theintercept.com/2017/10 /01/anti-monopoly-candidates-are-testing-a-new-politics-in-the-midterms/; Brian Beutler, "How Democrats Can Wage War on Monopolies—And Win," *New Republic*, September 16, 2017, https://newrepublic.com/article /144675/democrats-elizabeth-warren-can-wage-war-monopolies-and-win.

48. Baker 2006, 489–490. Compare Hacker and Pierson 2005.
49. Compare Hall and Thompson 2018.
50. There is no mechanism by which interest group politics necessarily or automatically leads to the adoption of institutions that enhance overall welfare. Baker 2006, 492–493. Compare North et al. 2009, 129–133, 230.
51. Antitrust was expressly understood and defended as a way to head off extensive governmental regulation. Jackson 1937a, 575, 576–577.
52. The adoption of a competition policy bargain did not lead to the immediate deregulation of those sectors of the economy that had been subject to ongoing regulatory supervision—transportation, financial services, electric power, and communications. But the deregulation movement that began during the 1980s followed its logic by narrowing regulation in these sectors to more closely mirror the scope of likely natural monopolies (where competition is not feasible). The competition policy bargain also did not affect the legitimacy of economic regulation intended to create competitive markets or address market failures such as externalities (like pollution), provision of public goods, natural monopoly, problems with markets arising from asymmetric information (such as moral hazard and adverse selection), or the high transactions costs of coordination and standard setting. Nor did it affect the legitimacy of social insurance.
53. If a substantial block of centrist voters accepts the political bargain, those voters can help maintain it politically. Compare Svolik 2017.
54. Baker 2006, 485–493, 524–530. An efficiency-enhancing competition policy bargain is possible in the underlying model if consumers and producers come to recognize that they interact politically in repeated play. The application of the Folk Theorem presumes either an infinitely repeated political interaction or, more plausibly in this context, a finitely repeated interaction with uncertain termination. Baker 2006, 524–530.
55. Chris Sagers attributes popular ambivalence toward market competition to the recognition that competition can be harmful to some market participants. Sagers 2019.
56. Social insurance has grown more extensive over time. In today's economy, it operates primarily through a combination of government-run insurance programs (including Social Security, Medicare, the Affordable Care Act, and unemployment insurance), direct governmental provision of services (including the welfare system and Head Start), and tax policy (including deductions for expenditures on childcare, education, and job training). The post–World War II moderation of business cycle fluctuations complemented the safety net before 2008, because a full employment economy makes it easier for workers who lose jobs to find new ones. Although owners of firms are also insulated from the vagaries of the market to some extent through the limited liability of corporate shareholders, the United States has not created a general safety net for producers. The corporate bailouts that took place during the most recent financial crisis were instead justified politically

as social insurance: aid to large automakers was intended to preserve high-paying manufacturing jobs and support for large banks was intended to prevent the severe economic depression that would result from a financial system collapse.

57. To similar effect, the literature on the political economy of international trade recognizes that political support for policies that increase social wealth while increasing risk of losses and dislocation to firms and their workers depends importantly on providing losers some form of social insurance protection. Rodrik 1998; Abdelal and Ruggie 2009.

58. If the political constraints fail, modifications to antitrust standards may undermine the bargain. Otherwise, modifications may implement it or improve it.

59. Baker 2010b.

60. Compare Baker 2006, 519–522.

61. Priest 2010, 4.

62. Priest 2010, 4.

63. Teles 2008, 101.

64. Teles 2008, 108.

65. See Phillips-Fein 2009, 156–160.

66. See Gavil 2002.

67. Three historical eras of antitrust interpretation are described in Baker 2002b.

68. See Posner 1976, 147–148; Telser 1960.

69. McGee 1958; Bork 1978, 144–155.

70. Compare Bork 1978, 429–440.

71. See the discussion of "Markets Self-Correct through Entry" in Chapter 5.

72. Bork defined a "naked" agreement as one that is not ancillary to cooperative productive activity engaged in by the firms and thus does nothing more than eliminate competition. Bork 1978, 263–264.

73. Bork 1978, 47–64, 406. See also Posner 1976, 933.

74. Bork 1978, 157, 406; Posner 1981.

75. Baker 2013b, 533–535.

76. Page 1995, 51, 70. See Kobayashi and Muris 2012, 153. For example, a rule that relied primarily on market concentration might continue to pay attention to that factor while raising the threshold of concern or allowing other factors like efficiencies and entry more readily to undermine the inference of harm to competition. Compare Landes and Posner 1980. On some occasions, the Court modified rules in small steps when the government had advocated larger ones. E.g., Monsanto v. Spray-Rite Service Corp., 465 U.S. 752, 761n7 (1984).

77. Cont'l T.V., Inc. v. GTE Sylvania Inc., 433 U.S. 36 (1977).

78. Brooke Grp. Ltd. v. Brown & Williamson Tobacco Corp., 509 U.S. 209 (1993); Matsushita Elec. Indus. Co., v. Zenith Radio Corp., 475 U.S. 574 (1986); Pac. Bell Tel. Co. v. linkLine Commc'ns, Inc., 555 U.S. 438 (2009).

79. Leegin Creative Leather Prods., Inc. v. PSKS, Inc., 551 U.S. 877 (2007) (overruling Dr. Miles Medical Co. v. John D. Park & Sons Co., 220 U.S. 373 (1911)). Although *Leegin* represented a doctrinal shift toward reduced antitrust enforcement overall, it expressly endorsed one basis for antitrust enforcement that the Court's prior resale price maintenance decisions did not: *Leegin* articulated and accepted exclusionary theories of anticompetitive effect in addition to collusive theories. *Leegin,* 551 U.S. at 893–894.

80. Brunswick Corp. v. Pueblo Bowl-O-Mat, Inc., 429 U.S. 477, 488 (1977) (antitrust injury doctrine); Matsushita Electric Industrial Co. v. Zenith Radio Corp., 475 U.S. 574 (1986) (standard for awarding summary judgment); Bell Atlantic Corp. v. Twombly, 550 U.S. 544 (2007) (standard for deciding motions to dismiss); Monsanto Co. v. Spray-Rite Service Corp., 465 U.S. 752 (1984) (standard for inferring that a manufacturer and its full-service dealers agreed on the resale price).

81. Broadcast Music, Inc. v. Columbia Broadcasting System, Inc., 441 U.S. 1 (1979).

82. McWane, Inc. v. FTC, 783 F.3d 814 (2015); Omega Envt'l, Inc. v. Gilbarco, Inc., 127 F.3d 1157 (9th Cir. 1997); U.S. Healthcare, Inc. v. Healthsource, Inc., 986 F.2d 589 (1st Cir. 1993). These courts interpreted Tampa Elec. Co. v. Nashville Coal Co., 365 U.S. 320 (1961), as allowing this approach.

83. United States v. Baker Hughes, Inc., 908 F.2d 981 (1990). See also Kovacic 2009, 143.

84. Compare United States v. Aluminum Co. of Am., 148 F.2d 416 (2d. Cir. 1945) *(Alcoa)* with E.I. du Pont de Nemours & Co., 96 F.T.C. 653 (1980).

85. See, e.g., McWane, Inc. v. FTC, 783 F.3d 814 (2015) (exclusive dealing); United States v. Dentsply Int'l, Inc., 399 F.3d 181 (3d Cir. 2005) (same); LePage's Inc. v. 3M, 324 F.3d 141 (3d Cir. 2003) (bundled discounts); United States v. Visa U.S.A., Inc., 344 F.3d 229 (2d Cir. 2003) (conduct tantamount to an exclusionary group boycott). See also Baker 2011, 36 (vertical merger enforcement).

86. See Chapter 3.

87. The debate took that form three decades ago as a dispute over antitrust's origins. Chicagoan Robert Bork read the legislative history to defend an aggregate surplus goal (which he termed, confusingly, a "consumer welfare" goal), while critic Robert Lande read it to defend a consumer surplus goal. Bork 1978, 56–66; Lande 1982, 1989. This argument over antitrust's origins foundered in part on the anachronism of interpreting the early understanding of the Sherman Act in terms of modern economic perspectives. The dispute over antitrust's origins is largely irrelevant to the goals of modern antitrust because the contemporary Supreme Court has accepted the Sherman Act's "dynamic potential." Bus. Elecs. Corp. v. Sharp Elecs. Corp., 485 U.S. 717, 732 (1988); Leegin Creative Leather Prods., Inc. v. PSKS, Inc., 551 U.S. 877, 888 (2007).

88. Baker 2013a, 2177–2179.
89. Mas-Colell et al. 1995, 332–333.
90. Mas-Colell et al. 1995, 332–333. For a nontechnical overview of economic concepts of cost see Gavil et al. 2017, 93–99.
91. Compare United States v. Anthem, Inc., 855 F.3d 345, 370 (D.C. Circuit 2017) (Millett, J., concurring).
92. Salop 2010, 339; Hovenkamp 2013; see Lopatka and Page 2002.
93. Bork 1978, 56–66.
94. The political economy argument for using an aggregate welfare standard was stronger during the late 1970s, when the Chicago school critics of structural era antitrust were writing.
95. Kovacic 2007. The Harvard school had a supporting role in the transformation of antitrust that began in the late 1970s, and not a co-leading role with the Chicago school. The Harvard school's focus on administrability could tie down the form that the rules take but not their substance. The Chicago school identified what antitrust rules should accomplish; the Harvard school helped determine how to implement them. Baker 2014, 4–6.
96. See Pitofsky 1987, 323–325. Other Chicago school critics also conceded this point. E.g., Sullivan et al. 2000, 7. Compare Kauper 2008, 42–44.
97. From the standpoint of political philosophy, noninterventionists focus on freedom from government control, while interventionists emphasize freedom from monopoly oppression. Compare Orbach 2017. Centrists see an open society with competing sources of wealth, status, and power as the best hope for aggregate prosperity, which antitrust pursues through a generalized efficiency goal, and for a reasonable distribution of the benefits of economic growth. Compare Walzer 1983. Perhaps the centrist position, which on this account acknowledges trade-offs and requires balancing, is one that all can appreciate but only an economist can love.
98. Oberlander 2003, 1099. When Governor Mitt Romney, the Republican candidate in the 2012 presidential election, expressed sympathy for government health insurance programs in his first debate with President Obama, commentators described his views as moving toward the center. Doyle McManus, "Moderate Mitt? Don't Count on It," *Los Angeles Times,* October 7, 2012.
99. See Derthick and Quirk 1985, 122–123; Behrman 1980, 120.
100. See Prasad 2006, 62–82.
101. Deregulation has, on the whole, been a success, particularly for consumers. Winston 1993. Financial deregulation is a partial exception, as is evident from the costly problems with savings and loans during the 1980s (White 1991) and with nonbank financial institutions and markets more recently. Gorton and Metrick 2012, 132; Lo 2012, 157–158, 161, 162–163. These problems arose in part because centrists misjudged the need for residual government supervision.
102. Federal Trade Commission Staff Report, *Competition and Consumer Protection Perspectives on Electric Power Regulatory Reform,* Washington,

D.C., September 2001, https://www.ftc.gov/sites/default/files/documents /reports/competition-and-consumer-protection-perspectives-electric-power -regulatory-reform-focus-retail/electricityreport.pdf. Similarly, rail deregulation did not eliminate the power to regulate shipping rates of dominant rail carriers. See James Calderwood, "Legal Briefs: Should Rail Rates Be Regulated Again?" *MH&L News*, April 4, 2006, http://mhlnews.com /transportation-amp-distribution/legal-briefs-should-rail-rates-be-regulated -again.

103. Neuchterlein and Weiser 2005, 88.
104. Benjamin et al. 2012, 456–457.
105. Transportation Research Board 1991, 169–198.
106. See Kalman 2010, 38–63; Blinder and Rudd 2013.
107. See Phillips-Fein 2009, 185–225.
108. Baker 2006, 505–515.
109. See Baker and Salop 2001, 339–354; Lewis 2004.
110. See Timothy Muris, Chairman, Federal Trade Commission, "Antitrust Enforcement at the Federal Trade Commission: In a Word—Continuity" (speech), Remarks at the American Bar Association Antitrust Section Annual Meeting, Chicago, IL August 7, 2001, https://www.ftc.gov/public -statements/2001/08/antitrust-enforcement-federal-trade-commission-word -continuity.
111. Baker and Shapiro 2008a.
112. See Baker 2006, 506–510, 512n107. During the Obama administration, however, the government tended to frame exclusion cases as unlawful agreements or mergers, not as monopolization or attempts to monopolize.
113. See also Baker 2010b, 621–628.
114. See Baker 2002b, 69–70; 2003.
115. See Chapter 4.
116. Conservatives have defended their political efforts to limit social insurance transfer programs on various grounds: as necessary to prevent excessive government spending and thereby allow lower taxes, as needed to enhance incentives to work, as requiring unduly intrusive regulation, and as aggrandizing in the federal government power that appropriately belongs to the states. Conservative opposition to social insurance may also have an unarticulated racial component. See Katznelson 2013.
117. See Baker and Salop 2015, 1–4; Raj Chetty et al. "The Fading American Dream: Trends in Absolute Income Mobility Since 1940," *Science*, April 28, 2017.
118. Helene Cooper and Jennifer Steinhauer, "Bucking Senate, Obama Appoints Consumer Chief," *New York Times*, January 4, 2012.
119. Peter Voskamp, "GOP Attempt to Overturn FCC's Net Neutrality Rules Fails in Senate," *Reuters*, November 10, 2011. During the Trump administration, the FCC abandoned net neutrality on a partisan division.
120. Ezra Klein, "Unpopular Mandate," *New Yorker*, June 25, 2012.
121. Bristol 2012.

122. Matt Stoller, "The False Dodd-Frank Narrative: Occupy Wall Street Attacks Huge Hot Money Loophole in the Law," *Naked Capitalism,* November 6, 2012, https://www.nakedcapitalism.com/2012/11/the-false -dodd-frank-narrative-occupy-wall-street-attacks-huge-hot-money-loophole -in-the-law.html.

123. See Oberlander 2003, 1136; Christine Hauser, "President Signs Medicare Bill Adding Prescription Drug Benefit," *New York Times,* December 8, 2003, http://www.nytimes.com/2003/12/08/politics/08CND-BUSH.html; Reihan Salam, "Brief Note on Paul Ryan and the Medicare Prescription Drug Benefit," *National Review Online,* August 12, 2012, http://www .nationalreview.com/agenda/313766/brief-note-paul-ryan-and-medicare -prescription-drug-benefit-reihan-salam#.

124. See Theda Skocpol, *Naming the Problem: What It Will Take To Counter Extremism and Engage Americans in the Fight Against Global Warning,* Cambridge, MA: Harvard University, January 2013, 39–44, http://www .scholarsstrategynetwork.org/sites/default/files/skocpol_captrade_report _january_2013_0.pdf; David M. Herszenhorn and Robert Pear, "Final Votes in Congress Cap Battle on Health Bill," *New York Times,* March 25, 2010, http://www.nytimes.com/2010/03/26/health/policy/26health.html; Jeff Zeleny and Robert Pear, "Kucinich Switches Vote on Health Care," *New York Times,* March 17, 2010, http://prescriptions.blogs.nytimes.com /2010/03/17/kucinich-switches-vote-on-health-care/.

125. Compare Tushnet 2003, 32.

126. A decade ago, leading antitrust conservative Judge Douglas Ginsburg called the per se rule against tying the "last man standing." The author heard Judge Ginsburg make this comment during his remarks at the Luncheon Round-table Discussion with Federal Courts of Appeals Judges at the ABA Section of Antitrust Law Spring Meeting on Mar. 25, 2009.

127. U.S. Department of Justice, "Justice Department Withdraws Report on Antitrust Monopoly Law," May 11, 2009 (regarding the U.S. Department of Justice, *Competition and Monopoly: Single-Firm Conduct Under Section 2 of the Sherman Act,* September 2008 report). The controversy over the monopolization report is discussed in Baker 2010b, 606–607.

128. *Trinko,* 540 U.S. at 407. Three Justices concurred in the judgment without commenting on this rhetoric, and none dissented.

129. The Court held that an antitrust claim could not proceed in a setting in which a separate statutory scheme provided for extensive regulation aimed at promoting competition.

130. *Trinko,* 540 U.S. at 414.

131. Credit Suisse Securities (USA) LLC v. Billing, 551 U.S. 264, 281–82 (2007). Wariness about private antitrust enforcement also helps explain why a conservative Supreme Court would prefer regulation to antitrust in *Trinko* and *Credit Suisse.*

132. Bell Atlantic Corp v. Twombly, 550 U.S. 544 (2007).

133. Comcast Corp. v. Behrend, 133 S. Ct. 1426 (2013).

134. Am. Express Co. v. Italian Colors Rest., 133 S. Ct. 2304 (2013).

135. Crane 2011, 62–63. Compare Engstrom 2013, 619.

136. Working with a conservative Congress, the Trump administration has sought to repeal the Affordable Care Act, overturn net neutrality, reform social security, and undo financial services regulation. Compare John Wagner and Juliet Eilperin, "Once a Populist, Trump Governs Like a Conservative Republican," *Washington Post,* December 6, 2017; Matt Grossmann and David A. Hopkins, "Trump Isn't Changing the Republican Party. The Republican Party Is Changing Trump," *Washington Post,* August 2, 2017; Harry Enten, "Voters Used to See Moderation in Trump. Not Anymore," *FiveThirtyEight,* January 5, 2018.

137. See Salop and Shapiro 2017.

138. Ryan Grim, "Steve Bannon Wants Facebook and Google Regulated Like Utilities," *The Intercept,* July 27, 2017; Daniel Kishi, "Time for a Conservative Anti-Monopoly Movement," *The American Conservative,* September 19, 2017; John Kehoe, "Kenneth Rogoff Concerned by the Dark Side of the Technology Revolution," *Financial Review,* March 9, 2018. See also Eleanor Clift, "Bill Galston and Bill Kristol's New Center Project Takes Aim at the Tech Oligarchs," *The Daily Beast,* September 11, 2017; Robert Kraychik, "Exclusive—Ted Cruz: Use Antitrust Laws to Break 'Massive Power' of Tech Lords to 'Subvert Our Democratic Process'," *Breitbart,* April 25, 2018.

139. David Dayen, "This Budding Movement Wants to Smash Monopolies," *The Nation,* April 4, 2017); Gilad Edelman, "The Democrats Confront Monopoly," *Washington Monthly,* November / December 2017.

140. Barry C. Lynn and Phillip Longman, "Populism with a Brain," *Washington Monthly,* June / July / August 2016; Zephyr Teachout, "Neil Gorsuch Sides with Big Business, Big Donors and Big Bosses," *Washington Post,* Feb. 21, 2017; Matt Stoller, "How Democrats Killed Their Populist Soul," *The Atlantic,* Oct. 24, 2016.

141. Barry C. Lynn, "Breaking the Chain: The Antitrust Case Against Wal-Mart," *Harpers* 29, July 2006; Marshall Steinbaum, "Antitrust in the Labor Market: Protectionist, or Pro-Competitive?" *Pro-Market,* Sept. 20, 2017, https://promarket.org/antitrust-labor-market-protectionist-pro-competitive/. A related progressive claim, that downstream market concentration leads to upstream supply chain fragility when geographically concentrated suppliers are vulnerable to common political risks or natural disaster threats, may or may not be correct. Any downstream producer would be expected to trade off the risk-reduction benefits of sourcing from suppliers in multiple locations (e.g., selecting some suppliers in Taiwan and others in Mexico) against the input price reductions it can achieve through limited sourcing. Downstream firms may save by making an all-or-nothing offer to a single supplier, as the progressive story supposes, but they may instead prefer to lessen risks by sourcing from multiple suppliers, particularly if purchasing

economies are exhausted at limited scale. Even if downstream firms single-source, moreover, suppliers would have an incentive to reduce risks by operating plants in multiple locations. Some downstream firms may be willing to pay more to a supplier that offers diversity in supply. If so, it is possible that the supply chain would be equally risky regardless of the downstream market structure.

142. Meghna Chakrabarti, "Are Tech Giants Like Amazon, Facebook and Google Monopolies?" September 4, 2017 (*Here and Now* interview with Matt Stoller), http://www.wbur.org/hereandnow/2017/09/04/amazon -facebook-google-monopolies. See also Foer 2017; Taplin 2017.

143. Khan and Vaheesah 2017, 237, 279–285.

144. Barry C. Lynn and Phillip Longman, "Populism with a Brain," *Washington Monthly*, June/July/August 2016; Mike Konczal, "Monopoly Power Is on the Rise in the US. Here's How to Fix That," *The Nation*, May 20, 2016.

145. But not necessarily. It is possible to imagine a progressive juggernaut, fueled by revulsion against policies of the Trump administration and the Republican Congress. If that movement is strong enough to overcome the electoral biases that presently favor Republicans (such as gerrymandering, the overweighting of less populous states in the Senate and Electoral College, inadequate regulation of political campaign spending, and restrictive voter registration rules), it could conceivably capture the Democratic party and end up controlling both Congress and the Presidency. On the other hand, populism has moved politics to the right in Europe, and not in a progressive direction. William A. Galston, "The Rise of European Populism and the Collapse of the Center-Left," *Brookings*, March 8, 2018, https://www .brookings.edu/blog/order-from-chaos/2018/03/08/the-rise-of-european -populism-and-the-collapse-of-the-center-left/. See also Dani Rodrik, "What Does a True Populism Look Like? It Looks Like the New Deal," *New York Times*, February 21, 2018. Compare Dani Rodrik, "What's Been Stopping the Left?" *Project Syndicate*, April 13, 2018, https://www.project -syndicate.org/commentary/left-timidity-after-neoliberal-failure-by-dani -rodrik-2018-04.

146. Kovacic 1989, 1139–1144.

147. The progressive wing of the Democratic party is attempting to mobilize popular support for a broad-based attack on dominant firms and market concentration. David Weigel, "Breaking from Tech Giants, Democrats Consider Becoming an Antimonopoly Party," *Washington Post*, September 4, 2017. But it remains to be seen whether voters will respond. See David Dayen, "Anti-Monopoly Candidates Are Testing a New Politics in the Midterms," *The Intercept*, October 1, 2017; Brian Beutler, "How Democrats Can Wage War on Monopolies—And Win," *New Republic*, September 16, 2017.

148. See Rahman 2018. See also Brodley 1987, 1023n11.

149. Jackson 1937a, 577.

3. Preventing the Political Misuse of Antitrust

1. Rill and Turner 2014, 587 (citing Caro 2012, 523–527).
2. Rill and Turner 2014, 587; Emery 1994, 101–102. The Justice Department eventually reached a settlement with ITT.
3. Salop and Shapiro 2017, 19.
4. George Lardner Jr., "Mitchell Tied to Hughes Bid," *Washington Post,* June 23, 1974. The deal reportedly fell through for financial reasons unrelated to antitrust issues.
5. Partisan misuse undermines the legitimacy of the laws abused. Kovacic 2014.
6. Antitrust enforcement should also be insulated from direct Congressional influence. This possibility is raised by the close attention the Federal Trade Commission (FTC) pays to Congress. Kovacic 1982.
7. E.g., Zephyr Teachout, "Neil Gorsuch Sides with Big Business, Big Donors and Big Bosses," *Washington Post,* February 21, 2017; Barry C. Lynn and Phillip Longman, "Populism with a Brain," *Washington Monthly,* June /July/August 2016; Matt Stoller, "How Democrats Killed Their Populist Soul," *The Atlantic,* October 24, 2016. On this account, deconcentration would interdict the vicious cycle of crony capitalism and support a democratization of the domestic political and economic spheres.
8. Gavil et al. 2017, 1345–1347; ABA Section of Antitrust Law 2015.
9. See Dal Bó 2006, 203 (narrow definition). Dal Bó's broad definition of regulatory capture resembles the usage of the term "special-interest protectionism" here.
10. E.g., Bork 1978, 159–160, 347–349.
11. Zingales 2012, 29.
12. Acemoglu and Robinson 2012, 335–367. See also Olson 1982. Compare Mokyr 1990, 176–183.
13. Winters 2011, 6.
14. See Winters 2011, 249; Gilens 2012, 85. See also Bartels 2008, 252–83; Byrne Edsall 1984, 241–242; Gilens and Page 2014, 576. But compare Branham et al. 2017; Dylan Matthew, "Studies: Democratic politicians represent middle-class voters. GOP politicians don't," *Vox,* April 2, 2018, https://www.vox.com/policy-and-politics/2018/4/2/16226202/oligarchy -political-science-politician-congress-respond-citizens-public-opinion.
15. Ulfelder 2010, 16–17, 60–61.
16. Editorial Board, "A Historic Tax Heist," *New York Times,* December 2, 2017; Jacob Hacker and Paul Pierson, "The GOP is Trying to Pass a Super-Unpopular Agenda—and That's a Bad Sign for Democracy," *Vox,* December 7, 2017, https://www.vox.com/the-big-idea/2017/12/7/16745584 /republican-agenda-unpopular-polls-tax-reform; Matthew Yglesias, "We're Witnessing the Wholesale Looting of America," *Vox,* December 19, 2017, https://www.vox.com/policy-and-politics/2017/12/19/16786006/looting-of

-america. See also Maggie Severns, "Big Donors Ready to Reward Republicans for Tax Cuts," *Politico,* January 29, 2018.

17. Brian Fung, "Why Trump Might Not Block the AT&T-Time Warner Merger, After All," *Washington Post,* November 11, 2016; David Goldman, "Donald Trump's War on Jeff Bezos, Amazon and the Washington Post," *CNN tech,* May 13, 2016, http://money.cnn.com/2016/05/13/technology /donald-trump-jeff-bezos-amazon/.

18. David McLaughlin and Todd Shields, "Trump's Talks with Dealmaking CEOs Rattle Antitrust Lawyers," *Bloomberg,* January 13, 2017, https://www .bloomberg.com/news/articles/2017-01-13/trump-s-talks-with-dealmaking -ceos-rattle-antitrust-lawyers; Chris Sagers, "Buyer Beware," *Slate,* January 13, 2017, http://www.slate.com/articles/news_and_politics/jurisprudence /2017/01/donald_trump_s_high_profile_apparent_merger_meetings_are_a _major_cause_for.html.

19. See Scott Colm, "Trump's Carrier Deal Is Not Living Up to the Hype—Jobs Still Going to Mexico," *CNBC,* June 22, 2016, https://www.cnbc.com/2017 /06/22/trumps-carrier-jobs-deal-is-just-not-living-up-to-the-hype.html.

20. Peter Baker, "'Very Frustrated' Trump Becomes Top Critic of Law Enforcement," *New York Times,* November 3, 2017. Compare Benjamin Wittes, "'The Saddest Thing': President Trump Acknowledges Constraint," *Lawfare,* November 3, 2017, https://lawfareblog.com/saddest-thing-president-trump -acknowledges-constraint; Frank Bowman, "President Trump Committed Another Impeachable Offense on Friday," *Slate,* November 3, 2017, http://www .slate.com/articles/news_and_politics/jurisprudence/2017/11/president _trump_committed_another_impeachable_offense_on_friday.html. One commentator suggested that Trump's criticism of the Justice Department for not investigating his political rivals created pressure on the Justice Department to challenge a high-profile merger involving a news network Trump had disparaged. Brian Stelter, "New Questions about Trump Administration's Review of AT&T-Time Warner Deal," *CNN,* November 4, 2017, http://money.cnn.com/2017/11/03/media/att-time-warner-department-of -justice/index.html.

21. Scott Moritz, "AT&T CEO, Among Trump's 'Defenders,' Felt Blindsided by DOJ Suit," *Bloomberg,* November 29, 2017, https://www.bloomberg.com /news/articles/2017-11-29/at-t-ceo-among-trump-s-defenders-felt -blindsided-by-doj-suit.

22. This is an issue with Justice Department enforcement actions only. The president arguably has the power to instruct the Justice Department on the exercise of prosecutorial discretion but can at most advise the FTC, an independent agency. Moreover, the scope and magnitude of President Trump's personal financial interests has not been disclosed. Enforcement decisions that benefit those interests could potentially violate the emoluments clauses of the Constitution. Litigation over these constitutional issues would raise questions about the standing of potential plaintiffs and the availability of remedies beyond impeachment and removal, however.

23. See David Dayen, "Don't Let AT&T Exploit Your Distrust of Trump," *The Nation*, November 9, 2017, https://www.thenation.com/article/dont-let-att-exploit-your-distrust-of-trump/.

24. Theodore Roosevelt played a larger role in antitrust enforcement, particularly in dealing with consolidations sponsored by J.P. Morgan.

25. David McLaughlin and Todd Shields, "Trump's Talks with Dealmaking CEOs Rattle Antitrust Lawyers," *Bloomberg*, January 13, 2017, https://www.bloomberg.com/news/articles/2017-01-13/trump-s-talks-with-dealmaking-ceos-rattle-antitrust-lawyers.

26. Joe Crowe, "DOJ's Antitrust Division Leader: Will Look Closely at Mergers," *Newsmax*, October 30, 2017, https://www.newsmax.com/us/makan-delrahim-department-of-justice-antitrust/2017/05/30/id/793042/.

27. Pitofsky 1979. See also Blake and Jones 1965, 383. Compare Green 1972, 17–21; Crane 2018a.

28. United States v. Aluminum Co. of America, 148 F.2d 416, 427–429 (1945) (L. Hand, J.) *(Alcoa)*. This theme also underlays the Depression-era Robinson-Patman Act.

29. Brown Shoe Co. v. United States, 370 U.S. 294, 316 and n28 (1962).

30. United States v. Topco Associates, Inc., 405 U.S. 596, 610 (1972).

31. Brown Shoe Co. v. United States, 370 U.S. 294, 320 (1962).

32. Bork and Bowman Jr. 1965, 369, 374.

33. Blake and Jones 1965, 384.

34. Pitofsky 1979, 1067.

35. Pitofsky 1979, 1059.

36. See Brown Shoe Co. v. United States, 370 U.S. 294, 344 (1962).

37. *Brown Shoe*, 370 U.S. at 316, 333.

38. Pitofsky 1979, 1070.

39. Pitofsky 1979, 1068.

40. While such cases were not routine during the 1950s and 1960s (Kovacic 1989, 1122), their frequency declined substantially after the mid-1970s. Kovacic 2003, 449 (table 4).

41. Kovacic 1989, 1131–1132, 1135–1136. It is hard to assess the relative importance of political concerns and contemporaneous worries about the economic harms from monopoly and oligopoly conduct, which also spurred deconcentration efforts. Kovacic 1989, 1134. Deconcentration advocates minimized the likelihood of efficiency losses from that policy (Kovacic 1989, 1135), in parallel with the way that Chicago-oriented commentators minimized the risks of market power from the antitrust reforms they proposed.

42. Kovacic 1989, 1105. Depression-era legislation did successfully break apart public utility holding companies and split the deposit and investment banking functions of banks, however. Kovacic 1989, 1117.

43. Compare Horton 2018. Various contemporary voices have recommended that antitrust seek to protect, for example, the competitive process, consumer choice, equal economic opportunity, diversity of voices, local community ties, democratic decision making, jobs, entrepreneurial opportunities, and

less concentrated market structures (even when concentration or a trend toward dominance is not linked to higher prices). Some of these could also be understood as economic goals.

44. Even a limited approach, such as treating the reduction of inequality as an explicit antitrust goal, would raise difficult implementation problems. Baker and Salop 2015, 24–26.

45. Mike Ananny et al., Letter from Professors of Law, Economics, Business, Communication, and Political Science to the Federal Trade Commission on Net Neutrality, January 29, 2015, http://www.pijip.org/wp-content/uploads /2015/01/Net-Neutrality-Prof-Letter-01292015.pdf.

46. Compare Hovenkamp 2018a.

47. Noel 2013, 14, 19–22.

48. Compare Noel 2013, 9, 10, 19.

49. See Noel 2013, 14. All of a coalition's members prefer to remain in it in order to implement its program. They are each better off doing so than leaving to join some other coalition: the other coalition may not have a majority or, if it becomes a majority coalition, the voter or interest group may not like its program, overall, as much.

50. An agency that operates primarily through rule making is more likely to conceive its role as implementing an interest group bargain than is an agency that operates primarily through adjudication. Baker 2013c.

51. Some theories of statutory interpretation call on courts to enforce the interest group bargain underlying the legislation. That approach has little relevance to the interpretation of the antitrust laws, particularly a century after enactment, because their prohibitions are broad and general. One exception may be the interpretation of a specific rule in an area where Congress had been active, though the majority and dissent interpreted the significance of recent congressional action differently in a prominent recent decision. Leegin Creative Leather Prods., Inc. v. PSKS, Inc., 551 U.S. 877 (2007).

52. A recent study purporting to find otherwise merely shows that political considerations may affect the care with which the agencies conduct a merger investigation, not the resolution of that investigation. Mehata et al. 2017. The authors' "outcome" measure is largely driven by agency decisions not to grant early termination.

53. Compare Kovacic and Winerman 2015, 2098, 2108. In addition, Congressional oversight of enforcement approaches and decisions is important to assure that law enforcers are held accountable for the way they exercise their responsibility to the public and use the powers with which they are entrusted. See Kovacic and Winerman 2015, 2088–2091.

54. Contribution of the United States on Independence of Competition Authorities, OECD Global Forum on Competition, DAF/COMP/GF/WD(2016)71, November 7, 2016, ¶¶ 6, 14.

55. In some instances, though, these devices could generate subtle political pressure. Kovacic and Winerman 2015, 2100–2108.

56. It is not surprising to find that some of the expert professionals that work with firms have ideological perspectives sympathetic to firm goals, and that those professionals bring those perspectives to their work in and out of government. But that does not mean they take positions in government to advance the interests of certain firms. Nor is it obvious whether senior officials concerned with future employment would do better by acting tough or easy with regulated firms. See Dal Bó 2006, 214–215. Moreover, regulatory capture theories that rely on the "revolving door" have only weak empirical support. The empirical literature has difficulty distinguishing the influence of prior or prospective employment from personal characteristics (which might include ideological perspectives). Carpenter 2014, 57, 66; Dal Bó 2006, 217–218. See also Makkai and Braithwaite 1992. But see Tabakovic and Wollman 2018.

57. In 2002, the Assistant Attorney General for Antitrust, Charles James, described an unprecedented growth in third-party advocacy, including lobbying the Justice Department, since his previous service there as a senior official a decade before. James 2002, 18. Much of that activity was likely associated with James's role in settling the *Microsoft* case, which had an extraordinarily high political profile, though James described lobbying as occurring more widely.

58. E.g., Bliss 2016; Kim Hart and Anna Palmer, "AT&T's T-Mobile Merger Lobbying Campaign Falls Short," *Politico,* September 1, 2011.

59. E.g., Justin Elliott, "The American Way," *ProPublica,* October 11, 2016, https://www.propublica.org/article/airline-consolidation-democratic -lobbying-antitrust; Brent Kendall et al., "Behind Google's Antitrust Escape," *Wall Street Journal,* January 5, 2013.

60. Alex Byers and Tony Romm, "Collapse of Comcast-Time Warner Cable merger shows limits of lobbying," *Politico,* April 24, 2015.

61. Fidrmuc et al. 2017.

62. Lao 2014, 686; Salop 2014, 648.

63. Compare Stimson 2015; Page 2008, 1, 2 (quoting Sowell 1987, 14). But compare Noel 2013, 14, 19; Ezra Klein, "For elites, politics is driven by ideology. For voters, it's not," *Vox,* November 9, 2017, https://www.vox.com /policy-and-politics/2017/11/9/16614672/ideology-liberal-conservatives.

64. Ideology also operates to signal important aspects of social identity for some group members. See Mason 2018.

65. This discussion assumes that rules that increase average deterrence also increase marginal deterrence. That is a reasonable assumption for antitrust rules as a whole, but might not always hold in individual cases. Schwartz 2000.

66. Compare McMurray 2017; Gavil et al. 2017, 443–444 (Figure 4–1).

67. For example, politics matters more at the Federal Communications Commission (FCC) than at the antitrust agencies, in part because that agency focuses on a single sector of the economy. In addition, the typical FCC matter is a rule making, which is often a quasi-legislative activity, while the

typical FTC matter is adjudicative. As a result, legislative norms guide the FCC—the agency aims, at least at times, to work out an interest group bargain—while judicial norms of basing decisions on law and policy guide the FTC. At the FTC, politics matters indirectly: the incumbent administration selects agency leadership in part based on ideology. However, agency leadership almost invariably puts aside direct political considerations when resolving individual matters. See generally Baker 2013c.

68. Compare Waller 2019; Gibson and Nelson 2017; Balkin and Levinson 2006.

69. Crane 2011, 70.

70. Behavioral economics has begun to influence industrial organization economics. While it has not yet had substantial influence on antitrust analysis, one would expect enforcers and courts to take into account well-established and systematic behavioral regularities that influence firm behavior when evaluating the competitive effects of firm conduct. For example, suppose that multiproduct pharmaceutical firms systematically limit price increases when they obtain market power to protect their corporate reputation for fairness and thereby protect sales of other products. Then the sale of a product with market power to a stand-alone firm unconcerned about reputation could lead to higher prices. That transaction would harm competition and could be challenged under the Clayton Act.

71. The relationship between economic development and legal change is not simple. Baker 2002b, 69.

72. But compare William Davies, "Populism and the Limits of Neoliberalism," *The London School of Economics and Politics Blog,* April 30, 2017, http://blogs .lse.ac.uk/europpblog/2017/04/30/essay-populism-and-the-limits-of -neoliberalism-by-william-davies/.

73. These problems may arise regardless of the strength of democratic political institutions. Compare Iyigun 2012, 6.

74. In legal fields not governed by judicial development of rules pursuant to general statutes, a similar process would require the modification of statutes and administrative rules.

75. Of course, trial courts have substantial practical discretion in resolving cases that turn on witness credibility or on the evaluation of sophisticated and complex economic analyses presented by competing experts, as it is unlikely that an appellate court will second guess factual findings that rely on judgments about such evidence. But compare Kolasky 2001.

76. Compare American Bar Association Section of Antitrust Law 2006; Haw 2012.

77. Hospital Corp. of Am. v. FTC, 807 F.2d 1381 (7th Cir. 1986) (Posner, J.) (affirming the FTC's decision that a hospital merger violated the antitrust laws).

78. FTC v. Advocate Health Care Network, 841 F.3d 460 (7th Cir. 2016) (reversing a district court's denial of a preliminary injunction against a hospital merger challenged by the FTC).

79. Baker 2013b, 544–550.

80. Some courts, applying a sliding scale, may also make it more difficult for the defendant to meet its burden of production when the plaintiff's prima facie case is strong. If a court does not credit a speculative efficiency when a plaintiff offers compelling evidence of anticompetitive effects, for example, it could describe its decision to condemn the practice either as turning on the defendant's failure to meet its burden of production or on the plaintiff's meeting its burden of persuasion after defendant showed a plausible but weakly supported efficiency justification.

81. E.g., United States v. Apple, Inc., 952 F. Supp. 2d 638, 694 (S.D.N.Y. 2013), aff'd, 791 F.3d 290 (2d Cir. 2015).

82. E.g., Polygram Holding, Inc. v. FTC, 416 F.3d 29 (D.C. Cir. 2005).

83. Carrier 1999.

84. FTC v. H.J. Heinz Co., 246 F.3d 708, 724 (D.C. Cir. 2001).

85. Resisting them requires strong political institutions too. See Acemoglu and Robinson 2012, 319–325.

86. See, e.g., Baker and Shapiro 2008a, 241–44 (discussing United States v. Oracle Corp., 331 F. Supp. 2d 1098 [N.D. Cal. 2004]). District courts can also limit the practical scope of appellate review by relying heavily on witness credibility.

87. There are three reasons. First, private plaintiffs would not be expected to take into account the economy-wide deterrent effect of their litigation efforts when deciding to bring cases, so may decline to challenge some conduct that an enforcement agency would challenge. See Segal and Whinston 2006. Second, damages may be too low relative to what efficient deterrence would require. See Gavil et al. 2017, 1394–1395. Third, the threat of damages would not deter violators to the extent they anticipate that they will be required to pay antitrust damages in the future. If so, they will pass through the expected damages payment to buyers in advance, in the form of higher prices. Baker 1988b; Salant 1987. But compare Segal and Whinston 2006.

4. Recalibrating Error Costs and Presumptions

1. E.g., Joe Nocera, "Google Isn't the Problem. U.S. and EU Regulators Are," *Bloomberg*, June 28, 2017.

2. Compare Statement of the Federal Trade Commission [FTC] Regarding Google's Search Practices, *Google Inc.*, No. 111–0163 (F.T.C. January 3, 2013) with Google Search (Shopping) (Case AT.39740), Commission Decision C (2017) 4444 final (June 27, 2017).

3. In the United States, most claims are settled in the shadow of litigation. Otherwise, a government or private plaintiff must prove anticompetitive harm to a district court judge or to the FTC in nonmerger matters or cases involving consummated mergers challenged by that Commission. By contrast, the Competition Directorate of the European Commission

(DG-Comp), a neutral-expert body, acts as prosecutor and judge. It investigates claims, makes findings, and assesses penalties. A review by European courts looks more like U.S. appellate review than a district court trial. The administrative enforcement model is more consistent with the civil law tradition of continental Europe than with the Anglo-Saxon adversarial approach. In practice, the European system gives defendants due process rights, including an impartial tribunal, notice of the charges against them, the opportunity to be heard in their defense, and findings and reasons. DG-Comp employs a "market test" to develop remedies, which gives an explicit role to excluded rivals in its decision-making process. Doing so does not mean that DG-Comp is captured by complaining rivals, any more than the ability of such firms to bring a private case in the United States means that U.S. courts are captured.

4. Faull and Nikpay 2014, § 9.06.

5. See Behrens 2015.

6. Germán Gutiérrez and Thomas Philippon argue that European markets became more competitive than U.S. markets after 2000, attribute that divergence to stronger antitrust enforcement in Europe, and argue that European institutions are tougher on anticompetitive conduct because they are more insulated from politics than U.S. institutions. Gutiérrez and Philippon 2018. But they do not explain why U.S. institutions became more susceptible to political influence around 2000, or European institutions less susceptible, as their argument requires. Rather, U.S. antitrust rules became less interventionist two decades earlier, and European merger enforcement moved toward the U.S. approach in the early 2000s. They also equate political influence with corporate lobbying, without recognizing that while U.S. antitrust institutions respond to ideological shifts (as detailed in Chapter 3), they are largely free from direct political influence.

7. Pate 2004; Kolasky 2002a, 2002b. Compare Shelanski 2013, 1698–1699. More recently, U.S. officials have been more diplomatic. They now prefer to emphasize areas of convergence and refer to divergences only obliquely. E.g., Baer 2015.

8. Europe's Competition Commissioner recently claimed European markets are less concentrated than U.S. markets and implicitly attributed that difference to stricter antitrust enforcement in Europe. Mike Konczal, "Meet the World's Most Feared Antitrust Enforcer," *The Nation*, March 12, 2018, https://www.thenation.com/article/meet-the-worlds-most-feared-antitrust -enforcer/.

9. Cooper and Kovacic 2010, 1556.

10. E.g., Baker and Scott Morton 2018.

11. See generally Hovenkamp 2018b.

12. Ehrlich and Posner 1974; Posner 1973.

13. Joskow and Klevorick 1979, 222–225.

14. Easterbrook 1984.

15. See Verizon Commc'ns Inc. v. Law Offices of Curtis V. Trinko, LLP, 540 U.S. 398, 414 (2004). The error costs of any particular substantive antitrust rule depend in part on other rules of antitrust law and beyond, such as procedural rules governing litigation, rules about remedy determination, the scope of intellectual property rights, and whether state unfair competition laws cover the same conduct. See generally Kaplow 2012; Wickelgren, 2012, 54.

16. See Beckner and Salop 1999, 43–52.

17. Mistaken resolution of cases leads to winners and losers, but implementation errors are costly overall.

18. The primary benefits and costs of antitrust enforcement likely come from deterring anticompetitive conduct and chilling beneficial conduct by firms that must comply with antirust rules in markets beyond those at issue in any particular case. See generally Baker 2003a, 27; compare Kaplow 2012.

19. For example, restricting analysis to the parties before the court would yield the misimpression that draconian punishments for parking in front of a fire hydrant will eliminate error costs. The prospect of such punishments would lead to 100 percent compliance with the no-parking rule, so there would be no court cases, no possibility for a court erroneously to convict or acquit a defendant, and no litigation expenditures. Yet such punishments would also chill parking in front of a hydrant when its social benefits (e.g., allowing a doctor to arrive in time to save a life) would outweigh its social costs. Such punishments would also discourage socially beneficial parking *near* hydrants (by drivers who fear that an aggressive parking enforcer would wrongly conclude that the hydrant is blocked and that a court would uphold the ticket). Restricting analysis to the parties before the court would yield the same misimpression with respect to an enforcement policy taken to the opposite extreme: A complete absence of enforcement of the rule prohibiting parking in front of hydrants would also lead to no court cases, and so would generate no judicial errors and no transaction costs of litigation. Yet such a rule would not deter parking in front of hydrants when the social cost (the cost of impeding fire-department access in the event of a fire discounted by the probability that a need for access would arise) would exceed the social benefit. The complex relationship between deterrence and litigation is explored in White 1988.

20. Compare First and Waller 2013, 2571.

21. See generally Schwartz 2000.

22. A rule change that increases the frequency or cost (penalty) of false positives may increase deterrence, but it could also do the reverse. The latter may occur if more false positives mean that firms no longer obtain enough benefit from staying within the line separating legal and illegal behavior to justify being careful. For this reason, uncertainty about a rule or its application can reduce compliance. See generally Salop 2013, 2668–2669, 2669n60; Lando 2006, 329–330; Posner 1999, 1483–1484.

23. Board of Trade of City of Chicago v. United States, 246 U.S. 231 (1918) (Chicago Board of Trade).

24. United States v. Socony-Vacuum Oil Co., 310 U.S. 150 (1940).

25. More generally, the consequences of bright-line rules are triggered once the facts are settled, while a comprehensive standard requires a judgment about the facts. Farnsworth 2007, 71, 164. Bright-line rules prevent that judgment by limiting what evidence is considered or the weight some types of evidence are given, and by specifying in advance which factual elements or combinations of elements would give rise to liability and which do not (covering all cases).

26. See Baker 2013b, 546–551. In Ohio v. American Express Co., 138 S. Ct. 2274 (2018), the majority and dissent differed on aspects of the application of the burden-shifting framework.

27. Timothy Bresnahan and I have proposed two other ways to reduce error costs in an environment in which antitrust litigation increasingly relies on complex economic evidence. First, we suggested that empirical economists develop a catalogue of generalizations about the competitive consequences of firm conduct in various groups of related industries, which courts could rely upon to develop presumptions. Second, we proposed that courts appoint economic experts to help clarify for them the nature of the dispute between the economic experts working on behalf of the opposing parties. Such an expert would undertake a limited task: reviewing the reports of the opposing experts for the parties and writing a report to explain where the experts disagree and why, without necessarily taking a view on the resolution of key disputes. Baker and Bresnahan 2008, 30–31.

28. Compare Baker 1991, 740n29.

29. Salop 2017, § III.A.

30. Areeda and Turner 1975, 699.

31. In merger cases, courts treat efficiencies as a defense—that is, a reason to think competition would not be harmed—but not as an affirmative defense that would justify a merger that would raise prices or harm competition in some other way. This approach structures the allocation of burdens of production and persuasion with respect to efficiency claims the same way such burdens are typically allocated elsewhere in merger enforcement and, more generally, civil procedure. With a "defense," the defendant has the burden of production but not the burden of persuasion. With an "affirmative defense," the defendant bears both burdens. *Antitrust Modernization Commission: Public Hearing, Panel II: Treatment of Efficiencies in Merger Enforcement* (November 17, 2005) (statement of Prof. Jonathan Baker, American University, Washington College of Law), http://govinfo.library.unt.edu/amc /commission_hearings/pdf/Baker_Statement.pdf.

32. United States v. Baker Hughes, Inc., 908 F. 2d 981 (D.C. Cir. 1990); Federal Trade Comm'n v. H.J. Heinz Co., 246 F.3d 708 (2001).

33. United States v. General Dynamics Corp., 415 U.S. 486 (1974). Because the predicate for the presumption was not satisfied, moreover, the presumption

would not be given any weight in resolving whether competition was harmed in the event the plaintiff was able to satisfy its initial burden with evidence not involving market concentration.

34. Salop 2017, § III.A. Salop provides three antitrust examples: the refusal of courts to inquire whether competition is good, Nat'l Soc'y of Prof'l Eng'rs v. United States, 435 U.S. 679, 695 (1978); the presumption that price fixing harms the economy's "central nervous system," United States v. Socony-Vacuum Oil Co., 310 U.S. 150, 224n59 (1940); and the concern that concentrated economic power would threaten non-economic values, Brown Shoe Co. v. United States, 370 U.S. 294, 316 (1962).

35. United States v. Philadelphia Nat'l Bank, 374 U.S. 321 (1963).

36. United States v. Von's Grocery Co., 384 U.S. 270, 301 (1966) (Stewart, J. dissenting).

37. *Baker Hughes*, 908 F.2d at 984, 987.

38. *Baker Hughes*, 980 F.2d at 991.

39. Federal Trade Comm'n v. H.J. Heinz Co., 246 F.3d 708, 726 (2001). One district court has interpreted this language to mean that as the plaintiff's prima facie case becomes more compelling, the defendant must show more to meet its burden of production (not just that the defendant must show more to meet its practical burden of persuasion). United States v. H & R Block, Inc., 833 F. Supp. 2d 36, 77 (D.D.C. 2011).

40. E.g., Chamberlin 1933, 48. Many commentators took from Chamberlin the lesson that supracompetitive prices were nearly inevitable in oligopolies. See generally, Hale and Hale 1958, 122–123, 131–137.

41. Stigler 1964.

42. See Schmalensee 1989.

43. Demsetz 1974.

44. Douglas Ginsburg and Joshua Wright make this argument without considering how the factual and error cost bases for the structural presumption have changed since 1990. Ginsburg and Wright 2015.

45. Baker 2002a, 188–189, n286.

46. Moreover, Steven Salop suggests that absent a presumption, merger law is more likely to underdeter than overdeter because errors in either detection tend to lessen legal compliance, firms have large incentives to undertake anticompetitive mergers, and the enforcement agencies tend to be gun-shy about litigating. Salop 2015, 297.

47. Beyond the economic rationales discussed in the text, some suggest preventing market concentration for noneconomic reasons. Chapter 3 cautions against relying on this overarching policy goal as a basis for developing or modifying antitrust rules, but some modern commentators see it as a further reason to strengthen the structural presumption. Peter Carstensen argues for strengthening the structural presumption in part on the basis of a concern with the political consequences of concentrated economic power. Carstensen 2015. Harry First and Eleanor Fox contend that the Supreme Court, in *Philadelphia National Bank*, was wrong to reject explicit consideration of

noncompetition factors such as saving jobs, preserving entrepreneurial opportunities, and preventing excessive concentration or a trend toward dominance even when not linked to higher prices. First and Fox 2015.

48. In addition, the structural presumption could be strengthened legislatively. See Hovenkamp and Shapiro 2018.

49. Beyond these two bases for presumptions, Steven Salop discusses inferences of competitive harm from high price-cost margins and from a history of industry collusion. Salop 2015, 299–305.

50. Baker and Shapiro 2008a, 34–35. Diversion ratios would be calibrated by price-cost margins. See generally Gavil et al. 2017, 806–810 (Sidebar 5–8).

51. U.S. Department of Justice and Federal Trade Commission 2010, § 6.1.

52. Baker and Shapiro 2008a, 33–34. See Baker 2002a, 174–177.

53. U.S. Department of Justice and Federal Trade Commission 2010, § 7.1.

5. Erroneous Arguments against Enforcement

1. Compare Field 2017, 1152–1154.

2. Most contemporary conservative antitrust commentators accept that antitrust has some useful role to play, so most are unlikely to agree with every one of the views that I describe the antitrust right as holding. It is hard to see how someone who simultaneously accepted all of them would want to support the antitrust enterprise.

3. For example, Justice Stephen Breyer endorsed the "single monopoly profit" theory in Town of Concord v. Boston Edison Co., 915 F.2d 17, 23, 32 (1st Cir. 1990) and authored the majority opinion in Credit Suisse Securities (USA) LLC v. Billing, 551 U.S. 264 (2007), discussed below. Yet, as author of the dissent in Leegin Creative Leather Products, Inc. v. PSKS, Inc., 551 U.S. 877 (2007), he took issue with the majority's noninterventionist approach. His antitrust positions often reflect concerns about the administrability of legal rules and the capacity of antitrust institutions, and so do not invariably follow the non-interventionist fault line emphasized here.

4. For another effort with a similar goal, though focused more on the specific doctrinal rules the courts have adopted, see Pitofsky 2008. For conservative criticism of that book, see Wright 2009.

5. Compare Devlin and Jacobs 2010.

6. Easterbrook 1984, 2–3, 15; Bork 1978, 133. See also Wright 2012a, 245.

7. The possibility of market self-correction through expansion by existing rivals is addressed separately below.

8. The antitrust economics literature frequently refers to "ease" of entry and "barriers" to entry, and that usage has been adopted here. These terms mislead, however, to the extent they suggest that entry conditions can be analyzed in the abstract, without reference to a competitive concern. The relevant question for antitrust enforcement and policy is typically whether

new competition will counteract or deter competitive harm from the specific business conduct at issue. The answer may vary with the nature of the conduct.

9. Conversely, as antitrust conservatives properly recognize, if entry is not easy, the self-correcting process can work slowly, giving antitrust enforcement a role to play. Easterbrook 1984, 2; see, e.g., Evans and Padilla 2005, 84; Bork 1978, 311; compare Wright 2012a, 245.

10. McChesney 2004, 50.

11. In what is termed a "contestable" market, the potential for rapid and inexpensive entry would deter or counteract any exercise of market power, no matter how small the number of incumbent firms. See, e.g., Baumol et al. 1988. Those suggesting application of this idea to the airline industry pointed out that aircraft were not committed to any particular route and that airlines could readily shift aircraft to new city-pairs in response to profit opportunities. See Bailey and Panzar 1981.

12. See Baumol and Willig 1986, 24–27. The reasons and evidence that airline markets are not contestable are surveyed in Baker 2002a, 170–172 and n153. Moreover, the flawed claim that competition from small rivals and potential entrants prevents competitive harm is at odds with the equally flawed argument made by some conservatives that the exclusion of inefficient entrants does not harm competition. See Salop 2008, 152–155 (criticizing the equally efficient entrant standard).

13. Evans and Padilla 2005, 84.

14. United States v. Microsoft Corp., 253 F.3d 34 (D.C. Cir. 2001) (en banc) (per curiam); Standard Oil Co. v. United States, 221 U.S. 1 (1911). See also United States v. Dentsply Int'l, Inc., 399 F.3d 181 (3d Cir. 2005); United States v. Aluminum Co. of Am. *(Alcoa)*, 148 F.2d 416 (2d Cir. 1945).

15. See Baker 2013b, 535–536, 559–560.

16. See generally *Microsoft*, 253 F.3d 34.

17. Lorain Journal Co. v. United States, 342 U.S. 143 (1951).

18. See United States v. Visa U.S.A., Inc., 344 F.3d 229, 241 (2d Cir. 2003); Baker 2013b, 559–560 and n160.

19. Levenstein and Suslow 2011, 463. Compare Hyytinen et al. Forthcoming; Harrington and Wei 2017; Bryant and Eckard 1991. Harrington and Wei 2017 find that cartel duration can be inferred reliably from data on discovered cartels.

20. A number of cartels lasted at least forty years. Levenstein and Suslow 2006, 53 (table 2).

21. Ezrachi and Gilo 2009; Baker 2003c, 194–195; Stiglitz 1987.

22. Bork 1978, 196. The exercise of market power would be expected to lead to higher prices and reduced output industry-wide when products are homogeneous. When applied correctly, the output standard is concerned with industry-wide output, not with the output of the firms alleged to have harmed competition, as firms that exercise market power by excluding rivals

and raising price could increase their own output even as industry output falls. Judge Easterbrook erroneously focused on the output of the firms alleged to have harmed competition in Easterbrook 1984, 31.

23. See Posner 1976, 53.

24. Cowling and Waterson 1976; Dansby and Willig 1979; see generally Kaplow and Shapiro 2007, 1083–1086; Shapiro 1989, 1:333–336.

25. Stigler 1964. See generally Baker 2010a, 238, 238n20.

26. Schmalensee 1989, 988 (Stylized Fact 5.1); Weiss 1989, 266–284. See also Bresnahan and Suslow 1989, 267; Baker 1999. Compare Kwoka 2017b. Endogeneity issues in relating concentration and price are addressed in Evans et al. 1993. Identification issues are discussed in Chapter 1, in endnotes to the section on "Oligopolies Are Common and Concentration is Increasing in Many Industries."

27. William J. Kolasky, Deputy Assistant Att'y Gen., Antitrust Div., U.S. Dept. of Justice, "Coordinated Effects in Merger Review: From Dead Frenchmen to Beautiful Minds and Mavericks" (speech), Address at the ABA Section of Antitrust Law Spring Meeting, April 24, 2002, 18, http://www.justice.gov/atr/public//.htm.

28. Baker and Shapiro 2008a, 253.

29. *Trinko*, 540 U.S. 398 (2004).

30. *Trinko*, 540 U.S. at 407.

31. *Trinko*, 540 U.S. at 407–408.

32. Evans and Hylton 2008, 220. Accord Padilla et al. 2018, 11. For a critical response to Evans and Hylton, see Baker 2008a.

33. Baker 2016a.

34. See generally Shapiro 2012; Baker 2007a, 579–586. Antitrust law has long recognized a monopolist's incentive to enjoy a quiet life. United States v. Aluminum Co. of Am. *(Alcoa)*, 148 F.2d 416, 427 (2d Cir. 1945).

35. E.g., United States v. Microsoft Corp., 253 F.3d 34, 76–79 (D.C. Cir. 2001) (en banc) (per curiam); United States v. Visa U.S.A., Inc., 344 F.3d 229, 241 (2d Cir. 2003); Lorain Journal Co. v. United States, 342 U.S. 143 (1951).

36. The "single monopoly profit" claim is most often made when analyzing restrictions that a dominant firm imposes on vertically related firms. Compare Evans and Padilla 2005, 77.

37. Bork 1978, 137–138, 140.

38. Bork 1978, 372, 380–381.

39. E & L Consulting, Ltd. v. Doman Indus., 472 F.3d 23, 29–30 (2d Cir. 2006); G. K. A. Beverage Corp. v. Honickman, 55 F.3d 762, 767 (2d Cir. 1995); Town of Concord v. Boston Edison Co., 915 F.2d 17, 23, 32 (1st Cir. 1990) (Breyer, C.J.); see Jefferson Parish Hosp. Dist. No. 2 v. Hyde, 466 U.S. 2, 36–37 (1984) (O'Connor, J., concurring).

40. Schor v. Abbott Labs., 457 F.3d 608, 611 (7th Cir. 2006) (Easterbrook, J.). The Supreme Court has ruled out the possibility that a monopolist can violate Sherman Act § 2 through monopoly leveraging in the absence of

proof that the defendant had a dangerous probability of success of obtaining monopoly power in the second market, *Trinko,* 540 U.S. at 415n4, but without reference to the single monopoly profit theory.

41. Crane and Wright 2009, 209–210 (bundled discounts); Evans 2006 (tying); Ramseyer and Rasmusen 2014 (exclusionary conduct).
42. See Gavil et al. 2017, 359–365; see also Salop 2008,144–148; Kaplow 1985; Bresnahan 2010; Nalebuff 2004; Salop and Romaine 1999, 624–630; compare O'Brien 2008, 78.
43. Gavil et al. 2017, 959–965. A dominant firm or coordinating firms can also exercise additional market power through exclusionary conduct that permits the evasion of rate regulation or through conduct that facilitates harmful price discrimination.
44. Cooper et al. 2005a, 648; Hylton and Salinger 2001, 471; McWane, Inc., FTC Docket No. 9351, 2014–1 Trade Cas. (CCH) ¶ 78,670, aff'd, 738 F. 3d 914 (11th Cir. 2015) at 129, 293 (Wright, Comm'r, dissenting).
45. Easterbrook 1984, 15; Evans and Padilla 2005, 81–82.
46. See Eastman Kodak Co. v. Image Technical Servs., Inc., 504 U.S. 451, 488 (1992) (Scalia, J., dissenting).
47. Levenstein and Suslow 2014. The vertical restraints allowed the colluding firms to discourage cheating or entry while keeping their collusive horizontal agreement secret.
48. See Baker and Chevalier 2013 (best-price guarantees).
49. See U.S. Dep't of Justice & Fed. Trade Comm'n, *Horizontal Merger Guidelines* § 10, 2010, http://www.justice.gov/atr///hmg-2010.pdf.
50. But compare Ippolito 1991.
51. Other relevant background institutions include, for example, antitrust rules governing burdens of proof and remedy determination, the procedural rules governing litigation, state unfair competition laws, and laws granting intellectual property rights. See generally Kaplow 2012; Wickelgren 2012, 54.
52. Procompetitive consequences may be systematically more visible than anticompetitive consequences, particularly if firms can take steps to disguise the latter. See Davies and Ormosi 2013; Baker 2001, 825.
53. MacKay and Smith 2014. Prior studies of the consequences of resale price maintenance did not address the identification problem highlighted here, and did not suggest a uniform interpretation. See generally, Baker 2015, 20n79.
54. Baker 2015, 12–13. Product "modules" (categories) included "light beer" and "sleeping aids."
55. MacKay and Smith 2014.
56. MacKay and Smith 2014, 15–17.
57. Under the leading procompetitive theory, the price increase reflects higher product quality or improved service, quality-adjusted prices fall, and industry output increases. The most likely interpretation of a price increase

combined with an output reduction across the group of branded retail products analyzed is the one adopted by the study's authors: that competition was harmed on average. MacKay and Smith 2014, 3, 16, 17–18. It is possible, however, that total output fell yet consumers in aggregate benefited. This could have happened, for example, if inframarginal purchasers valued point-of-sale services induced by resale price maintenance a great deal while marginal purchasers did not value such services much.

58. MacKay and Smith 2014, 4–5, 10, 13, n36. The results reflect the combined consequences of conduct that would be treated as resale price maintenance under the Sherman Act (including finding an agreement between the manufacturer and distributor) and conduct that has a similar effect but could not have been challenged. They measure the consequences of a more permissive legal environment for all practices that may have been chilled by the per se prohibition against resale price maintenance.

59. Hence, the study's results caution against abandoning antitrust law's concern with resale price maintenance. But see Joshua Wright, Comm'r, Federal Trade Commission (FTC), "The Economics of Resale Price Maintenance and Implications for Competition Law and Policy" (speech), Remarks Before the British Institute of International and Comparative Law, April 9, 2014, 19–21, https://www.ftc.gov/public-statements/2014/04/economics -resale-price-maintenance-implications-competition-law-policy-0; Lambert and Sykuta 2013.

60. See generally Sokol 2014, 1004n8.

61. One study found that exclusive dealing arrangements between certain brewers and their Chicago distributors did not raise the distribution costs of potentially foreclosed brewers. Asker 2016. Another study found that exclusive distributors sold more beer than nonexclusive distributors. Sass 2005. The findings of a third study suggest that exclusive dealing has harmed competition in the beer industry. The study, which addressed the identification issue by exploiting differences in rules across states and within states over time, found that beer sales were lower when rules permitted distributors to engage in exclusive dealing. Klick and Wright 2008, 20–21.

62. Cooper et al. 2005a, 662.

63. Hylton and Salinger 2001, 514, n138. Accord Evans and Padilla 2005, 95.

64. Kobayashi and Muris 2012, 153. Kobayashi and Muris's recommendation that courts ignore post-Chicago school theoretical modeling demonstrating the possible rationality of predatory pricing (Kobayashi and Muris, 166) gives no weight to recent empirical literature that finds examples of successful price predation during eras in which enforcement against predatory pricing was lax (during the early twentieth century or, more recently, following the Supreme Court's decisions in *Matsushita* and *Brooke Group*). See Burns 1986; Elzinga and Mills 2009; Genesove and Mullin 2006; Lerner 1995; Scott Morton 1997; Weiman and Levin 1994. In a literature survey, Kobayashi recognizes that four of these articles "provide evidence consistent with the use of predatory pricing," but dismisses three of the four

on the ground that "we do not know whether these price wars would be unlawful under modern predation standards"—an issue not relevant to assessing their plausibility—"or whether such episodes resulted in reductions to welfare"—a rhetorical device that presumes implausibility and sets a high bar against relying on relevant evidence that suggests otherwise. Kobayashi 2010, 127.

65. Manne and Wright 2010, 196, 200.

66. See Baker 2013b, 580–81.

67. Easterbrook 1984, 2; compare Page 2010, 47.

68. Easterbrook 1984, 15.

69. For a recent example in which the Supreme Court corrected the erroneous decisions of multiple appellate courts, see FTC v. Actavis, Inc., 570 U.S. 136 (2013). Compare Carrier 2012. Moreover, appellate courts can correct their own errors. Compare Blue Cross & Blue Shield United v. Marshfield Clinic, 65 F.3d 1406, 1415 (7th Cir. 1995) (Posner, C.J.) (assuming that a contractual most-favored-nations provision would help a firm bargain with its suppliers for low prices and deeming the theory that the provision would discourage price cutting as "an ingenious but perverse argument"), with In re Brand Name Prescription Drugs, 288 F.3d 1028, 1033 (7th Cir. 2002) (Posner, J.) (noting authority for prohibiting industrywide adoption of most-favored-nations provisions, "which make discounting more costly").

70. Today, three of the Supreme Court cases described as creating erroneous precedents in this paragraph and the accompanying notes (*Appalachian Coals, Schwinn,* and *Von's*) are widely considered wrongly decided. The merits of a fourth, *Dr. Miles,* remain controversial. See Dr. Miles Med. Co. v. John D. Park & Sons Co., 220 U.S. 373 (1911), *overruled by* Leegin Creative Leather Prods., Inc. v. PSKS, Inc., 551 U.S. 877 (2007).

71. Appalachian Coals, Inc. v. United States, 288 U.S. 344 (1933), *abrogated by* United States v. Socony-Vacuum Oil Co., 310 U.S. 150, 221 (1940).

72. United States v. Arnold, Schwinn & Co., 388 U.S. 365 (1967), *overruled by* Cont'l T.V., Inc. v. GTE Sylvania Inc., 433 U.S. 36 (1977). One could argue that *Schwinn* barely lasted at all, given the hostility with which lower courts and commentators received it. E.g., *Tripoli Co. v. Wella Corp.,* 425 F.2d 932, 936–38 (3d Cir. 1970) (en banc).

73. See section above on "Markets Self-Correct Through Entry."

74. *See Sylvania,* 433 U.S. at 48, 48n14; Gavil et al. 2017, 697–700 (Sidebar 5–1); Baker and Shapiro 2008a, 238.

75. See generally Christiansen and Eskridge 2014; compare Widiss 2014; Nourse 2013. If the historical per se prohibition on resale price maintenance, overruled in 2007, is considered an error, as today's antitrust conservatives hold, then the decision by Congress to give states the authority to permit resale price maintenance agreements in certain industries, which was in effect between 1952 and 1975, would constitute a form of legislative correction.

76. The Supreme Court's decision in *Dr. Miles*, which took nearly a century to overturn, was limited substantially after seven years by United States v. Colgate & Co., 250 U.S. 300 (1919). Moreover, during a period when the Supreme Court likely considered the precedent treating resale price maintenance as illegal per se to be wrongly decided, but before the Court overruled that precedent, it raised the burden of proof for plaintiffs in Monsanto Co. v. Spray-Rite Service Corp., 465 U.S. 752 (1984), and Business Electronics Corp. v. Sharp Electronics Corp., 485 U.S. 717 (1988), and abandoned the per se rule for maximum resale price maintenance. State Oil Co. v. Khan, 522 U.S. 3 (1997). The Supreme Court has also deployed its tools for narrowing past decisions by limiting the per se rule against horizontal agreements to naked restraints, Broad. Music, Inc. v. CBS, Inc., 441 U.S. 1 (1979), and by circumscribing the impact of *Aspen Skiing*, a monopolization precedent I do not consider erroneous. See Verizon Commc'ns Inc. v. Law Offices of Curtis V. Trinko, LLP, 540 U.S. 398, 409 (2004). If an erroneous precedent that discourages efficient conduct is construed narrowly, its adverse impact may be muted, as the affected firms may find other ways to achieve the desired efficiencies at little additional cost. Devlin and Jacobs 2010, 98.

77. See section above on "Markets Self-Correct Through Entry." See also Devlin and Jacobs 2010, 98–99.

78. Easterbrook 1984, 34.

79. Easterbrook 1984, 36; compare Snyder and Kauper 1991.

80. Easterbrook 1984, 35.

81. Easterbrook 1984, 36. The "antitrust injury" doctrine requires plaintiffs to prove "injury of the type the antitrust laws were intended to prevent and that flows from that which makes defendants' acts unlawful." Brunswick Corp. v. Pueblo Bowl-O-Mat, Inc., 429 U.S. 477, 489 (1977).

82. See Easterbrook 1984, 35–39.

83. Easterbrook 1984, 38–39.

84. Monsanto Co. v. Spray-Rite Serv. Corp., 465 U.S. 752 (1984); Bus. Elecs. Corp. v. Sharp Elecs. Corp., 485 U.S. 717 (1988). The demise of the per se rule against vertical price fixing will likely further reduce the attractiveness of such suits. Leegin Creative Leather Prods., Inc. v. PSKS, Inc., 551 U.S. 877 (2007).

85. Hovenkamp 2005, 71.

86. David J. Theroux, "Open Letter on Antitrust Protectionism," *Independent Institute*, June 2, 1999, http://www.independent.org/issues/article.asp?id =483; Easterbrook 1984, 34; DiLorenzo 2004. But see Page and Lopatka 2007, 31–32.

87. Government monopolization cases are infrequent: over the long term, the average is less than one per year per agency (DOJ or FTC). See Kovacic 2003, 449 tbl.4. But the antitrust laws also allow private suits, and some "big cases" against single firm defendants—most notably, in recent years, Microsoft—can take on outsize importance.

88. *2010 Merger Guidelines* § 2.2; See *FCC Staff Analysis and Findings* ¶ 83, n255, *In re* Applications of AT&T, Inc. & Deutsche Telekom AG, WT Docket No. 11–65, November 29, 2011 (describing interests of merging firms and merger opponents and their possible alignment with the public interest), http://hraunfoss.fcc.gov/edocs_public/attachmatch/DA-11-1955A2 .pdf. Compare Hosp. Corp. of Am. v. FTC, 807 F.2d 1381, 1391–92 (7th Cir. 1986) (Posner, J.) ("Hospital Corporation's most telling point is that the impetus for the Commission's complaint came from a competitor"), with 807 F.2d at 1387 (the FTC could have concluded that colluding hospitals could manipulate certificate of need laws "to delay any competitive sally by a noncolluding competitor").

89. Hovenkamp 2005, 70.

90. FTC v. Actavis, Inc., 570 U.S. 136 (2013).

91. E.g., FTC v. Watson Pharms., Inc., 677 F.3d 1298, 1312 (11th Cir. 2012), *rev'd sub nom. Actavis,* 570 U.S. 136 (2013). The most sustained court challenges to these practices were not brought by complaining excluded rivals, but by the Federal Trade Commission or by classes of buyers. E.g., *Actavis; In re* K-Dur Antitrust Litig., 686 F.3d 197 (3d Cir. 2012); Valley Drug Co. v. Geneva Pharm., Inc., 344 F.3d 1294 (11th Cir. 2003).

92. Allied Orthopedic Appliances Inc. v. Tyco Health Care Grp., 592 F.3d 991, 997 (9th Cir. 2010); Concord Boat Corp. v. Brunswick Corp., 207 F.3d 1039, 1059 (8th Cir. 2000); Omega Envtl., Inc. v. Gilbarco, Inc., 127 F.3d 1157, 1163 (9th Cir. 1997); Paddock Publ'ns, Inc. v. Chi. Tribune Co., 103 F.3d 42, 47 (7th Cir. 1996); U.S. Healthcare, Inc. v. Healthsource, Inc., 986 F.2d 589, 596 (1st Cir. 1993); Roland Mach. Co. v. Dresser Indus., 749 F.2d 380, 395 (7th Cir. 1984).

93. *See Allied Orthopedic,* 592 F.3d at 996–997; *Omega Environmental,* 127 F.3d at 1163. Judge Bork recognized that foreclosure could in theory (might "conceivably") occur through disruption of optimal distribution patterns, but suggested that anticompetitive outcomes were implausible. See Bork 1978, 156.

94. Compare Hovenkamp 2016, 598n316, 599n317; American Bar Association Section of Antitrust Law 2017, 1:214–216; Gavil et al. 2017, 1015.

95. United States v. Dentsply Int'l, 399 F.3d 181, 185, 193 (3d Cir. 2005); United States v. Microsoft Corp., 253 F.3d 34, 366–67 (D.C. Cir. 2001) (en banc) (per curiam). See also McWane, Inc. v. Federal Trade Commission, 783 F.3d 814 (11th Cir. 2015).

96. Joshua Wright, Comm'r, FTC, "Defining the Federal Trade Commission's Unfair Methods of Competition Authority" (speech), Remarks at the Executive Committee Meeting of the New York State Bar Association's Antitrust Section: Section 5 Recast, June 19, 2013, 24, https://www.ftc.gov /sites/default/files/documents/public_statements/section-5-recast-defining -federal-trade-commissions-unfair-methods-competition-authority /130619section5recast.pdf.

97. Bork 1978, 49; Manne and Wright 2010, 157.

98. See Leegin Creative Leather Prods., Inc. v. PSKS, Inc., 551 U.S. 877, 916–17 (2007) (Breyer, J., dissenting); Bork 1978, 429–440.

99. See generally Baker 2013b.

100. Compare Shelanski 2011, 712.

101. See Joshua D. Wright, Comm'r, FTC, "Proposed Policy Statement Regarding Unfair Methods of Competition Under Section 5 of the Federal Trade Commission Act," June 19, 2013, 8, https://www.ftc.gov/public -statements/2013/06/statement-commissioner-joshua-d-wright; compare Maureen K. Ohlhausen, Comm'r, FTC, "Principles of Navigation" (speech), Remarks at the U.S. Chamber of Commerce: Section 5, July 25, 2013, 1–2, 7–8, https://www.ftc.gov/public-statements/2013/07/section-5-principles -navigation.

102. A need to reduce false positives and to mitigate their chilling effect on efficient conduct was frequently cited as a ground for abandoning some of the per se rules that prevailed prior to the late 1970s, especially with regard to vertical restraints. E.g., Posner 1975a. During the 1960s, the strong presumption of harm to competition from horizontal mergers when market concentration is high and increasing was questioned on similar grounds. E.g., United States v. Von's Grocery Co., 384 U.S. 270, 287–88 (1966) (Stewart, J., dissenting).

103. For example, Areeda and Turner argued that a dominant firm's below-cost pricing should create an irrebuttable presumption of monopolization. Areeda and Turner 1975, 712; see Pac. Eng'g & Prod. Co. v. Kerr-McGee Corp., 551 F.2d 790, 797 (10th Cir. 1977).

104. Compare FTC v. Actavis, Inc. 570 U.S. 136, 159–160 (2013).

105. Lande and Davis 2008, 880. A substantial fraction of the private cases studied did not follow federal, state, or EU government enforcement actions, and others had a mixed public/private origin. Lande and Davis 2008, 897. For criticisms of the Lande and Davis study, and the authors' responses to those criticisms, see Werden et al. 2011, 227–233; Crane 2011, 168–272; Davis and Lande 2013. The private damages remedy has a deterrent effect only to the extent that violators do not anticipate that they will be required to pay antitrust damages in the future. Otherwise, they will pass through the expected damages payment to buyers in advance, in the form of higher prices. See generally Baker 1988b; Salant 1987; Segal and Whinston 2006.

106. See generally Bone 2003, 259–291.

107. Verizon Commc'ns Inc. v. Law Offices of Curtis V. Trinko, LLP, 540 U.S. 398 (2004); Credit Suisse Secs. (USA) LLC v. Billing, 551 U.S. 264 (2007); Bell Atl. Corp v. Twombly, 550 U.S. 544 (2007); Comcast Corp. v. Behrend, 569 U.S. 27 (2013); Am. Express Co. v. Italian Colors Rest., 570 U.S. 228 (2013). These decisions are reasonably described as conservative with respect to antitrust because they restrict antitrust plaintiffs' access to court. See generally Crane 2011, 62–63; Engstrom 2013, 619.

108. *Trinko* and *Credit Suisse* required regulatory resolution of antitrust disputes; *American Express* relegated antitrust disputes to individual arbitration.

109. The Court also did not consider whether a wholly different remedial approach of restricting the litigation tactics available to large-firm defendants would address the social costs of private litigation more effectively than the approach it chose: of restricting private plaintiffs' access to the courts. But compare *Twombly,* 550 U.S. at 560n6. Empirical studies of the costs associated with pretrial civil litigation and the costs of class action litigation are reviewed in Kessler and Rubinfeld 2007, 378–381, 390.

110. See generally Crane 2011, 59–60. The Class Action Fairness Act of 2005, Pub. L. No. 109–2, 119 Stat. 4 (codified as amended in scattered sections of 28 U.S.C.), required, in part, greater judicial scrutiny of "coupon settlements," such as settlements awarding consumers discounts on new purchases from defendant firms. This requirement addressed an agency problem: a concern about the incentive of plaintiffs' attorneys to reach settlements that awarded attorneys' fees that were generous relative to the compensation awarded class members. See *In re* HP Inkjet Printer Litig., 716 F.3d 1173, 1177–78 (9th Cir. 2013); see generally Vance 2006. That incentive could lead counsel to bring non-meritorious suits and settle meritorious cases too cheaply from an optimal-deterrence perspective. Compare Bone 2003, 275–280.

111. Monsanto Co. v. Spray-Rite Serv. Corp., 465 U.S. 752 (1984); Bus. Elecs. Corp. v. Sharp Elecs. Corp., 485 U.S. 717 (1988). The Supreme Court has not revisited *Monsanto* or *Sharp* since it overruled the per se prohibition against resale price maintenance. That change in the substantive rule, however, reduces the apparent benefits of *Monsanto*'s and *Sharp*'s procedural rules and calls into question whether those rules' benefits continue to exceed the costs of the limits that the rules place on terminated dealers' access to courts. The interplay among substantive and procedural rules in antitrust is described in Calkins 1986, 1127–1139.

112. Ill. Brick Co. v. Illinois, 431 U.S. 720 (1977).

113. Matsushita Elec. Indus. v. Zenith Radio Corp., 475 U.S. 574 (1986).

114. See Crane 2011, 63–67; see Shelanski 2011, 714; Salop 2014, 635–636.

115. See DeBow 1988, 44; compare Robert D. Hershey, "Courts Assailed by Antitrust Chief," *New York Times,* November 9, 1985.

116. See Bell Atl. Corp v. Twombly, 550 U.S. 544, 559 (2007).

117. Credit Suisse Secs. (USA) LLC v. Billing, 551 U.S. 264, 281–82 (2007).

118. Crane 2011, 60–62. Crane associates these concerns with a Harvard school perspective, distinct from the views of the Chicago school.

119. See Gavil 2007, 24.

120. See Gavil 2007, 25.

121. See Baker 2003a, 42–45.

122. Gavil 2007, 21.

6. Inferring Agreement and Algorithmic Coordination

1. Constance L. Hays, "Variable-Price Coke Machine Being Tested," *New York Times,* October 28, 1999.
2. Sam Schechter, "Why Do Gas Station Prices Constantly Change? Blame the Algorithm," *Wall Street Journal,* May 8, 2017; see Mehra 2017.
3. James Walker, "Researchers Shut Down AI that Invented Its Own Language," *Digital Journal,* July 21, 2017, http://www.digitaljournal.com/tech -and-science/technology/a-step-closer-to-skynet-ai-invents-a-language -humans-can-t-read/article/498142; Abigail Constantino, "No, Facebook Did Not Shut Down AI Program for Getting Too Smart," *WTOP,* August 1, 2017, https://wtop.com/social-media/2017/08/facebook-artificial-intelligence -bots/; Adrienne Lafrance, "An Artificial Intelligence Developed Its Own Non-Human Language," *Atlantic,* June 15, 2017.
4. Information, United States v. David Topkins, No. 3:15-cr-00201-WHO (N.D. Cal. April 6, 2015). Compare U.K. Competition and Markets Authority, "CMA Issues Final Decision in Online Cartel Case," press release, August 12, 2016.
5. Mehra 2016; Stucke and Ezrachi 2015; Deck and Wilson 2003. Compare Calvano et al. 2018. But compare Ittoo and Petit 2017; James Somers, "Is AI Riding a One-Trick Pony?" *MIT Technology Review,* September 29, 2017.
6. Compare Kaplow 2013, 431.
7. Compare United States v. Container Corp., 393 U.S. 333 (1969).
8. Humans can simplify that task by responding identically across markets, but the resulting coordinated consensus would probably be imperfect. See Baker 1993, 164–167.
9. Compare Bernheim and Madsen 2017.
10. See generally Harrington 2018. Compare Deng 2017.
11. Firms may be able to coordinate without rapid price matching by employing pricing algorithms that combine price leadership with substantial price reductions in the event rivals do not follow. Gal 2018, § II.B.2. Algorithms that implement grim punishment strategies may not be credible (subgame perfect), however.
12. See generally Gavil et al. 2017, 838–847.
13. See Deck and Wilson 2003.
14. Algorithm design would also need to address the length of time that rival price cuts would be matched before reverting to prior prices. That timing would presumably depend on what the firm knows about the frequency and magnitude of shocks to cost and demand, and its uncertainty as to whether the price reduction reflects cheating on a coordinated consensus or a negative demand shock.
15. This discussion also assumes that the firms and their algorithms do not seek to identify key features of rivals' algorithms (such as setting predetermined

maximum prices, optimal price adjustment increments, and optimal time periods before making price adjustments) by monitoring rivals' responses to the firm's own pricing decisions. Were they do to so, and to condition their own decisions on those inferences, it may no longer be appropriate to refer to the pricing algorithms as exhibiting (mere) leader-follower conduct.

16. This assumption also puts aside the possibility that the firms would hire the same third-party vendor, acting as a cartel manager, to develop or select the pricing algorithm for them. See Ezrachi and Stucke 2016, 46–55.

17. If the algorithm leads firms to match rivals' prices quickly, before most buyers respond to one firm's price cuts, for example, it is implausible that any firm would find it profitable to introduce a new algorithm that undercuts rivals. The incremental profits from attracting new customers would almost surely be outweighed by the incremental losses from cutting prices to the customers that the firm also would have served had it maintained the higher price. Hence, if all firms adopt this pricing algorithm, none may find it in its interest to change to another pricing algorithm.

18. The prospects for coordination are enhanced when algorithms can decode the strategies of rival algorithms. Salcedo 2015.

19. Compare Bernheim and Madsen 2017; Green and Porter 1984.

20. The interpretation would be similar if Coke's algorithm induced Pepsi's algorithm to conclude that price cutting would not be profitable absent a shift in cost or demand by lowering the price in Boston even below $1.00 (Coke's predetermined maximum)—say, to $0.80.

21. Gal and Elkin-Koren 2017.

22. This frame interprets the plus factors as a policy choice based on balancing error costs. Louis Kaplow argues that the plus factors perform poorly in balancing error costs and questions particularly the way some courts and commentators rely on the plus factors to treat communication among rivals as a prerequisite for inferring agreement. Kaplow 2013, 1–2, 109–114, 122–123.

23. Theatre Enters., Inc. v. Paramount Film Distrib. Corp., 346 U.S. 537, 541 (1954). In 1986, the Supreme Court further encouraged a cautious approach. The Court held that in a private damages action under Sherman Act § 1, a plaintiff seeking to demonstrate an agreement "must present evidence 'that tends to exclude the possibility' that the alleged conspirators acted independently" in order to survive a defense motion for summary judgment or for judgment as a matter of law. The Court also observed that "if the factual context renders respondents' claim implausible—if the claim is one that simply makes no economic sense—respondents must come forward with more persuasive evidence to support their claim than would otherwise be necessary." Matsushita Electric Indus. Co. v. Zenith Radio Corp. 475 U.S. 574, 577–578 (1986) (citing *Monsanto Co. v. Spray-Rite Service Corp.*, 465 U.S. 752, 764 [1984]). In a civil case, where the inference of agreement requires a preponderance of the evidence, *Matsushita* should not be read to

insist on near certainty. In re Publication Paper Antitrust Litigation, 690 F.3d 52, 62–63 (2d. Cir. 2012); In re Brand Name Prescription Drugs Antitrust Litigation, 186 F.3d 781, 787 (7th Cir. 1999) (Posner, C.J.). The standard set forth in *Matsushita* applies in a setting in which courts must construe facts in the light most favorable to plaintiffs and thus a setting in which the possibility of false negatives has been minimized. The "more persuasive evidence" requirement applies only when the claim "makes no economic sense." This is an allusion to the demanding substantive standard for testing predatory pricing claims, the violation alleged in *Matsushita*. It does not apply to claims the Court would find more plausible, as when the alleged agreement involves price fixing or market division among horizontal rivals.

24. See United States v. Airline Tariff Publ'g Co., 59 Fed. Reg. 15,225 (March 31, 1994); United States v. Airline Tariff Publ'g Co., 58 Fed. Reg. 3971 (January 12, 1993).

25. There is no reason to think that an increase in average deterrence would be accompanied by a reduction in marginal deterrence, notwithstanding the theoretical possibility. See Schwartz 2000.

26. The Turner/Posner debate on conscious parallelism is described in Gavil et al. 2017, 322–326.

27. Perhaps the firm could instead try to defend its new price as no more than what it would obtain in a competitive market. But doing so would either require comparing price with cost of the marginal producer—an approach that would raise similar problems to proving the magnitude of a cost increase—or require comparing price with the price charged in some similar market known to be competitive. The latter approach would require a demonstration that the benchmark price is competitive, as well as a potentially challenging adjustment to the benchmark price for differences in cost and product quality between the markets.

28. Kaplow 2013, 324–336, 344–345.

29. Turner 1969, 1217–1231.

30. Although the economic tools for identifying price elevation in repeated oligopoly interactions have increased in sophistication since the time Turner wrote, it will still often be difficult to determine the competitive price reliably. But compare Miller and Weinberg 2017. The most plausible definition of a competitive price, against which market prices would need to be compared, is the price that would arise as the outcome of oligopoly conduct without repeated interaction (i.e., in a one-shot interaction). Compare Kaplow 2013, 269–275, 353–367; Werden 2004, 779–780. This way of distinguishing competition and coordination can be understood as updating Richard Posner's position in the Turner/Posner debate on conscious parallelism. See generally Gavil et al. 2017, 322–326. Alternatively, the competitive price could be defined to equal marginal cost. Marginal cost may be difficult to measure for a range of conceptual and practical reasons, however. Doing so

would be particularly challenging in markets in which fixed costs are substantial, and the competitive price is the average cost of a hypothetical efficient entrant (which is the industry's marginal cost in a free-entry equilibrium).

31. Turner 1969, 1217–1231.
32. Kaplow 2013, 188–189, 261, 269. Kaplow recommends that courts look to pricing patterns, price elevation, facilitating practices, and the conduciveness of market conditions in order to identify oligopolistic coordination. Kaplow 2018a (In press), § 3.2.1.
33. Werden 2004, 779.
34. Additional reasons are discussed below in the section on "Algorithmic Decision Makers."
35. As with administrability arguments generally, the problems raised by Turner influenced the form of antitrust law's response by leading courts to adopt the plus factor approach, but it did not tie down the substance of the plus factors.
36. If parties negotiate by proposing quid pro quo conduct ("if you do X, then, and only then, I will do Y"), for example, they can be said to have reached an agreement when they identify a consistent set of proposals and allow them to take effect. Proposals of this form include assurances that party would follow through if the others go along.
37. If the firms are not already coordinating, they must also identify which market participants would join in a coordinated arrangement.
38. In re Text Messaging Antitrust Litigation, 630 F.3d 622 (7th Cir. 2010).
39. Five years later, in the same case but on a more extensive record, the same appellate panel viewed the plus factors differently: as implicitly showing that the firms did not need to engage in the forbidden process in order to coordinate. In re Text Messaging Antitrust Litigation, 782 F.3d 867 (7th Cir. 2015). The court also raised the possibility that firms did not have to coordinate at all in order to achieve higher prices. I was an economic expert for one of the defendants in the case.
40. Blomkest Fertilizer, Inc. v. Potash Corp., 203 F.3d 1028, 1046 (8th Cir. 2000) (Gibson, J., dissenting). The dissent also argued that prices had increased more than could be explained by the two types of governmental action referenced by the majority: a settlement in a dumping case that set a price floor and the privatization of a major producer that induced it to reduce output. Compare Hovenkamp 2005, 136.
41. See generally Gavil et al. 2017, 366–372.
42. Competitively sensitive information might include, for example, sales to specific customers; advance notice of price changes, especially if not disclosed to customers; or verification of the price the firm charged in specific past transactions. The timing of communication may also be important: the inference of an agreement may be stronger when communication or its opportunity is closely followed in time by parallel price

increases because that coincidence suggests the firms met covertly to fix the price. United States v. Foley, 598 F.2d 1323 (4th Cir. 1979). A number of courts have held, as the Seventh Circuit recently put it, that "an express, manifested agreement, and thus an agreement involving actual, verbalized communication, must be proved in order for a price fixing conspiracy to be actionable under the Sherman Act." In re High Fructose Corn Syrup Antitrust Litig., 295 F.3d 651, 654 (7th Cir. 2002) (Posner, J.). But commentators who treat "communications" as a prerequisite for inferring an agreement interpret the term more broadly than verbal exchanges. Page 2013, 218; Werden 2004, 780; Page 2015. Louis Kaplow argues that communications should not be a prerequisite for inferring agreement. Kaplow 2013, 1–2.

43. Examples of the latter may include a sudden and substantial change in industry conduct; complex and seemingly arbitrary revisions to the pattern of prices on price lists; firms purchasing products at wholesale from a competitor that they could have produced more cheaply internally; or firms with excess low-cost capacity declining to compete for the business of buyers that are customers of their rivals or declining to offer a secret discount to obtain a large increment of business. Other examples may include firms not adjusting prices when supply or demand conditions change substantially, as by declining to lower a high price when costs or demand are falling; multiproduct producers raising prices substantially on products where their firm's demand is elastic but industry demand is less elastic; or rival firms standardizing or simplifying product grades, publishing price lists, or announcing price changes in advance in situations where these practices provide little or no customer benefit. Compare City of Tuscaloosa v. Harcros Chems., Inc., 158 F.3d 548, 572 (11th Cir. 1998); Kovacic et al. 2011, 435–436.

44. Matsushita Elec. Indus. Co. v. Zenith Radio Corp., 475 U.S. 574, 587, 596, 597–598 (1986). Accord Eastman Kodak Co. v. Image Technical Servs., Inc., 504 U.S. 451, 468 (1992).

45. These plus factors include industry features thought to facilitate coordination, such as few firms, homogeneous products, difficult entry conditions, large numbers of purchasers, small and frequent transactions, or transparent prices. They also include a past history of industry coordination. Conversely, many firms, heterogeneous products, easy entry conditions, few purchasers, large and infrequent transactions, and secret prices tend to cast doubt about the feasibility of coordinated conduct, whether through agreement or otherwise. To similar effect, if industry demand is relatively elastic before coordination is said to have occurred, the gains from coordination would be limited, calling into question whether firms have a rational motive to bear the costs of behaving collectively. If demand is inelastic after coordination is said to have occurred, though, that means that any coordination is far from complete (as inelastic demand means that price must be below the level that

maximizes joint profits). That is not inconsistent with coordinated conduct, as coordination need not be complete to be harmful and demand might have been even less elastic before coordination.

46. These may include sustained and substantial profitability; prices rising when costs fall; the stability of market shares over time despite substantial shifts in buyer demand or costs likely to affect firms differentially; or prices that are high relative to costs for products not strongly differentiated when firms have excess capacity. They may also include the adoption by leading firms of practices that might facilitate coordination, such as preannouncement of price increases, use of common price lists, or exchange of information about prices, costs, output, capacity, or sales. Actions that would be contrary to self-interest unless pursued collectively also may indicate that firms are exercising market power.

47. William J. Kolasky, Deputy Assistant Att'y Gen., "Coordinated Effects in Merger Review: From Dead Frenchmen to Beautiful Minds and Mavericks" (address), The ABA Section of Antitrust Law Spring Meeting, Washington, D.C., April 24, 2012.

48. See In re Text Messaging Antitrust Litigation, 782 F.3d 867, 871 (7th Cir. 2015); Williamson Oil Co. v. Phillip Morris USA, 346 F.3d 1287, 1307 (11th Cir. 2003). This logic may lead to the question of whether the plus factors in the second group prove too much: if the industry is conducive to coordination, why did the firms need to risk liability by doing so through agreement? Or, to similar effect, if the firms adopted facilitating practices unilaterally and in parallel, what more could they accomplish through an agreement? See Baker 1993, 190–191; compare Kaplow 2013, 1215–1273. The answer is that coordination absent an agreement is not always successful nor invariably incomplete. Hence even in an industry conducive to that outcome, coordination may become more effective with an agreement. The economic concept of coordination differs from the legal concept of agreement. Baker 1993, 152n16.

49. Relatedly, computerized algorithms could develop and employ complex algorithms that humans could not practically implement.

50. Such justifications may also be called into question if competing firms adopt algorithms that ignore obvious potential influences on demand or cost, do not rely on the best data when formulating prices, train their algorithms on similar case studies when better examples are available, or lock their algorithms rather than continuing to learn. Gal 2018, § IV.A.2.

51. As previously observed, this may be plausible, for example, if buyers are numerous, make small purchases, and cannot easily store inventories.

52. Compare Kaplow 2013, 431.

53. Explanations help because machine learning techniques are prone to overfitting (making predictions based on spurious correlations). See Cliff Kuang, "Can A.I. Be Taught to Explain Itself?" *New York Times Magazine*, November 21, 2017; James Mackintosh, "Robotic Hogwash! Artificial

Intelligence Will Not Take Over Wall Street," *Wall Street Journal*, July 17, 2017; compare Christopher Mims, "Career of the Future: Robot Psychologist," *Wall Street Journal*, July 9, 2017.

54. By matching prices market-by-market, the simple firm is led to incorporate in its prices the information about shifts to cost and demand that can be learned from changing market prices. It may also learn about industry-wide shifts in costs and demand in other ways.

55. Compare Harrington 2018, § 4.

56. U.S. Dep't of Justice and Federal Trade Commission, *Horizontal Merger Guidelines* § 7 (2010). The *Horizontal Merger Guidelines* describe three types of coordination: (1) "the explicit negotiation of a common understanding of how firms will compete or refrain from competing," (2) "a similar common understanding that is not explicitly negotiated but would be enforced by the detection and punishment of deviations" that would undermine it, and (3) "parallel accommodating conduct not pursuant to a prior understanding." The narrow definition in the text encompasses the first two types; the broad definition adds the third.

57. If a firm adopted an algorithm likely to facilitate coordination given the algorithms employed by rivals or given the ability of rivals to identify the algorithm and match it, the Federal Trade Commission could potentially challenge the adoption of the algorithm as an invitation to collude.

58. Harrington 2018. See Calvano et al. 2018; Deng 2018.

59. But compare Harrington 2018, § 6.2. It would likely be the most difficult to make that distinction in markets in which the primary impediment to successful coordination among rivals is identifying what price to charge (rather than deterring cheating or preventing entry), and the firms solve the problem of reaching a coordinated consensus on price through leader-follower behavior. When it is difficult to distinguish repeated interactions from one-shot interactions with learning from prices, moreover, courts cannot easily craft injunctions to prevent continuing repeated interactions. It may be less difficult to make the necessary distinction in markets where coordination is impeded primarily by the threat of cheating, however, if firms employ strategies that induce steep price cutting in response to price reductions by rivals.

60. But see U.S. v. H&R Block, Inc., 833 F. Supp. 2d 36 (D.D.C. 2011).

61. Unilateral effects theories have played a prominent role in horizontal merger enforcement at the antitrust agencies since the late 1980s. Baker 2003d.

62. F.T.C. v. CCC Holdings Inc., 605 F. Supp. 2d 26 (D.D.C. 2009).

63. Since airline deregulation in 1978, the Justice Department has also brought several nonmerger cases involving the airline industry. It challenged one major airline's attempt to collude with another, United States v. American Airlines, Inc., 743 F.2d 1114 (5th Cir. 1984), and attacked one airline's acquisition of takeoff and landing slots at a slot-constrained airport from another airline, U.S. Dept. of Justice, Antitrust Div., "Justice Department

Files Antitrust Lawsuit to Block United's Monopolization of Takeoff and Landing Slots at Newark Airport," press release, November 10, 2015. But the government was unsuccessful when it attempted to stop exclusionary conduct by a large network carrier against a small low-cost rival that threatened the large carrier's market power at its hub airports. United States v. AMR Corp., 335 F.3d 1109 (10th Cir. 2003).

64. Borenstein and Rose 2014; Baker 2002a, 166–173; Proposed Final Judgment and Competitive Impact Statement, United States v. Airline Tariff Publ'g Co., 59 Fed. Reg. 15, 225 (March 31, 1994); Proposed Final Judgment and Competitive Impact Statement, United States v. Airline Tariff Publ'g Co., 58 Fed. Reg. 3,971 (January 12, 1993); Ciliberto and Williams 2014, 765, 789; Evans and Kessides 1994, 365. Compare Aryal et al. 2018. In the Justice Department's coordination case against the major airlines in the early 1990s, the government found that when a rival reduced fares, a carrier would commonly match on that route and also on another route that was a more important route to the airline that cut fares (e.g., a route with an end point at the discounter's hub). The airlines continue to employ such "cross-market initiatives" to deter discounting and prevent fare wars. Amended Complaint, United States v. U.S. Airways Group, Inc., No. 1:13-cv-01236-CKK, ¶ 43 (D.D.C. September 5, 2013). (The airlines may also exercise market power unilaterally on routes where they have a dominant position.)

65. J. Bruce McDonald, Deputy Assistant Att'y Gen., "Antitrust for Airlines" (speech), presented to the Regional Airline Association, President's Council Meeting, November 3, 2005. When economists who had worked on a number of agency merger reviews evaluated the consequences of three major mergers involving legacy carriers, they found it natural to employ a statistical technique—difference-in-difference analysis—that was appropriate for evaluating the trade-off between unilateral effects and efficiencies but was incapable of evaluating whether the mergers had facilitated coordination across merging and non-merging airlines. Carlton et al. 2017.

66. U.S. Dept. of Justice, Antitrust Div., "Statement by Assistant Attorney General R. Hewitt Pate Regarding the Closing of the America West/US Airways Investigation," press release, June 23, 2005; U.S. Dept. of Justice, Antitrust Div., "Statement of the Department of Justice's Antitrust Division on Its Decision to Close Its Investigation of the Merger of Delta Airlines Inc. and Northwest Airlines Corporation," press release, October 29, 2008.

67. U.S. Dept. of Justice, Antitrust Div., "Statement of the Department of Justice Antitrust Division on Its Decision to Close Its Investigation of Southwest's Acquisition of Airtran," press release, April 26, 2011.

68. U.S. Dept. of Justice, Antitrust Div., "United Airlines and Continental Airlines Transfer Assets to Southwest Airlines in Response to Department of Justice's Antitrust Concerns," press release, August 27, 2010.

69. U.S. Dept. of Justice, Antitrust Div., "Department of Justice and Several States Will Sue to Stop United Airlines from Acquiring US Airways," press release, July 27, 2001.

70. See Trial brief of the United States, United States v. Northwest Airlines Corp., CA No. 98–74611 (E.D. Mich. October 24, 2000). I was an economic expert for the Justice Department in this case.

71. Amended Complaint, United States v. U.S. Airways Group, Inc., No. 1:13-cv-01236-CKK (D.D.C. September 5, 2013).

72. These are important dimensions on which competition could be harmed by a merger, but they are not the only dimensions on which airline coordination could become more effective. For example, there is anecdotal evidence that Southwest was acting to constrain more effective coordination in system-wide fare increases, stepping into the role that Northwest had played in 2000. Kwoka et al. 2016, 252. If so, a hypothetical future merger between Southwest and one of the other network carriers (American, Delta, or United) would further enhance the effectiveness of airline industry coordination system wide.

73. United States v. H&R Block, Inc., 833 F.3d 36 (D.D.C. 2011); Complaint, United States v. Anheuser-Busch InBEV SA/NV, No.1:13-cv-00127 (D.D.C. January 31, 2013); FCC Staff Analysis and Findings, In re Applications of AT&T, Inc. & Deutsche Telekom AG, WT Docket No. 11–65 (November 29, 2011).

74. See Baker 2002a, 174–177. It will often be plausible to suppose that firms would deviate from a coordinated outcome by cutting the coordinated price (cheating on the "reward state"). Then a maverick would be nearly indifferent between going along with a high coordinated price and cheating on that price. It is also possible that firms would deviate by declining to punish cheating rivals (cheating on the "punishment state"). Then a maverick would be nearly indifferent to participating in the punishment of cheaters. Compare Kühn 2015. The definition of a maverick as a firm that constrains the effectiveness (including existence) of coordinated conduct supposes that the oligopolists coordinate imperfectly through repeated interaction. (Coordination may be imperfect, for example, when the firms cannot employ communication and side payments.) In that setting a maverick need not be observably disruptive, though it could be. Others employ the term maverick more broadly: to also include a firm that invests in market share or otherwise competes more aggressively than its rivals when oligopolists are not coordinating through repeated interaction. E.g., Kwoka 1989, 410.

75. Baker 2002a, 178–179.

76. Enforcers also might increase their efforts to identify and prevent practices facilitating coordination. Unilateral facilitating practices adopted in parallel by rivals may be difficult to reach under the Sherman Act but the FTC may be able to interdict them through competition rulemaking. Baker 1993, 207–219.

7. Exclusionary Conduct by Dominant Platforms

1. Senator Elizabeth Warren, "Reigniting Competition in the American Economy" (speech), Keynote Remarks at New America's Open Markets Program Event, June 29, 2016, https://www.warren.senate.gov/files /documents/2016-6-29_Warren_Antitrust_Speech.pdf.

2. E.g., Matt Stoller, "Are Tech Giants Like Amazon, Facebook and Google Monopolies?" interview by Meghna Chakrabarti, *Here and Now,* September 4, 2017, http://www.wbur.org/hereandnow/2017/09/04/amazon -facebook-google-monopolies; see also Foer 2017; Taplin 2017.

3. Ryan Grim, "Steve Bannon Wants Facebook and Google Regulated Like Utilities," *The Intercept,* July 27, 2017, https://theintercept.com/2017/07/27 /steve-bannon-wants-facebook-and-google-regulated-like-utilities/; Daniel Kishi, "Time for a Conservative Anti-Monopoly Movement," *The American Conservative,* September 19, 2017, http://www.theamericanconservative .com/articles/amazon-facebook-google-conservative-anti-monopoly -movement/; John Kehoe, "Kenneth Rogoff Concerned by the Dark Side of the Technology Revolution," *Financial Review,* March 9, 2018. See Eleanor Clift, "Bill Galston and Bill Kristol's New Center Project Takes Aim at the Tech Oligarchs," *The Daily Beast,* September 11, 2017, https://www .thedailybeast.com/bill-galston-and-bill-kristols-new-center-project-takes -aim-at-the-tech-oligarchs.

4. Statement of the Federal Trade Commission Regarding Google's Search Practices, *Google Inc.,* No. 111-0163 (F.T.C. January 3, 2013).

5. E.g., Statement of the Commission Concerning Google / AdMob, No. 101–0031 (F.T.C. May 21, 2010); Statement of the Federal Trade Commission Concerning Google / DoubleClick, No. 071–0170 (F.T.C. December 20, 2007). But see Final Judgment, United States v. Google Inc., No. 1:11-cv-00688 (D.D.C. 2011) (accepting consent settlement resolving competitive issues raised by Google's acquisition of ITA); U.S. Department of Justice Antitrust Division, "Yahoo! Inc. and Google Inc. Abandon Their Advertising Agreement," press release, November 5, 1995, https://www .justice.gov/archive/atr/public/press_releases/2008/239167.htm. U.S. and European decisions not to bring enforcement actions against Google's acquisitions of Next Labs, Dropcam, and Waze, and Facebook's acquisition of WhatsApp, are criticized in Stucke and Grunes 2016, § 6.

6. Major enforcement initiatives against Google in Europe and elsewhere are surveyed in Elena Perotti, *Google's Antitrust Woes Around the World,* WAN-IFRA Public Affairs and Media Policy Briefing, July 27, 2017.

7. See Baker and Scott Morton 2018.

8. United States v. Visa U.S.A., Inc., 344 F.3d 229 (2d Cir. 2003); Ohio v. American Express Co., 138 S. Ct. 2274 (2018).

9. Of the eight questions about platform market power raised in a recent article, four are concerned with exclusion primarily. Bamberger and Lobel 2017.

10. Baker 2013b, 556–558.

11. Platform conduct can also raise coordinated effects concerns, as with the platform most-favored nation (MFN) provisions discussed below. In addition, critics of dominant platforms have identified issues that go beyond the competitive problems discussed in this chapter, including threats to privacy and speech values and the ability of the firms controlling such platforms to exploit their market power inappropriately to influence the political process. Information technology platforms can also, of course, provide immensely valuable products and services.

12. According to Robert Bork in *The Antitrust Paradox,* courts should almost never credit the possibility that a firm could exclude rivals through predatory pricing or by refusing to deal with suppliers or distributors or otherwise forcing rivals to bear higher distribution costs. Bork 1978, 155, 156, 346; but see Bork 1978, 159, 344–346. (After the book was published, Bork also took the view that Microsoft had harmed competition through exclusionary conduct.) Frank Easterbrook suggested that courts adopt a rule of per se legality for all alleged predatory conduct. Easterbrook 1981, 336–337. Bork and Easterbrook argued that the chill to procompetitive behavior from antitrust enforcement against exclusionary conduct almost invariably outweighs the benefits from deterring possible competitive harms, even when the conduct is undertaken by a dominant firm. Easterbrook 1981, 336–367; Bork 1978, 157. On the other hand, Richard Posner has come to recognize the competitive danger when a firm with "a monopoly share of some market in a new-economy industry" acts to "ward off new entrants." Posner 2001, 251.

13. Baker 2013b, 527–529, 534–535.

14. Baker 2013b, 527–529.

15. Baker 2013b, 532–533, 535.

16. Baker 2013b, 535–537.

17. Baker 2013b, 546–555. But some aspects of the burden-shifting framework were described differently by the majority and dissent in Ohio v. American Express Co., 138 S. Ct. 2274 (2018).

18. See Shelanski 2013, 1665–1666, 1677. Multisided platforms often perform three functions: facilitating exchange by matching end users on the sides, building participation on the sides to increase the likelihood that end users will find a suitable match, and sharing resources to reduce the costs of providing services to end users on the sides. American Bar Association Section of Antitrust Law 2012, 441. Timothy Bresnahan and Shane Greenstein define a platform as "a bundle of standard components around which buyers and sellers coordinate efforts." Bresnahan and Greenstein 1999, 4.

19. It does not matter for this purpose whether e-book readers license rights to the book or purchase it.

20. Bresnahan and Greenstein 1999, 3, emphasize the possibility of divided technical leadership. On shared platforms, technical leadership is divided

among firms providing complementary services. In such settings, firms' incentives to foster competition among sellers of complements help constrain the exercise of market power.

21. The magnitude of network effects may depend on the type or location of users as well as the number of users when some users are valued more than others. Tucker 2018.

22. Hence some definitions of platform reference cross-platform network effects. E.g., Katz 2018, 103, 203. But compare Katz 2018, 110.

23. See generally Shelanski et al. 2018, 189.

24. Dominant platforms may also benefit from analogous feedback effects when third parties produce complementary products tied to the platform, not readily available to users of rival platforms. Shelanski 2013, 1683.

25. Many large platforms have a substantial rival—such as Google with Bing, Amazon with Walmart.com, Uber with Lyft, and Android with iOS. Sometimes new platforms have supplanted formerly dominant platforms, as when social network users migrated from MySpace to Facebook. Tucker 2018.

26. See Justus Haucap, "A German Approach to Antitrust for Digital Platforms," *Pro-Market*, April 2, 2018, https://promarket.org/german-approach-antitrust-digital-platforms/ (identifying capacity constraints, multihoming, and differentiation as features potentially limiting concentration in platform markets, notwithstanding network effects and scale economies in supply).

27. See Shapiro 1999, 682–683.

28. See Shapiro 1999, 677–678.

29. A platform would also benefit from economies of scope if it can produce multiple services more cheaply than can separate firms.

30. The relevant price and participation elasticities depend in part on the extent of competition between platforms. The optimization problem of a firm controlling a multisided platform is analogous to the familiar pricing problem that faces a multiproduct seller of demand complements. The latter firm has an incentive to reduce the prices of its products below what it would charge if demands were independent and may set one product's price below marginal cost in order to raise demand for its other products. Similarly, a firm operating a multisided platform subject to network effects may set the price on one side below cost, in order to attract the participation of buyers on other sides, though it could also charge prices above cost on all sides. The key difference between the two settings is on the buyer's (user's) side: buyers of demand complements internalize the benefits of purchasing one product for their purchases of the other, while the network effects that often benefit platform users are not internalized by buyers. Compare Boik 2018.

31. Some platforms charge end users indirectly, based on their usage of a complementary product. For example, a smartphone platform may earn a commission on in-game purchases.

32. See, e.g., Farhad Manjoo, "Why We May Soon Be Living in Alexa's World," *New York Times*, February 21, 2018.

33. Compare Shelanski 2013, 1676.
34. Users of "free" services offered by an information technology platform can be harmed by anticompetitive conduct on non-price dimensions such as privacy, website experience, or quality of services provided. Market definition issues involving services where users are not directly charged are considered briefly in Chapter 9.
35. A business school professor singled out Amazon, among all the large information technology firms, as having the greatest potential for future dominance of search, hardware, and cloud computing. Scott Galloway, "Amazon Takes over the World," *Wall Street Journal*, September 22, 2017. A well-known law review note argued that antitrust law has not successfully addressed Amazon's exercise of market power. Khan 2017.
36. Salop 2018. As with many exclusionary practices, vertical mergers can also harm competition by facilitating coordination. See Gavil et al. 2017, 881, 889. It would also be possible for a vertical merger to facilitate anticompetitive price discrimination.
37. This hypothetical transaction might also be understood as a potential competition merger with collusive effects.
38. The profitability analysis may be complicated by counterstrategies employed by excluded firms. When rivals denied access to one distributor by a large firm's exclusivity arrangement reach exclusive contracts with other distributors, the large firm's profits may be affected but its exclusionary strategy may remain profitable, particularly if marginal cost increases more for smaller firms. The profitability analysis becomes further complicated when products are differentiated, buyers have a taste for product variety, and sellers do not know the valuation individual buyers place on their products. See Calzolari and Denicolò 2015.
39. Vertical integration may help firms make their products and services better and cheaper, as by aligning the incentives of the firms and eliminating double marginalization. On the other hand, vertical integration can raise costs or reduce quality, as by making the merged firm less flexible. Its sunk organizational investments in working with the acquired supplier or distributor may make it costly for the firm to switch to a rival supplier or distributor that later develops a better or cheaper product or service—leading the merged firm to bear higher costs or offer lower quality products and services than if it were unintegrated. To similar effect, after an acquisition rival suppliers and distributors may prefer to work with unintegrated downstream and upstream partners, respectively, than to deal with the merged firm. An analogous trade-off arises when sellers of complements collaborate to develop services by adopting an industry standard. Those standards can be "open" (allowing nondiscriminatory access to all providers of complements) or "closed" (limiting compatibility to specified sellers of complements). Both open access and closed access regimes can be competitive, and competition among integrated systems is not necessarily more or less competitive than competition among components.

40. Stucke and Grunes 2016, § 2.01.
41. See Shelanski 2013, 1678–1679.
42. Compare Joanna Stern, "Facebook Really Is Spying on You, Just Not Through Your Phone's Mic," *Wall Street Journal*, March 7, 2018; James P. Bagrow, Xipei Liu, and Lewis Mitchell, "Information Flow Reveals Prediction Limits in Online Social Activity," arXiv:1708.04575 [physics. soc-ph], August 15, 2017, https://arxiv.org/abs/1708.04575.
43. See Lina M. Khan, "What Makes Tech Platforms So Powerful?" *Pro-Market*, April 5, 2018, https://promarket.org/makes-tech-platforms -powerful/. Compare Josh Marshall, "A Serf on Google's Farm," *Talking Points Memo*, September 1, 2017, https://talkingpointsmemo.com/edblog/a -serf-on-googles-farm (describing the information Google obtains about a content provider that uses Google's services).
44. Some Internet applications give consumers open access to their online activities in exchange for free services. Natasha Singer, "Do Not Track? Advertisers Say 'Don't Tread on Us,'" *New York Times*, October 13, 2012.
45. Federal Trade Commission, *Data Brokers: A Call for Transparency and Accountability*, May 2014; compare Kaveh Waddell, "When Apps Secretly Team Up to Steal Your Data," *The Atlantic*, April 7, 2017.
46. See Mikians et al. 2012, 2013.
47. See Garcés 2018; Erik Larson, "Turner Cites AT&T's Trove of Customer Data in Defense of Merger," *Bloomberg*, March 28, 2018, https://www .bloomberg.com/news/articles/2018-03-28/turner-cites-at-t-s-trove-of -customer-data-in-defense-of-merger.
48. This was a potential competitive concern with Google's proposed joint venture with Yahoo!, though it was not highlighted in the Justice Department's statement. U.S. Department of Justice Antitrust Division, "Yahoo! Inc. and Google Inc. Abandon Their Advertising Agreement," press release, November 5, 1995, https://www.justice.gov/archive/atr/public/press_releases /2008/239167.htm.
49. When the scale economies are in supply, smaller firms have higher average costs. When scale economies come from network effects, smaller firms must pay more than their rivals to attract incremental customers. See, e.g., United States v. Bazaarvoice, Inc., 2014 WL 203966, 2014–1 Trade Cases P 78, 641 (N. D. Calif. January 8, 2014).
50. But compare Anita Balakrishnan, "Apple's deal for Shazam draws 'in-depth investigation' from Europe," *CNBC*, April 23, 2018, https://www.cnbc.com /2018/04/23/european-commission-annouces-in-depth-investigation-into -apples-shazam-deal.html.
51. Amazon undoubtedly learns about households through their online shopping history. It is possible that Amazon would gain an information advantage over rivals if it handles many more transactions from customers than do those other firms. Shelanski 2013. Compare Josh Marshall, "Data Lords: The Real Story of Big Data, Facebook and the Future of News," *Taking Points Memo*, April 8, 2018, https://talkingpointsmemo.com

/edblog/data-lords-the-real-story-of-big-data-facebook-and-the-future-of
-news.

52. To similar effect, Amazon could offer bundled discounts to the targeted customers.

53. Laura Stevens, "Amazon Snips Prices on Other Sellers' Items Ahead of Holiday Onslaught," *Wall Street Journal,* November 5, 2017.

54. To similar effect, a multimarket monopolist may develop a reputation for aggressive competition by cutting prices in response to entry in one market and profit from doing so by discouraging entry in other markets, thereby protecting its market power in those other markets. Bolton et al. 2000, 2300–2301.

55. Amazon's private label products are reportedly successful and expanding. Sarah Perez, "Amazon's Private Label Brands are Taking over Market Share," *TechCrunch,* November 3, 2016, https://techcrunch.com/2016/11/03 /amazons-private-label-brands-are-killing-it-says-new-report/; Greg Bensinger, "Amazon to Expand Private-Label Offering—From Food to Diapers," *Wall Street Journal,* May 15, 2016.

56. See Khan 2017, 780–782. Compare Shelanski 2013, 1700; Zhu and Liu 2018.

57. This chapter focuses on competitive harms in current product markets—in this case from Amazon's ability to obtain or maintain supracompetitive diaper prices. Chapter 8 considers harms to innovation competition and competition in future products from similar scenarios.

58. This possibility is similar to the Google "search bias" allegations. Gilbert 2019. This means of exclusion may be particularly effective in a product category in which many customers are new to the product. Search bias potentially excludes by reducing rivals' scale economies as well as by targeting rivals' customers through price discrimination.

59. Shapiro and Varian 1999, 19–81.

60. Gavil et al. 2017, 322–326 (Sidebar 5–4).

61. If a monopolist were able to use "big data" to identify each customer's willingness to pay, it is possible in theory that it could charge customer-specific prices close to those levels. See McSweeney and O'Dea 2017, 77. In the limiting case of perfect (first-degree) price discrimination, consumer welfare would be harmed, because the monopolist would appropriate the available consumer surplus. But allocative efficiency would be enhanced, because all buyers willing to pay a price that covers the variable cost of producing for them would purchase the monopolist's product. Whether the antitrust laws would or should reach this theoretical possibility thus turns in part on the welfare standard.

62. See Braghieri 2017.

63. In the limiting case of highly competitive (free-entry) markets, firms are constrained to earn competitive profits only. Hence they are led to temper the extent to which they charge higher prices to less price-sensitive customers.

64. See, e.g., Global Antitrust Institute 2017.
65. This outcome most plausibly arises under conditions of "best-response asymmetry," in which firms that compete for multiple customer groups (e.g., in multiple markets) find different groups to be more valuable. That is, one firm's strong market—one in which it prefers to set high prices relative to costs when able to discriminate—is another's weak market, in which it prefers to set low prices, and vice versa. Best-response asymmetry plausibly characterizes settings in which firms' most loyal customers are concentrated in different markets. Cooper et al. 2005b; Armstrong and Vickers 2001, 584; Corts 1998. But compare Rhee 2017. The procompetitive effects of price discrimination in oligopoly markets when firms are equally vulnerable may dissipate, however, if the firms place a similar value on each customer group. That is, price discrimination may discourage price competition under conditions of best-response symmetry, in which firms agree on their ranking of strong and weak markets. See Stole 2007, 2238.
66. Kutsoati and Norman n.d.
67. See Hemphill and Wu 2013.
68. See Bernheim and Whinston 1990; Ciliberto and Williams 2014, 765, 789; Evans and Kessides 1994, 365.
69. Absent exclusion or collusion, a dominant firm that is better able to discriminate in price than its rivals may raise price to its most valuable customers while simultaneously finding it profitable to compete more aggressively for its rivals' most valuable customers. The dominant firm's best customers would pay more and its rivals' best customers would pay less relative to uniform pricing. See Gehrig et al. 2011. Compare Belleflamme et al. 2017.
70. In other markets, competition may also be harmed by enhancing coordination. If coordinating oligopolists collectively have a greater ability to target the customers of noncoordinating rivals or entrants than the reverse, the coordinating firms may be able to use that threat to discourage rivalry that would threaten their coordinated arrangement.
71. See Armstrong and Vickers 1993; Katz and Shapiro 1999, 78. Compare Fumagalli and Motta 2013; Patterson 2017, 179.
72. Compare Creighton et al. 2005, 977.
73. Price matching guarantees raise a range of issues that do not arise when dominant firms with an information advantage can target rivals with selective discounts when their rivals cannot effectively target them in return, however. The issues include the possibility that meeting competition guarantees are costly for consumers to take advantage of, the extent to which consumers would compare prices and switch to lower-priced sellers absent price guarantees, the extent to which rivals would learn about their competitors' prices absent price guarantees, and the possibility that price matching guarantees could signal otherwise uniformed consumers that a seller has low costs and prices.

74. Edlin 1997; Salop 1986. See also Motta 2004.
75. Compare Deck and Wilson 2003.
76. Lorain Journal Co. v. United States, 342 U.S. 143 (1951).
77. The leading pre-Internet platform connecting consumers wishing to purchase flowers for delivery with a florist near the delivery location maintained its market power by preventing its members from participating in other networks. See American Floral Services, Inc. v. Florists' Transworld Delivery Ass'n, 633 F. Supp. 201, 204 n.5 (N.D. Ill. 1986) (citing United States v. Florist's Telegraph Delivery Ass'n, 1956 Trade Cas. (CCH) ¶ 68,367 (E.D.Mich.1956)); United States v. Florist's Telegraph Delivery Ass'n 1996 Trade Cas. (CCH) ¶ 71,394 (E.D.Mich.1990); U.S. Justice Department Antitrust Division, "Justice Department Settles Charges Against FTD, The Leading Flowers-by-Wire Company, for Violating 1990 Consent Decree," press release, August 2, 1995.
78. United States v. Visa, 344 F.3d 229 (2d Cir. 2003).
79. FTC Staff Report, *Entering the 21st Century: Competition Policy in the World of B2B Electronic Marketplaces* Part 3B1 (October 2000). See also Katz 2018, 114–115.
80. A number of these practices have been termed "conditional pricing" arrangements. These are practices such as loyalty programs and bundled prices under which prices for a product or product mix depend, explicitly or de facto, on the share or the volume bought or sold. In various settings, conditional pricing practices can harm competition by excluding rivals or by facilitating coordination, or benefit competition by allowing firms to capture efficiencies.
81. See International Travel Arrangers, Inc. v. Western Airlines, Inc., 623 F.2d 1255 (8th Cir. 1980). Compare Farrell et al., 2010, 268. But compare Retractable Technologies, Inc. v Becton Dickinson & Co., 842 F.3d 883 (5th Cir. 2016).
82. In theory, platform users may be able to overcome the switching costs associated with foregone network effect benefits by coordinating a shift to another platform with other users, but it will often be impractical for them to do so. This discussion also supposes that small rivals or potential entrants would have an incentive to compete with the platform leader rather than to reach an accommodation with the leader or be acquired by it.
83. Put differently, scale economies in demand or supply do not insulate even a dominant firm from rivalry unless enough of its customers are captive (insensitive to price). Absent customer captivity, a dominant firm's attempt to exercise market power could be undermined by rivals able to take away enough customers to obtain comparable scale economies by undercutting the dominant firm's price.
84. For example, a small firm could have proprietary technologies (as from product or process patents); lower costs arising from greater experience in employing a complex production process (moving farther down the learning

curve than its rivals); or privileged access to raw materials, geographic locations, or other critical inputs.

85. While this chapter focuses on dominant firms, oligopolists exercising market power in markets in which scale economies are important can also obtain, extend, or protect market power by increasing customer captivity. For example, hospitals and health insurers, vying for control of patients through vertical merger or otherwise, may raise switching costs in their markets. See Reed Abelson, "Hospital Giants Vie for Patients in Effort to Fend Off New Rivals," *New York Times,* December 18, 2017.

86. Some commentators incorrectly suppose that input or customer foreclosure of rivals cannot harm competition unless rivals are forced below an efficient scale. E.g., Wright 2012b, 1166.

87. Geoffrey A. Fowler, "Why You Cannot Quit Amazon Prime—Even If Maybe You Should," *Washington Post,* January 31, 2018. One might instead think of Amazon Prime as offering customers the opportunity to accept a two-part tariff (a fixed fee plus a product price with free rapid shipping). But only some customers subscribe to Amazon Prime, so it is appropriate to characterize the program as charging a fee for fast delivery.

88. Compare Gans 2018. Facebook plans to make it easier for users to transfer information. Natasha Tiku, "Facebook Will Make It Easier for You to Control Your Personal Data," *Wired,* March 28, 2018, https://www.wired.com/story/new-facebook-privacy-settings/.

89. Platform MFNs differ from simple MFNs. In the latter agreements, a seller promises that it will not charge a lower price to any other buyer. The competitive consequences of simple MFNs are discussed in Baker and Chevalier 2013.

90. Baker and Scott Morton 2018. Platform MFNs can also be used to facilitate coordination, either among platforms or the vendors that are its end users.

91. The Morning Pioneer, Inc. v. The Bismarck Tribune Co., 493 F.2d 383 (8th Cir. 1974).

92. Khan 2017, 746, 753, 755. With her Amazon theory in mind, she recommends, among other things, that courts presume competitive harm when a dominant platform prices below cost. Khan 2017, 790–792. She also proposes that the antitrust laws treat more skeptically vertical integration by a dominant platform (Khan 2017, 792–797), and discusses regulatory approaches to address the exercise of market power by dominant platforms. Khan 2017, 797–802.

93. Khan 2017, 747.

94. Khan 2017, 755.

95. Khan 2017, 786–788.

96. For goods Amazon obtains through an agency distribution model, under which the vendor sets the selling price, Amazon could depress payments to suppliers by negotiating commissions at a higher percentage of seller revenues. Amazon may be unable to raise directly the prices charged to

buyers for such goods. But if competing vendors are constrained to earn zero economic profits in equilibrium through entry and exit, sellers keeping a smaller percentage of revenues may respond by increasing selling prices.

97. Compare Brynjolfsson et al. 2017.

98. During 2009, Amazon's retail e-book prices for many best sellers and new releases were below the wholesale prices that Amazon paid the publishers. Baker 2019, § III.B.

99. This possibility is suggested by an empirical study that finds that in 2012 and 2013, Amazon's physical book prices were consistently well below static profit-maximizing levels. Reimers and Waldfogel 2017. The study concludes that Amazon set physical book prices close to, but not below, marginal cost, but that its price-cost margins were well below what it would be expected to charge given the elasticity of the demand it faced.

100. Baker 2013b, 562–563.

101. It is possible that e-books are demand complements for physical books rather than substitutes but the evidence is mixed. See Gilbert 2015, 169–170. It is also possible that online sales are transaction complements: that once a customer decides to purchase a physical book online, it fills its shopping cart with other products that it might otherwise have purchased elsewhere.

102. Perhaps a customer who buys a physical book is more likely to buy a sequel, books by the same author, or a book on a similar topic. Or that customers who start buying from Amazon, regardless of product category, tend to become more loyal Amazon customers generally.

103. Posner 1979, 937.

104. Posner 1979, 937–938 (citing Kaysen and Turner 1959, 133).

105. E.g., Brown Shoe Co. v. US, 370 U.S. 294 (1962).

106. Posner 1979, 938 (citing Areeda and Turner 1978, ¶ 726b). Robert Bork similarly viewed vertical integration as virtually always procompetitive. Bork 1978, 232, 234, 236.

107. Reazin v. Blue Cross and Blue Shield of Kan., Inc., 663 F. Supp. 1360, 1489 (D. Kan. 1989), aff'd, 899 F.2d 951 (10th Cir. 1990). For an example of antitrust's hospitality to vertical integration during the 1980s, see O'Neill v. Coca-Cola Co., 669 F. Supp. 217 (N.D. Ill. 1987).

108. See generally Riordan and Salop 1995; Salop and Culley 2016. See also Luco and Marshall 2018; Baker et al. 2017; Dafny et al. 2016; Houde 2012; Baker et al. 2011; Hastings and Gilbert 2005. Vertical integration can also benefit competition. Crawford et al. 2018. A study involving concrete producers found that vertically integrated downstream firms were more efficient than their unintegrated counterparts but attributed that outcome to horizontal coordination among downstream plants that could have been achieved without vertical integration. Hortaçsu and Syverson 2007.

109. Final Judgment, United States v. Google Inc., No. 1:11-cv-00688 (D.D.C. 2011) (accepting consent settlement resolving competitive issues raised by Google's acquisition of ITA).

110. The Justice Department relied on modern economic learning to frame its case. The district court concluded that the DOJ had not proven its allegations on the facts. The government has appealed.

111. Barry C. Lynn & Phillip Longman, "Populism with a Brain," *Washington Monthly,* June/July/August 2016.

112. Tony Hsieh, CEO, "Letter to All Zappos Employees," *Zappos.com,* July 22, 2009, https://www.zappos.com/ceoletter.

113. Robin Wauters, "Confirmed: Amazon Spends $545 Million On Diapers .com Parent Quisdi," *TechCruch,* November 8, 2010, https://techcrunch.com /2010/11/08/confirmed-amazon-spends-545-million-on-diapers-com-parent -quidsi/. Amazon shut down the Quisdi sites months after consummating the transaction. Ari Levy, "New Details on Amazon's Move to Shutter the Company It Bought for $545 Million," *CNBC,* April 3, 2017.

114. Wikipedia, "List of Mergers and Acquisitions by Alphabet," https://en .wikipedia.org/wiki/List_of_mergers_and_acquisitions_by_Alphabet.

115. This possibility is not surprising: a firm may have an incentive to create competition for a supplier or distributor, or a seller of complements more generally, and it may have key assets or capabilities that would give it a leg up on de novo entrants in doing so.

116. Steven Salop recommends that courts adopt a neutral presumption toward most vertical mergers, excepting a modest anticompetitive presumption for mergers involving dominant firms in markets with significant scale economies or network effects and a procompetitive presumption for vertical mergers involving firms with low market shares. Salop 2018.

117. In United States v. Apple Inc., 952 F. Supp. 2d 638 (S.D.N.Y. 2013), aff'd, 791 F.3d 290 (2d Cir. 2015), the courts properly concluded that a price-fixing agreement among e-book publishers, facilitated in part through platform MFNs imposed through vertical distribution contracts with Apple's iBookstore, was illegal per se and found Apple liable on this basis for its role in orchestrating the cartel. The district court held in the alternative that Apple's conduct violated the Sherman Act though application of the rule of reason.

118. Significance is discussed in Baker 2013b, 548n97, 549n102, 551–552.

119. Baker 2013b, 548–550.

120. Baker 2013b, 549–550.

121. Toys "R" Us, Inc., 126 F.T.C. 415, 590–608 (1998), aff'd, 221 F.3d 928 (7th Cir. 2000). To similar effect, the Tenth Circuit has explained that evidence of defendant market power and entry barriers suggests a triable issue of fact concerning recoupment in a predatory pricing case, Multistate Legal Studies, Inc. v. Harcourt Brace Jovanovich Legal and Prof'l Publ'ns, Inc., 63 F.3d 1540, 1549, 1555–1556 (10th Cir. 1995), and the Supreme Court indicated that an exclusionary group boycott can be condemned on finding exclusion, market power, and the absence of efficiencies. Nw. Wholesale Stationers, Inc. v. Pac. Stationery & Printing Co., 472 U.S. 284 (1985).

122. In *Toys*, the FTC applied the rule to a firm it found to have a market share of more than 30 percent in the areas in which it did business and between 40 percent and 50 percent in many cities. *Toys*, 126 F.T.C. at 597–599.

123. Utah Pie Co. v. Continental Baking Co., 386 U.S. 685 (1967) is better understood as a predatory pricing case than as a targeted discounting case. Regardless of how it is interpreted, the plaintiff should not have prevailed. The plaintiff had a cost advantage arising from the location of its plant, 386 U.S. at 690, and did not appear to be excluded by the conduct of any of its rivals, notwithstanding the Court's suggestion that a firm forced by its competitors to charge an unusually low price "will in time feel the financial pinch and will be a less effective competitive force." 386 U.S. at 699–700. Nor did the Court explain how competition would have been harmed were the plaintiff excluded. For example, there was no suggestion that any producer other than the plaintiff could have been excluded by the rivals' conduct.

124. To apply a truncated rule in an attempt to monopolize case, a court would need to interpret the market power predicate as concerned with postexclusion market power or else conclude that the defendant's pre-exclusion market power, which was presumably less than what would be needed to plead a monopolization case, was sufficient to give it the ability to exclude rivals.

125. In lieu of truncated condemnation, it may be possible to challenge exclusion through targeted price discounts under the Robinson-Patman Act, which bars unlawful price discrimination. This legal strategy was suggested by Aaron Edlin for attacking the anticompetitive consequences of price matching guarantees. Edlin 1997. However, that strategy could be employed only with respect to the sale of goods, as Robinson-Patman's prohibitions do not apply to sales of services. Nor can it be employed with respect to sales to end-use consumers, as those sales would not satisfy the competitive injury requirement of the act under current interpretations. Even then, such an action appears likely to founder on the act's meeting competition defense.

126. See Lao 2018. Compare Shelanski 2013, 1687–1688.

127. See Brooke Grp. Ltd. v. Brown & Williamson Tobacco Corp., 509 U.S. 209 (1993) (applying Sherman Act principles in a Robinson-Patman Act decision).

128. Baker 2013b, 566–567. See also Baker 1994, 594; Kaplow 2018b.

129. In some cases, this inquiry would distinguish procompetitive interpretations from anticompetitive ones. If an alleged exclusionary strategy requires participation by multiple excluding firms, for example, it would not be plausible unless it reasonably appears profitable in prospect for each. Profitability is measured relative to the expected profits from the strategy the alleged predator would otherwise have adopted. Ibid.

130. In many retrospective exclusion cases, whether or not they involve predatory pricing, profitability may be inferred without detailed analysis from observing higher prices or other harms to competition.

131. Hemphill and Weiser 2018, § II.A.
132. This possibility has been acknowledged in the case law. Spirit Airlines, Inc. v. Nw. Airlines, Inc., 431 F.3d 917, 921–924 (6th Cir. 2005).
133. See generally Bolton et al. 2000; Edlin 2002.
134. Fumagalli and Motta 2013.
135. Motta and Vasconcelos 2012.
136. For example, it could show that it set low prices for e-books for procompetitive reasons: to sell more Kindle e-book readers or because customers shopping for e-books were more likely to shop for backlisted e-books or other products on Amazon's site.
137. These are profits relative to a but-for world in which the dominant platform was unable to maintain its market power.
138. Khan finds competitive harm plausible, so proposes that courts abandon the recoupment requirement when a dominant platform prices below cost. Khan 2017, 701.
139. Areeda and Turner 1975, 712. See Pac. Eng'g & Prod. Co. v. Kerr-McGee Corp., 551 F.2d 790, 797 (10th Cir. 1977).
140. Brooke Grp. Ltd. v. Brown & Williamson Tobacco Corp., 509 U.S. 209, 223, 226 (1993).
141. Baker 1994, 587–589. See also Katz 2018, 108–109, 109n25.
142. Brooke Grp. Ltd. v. Brown & Williamson Tobacco Corp., 509 U.S. 209, 227 (1993).
143. Elzinga and Mills 2009; Burns 1986; Genesove and Mullin 2006; Scott Morton 1997, 679, 714; Weiman and Levin 1994.
144. Edlin 2002. See also Lehman 2005; Edlin et al. 2017.
145. Baker 2013b, 562–567.
146. One reason cost allocation is arbitrary is that the economic classification of costs as fixed versus variable depends on the decision the firm is making. For an airline, for example, the cost of an aircraft is a fixed cost with respect to a decision to serve another passenger on a flight, but a variable cost with respect to a decision to add another daily flight on a route. Another reason is that there arc invariably multiple ways to allocate the fixed expenditures that a multiproduct firm uses to produce multiple products across those products. For example, there is no unique way to allocate the cost of building a hospital operating room across the many types of procedures that surgeons perform in it (thinking of each type of procedure as a different product market served by the hospital).
147. Some courts decline to find that firms price below cost when the discounts are selective and not undertaken across an entire product line. American Bar Association Section of Antitrust Law 2017, 287. But this approach was not mandated by the Supreme Court in its leading modern predatory pricing decision: the Court accepted that the below-cost pricing requirement could be satisfied in that case by discounts limited to a market segment, while holding for defendant on other grounds. Brooke Group Ltd. v. Brown &

Williamson Tobacco Corp., 509 U.S. 209 (1993). Other courts have similarly declined to insist that predatory pricing take place across an entire product line. See American Bar Association Section of Antitrust Law 2017, 287n431.

148. Novell, Inc. v. Microsoft Corp., 731 F.3d 1064, 1075 (10th Cir. 2013). See generally Gavil et al. 2017, 596–600 (Sidebars 4–8).

8. Threats to Innovation from Lessened Competition

1. See Chapter 1.
2. Compare Katz and Shelanski 2007, 3–5.
3. See Baker 2007a.
4. United States v. Microsoft Corp., 253 F.3d 34 (D.C. Cir. 2001) (en banc).
5. Lorain Journal Co. v. United States, 342 U.S. 143 (1951).
6. United States v. Visa, 344 F.3d 229 (2d Cir. 2003).
7. U.S. Dep't of Justice and Federal Trade Commission (FTC), *Horizontal Merger Guidelines* § 0.1 note 6 (1992). See also Joseph Farrell, Deputy Assistant Att'y Gen., U.S. Dept. of Justice, "Thoughts on Antitrust and Innovation" (speech), National Economists' Club, Washington, D.C., January 25, 2001, https://www.justice.gov/atr/speech/thoughts-antitrust -and-innovation.
8. Gilbert and Greene 2015, 1921–1922.
9. Gilbert and Greene 2015, 1941–1942.
10. See Shelanski 2013, 1685.
11. Microsoft framed its challenge as an alleged failure to show a causal link between the anticompetitive conduct and the competitive harm. *Microsoft*, 253 F.3d at 78–80. The court concluded that it could infer causation even though it was impossible to "confidently reconstruct" the counterfactual "world absent the defendant's exclusionary conduct." *Microsoft*, 253 F.3d at 78–80.
12. United States v. Baker Hughes, Inc., 908, 984 F.2d 981 (D.C. Cir. 1990) (emphasis in original).
13. In potential competition cases, courts treat as a horizontal rival in current products an acquired firm that plans to enter the market in which the acquiring firm now competes within a reasonable time. FTC v. Steris Corp., 133 F. Supp. 3d 962, 978 (N.D. Ohio 2015).
14. The possibility that a court may have no practical way to restore lost competition in rapidly changing industries is no reason to avoid enforcement. In monopolization cases, when the competitive harm has occurred in the past, courts may not always be able to fashion structural or behavioral relief that restores competition. Even then, though, sanctions against violators will have deterrent effect throughout the economy, as by discouraging dominant firms in other innovative sectors from engaging in anticompetitive conduct. As Douglas Melamed has observed, "We don't refrain

from enforcing murder laws because we can't resurrect the corpse." Victor
Luckerson, "'Crush Them': An Oral History of the Lawsuit that Upended
Silicon Valley," *The Ringer,* May 18, 2018, https://www.theringer.com/tech
/2018/5/18/17362452/microsoft-antitrust-lawsuit-netscape-internet-explorer
-20-years.

15. See Katz and Shelanski 2007, 6.
16. See Baker 2003d, 35–36.
17. In addition, a merger can harm competition by facilitating coordination to
    limit research and development (R&D). That possibility is not fanciful. See,
    e.g., United States v. Automobile Manufacturers Ass'n, 307 F. Supp. 617
    (C.D. Cal. 1969), aff'd in part and appeal dismissed in part sub nom City of
    New York v. United States, 397 U.S. 248 (1970). In a market conducive to
    R&D coordination, the acquisition of a disruptive innovator could lead to a
    reduction in R&D effort. On the other hand, many markets may not be
    conducive to coordination in the Stiglerian deterrence sense (in which a
    coordinated consensus can be sustained through punishment threats),
    because of difficulties deterring cheating in R&D. The coordinated suppres-
    sion of R&D remains possible if the merger dampens R&D competition
    through what the 2010 *Horizontal Merger Guidelines* term "parallel accom-
    modating conduct." That coordinated outcome may be the most plausible if
    the merging firms' rivals treat R&D investments as strategic complements.
    Under such circumstances, the merged firm may find it profitable to cut
    back on R&D, recognizing that its rivals would follow.
18. Federico et al. 2017. Compare Wald and Feinstein 2004. The merged firm
    could also save by eliminating duplicative R&D activities. As with fixed
    cost savings generally, such efficiencies would not necessarily reverse the
    merger's potential to harm competition within the affected market.
    Chapter 9 discusses the appropriate treatment of cross-market welfare
    trade-offs.
19. If the merging firms are research labs, planning to license their intellectual
    property rather than using it to produce future products themselves, the
    licensing fee will rise.
20. See Katz and Shelanski 2007, 50–52.
21. Rapid entrants are treated as market participants under the *Merger Guide-
    lines.* U.S. Dep't of Justice and FTC, *Horizontal Merger Guidelines* § 5.1
    (2010). The acquisition of firms planning to compete in current products but
    less rapidly can also harm competition. Compare FTC v. Steris Corp.,
    133 F. Supp. 3d 962, 978 (N.D. Ohio 2015).
22. U.S. Dep't of Justice and FTC, *Horizontal Merger Guidelines* § 6.4 (2010).
23. See Deborah L. Feinstein, Director, Bureau of Competition, Fed'l Trade
    Comm'n, *The Forward-Looking Nature of Merger Analysis,* February 6, 2014,
    https://www.ftc.gov/public-statements/2014/02/forward-looking-nature
    -merger-analysis. See also Shelanski 2013, 1702–1704.
24. Hill et al. 2015, 431–434.

25. FTC, "Mallinckrodt Will Pay $100 Million to Settle FTC, State Charges It Illegally Maintained Its Monopoly of Specialty Drug Used to Treat Infants," press release, January 18, 2017. In its complaint, the FTC framed the case as monopolization, but it can equally be understood as a postconsummation merger challenge.

26. FTC, "FTC Puts Conditions on Nielsen's Proposed $1.26 billion Acquisition of Arbitron," press release, September 20, 2013. *See also* FTC, "FTC Approves Final Order Preserving Future Competition in the Market for Drug-coated Balloon Catheters Used to Treat Peripheral Artery Disease," press release, January 21, 2015.

27. Dow/DuPont (Case M.7932), Commission Decision C (2017) 1946 final (March 27, 2017). The European Commission found that five firms were active in developing innovative herbicides and insecticides, including discovery of new active ingredients, developing and testing them to achieve regulatory approval, and manufacturing and selling products that contain those ingredients worldwide. If so, only those five firms could be said to have the capabilities to compete in R&D to develop future herbicide products in various narrowly defined future product markets.

28. Gilbert 2018.

29. Cunningham et al. 2018 found that 7% of pharmaceutical mergers were "killer" acquisitions. Compare "Into the Danger Zone," *Economist*, June 2, 2018.

30. See Fudenberg et al. 1983.

31. See U.S. Dep't of Justice and FTC, *Antitrust Guidelines for the Licensing of Intellectual Property* § 3.2.3 (2017); J. Thomas Rosch, Commissioner, FTC, "Antitrust Regulation of Innovation Markets" (speech), Remarks before the ABA Antitrust Intellectual Property Committee, February 5, 2009, https://www.ftc.gov/public-statements/2009/02/antitrust-regulation -innovation-markets.

32. Compare Shelanski 2013, 1671–1673.

33. U.S. Dep't of Justice and FTC, *Antitrust Guidelines for the Licensing of Intellectual Property* § 3.2.3 (2017).

34. When initially proposed, innovation markets were limited to cases in which R&D is at an advanced stage, so the effects on downstream product markets could be reasonably predicted and the innovation market participants identified with reasonable certainty. Katz and Shelanski 2007, 42.

35. Compare Baker 2007b, 157–159.

36. See Baker 2002a, 198–199.

37. But see Katz and Shelanski 2007, 47.

38. Accord Katz and Shelanski 2007, 6, 30.

39. According to the 2010 *Horizontal Merger Guidelines*, if the postmerger Herfindahl-Hirschman Index (HHI) exceeds 2,500, corresponding to four equally sized firms, a market is highly concentrated, so all but the smallest mergers raise significant competitive concerns. U.S. Dep't of Justice and FTC, *Horizontal Merger Guidelines* § 5.3 (2010).

40. See Jullien and Lefouili 2018; Denicolò and Polo 2018; compare Bloom et al. 2018. Moreover, if a merger confers efficiencies, spillovers to non-merging firms could amplify the resulting social benefits.

41. Shapiro 2018, 27. Compare Randy Picker, "Platforms and Adjacent Market Competition: A Look at Recent History," *ProMarket*, April 16, 2018, https://promarket.org/platforms-adjacent-market-competition-look-recent -history/.

42. Shapiro 2018, 27.

43. See Competitive Impact Statement, United States v. Ticketmaster Enter-tainment, Inc., No. 1:10-cv-00139 (D.D.C. January 25, 2010); Christine A. Varney, Assistant Att'y Gen., U.S. Dept. of Justice, "The Ticketmaster / Live Nation Merger Review and Consent Decree in Perspective" (speech), Remarks Prepared for the South by Southwest, March 18, 2010, https://www .justice.gov/atr/speech/ticketmasterlive-nation-merger-review-and-consent -decree-perspective. On the success of the consent decree, compare Ben Sisario and Graham Bowley, "Live Nation Rules Music Ticketing, Some Say with Threats," *New York Times*, April 1, 2018 with Jared Smith, "Ticketing, Vertical Integration and the NYT's Recent Article," *Ticket-master Insider*, April 1, 2018, https://insider.ticketmaster.com/ticketing -vertical-integration-and-the-nyts-recent-article/.

44. Shapiro 2018, 28.

45. FTC, "FTC Closes Its Investigation Into Facebook's Proposed Acquisition of Instagram Photo Sharing Program," press release, August 22, 2012.

46. Anticipated Acquisition by Facebook Inc. of Instagram Inc., No. ME/5525/12 (Office of Fair Trading, August 22, 2012).

47. If the concern were solely with advertising price competition, not about the possibility that Instagram would develop new, better, or less expensive ways of reaching users with ads nor about the possibility that Instagram would evolve into a higher quality social network, the merger would instead raise exclusion issues like those discussed in Chapter 7.

48. Anticipated Acquisition by Facebook Inc. of Instagram Inc., No. ME/5525/12 (Office of Fair Trading, August 22, 2012) at ¶¶ 28–29.

49. Anticipated Acquisition by Facebook Inc. of Instagram Inc., No. ME/5525/12 (Office of Fair Trading Aug. 22, 2012) at ¶ 25.

50. Anticipated Acquisition by Facebook Inc. of Instagram Inc., No. ME/5525/12 (Office of Fair Trading Aug. 22, 2012) at ¶ 36. This discussion was framed in terms of asking whether the merged firm could harm competition with other social networks by impeding their access to photo-graphs posted by Instagram users.

51. Assuming that advertising on social media platforms was a future product market, as the UK's Office of Fair Trading (OFT) appears to have supposed at least for purpose of argument, the agency would need to have concluded that Instagram was potentially one of a handful of significant rivals to Facebook in that market. OFT suggested otherwise, but its two cursory arguments may not have survived an in-depth investigation. Its conjecture

that entry was easy could have foundered on the recognition that Instagram's success was built on exporting user lists of friends from Twitter (social-graph portability). Facebook and other social networks could have readily cut off that option, and all leading social networks have since reportedly done so. Ben Thompson, "Manifestos and Monopolies," *Stratechery,* February 21, 2017, https://stratechery.com/2017/manifestos-and -monopolies/. Under such circumstances, social networks with a substantial base of users would come to have a substantial advantage in competing for advertisers over networks with small user bases. Accordingly, an enforcer might reasonably conclude that only social networks with such a user base should be considered participants in a market for innovating in advertising on social networks. Alternatively, if the merger were allowed on the ground that entry and expansion were easy, an enforcement agency could potentially have challenged the later decision by leading social networks to cut off social graph portability as harming innovation competition by excluding potential rivals from access to a key input.

52. It is hard to know what the evidence would have shown about the likelihood that search advertising would be a close substitute for advertising over social networks, however. It is possible that search would have appeared the better channel for transaction advertising and social networks the better channel for brand advertising.

53. OFT also suggested that no rival other than Google was likely to become a significant competitor to Facebook as a vehicle for providing advertising on social networks. Yet an enforcer at the time could have recognized that Instagram's attraction to mobile Internet users would potentially give it an advantage in attracting end users to its network if (as turned out to be the case) mobile advertising became more important over time. See Eric Jackson, "Why the FTC Should Block Facebook's Acquisition of Instagram," *Forbes,* June 5, 2012; Somini Sengupta, "Why Would the Feds Investigate the Facebook-Instagram Deal?" *New York Times,* May 10, 2012. That feature could have given Instagram a source of R&D capital for developing future ways of advertising on social networks unavailable to many potential rivals, making it (along with Google) a significant future rival for Facebook in providing advertising over social networks, particularly in targeting users that reach the Internet through both fixed and mobile broadband connections. The agency might have found that advertising on other social networks, like Twitter, was a distant substitute.

54. Memorandum Opinion and Order, Applications of Comcast Corporation, General Electric Company, and NBC Universal, Inc. for Consent to Assign Licenses and Transfer Control of Licensees, MB Docket No. 10–56, FCC 11–4 ¶41 (released January 20, 2011).

55. By increasing switching costs, the firm would reduce churn and increase the fraction of current customers who accept upgrades.

56. Perhaps customers tend to stick with their current supplier when upgrading to next-generation products, but customers new to the market and ones that

overcome the costs of switching away from their existing supplier prefer to avoid getting locked in to any particular seller. In this setting, smaller firms may limit switching costs in order to attract new customers while larger firms benefit from increased customer captivity because they depend less on new customers and more on selling upgrades to existing customers. See Kyle Orland, "Sony is locking Fortnite accounts to PS4, and players are mad," *Ars Technica*, June 14, 2018, https://arstechnica.com/gaming/2018/06/sony-is -locking-fortnite-accounts-to-ps4-and-players-are-mad/.

57. Competition could also be harmed in markets for the complements, as was alleged in the IBM plug interface cases. Transamerica Computer Co. v. IBM, 698 F.2d 1377, 1383–84 (9th Cir. 1983); Cal. Computer Prods., Inc. v. IBM, 613 F.2d 727, 744 (9th Cir. 1979); Telex Corp. v. IBM, 510 F.2d 894 (10th Cir. 1975). See also C.R. Bard, Inc. v. M3 Sys., Inc., 157 F.3d 1340 (Fed. Cir. 1998).

58. The economics literature has long recognized the possibility that R&D investments can deter innovation rivalry. For example, a firm with a lead in a patent race can discourage rivalry from followers, unless, perhaps, the latter firms anticipate that they may leap ahead to become the leader. Fudenberg et al. 1983. In this way, innovation can become a source of persistent dominance.

59. Baker 2016a, 453n77. Compare Srinivasan 2018.

60. Compare Bloom et al. 2018, § 5.

61. A firm would tend to treat R&D rivalry as a strategic complement if it expects to have a substantial share of a postinnovation market (perhaps resulting from a strong brand name, reputation for quality, or high-quality distribution) or if it expects to lose substantial share if rivals innovate when it does not. Baker 2016a, 443–444. Mobile applications developers that react to Google's introduction of a rival app on the Android platform by reducing their investments in improving directly competitive apps are most likely treating their R&D as a strategic substitute for Google's investments because they expect that they will be unable to capture a substantial market share in competition with a platform-owned app. The same firms act as though Apple entry on the iPhone platform will quickly be emulated by Google on the Android platform, suggesting that they think Google treats Apple R&D investments as a strategic complement for its own R&D. See Wen and Zhu 2017.

62. The social cost of allowing the merger to remove the constraint the fringe firm creates for the dominant firm through potential competition in future products could be substantial even if the fringe firm has only a small likelihood of disrupting the industry, particularly when few or no other rivals have as good prospects for innovation success.

63. Baker 2016c, 285.

64. Baker 2016a, 444.

65. It is also possible that nondominant firms, acting alone or through coordination with competitors, would harm innovation by excluding rivals or

entrants. See, e.g., In re Fair Allocation System, 63 Fed. Reg. 43182 (FTC 1998).

66. United States v. Microsoft Corp., 253 F.3d 34, 54, 79 (D.C. Cir. 2001) (en banc).

67. *Microsoft*, 253 F.3d at 59–74.

68. *Microsoft*, 253 F.3d at 74–77.

69. See *Microsoft*, 253 F.3d at 53–56.

70. The monopolization allegations focused on competitive harms in an operating system market. These were the primary concern of the litigation and the opinions of the district and appeals courts. The public debate over Microsoft's conduct was also concerned with possible competitive harms in a browser market.

71. See generally Baker 2013b, 547–550, 555. Compare Shelanski 2013, 1696–1697.

72. Compare Statement of the Federal Trade Commission Regarding Google's Search Practices, Google Inc., No. 111-0163 (F.T.C. January 3, 2013) with Google Search (Shopping) (Case AT.39740), Commission Decision C (2017) 4444 final (June 27, 2017).

73. *Microsoft*, 253 F.3d at 65.

74. *Microsoft*, 253 F.3d at 67. Had Microsoft met its burden of production, the government would have been required to show that Microsoft's justification was insufficient to overcome the competitive harm. Abbott Labs. v. Teva Pharms. USA, Inc., 432 F.Supp. 2d 408, 420–424 (D. Del. 2006). See also Caldera, Inc. v. Microsoft Corp., 72 F. Supp. 2d 1295, 1313 (D. Utah 1999); In re IBM Peripheral EDP Devices Antitrust Litig., 481 F. Supp. 965, 1003 (N.D. Cal. 1979), aff'd sub nom, Transamerica Computer Co. v. IBM Corp., 698 F2d 1377 (9th Cir. 1993). Contra, Allied Orthopedic Appliances, Inc., v. Tyco Healthcare Group LP, 592 F.3d 991, 1000 (9th Cir. 2010). The appeals court also declined to uphold the district court's finding that competition was harmed by another product design decision—to override a user's default browser choice under some circumstances. After Microsoft met its burden of production to justify that decision, the government failed to meet its burden of persuasion. *Microsoft*, 253 F.3d at 67.

75. See Northeastern Tel. Co. v. AT&T Co., 651 F.2d 76, 94–96 (2d Cir. 1981); Berkey Photo, Inc. v. Eastman Kodak Co., 603 F.3d 263, 287n39 (2d Cir.1979); compare C.R. Bard, Inc. v. M3 Sys., Inc., 157 F.3d 1340 (Fed. Cir. 1998) But see Allied Orthopedic Appliances, Inc., v. Tyco Healthcare Group LP, 592 F.3d 991, 998–999, 1002 (9th Cir. 2010). If the rivals are not innovating, competition could still be harmed in existing products, leading to higher prices rather than reduced incentives to innovate.

76. Bruce B. Wilson, Deputy Assistant Att'y Gen., "Patent and Know-How License Agreements: Field of Use, Territorial, Price and Quantity Restrictions" (speech), Remarks before the Fourth New England Antitrust Conference, November 6, 1970, reprinted in *Antitrust Primer: Patents,*

Franchising, Treble Damage Suits, Proceedings of the Fourth New England Antitrust Conference, edited by Sara-Ann Sanders, 11 (Boston: Warren, Gorham and Lamont, 1970). Some of the cited practices restricted the way a licensee could use products other than those within the scope of the patent. One required the licensee to grant back subsequent patents. Others, including resale price maintenance and restrictions on resale, can be thought of as vertical restraints. Patent licensing practices aside from those cited could be unlawful too, if found unreasonable. See generally Gilbert and Shapiro 1997, 283.

77. E.g., United Shoe Machinery Corp. v. U.S., 110 F. Supp. 295, 351 (1953), aff'd, 347 U.S. 521 (1954); Xerox Corp., 86 F.T.C. 364 (1975) (Decision and Order).

78. See U.S. Dep't of Justice, *Antitrust Enforcement Guidelines for International Operations* § 3.62 (1989). Compare Baker and Rushkoff 1990.

79. U.S. Dep't of Justice and FTC, *Antitrust Guidelines for the Licensing of Intellectual Property* (1995); U.S. Dep't of Justice and FTC, *Antitrust Guidelines for the Licensing of Intellectual Property* (2017).

80. A senior Justice Department official who later became Assistant Attorney General for Antitrust took the view that patent licenses should not be condemned without a clear showing that they are anticompetitive. That suggestion heightens the burden on the government to demonstrate competitive harm relative to what courts require under the rule of reason. Rule 1986, 370.

81. Rule 1986, 368.

82. Exclusionary license restrictions are not insulated from antitrust liability by the intellectual property laws. See *Microsoft,* 253 F.3d at 62–63. Vickers 2010, 383–390 sets forth and critiques the theoretical case for a laissez-faire competition policy toward the exercise of intellectual property rights.

83. Walker Process Equipment, Inc. v. Food Mach. & Chem. Corp., 382 U.S. 172 (1965).

84. Relatedly, firms can exclude innovative rivals, harming competition, by manipulating product and safety standards incorporated into local building codes. American Society of Mechanical Engineers, Inc. v. Hydrolevel Corp., 456 U.S. 556 (1982).

85. Rambus Inc. v. FTC, 522 F.3d. 456 (D.C. Cir. 2008); Broadcom Corp. v. Qualcomm Inc., 501 F. 3d 297 (3d Cir. 2007); Funai Electric Co. v. LSI Corp., 2017 WL 1133513 (N.D. Cal. 2017); Zenith Electronics, LLC v. Sceptre, Inc., 2015 WL 12765633 (C.D. Cal. 2015).

86. Often, some standard setting organization (SSO) members will have an incentive to prefer that the patent owners exercise market power, while others will prefer to keep downstream prices low by preventing patent owners from doing so. When the incentives of SSO members vary, consensus SSO standards may not fully prevent ex post opportunism by patent holders.

87. See generally Melamed and Shapiro 2018. Such cases do not challenge as antitrust violations the mere lawful exploitation of pre-existing market power by firms that raise price: they challenge conduct that allows firms to exercise market power. The current Assistant Attorney General for Antitrust takes a contrary view. He argues that ex post opportunism by owners of patents included in a standard is an issue for contract law, with no role for antitrust enforcement, and that the harms from patent "holdup" (ex post opportunism by patent holders) are likely small relative to the harms from patent "holdout": the possibility that the patent licensees (e.g., SSO members) might decline to take a fair, reasonable, and nondiscriminatory (FRAND) license or delay doing so in order to drive down license fees. Delrahim 2017.

88. The conduct might, for example, reduce the likelihood that a rival would imitate a dominant firm's product improvements or make it more difficult for a rival to compete in future products. For appropriability to matter to investment incentives, the investments must confer benefits that cannot be internalized by contracting with the beneficiaries. See Segal and Whinston 2000.

89. See generally Baker 2016a.

90. Richard L. Schmalensee, Direct Testimony ¶¶ 616, 623, United States v. Microsoft Corp., Nos. 98–1232, 98–1233, 1999 WL 34757070 (D.D.C. January 13, 1999).

91. Hemphill 2013; Bourreau and Julien 2017.

92. Eastman Kodak Co. v. Image Technical Servs., Inc., 504 U.S. 451, 485 (1992).

93. United States v. United Shoe Mach. Corp., 110 F. Supp. 295, 345 (D. Mass. 1953), aff'd, 347 U.S. 521 (1954).

94. Verizon Commc'ns Inc. v. Law Office of Curtis V. Trinko, LLP, 540 U.S. 398, 407–408 (2004).

95. Berkey Photo, Inc. v. Eastman Kodak Co., 603 F.2d 263, 284–285 (2d Cir. 1979). See also SCM Corp. v. Xerox Corp., 463 F. Supp. 983, 1001 (D. Conn. 1978), remanded, 599 F.2d 32 (2d Cir. 1979). Cf. Novell, Inc. v. Microsoft Corp., 731 F.3d 1064, 1073 (10th Cir. 2013); Shelanski 2013, 1694–1695.

96. Keith Hylton and Haizhen Lin view antitrust enforcement against the exclusionary conduct of dominant firms as benefiting society by lowering postinnovation consumer prices, while harming society by discouraging innovation. Hylton and Lin 2010, 255. They implicitly take a Schumpeterian perspective on innovation that does not account for the dynamic benefits of pre-innovation competition in providing an incentive to innovate. Contrary to what they suppose, there is no necessary trade-off between static and dynamic efficiencies. Nor are the price and innovation channels necessarily independent: in the merger context, if an acquisition increases pre-innovation profits by more than it increases postinnovation profits, it can

lessen the firm's incentive to escape competition by investing in R&D. Federico et al. 2018.

97. See generally Baker 2016a.

98. On the other hand, when a new product introduction is expected to increase the sales of complementary products, and those sales would be very profitable to the dominant firm (as when it is the only seller of the complementary goods), the dominant firm would care mainly about ensuring that *some* firm introduces a new product. Its incremental gain from upgrading its own product conditional on its rival introducing a new product would be small. That would limit the dominant firm's incentive to increase its R&D effort in response to greater rival R&D investment.

9. Harms to Suppliers, Workers, and Platform Users

1. United States v. Anthem, Inc., 855 F.3d 345 (D.C. Cir. 2017), aff'g 236 F. Supp. 3d 171 (D.D.C. 2017). Prior to the trial, I consulted with one defendant on a limited issue related to the litigation.

2. This discussion ignores the merger's adverse consequences for small employers, who were not self-insured and so paid the defendants for full insurance. It also ignores the merger's particular effects in the Richmond area.

3. The dissenting judge expected the merging health insurers to exploit their greater size to negotiate lower rates for providing medical services from hospitals and doctors. See 855 F. 3d at 372, 374, 379 (indicating that lower provider rates negotiated by the health insurers would be passed through to employers fully). Under such circumstances, any competitive harm to customers would take the form of higher administrative fees charged to employers.

4. 855 F.3d at 353–355. The majority recognized efficiencies as a defense—that is, a reason to think competition would not be harmed—but not as an affirmative defense that would justify a merger that would raise prices or harm competition in some other way.

5. This claim would have been litigated in a second phase of the trial, had the defendants prevailed in the first phase. 236 F. Supp. 3d at 179.

6. 855 F.3d at 377, 381 (Kavanagh, J., dissenting). The dissenting judge thought the record supported the merging firm's efficiency claims, and that the district court's conclusion otherwise was clear error. 855 F.3d at 375. He also contended that merging firms were legally entitled to raise efficiencies in their defense. His conclusion that customers would benefit from lower prices meant that in his view, the government had not demonstrated that the merger would harm competition in a market for the sale of services to sellers.

7. Rybincek and Wright 2014.

8. E.g., Todd v. Exxon Corp., 275 F.3d 191 (2d Cir. 2001). See Weyerhaeuser Co. v. Ross-Simmons Hardwood Lumber Co., 549 U.S. 312, 321, n2

(2007). Some read *Weyerhaeuser* more narrowly, to hold that an input monopsonist can harm competition only if its input rivals are the same as its output rivals.

9. Antitrust law treats buyer cartels identically to seller cartels. See Mandeville Island Farms v. American Crystal Sugar Co., 334 U.S. 219, 235 (1948). Absent a legitimate business justification, they are illegal per se. United States v. Socony-Vacuum Oil Co. 310 U.S. 150, 223 (1940). See also Nat'l Macaroni Mfrs. Ass'n v. Fed. Trade Commission, 345 F.2d 421, 427 (7th Cir. 1965); United States v. Seville Indus. Mach. Corp., 696 F. Supp. 986 (D.N.J 1988); Doe v. Ariz. Hosp. & Healthcare Ass'n, 2009 WL 1423378 (D. Ariz. 2009). Compare Knevelbaard Dairies v. Kraft Foods, 232 F.3d 979 (9th Cir. 2000). See generally Lindsay et al. 2016. As with seller cartels, buyer cartels may be prosecuted criminally. E.g., United States v. Romer, 148 F.3d 359 (4th Cir. 1998); United States v. Seville Indus. Mach. Corp., 696 F. Supp. 986 (D.N.J 1988).

10. The dissenting judge in *Anthem* accepted that a merger creating monopsony power could harm competition. 855 F.2d at 378. The Supreme Court has recognized that unilateral conduct depressing prices can violate Sherman Act § 2. Weyerhaeuser Co. v. Ross-Simmons Hardwood Lumber Co., 549 U.S. 312 (2007).

11. See generally Naidu et al. 2018.

12. See Competitive Impact Statement, United States v. Adobe Systems, Inc., Case No. 1:10-cv-01629 (D.D.C. September 24, 2010). See also United States v. Lucasfilm, Inc., 2011 WL 2636850 (D.D.C. 2011). The underlying conduct generated related private litigation. E.g., In re High-Tech Employee Antitrust Litig., 2015 WL 5159441 (N.D. Cal. 2016). For a Federal Trade Commission case challenging anticompetitive harm to workers, see Complaint, In re Your Therapy Source, FTC No. 171-0134 (2018).

13. Steven Greenhouse, "Suit Claims Hospitals Fixed Nurses Pay," *New York Times,* June 21, 2006. In several cases, the hospital defendants reached settlements with the plaintiff classes. See generally Rob Wolff, "Nurse Wage-Fixing Cases—An Update," *Littler,* August 4, 2010, https://www.littler.com/publication-press/publication/nurse-wage-fixing-cases-update.

14. O'Bannon v. NCAA, 802 F.3d 1049, 1057–1058 (9th Cir.2015).

15. Marinescu and Hovenkamp 2018.

16. See *Weyerhaeuser,* 549 U.S. at 321.

17. See Stucke 2013, 1513–1514 and n31.

18. See generally Noll 2005.

19. Orbach 2010, 138; see Williamson 1968.

20. See generally Hemphill and Rose 2018; Nevo 2014; Baker 1997. The antitrust concern is with conduct that increases the seller's bargaining leverage by eliminating or lessening the value of buyer alternatives (that is, with exclusionary conduct), not with conduct that increases the seller's bar-

gaining leverage by improving the seller's alternatives nor with increased bargaining leverage arising from improvements in the seller's negotiating skill or greater seller patience.

21. U.S. Dep't of Justice and Federal Trade Commission (FTC), *Horizontal Merger Guidelines* § 6.2 (1992). E.g., FTC v. ProMedica Health Sys., Inc., 2011-1 Trade Cas. (CCH) ¶ 77,395 (N.D. Ohio Mar. 29, 2011), aff'd, ProMedica Health Sys., Inc. v. FTC, 749 F.3d 559 (6th Cir. 2014). See Hemphill and Rose 2018.

22. See 855 F. 3d at 377–378.

23. Competitive Impact Statement, United States v. Charter Communications, Inc., No. 1:16-cv-00759 (D.D.C. 2016).

24. A firm can exercise monopsony power without violating the Sherman Act if its unilateral conduct merely exploits lawfully obtained buyer power. But the firm may violate the antitrust laws if it engages in predatory conduct to obtain, maintain, or extend its market power as a buyer, or if it exploits a low price paid to suppliers to help finance predatory pricing downstream, thereby obtaining, maintaining, or extending its market power as a seller. West Penn Allegheny Health Sys., Inc. v. UPMC, 627 F.3d 85, 103 (3d Cir. 2010); Ocean State Physicians Health Plan v. Blue Cross & Blue Shield, 883 F.2d 1101, 1110 (1st Cir. 1989); Kartell v. Blue Shield of Mass., Inc., 749 F.2d 922, 927, 928 (1st Cir. 1984) (Breyer, J.).

25. In both cases, input purchases are reduced by comparison with the but-for world.

26. See *Anthem*, 855 F.3d at 355. The exercise of countervailing power is not an efficiency. See Baker et al. 2008c. But compare Kirkwood 2014.

27. E.g., West Penn Allegheny Health Sys., Inc. v. UPMC, 627 F.3d 85, 105 (3d Cir. 2010); Federal Trade Comm'n v. H.J. Heinz Co., 246 F.3d 708, 718–719 (2001); see Knevelbaard Dairies v. Kraft Foods, 232 F.3d 979, 988 (9th Cir. 2000). But one court declined to hold an alleged buyer's cartel illegal per se because the alleged conspiracy might not be profitable if it also led to lower prices to downstream consumers. Balmoral Cinema, Inc. v. Allied Artists Pictures Corp., 885 F.2d 313, 317 (6th Cir. 1989).

28. Courts recognize that firms sometimes use their buyer power to exclude rivals, harming competition in downstream markets. When that happens, the competitive consequences are evaluated in the downstream market. E.g., U.S. v. Delta Dental of Rhode Island, 943 F. Supp. 172, 177 (D. R.I. 1996); see Been v. O.K. Industries, Inc., 495 F.3d 1217, 1234n12 (2007). Compare Kartell v. Blue Shield of Mass., Inc., 749 F.2d 922, 927, 931 (1st Cir. 1984) (Breyer, J.).

29. Telecor Communications, Inc. v. Southwestern Bell Telephone Co., 305 F.3d 1124, 1134 (10th Cir. 2002). See generally Stucke 2013, 144–145 (collecting cases). Accordingly, buyers that pay less can establish antitrust injury. Dyer v. Conoco, Inc., 49 F.3d 727 (5th Cir. 1995); New Mexico Oncology and Hematology Consultants, Ltd. v. Presbyterian Healthcare

Services, 54 F.Supp. 3d 1189, 1205 (D. N.Mex. 2016); White Mule Co. v. ATC Leasing Co. LLC, 540 F.Supp. 2d 869, 888 (N.D. Ohio 2008).

30. The OECD and European Commission have taken this view. Stucke 2013, 1541–1542.

31. If an upstream monopsonist sells into a competitive market so that its downstream demand is perfectly elastic, downstream prices will not change.

32. Compare Balmoral Cinema, Inc. v. Allied Artists Pictures Corp., 885 F.2d 313, 317 (6th Cir. 1989).

33. Baker 2007b, 132–133.

34. For discussion of a range of issues that arise in implementing the standard approach, see Baker 2007b, 139–152.

35. In practice, the agencies may undertake competitive effects analysis simultaneously with market definition. That may facilitate both analyses, particularly when the alleged harm is retrospective, because the hypothetical monopolist test looks at the profitability of an increase in price relative to the price in the but-for world absent the conduct at issue. Compare Baker 2007b, 162–167, 169–173. But competitive effects analysis is concerned with more economic forces than is market definition, so the two analyses are conceptually distinct.

36. Baker 2007b, 148–151. Compare Hatzitaskos et al. 2017. Moreover, market definition does not take place in a vacuum: demand substitution evidence must be evaluated with reference to each specific allegation of competitive harm.

37. Kaplow 2010. As Kaplow explains, it is not possible to identify the "best" market, namely the market for which market shares provide the best indicator of market power, without already having an estimate of market power derived through other means. That idea is related to the suggestion, once in the *Horizontal Merger Guidelines* but later removed, that a court should select the smallest market that satisfies the hypothetical monopolist test. Compare U.S. Dep't of Justice and FTC, *Horizontal Merger Guidelines* § 4.11 (2010) with U.S. Dep't of Justice and FTC, *Horizontal Merger Guidelines* § 1.0 (1992). Both ideas turn on the mistaken assumption that there is a single appropriate antitrust market for analyzing the competitive consequences of any particular conduct. Market definition is not incoherent or circular because it is concerned with evaluating the significance of demand substitution, not with finding the best market. It is not circular to evaluate the profitability of a price increase across the products and locations in a candidate market implemented by the market participants. In general, that evaluation depends on information about the elasticity of candidate market demand (and potentially additional demand parameters when firms are differentiated) and information about price-cost margins. It is not necessary to know whether firms are exercising market power in order to estimate demand parameters or infer margins from accounting data. The hypothetical monopolist test looks at the profitability of a price increase

relative to the price absent the conduct at issue (in the but-for world), but the but-for price need not be a competitive price.

38. Discarding market definition would mean that market shares could no longer be relied on when developing antitrust rules or evaluating market power. To adjust, antitrust law would presumably rework the rules to evaluate market power exclusively through other forms of economic evidence (such as information about demand and supply elasticities).

39. Ward 2017, 2061. See Evans and Noel 2005, 2008.

40. *E.g.*, Times-Picayune Publ'g Co. v. United States, 345 U.S. 594, 610, 612, and n61 (1953); United States v. Microsoft Corp., 253 F.3d 34 (D.C. Cir. 2001).

41. Ohio v. American Express Co., 138 S. Ct. 2274 (2018). The Court defined a cluster market encompassing both sides of a two-sided platform in a narrow setting: when users on different sides are matched in a single, simultaneous transaction, 138 S. Ct. at 2286, and when network effects are so strong as to make it impossible for firms other than transaction platforms to compete on either side. 138 S. Ct. at 2287.

42. The sale of demand complements by a multiproduct firm differs from the sale of products or services on different sides of a platform on the buyer side but not the seller side of the transaction. Buyers of demand complements internalize the benefits of purchasing one product for their purchases of the other, while the network effects that often benefit platform users are not internalized by buyers. This distinction is not surprising: the purchasers of left and right shoes (demand complements) are the same, but magazine advertisers and subscribers (platform users) are different.

43. See Baker 2007b, 134.

44. A similar problem arises when courts define "cluster markets" like commercial banking services or inpatient hospital services, which combine demand complements as well as substitutes. Cluster markets may mislead as to competitive effects when competition from sellers of a partial line of products or services constrains the pricing of the full-line sellers offering the cluster. Baker 2007b, 157–159.

45. Nor is it necessary to incorporate the feedback analysis in market definition in order to account for it fully when evaluating competitive effects.

46. Some aspects of rivalry among market participants might remain unincorporated.

47. To similar effect, a multiproduct firm alleged to have raised the price of one product anticompetitively, or one alleged to have the incentive to do so, can counter by demonstrating that a price increase would be unprofitable after accounting for the harm to its sales of a demand complement. See Baker 1988a, 131–134.

48. United States v. Philadelphia Nat'l Bank, 374 U.S. 321 (1963).

49. U.S. Dep't of Justice and FTC, *Horizontal Merger Guidelines* § 10 n. 14 (2010). The extent to which the enforcement agencies make cross-market

welfare trade-offs in markets that are inextricably linked is qualified by the *Merger Guidelines'* insistence that efficiencies are not cognizable if they are not merger-specific and substantiated, or arise from anticompetitive reductions in output or service.

50. E.g., Miss. River Corp. v. FTC, 454 F.2d 1083, 1089 (8th Cir. 1972); United States v. Ivaco, Inc., 704 F. Supp. 1409, 1427 (W.D. Mich. 1989). Compare NCAA v. Board of Regents, 468 U.S. 85, 116–117 (1984). See generally Crane 2015, 399–400. But see Werden 2017, 122–126. But compare Baker 2008b, 171–172.

51. United States v. Topco Assocs., Inc., 405 U.S. 596, 610–611 (1972). *Topco* has been treated by lower courts as precluding cross-market welfare trade-offs in non-merger litigation. E.g., Law v. NCAA, 902 F. Supp. 1394, 1406 (D. Kan. 1995), aff'd 134 F.3d 1010 (10th Cir. 1998). But see O'Bannon v. National Collegiate Athletic Ass'n, 802 F.3d 1049, 1073 (2015). But compare Sullivan v. National Football League, 34 F.3d 1091 (1st Cir. 1994). Gregory Werden contends that that a prohibition on cross-market welfare trade-offs would be inconsistent with ancillary restraints analysis and tying precedents and create tensions with post-*Topco* Supreme Court precedent allowing reasonableness review of vertical restraints. Werden 2017, 127–132. But ancillary restraints analysis is an historical artifact that has since been integrated into the modern structured approach to applying the rule of reason. Gavil et al. 2017, 229–230 (Sidebar 2–5). Nor is there an inconsistency with tying precedents. The reasonableness evaluation of tying is generally concerned with competitive benefits or harms in the market that includes the tied product. Courts will look to the tying-product market to identify the challenged conduct (whether there is a tie), but whether that conduct is harmful depends in the first instance on whether it confers market power in the tied-product market. See Jefferson Parish Hospital Dist. No. 2 v. Hyde, 466 U.S. 2, 36–37, 38 (1984) (O'Connor, J., concurring). It has been suggested that harm in the tied-product market could be justified by benefits in protecting the seller's reputation in the tying-product market "if failure to use the tied product in conjunction with it may cause it to misfunction." Fortner Enterprises, Inc. v. U.S. Steel Corp., 394 U.S. 495, 512 n. 9 (1969) (White, J., dissenting), but when tying has been justified as protecting seller goodwill, the reputational benefits typically if not invariably accrue in the same market as the competitive harm. In general, moreover, the reasonableness review of vertical restraints does not require cross-market welfare trade-offs. Suppose that a manufacturer adopts exclusive retail distribution territories. In the usual case, an excluded retailer contends that the loss of intrabrand rivalry leads to higher retail prices while the manufacturer responds that greater interbrand rivalry among manufacturers leads to lower retail prices and the latter effect dominates. In that case, harms and benefits are in the same market—a downstream retail market.

52. E.g., Kottras v. Whole Foods Market, Inc., 281 F.R.D. 16, 25 (D.D.C. 2012).

53. See Crane 2015, 407–408. The cross-market welfare trade-off issue is distinct from the usual welfare standard question of whether antitrust law should seek to maximize consumer surplus or aggregate surplus, as discussed in Chapter 2. The $10 and $30 figures could represent either form of surplus. It would be possible conceptually for a court to balance benefits in one market against harms in another regardless of whether the benefits and harms are calculated in terms of consumer surplus or aggregate surplus. The possibility of cross-market welfare trade-offs should be limited to cognizable efficiencies on the benefit side, so arises after determining whether the defendant had a less restrictive alternative (or, in the merger context, whether the efficiencies were merger-specific).

54. Crane 2015, 409–410. Crane finds unpersuasive three other objections to undertaking cross-market welfare trade-offs in merger review: the assertion that it would justify a succession of mergers leading to monopoly, an objection based on the language of the Clayton Act, and the claim that it would lead to an unsavory explicit balancing of the interests of competing groups of consumers.

55. Members of these groups are often injured in cases in which anticompetitive conduct harming suppliers is alleged.

56. Even when final consumers or workers would receive concentrated benefits, that possibility would not be allowed to justify the harms. If the profits from a seller cartel are shared with workers by raising wages in labor markets, for example, the benefits to workers would not be counted in favor of the cartel. (That outcome is less likely to arise today than it would have been when a larger fraction of workers were unionized, however.)

57. Permitting courts to make cross-market trade-offs avoids the possibility that a merger, say, that benefits the buyers hugely in a large market would be stopped because it harms the buyers slightly in a small one. (When a court defines a price-discrimination market or a submarket to capture the harm to a group of targeted buyers (or suppliers) within a product and geographic market, for example, the market could be small. Compare Baker 2007b, 151–152.) The enforcement agencies have declined to challenge acquisitions on this ground. E.g., U.S. Dept. of Justice, Antitrust Div., "Statement of the Department of Justice Antitrust Division on Its Decision to Close Its Investigation of Southwest's Acquisition of Airtran," press release, April 26, 2011. It is easy to overstate the likelihood of this possibility, however, because it arises only in the absence of a less restrictive alternative. (It also supposes, more plausibly, that the harm would not be avoided through Coasian bargaining nor corrected through a robust tax and transfer system.) Accordingly, this possibility should not be taken to justify broadening markets to avoid making cross-market trade-offs and, more specifically, not to justify the holding in Ohio v. American Express Co., 138 S. Ct. 2274 (2018).

58. Were the safety net to become substantially stronger and more secure, this side payment would be less needed to protect antitrust's political support. If in addition, the primary error cost concern with antitrust rules became an excessive chill to procompetitive conduct rather than insufficient deterrence of harmful conduct, the primary concern today, courts might reasonably expand this exception by allowing cross-market trade-offs more freely.

10. Restoring a Competitive Economy

1. United States v. Microsoft Corp., 253 F.2d 34 (D.C. Cir. 2001).
2. Other than Microsoft, modern U.S. antitrust cases with broad public interest might include the government suit against AT&T that led to the breakup of that firm during the early 1980s, the lysine price-fixing conspiracy involving Archer Daniels Midland that was the subject of popular books and a film, and occasional merger challenges such as the government's actions to block AT&T's acquisition of T-Mobile.
3. Aspen Skiing Co. v. Aspen Highlands Skiing Corp., 472 U.S. 585 (1985).
4. Until those decisions, that evaluation had been governed by United States v. Aluminum Co. of Am., 148 F.2d 416 (2d. Cir. 1945) (Alcoa). It is evident from comparing *Microsoft* with another decision of the same court, Polygram Holding, Inc. v. FTC, 416 F.3d 29 (D.C. Cir. 2005), that the D.C. Circuit was setting forth a structured reasonableness test for Sherman Act Section 2, analogous to the approach applied under Section 1.
5. *Microsoft*, 253 F.3d at 78–89. The court's competitive analysis was discussed in Chapter 8.
6. *Microsoft*, 253 F.3d at 63.
7. Baker 2010b, 621.
8. Baker 2010b, 621–622.
9. Dan Morgan and Juliet Eilperin, "Microsoft Targets Funding for Antitrust Office," *Washington Post*, October 15, 1999.
10. Mike Allen, "Bush Hints He Would Not Have Prosecuted Microsoft," *Washington Post*, February 28, 2000.
11. See John Hendren, "Microsoft, Employees Throw Support to Gorton," *Seattle Times*, November 5, 2000; compare Donald Lambro, "Bush Camp Sees Him Saving Microsoft," *Washington Times*, April 10, 2000.
12. Ginsburg may be best known today for his unsuccessful Supreme Court nomination. He has been credited with coining the phrase "Constitution in exile" to capture the nostalgia on the right for the way the Supreme Court enshrined economic rights a century ago.
13. Ginsburg served as Assistant Attorney General for Antitrust during the Reagan administration. Although he tends to be skeptical of government challenges to exclusionary conduct, he has supported antitrust challenges to price-fixing cartels and to horizontal mergers that would create highly concentrated markets. See Ginsburg 1991b, 100. On the D.C. Circuit, he

wrote an antitrust opinion upholding an FTC decision challenging an agreement among rivals to divide markets. Polygram Holding, Inc. v. FTC, 416 F.3d 29 (D.C. Cir. 2005).

14. United States v. Jerrold Electronics Corp., 187 F. Supp. 545 (E.D. Pa. 1960), aff'd per curium, 365 U.S. 567 (1961).

15. Broadcast Music, Inc. v. Columbia Broadcasting System, Inc., 441 U.S. 1 (1979).

16. Berkey Photo, Inc. v. Eastman Kodak Co., 603 F.2d 263 (2d Cir. 1979); Transamerica Computer Corp. v. IBM, 698 F.2d 1377 (9th Cir. 1963); Northeastern Telephone Co. v. AT&T Co., 651 F.2d 76 (2d Cir. 1981). That interpretation was not compelled at the time, nor would it be compelled today. See *Microsoft*, 253 F.3d at 67; Abbott Labs. v. Teva Pharms. USA, Inc., 432 F.Supp. 2d 408, 422 (D. Del. 2006); Caldera, Inc. v. Microsoft Corp., 72 F. Supp. 2d 1295, 1313 (D. Utah 1999); In re IBM Peripheral EDP Devices Antitrust Litig., 481 F. Supp. 965, 1003 (N.D. Cal. 1979), aff'd sub nom, Transamerica Computer Co. v. IBM Corp., 698 F2d 1377 (9th Cir. 1993). But see Allied Orthopedic Appliances, Inc., v. Tyco Healthcare Group LP, 592 F.3d 991, 1000 (9th Cir. 2010).

17. U.S. Dep't of Justice and FTC, *Commentary on the Horizontal Merger Guidelines* § 4 (2006).

18. But see Page and Lopatka 2007. In addition, the appeals court's decision to evaluate specific practices individually rather than collectively undermined the narrative force of the district court's findings of fact. Page and Lopatka 2007, 43–44; Gavil and First 2014, 98.

19. *Microsoft*, 253 F.3d at 49–50.

20. Verizon Commc'ns Inc. v. Law Office of Curtis V. Trinko, LLP, 540 U.S. 398 (2004).

21. E.g., Nobody v. Clear Channel Communications, Inc., 311 F. Supp. 2d 1048, 1112–1114 (D. Colo. 2004). But see John Doe 1 v. Abbott Laboratories, 571 F.3d 930 (9th Cir. 2009).

22. See *Trinko*, 540 U.S. at 407–408.

23. Rep. F. James Sensenbrenner, Chairman, Committee on the Judiciary, U.S. House of Representatives, "Sensenbrenner Introduces Antitrust Study Commission Legislation," press release, June 27, 2001. See also *Antitrust Modernization Commission: Public Meeting* (July 15, 2004) (testimony of Hon. F. James Sensenbrenner).

24. *Antitrust Modernization Commission: Public Meeting* (July 15, 2004) (testimony of Hon. F. James Sensenbrenner), 5.

25. Americans for Tax Reform, "Comments Regarding Commission Issues for Study," September 9, 2004 (filed before the Antitrust Modernization Commission) (letter signed by Grover G. Norquist). Other commenters instead called for more enforcement.

26. Three horizontal merger complaints brought late during the George W. Bush administration alleged mergers to monopoly, so were pleaded with a

monopolization cause of action as well as under Section 7 of the Clayton Act. None involved exclusionary conduct. Complaint, United States v. Microsemi Corp., Civil Action No. 1:08cv1311 (ATJ/JFA) (E.D. Va. December 18, 2008); Complaint, United States v. Amsted Indus., Inc., Civ. No. 1: 07-CV-00710 (D.D.C. April 18. 2007); Complaint, United States v. Daily Gazette Co., 567 F. Supp. 2d 859 (S.D. W.Va. 2008).

27. U.S. Department of Justice (DOJ), "Justice Department Withdraws Report on Antitrust Monopoly Law," press release, May 11, 2009, https://www .justice.gov/opa/pr/justice-department-withdraws-report-antitrust -monopoly-law. See also Brief for the United States and the Federal Trade Commission as Amici Curiae Supporting Petitioner at 14, Verizon Commc'ns Inc. v. Law Offices of Curtis V. Trinko, LLP, 540 U.S. 398 (2004) (No. 02–682) (sec. II.A.1). The Section 2 report grew out of joint hearings on monopolization conduct by the FTC and DOJ, but the final report was issued only by the Justice Department. A majority of FTC Commissioners termed the DOJ report "a blueprint for radically weakened enforcement of Section 2 of the Sherman Act." *Statement of Commissioners Harbour, Liebowitz, and Rosch on the Issuance of the Section 2 Report by the Department of Justice* (September 8, 2008). Eight months later, after a new administration had taken office, the Justice Department withdrew the report and declared its intention to reinvigorate Section 2 enforcement. U.S. Department of Justice, "Justice Department Withdraws Report on Antitrust Monopoly Law," press release, May 11, 2009; Christine Varney, Asst. Att'y Gen. for Antitrust, "Vigorous Antitrust Enforcement in this Challenging Era" (speech), Remarks as Prepared for the U.S. Chamber of Commerce, May 12, 2009. Professor Herbert Hovenkamp, the primary author of the leading antitrust treatise, described the DOJ Section 2 report as "extremely tolerant of single-firm conduct." Hovenkamp 2010, 1613.

28. When antitrust law adopted Chicago-oriented rules two decades earlier, two branches of the federal government—the courts and the executive— were enthusiastic about the new approach. But Congress (as well as the states) questioned various aspects, helping ensure that the outcome was limited to reforming the political bargain rather than reneging on it. Baker 2006, 505–515.

29. The D.C. Circuit's unanimous decision on liability undermined Microsoft's legitimacy critique, and Microsoft itself no longer pressed that position once it settled with the government. Charles (Rick) Rule, an outside counsel for Microsoft and former head of the Justice Department's Antitrust Division, told the AMC that "in a perfect world," Section 2 could probably be repealed, but that as "a political realist" he recognized that that was not possible. He instead offered ten suggestions for modifying monopolization doctrine which, if accepted, would collectively mean "there wouldn't be a lot of behavior that would be caught by Section 2."

Antitrust Modernization Commission: Public Hearing, Panel I (September 29, 2005) (panelist Charles F. "Rick" Rule), https://govinfo.library.unt.edu/amc

/commission_hearings/pdf/050929_Exclus_Conduct_Transcript_reform
.pdf. Steven Salop, a leading defender of monopolization enforcement,
responded that Rule sought to fix antitrust "in more or less the way I fixed
our cat." *Antitrust Modernization Commission* (September 29, 2005) (panelist
Prof. Steven C. Salop) at 42.

30. See generally Baker 2002b. See also Kovacic 1989, 1139–1144.

31. See Kimble v. Marvel Entm't, LLC, 135 S.Ct. 2401, 2412–2413 (2015).

32. Baker 2003d.

33. The relationship between economic and legal change is not a simple one,
however. Baker 2002b, 69–70.

34. Antitrust law began to grapple with competitive issues involving information technology platforms in monopolization cases involving IBM during
the 1960s and 1970s and continued that effort in litigation against Microsoft during the 1990s, but these forms of business organization have since
become more influential.

35. U.S. Senate Democrats, "A Better Deal: Cracking Down on Corporate
Monopolies," July 24, 2017, https://www.democrats.senate.gov/imo/media
/doc/2017/07/A-Better-Deal-on-Competition-and-Costs-1.pdf. During the
2016 campaign, the Democratic party strongly supported antitrust, though
with differences between the mainstream and progressive wings. Neil Irwin,
"Liberal Economists Think Big Companies Are Too Powerful. Hillary
Clinton Agrees," *New York Times,* October 4, 2016; Timothy B. Lee,
"Hillary Clinton Just Took a Step toward Elizabeth Warren's View on
Monopolies," *Vox,* October 4, 2016.

36. On the other hand, FTC Chairman Joe Simons has emphasized his
willingness to follow the economic evidence, regardless of whether it leads
to more or less enforcement. Joe Simons, Chairman, Federal Trade Commission, Prepared Remarks (speech), Remarks at the Federal Trade
Commission Hearings on Competition and Consumer Protection in the
21st Century, Washington, D.C. September 13, 2018, https://www.ftc.gov
/public-statements/2018/09/prepared-remarks-chairman-joe-simons
-hearings-competition-consumer.

37. Michael Mandel, "How Ecommerce Helps Less-Educated Workers,"
Progressive Policy Institute, April 13, 2018, http://www.progressivepolicy.org
/blog/how-ecommerce-helps-less-educated-workers/; see Michael Mandel,
"The Ecommerce Counterfactual," *Progressive Policy Institute,* March 12,
2018, http://www.progressivepolicy.org/blog/the-ecommerce-counterfactual/.

38. Baker and Salop 2015, 1–2.

39. Rodrik 2018; German Lopez, "The Past Year of Research Has Made It Very
Clear: Trump Won Because of Racial Resentment," *Vox,* December 15,
2017; Thomas B. Edsall, "How Fear of Falling Explains the Love of
Trump," *New York Times,* July 20, 2017; Daniel W. Drezner, "I attended
three conferences on populism in 10 days. Here's what I learned." *Washington Post,* June 19, 2017. Compare Robert Tsai and Calvin TerBeek,
"Trumpism Before Trump," *Boston Review,* June 11, 2018.

40. See Dani Rodrik, "What Does a True Populism Look Like? It Looks Like the New Deal," *New York Times,* February 21, 2018. But see Thomas B. Edsall, "Why Is It So Hard for Democracy to Deal with Inequality?" *New York Times,* February 15, 2018.

41. Senator Elizabeth Warren, "Reigniting Competition in the American Economy" (speech), Keynote Remarks at New America's Open Markets Program Event, June 29, 2016, https://www.warren.senate.gov/?p=press_release&id=1169.

42. But see Crane 2018b; David Brooks, "Donald Trump is Not Playing by Your Rules," *New York Times,* June 11, 2018.

43. But see Mark Joseph Stern, "America Could Look Like North Carolina by 2020," *Slate,* April 27, 2017.

44. The way elites frame issues can shape public opinion. Zaller 1992.

45. As a basis for discussion, Congress might consider strengthening Clayton Act § 7 by allowing the plaintiff to prevail by showing merely an increased risk of competitive harm; legislation to overturn the Supreme Court's decision in Ohio v. American Express Co., 138 S. Ct. 2274 (2018) if the lower courts interpret that decision to undermine long-standing and sensible precedents governing market definition, the allocation of burdens in agreement cases, proof of competitive harm with direct evidence, or the concern with harm to non-output dimensions of competition; legislation to reduce procedural hurdles limiting access to the courts by private plaintiffs; Sherman Act modifications prohibiting invitations to collude and broadening the monopolization offense to include monopoly leveraging and anticompetitive unilateral conduct by non-dominant firms; legislation to ensure that the antitrust laws can be enforced in industries subject to extensive regulation; and legislation awarding the FTC market investigation powers similar to those of the UK's Competition & Markets Authority.

46. The Federal Trade Commission has the authority under Section 6(b) of the F.T.C. Act to compel answers to questions and obtain data in order to conduct wide-ranging economic studies without a specific law enforcement purpose. If it identifies competition problems, it can bring enforcement actions under Section 5 of the act, engage in competition rule making, or write a report highlighting the problem and recommending action by Congress, the states, or regulatory agencies. These powers do not quite add up to the wide-ranging ability of the UK's Competition & Markets Authority to conduct market investigations, but they may approach it. See Competition & Markets Authority, *Market Studies and Market Investigations: Supplemental Guidance on the CMA's Approach* §§ 1.5–1.6 (July 2017). Congress could usefully give the FTC similar authority.

47. Individuals could be named as defendants regardless of whether the cases are civil or criminal. Memorandum from Sally Yates, Deputy Att'y Gen., Dep't of Justice, to Assistant Att'y Gen., Antitrust Div., et al. (September 9, 2015).

48. For example, the United States funded an expansion in aluminum production capacity during World War II, paid the dominant incumbent firm (Alcoa) to build and run almost all the new plants to meet defense needs, then sold off the plants after the war to create new rivals. Balmer and Werden 1981, 99; Kovacic 1999, 1306; Roback 1946. The resulting decline in Alcoa's market share during the 1960s and 1970s led to lower prices. Bresnahan and Suslow 1989.

49. E.g., Executive Order, Steps to Increase Competition and Better Inform Consumers and Workers to Support Continued Growth of the American Economy, April 15, 2016, https://obamawhitehouse.archives.gov/the-press -office/2016/04/15/executive-order-steps-increase-competition-and-better -inform-consumers.

50. See also Collection 2018.

References

Abdelal, Rawi, and John G. Ruggie. 2009. "The Principles of Embedded Liberalism: Social Legitimacy and Global Capitalism." In *New Perspectives on Regulation,* edited by David Moss and John Cisternino, 151–162. Cambridge, MA: The Tobin Project.

Acemoglu, Daron, and James A. Robinson. 2012. *Why Nations Fail: The Origins of Power, Prosperity, and Poverty.* New York: Crown Publishing.

Alexander, Barbara J. 1994. "The Impact of the National Industrial Recovery Act on Cartel Formation and Maintenance Costs." *Review of Economics and Statistics.* 76, no. 2: 245–254.

———. 1997. "Failed Cooperation in Heterogeneous Industries Under the National Recovery Administration." *Journal of Economic History.* 57, no. 2: 322–344.

American Bar Association Section of Antitrust Law. 2006. *Economic Evidence Task Force, Final Report.* http://www.abanet.org/antitrust/at-reports/01-c-ii .pdf.

———. 2012. *Market Definition in Antitrust: Theory and Case Studies.* Chicago, IL: American Bar Association.

———. 2015. *Handbook on the Scope of Antitrust.* Chicago, IL: American Bar Association.

———. 2017. *Antitrust Law Developments.* 8th ed. 2 vols. Chicago, IL: American Bar Association.

Anderson, J. Jonas. 2014a. "Congress as a Catalyst of Patent Reform at the Federal Circuit." *American University Law Review.* 63, no. 4: 961–1018.

———. 2014b. "Patent Dialogue." *North Carolina Law Review.* 92, no. 4: 1049–1108.

Areeda, Phillip, and Donald F. Turner. 1975. "Predatory Pricing and Related Practices Under Section 2 of the Sherman Act." *Harvard Law Review.* 88, no. 4: 697–733.

———. 1978. *Antitrust Law,* vol. 3. Boston: Little, Brown.

Armstrong, Mark, and John Vickers. 1993. "Price Discrimination, Competition and Regulation." *Journal of Industrial Economics.* 41, no.4: 335–359.

———. 2001. "Competitive Price Discrimination." *RAND Journal of Economics.* 32, no. 4: 579–605.

Aryal, Gaurab, Federico Ciliberto, and Benjamin T. Leyden. 2018. "Public Communication and Collusion in the Airline Industry." University of Chicago Becker Friedman Institute Working Paper No. 2018–11. https://ssrn.com /abstract=3122560.

Ashenfelter, Orley C., Henry Farber, and Michael R Ransom. 2010. "Labor Market Monopsony." *Journal of Labor Economics.* 28, no. 2: 203–210.

Ashenfelter, Orley, and Daniel Hosken. 2010. "The Effect of Mergers on Consumer Prices: Evidence from Five Selected Case Studies." *Journal of Law and Economics* 53, no. 3: 417–466.

Asker, John. 2016. "Diagnosing Foreclosure Due to Exclusive Dealing." *Journal of Industrial Economics.* 64, no. 3: 375–410.

Auletta, Ken. 2001. *World War 3.0: Microsoft and Its Enemies.* New York: Penguin Random House.

Autor, David, David Dorn, Lawrence F. Katz, Christina Patterson, and John Van Reenen. 2017. "Concentrating on the Fall of the Labor Share." *American Economic Review.* 107, no. 5: 180–185.

Azar, José, Sahil Raina, and Martin Schmalz. 2016. "Ultimate Ownership and Bank Competition." Working Paper. http://ssrn.com/abstract=2710252.

Azar, José, Ioana Marinescu, and Marshall I. Steinbaum. 2017. "Labor Market Concentration." NBER Working Paper No. 24147. http://www.nber.org /papers/w24147.pdf.

Azar, José, Martin C. Schmalz, and Isabel Tecu. 2018a. "Anti-Competitive Effects of Common Ownership." *Journal of Finance.* 73, no. 4.

Azar, José A., Ioana Marinescu, Marshall I. Steinbaum, and Bledi Taska. 2018b. "Concentration in US Labor Markets: Evidence from Online Vacancy Data." NBER Working Paper No. 24395. http://www.nber.org/papers/w24395.pdf.

Backus, Matthew R. 2014. "Why Is Productivity Correlated with Competition?" Working Paper. http://www8.gsb.columbia.edu/researcharchive/articles /15059.

Baer, Bill. 2015. "Cooperation, Convergence, and the Challenges Ahead in Competition Enforcement." Remarks at the Georgetown Law 9th Annual Global Antitrust Enforcement Symposium, Washington, D.C., September 29, 2015. https://www.justice.gov/opa/file/782361/download.

Bailey, Elizabeth E., and John C. Panzar. 1981. "The Contestability of Airline Markets During the Transition to Deregulation." *Law and Contemporary Problems.* 44, no. 1: 125–146.

Baker, Donald I., and Bennett Rushkoff. 1990. "The 1988 Justice Department International Guidelines: Searching for Legal Standards and Reassurance." *Cornell International Law Journal.* 23, no. 3: 405–440.

Baker, Jonathan B. 1988a. "The Antitrust Analysis of Hospital Mergers and the Transformation of the Hospital Industry." *Law and Contemporary Problems*. 51, no. 2: 93–164.

———. 1988b. "Private Information and the Deterrent Effect of Antitrust Damage Remedies." *Journal of Law, Economics, & Organization*. 4, no. 2, 385–408.

———. 1989. "Identifying Cartel Policing Under Uncertainty: The U.S. Steel Industry, 1933–1939." *Journal of Law and Economics*. 32, no. 2, pt. 2: S47–S76.

———. 1991. "Per Se Rules in the Antitrust Analysis of Horizontal Restraints." *Antitrust Bulletin*. 36, no. 4: 733–743.

———. 1993. "Two Sherman Act Section 1 Dilemmas: Parallel Pricing, the Oligopoly Problem, and Contemporary Economic Theory." *Antitrust Bulletin*. 38, no. 1: 143–219.

———. 1994. "Predatory Pricing After Brooke Group: An Economic Perspective." *Antitrust Law Journal*. 62, no. 3: 585–603.

———. 1997. "Unilateral Competitive Effects Theories in Merger Analysis." *Antitrust*. 11, no. 2: 21–26.

———. 1999. "Econometric Analysis in *FTC v. Staples*." *Journal of Public Policy & Marketing*. 18, no. 1: 11–21.

———. 2001. "New Horizons in Cartel Detection." *George Washington Law Review*. 69, no. 5/6: 824–828.

———. 2002a. "Mavericks, Mergers and Exclusion: Proving Coordinated Competitive Effects Under the Antitrust Laws." *New York University Law Review*. 77, no. 1: 135–203.

———. 2002b. "A Preface to Post-Chicago Antitrust." In *Post Chicago Developments in Antitrust Law*, edited by Roger van den Bergh, Roberto Pardolesi and Antonio Cucinotta, 60–75. Northampton, UK: Edward Elgar.

———. 2003a. "The Case for Antitrust Enforcement." *Journal of Economic Perspectives*. 17, no. 4: 27–50.

———. 2003b. "Competitive Price Discrimination: The Exercise of Market Power Without Anticompetitive Effects." *Antitrust Law Journal*. 70, no. 3: 643–654.

———. 2003c. "Responding to Developments in Economics and the Courts: Entry in the Merger Guidelines." *Antitrust Law Journal*. 71, no. 1: 189–206.

———. 2003d. "Why Did the Antitrust Agencies Embrace Unilateral Effects?" *George Mason University Law Review*. 12, no. 1: 31–37.

———. 2006. "Competition Policy as a Political Bargain." *Antitrust Law Journal*. 73, no. 2: 483–530.

———. 2007a. "Beyond Schumpeter vs. Arrow: How Antitrust Fosters Innovation." *Antitrust Law Journal*. 74, no. 3: 575–601.

———. 2007b. "Market Definition: An Analytical Overview." *Antitrust Law Journal*. 74, no. 1: 129–173.

———. 2008a. "'Dynamic Competition' Does Not Excuse Monopolization." *Competition Policy International*. 4, no. 2: 243–251.

———. 2008b. "Efficiencies and High Concentration: Heinz Proposes to Acquire Beech-Nut (2001)." In *The Antitrust Revolution,* edited by John E. Kwoka Jr. and Lawrence J. White, 157–177. 5th ed. New York: Oxford University Press.

———. 2010a. "Market Concentration in the Antitrust Analysis of Horizontal Mergers." In *Antitrust Law and Economics,* edited by Keith N. Hylton, 234–260. 2nd ed. Cheltenham, UK: Edward Elgar. Corrected in a Working Paper available at http://ssrn.com/abstract=1092248.

———. 2010b. "Preserving a Political Bargain: The Political Economy of the Non-Interventionist Challenge to Monopolization Enforcement." *Antitrust Law Journal.* 76, no. 3: 605–652.

———. 2011. "Comcast / NBCU: The FCC Provides a Roadmap for Vertical Merger Analysis." *Antitrust.* 25, no. 2: 36–42.

———. 2013a. "Economics and Politics: Perspectives on the Goals and Future of Antitrust." *Fordham Law Review.* 81, no. 5: 2175–2196.

———. 2013b. "Exclusion as a Core Competition Concern." *Antitrust Law Journal.* 78, no. 3: 527–589.

———. 2013c. "Antitrust Enforcement and Sectoral Regulation: The Competition Policy Benefits of Concurrent Enforcement in the Communications Sector." *Competition Policy International.* 9, no. 1: 1–8.

———. 2014. "Channeling and Contending with Bill Kovacic." In *William E. Kovacic—Liber Amicorum: An Antitrust Tribute,* edited by Nicolas Charbit and Elisa Ramundo, vol. 2, 1–11. New York: Institute of Competition Law.

———. 2015. "Taking the Error Out of 'Error Cost' Analysis: What's Wrong with Antitrust's Right." *Antitrust Law Journal.* 80, no. 1: 1–38.

———. 2016a. "Evaluating Appropriability Defenses for the Exclusionary Conduct of Dominant Firms in Innovative Industries." *Antitrust Law Journal.* 80, no. 3: 431–461.

———. 2016b. "Overlapping Financial Investor Ownership, Market Power, and Antitrust Enforcement: My Qualified Agreement with Professor Elhauge." *Harvard Law Review Forum.* 129: 212–232.

———. 2016c. "Exclusionary Conduct of Dominant Firms, R&D Competition, and Innovation." *Review of Industrial Organization.* 48, no. 3: 269–287.

———. 2017. "Market Power in the U.S. Economy Today." Washington Center for Equitable Growth. http://equitablegrowth.org/research-analysis/market -power-in-the-u-s-economy-today/.

———. 2019 (Forthcoming). "Cartel Ringmaster or Competition Creator? The Ebooks Case Against Apple (2013)." In *The Antitrust Revolution: Economics, Competition, and Policy,* edited by John E. Kwoka Jr. and Lawrence J. White. 7th ed. New York: Oxford University Press.

Baker, Jonathan B., and Timothy F. Bresnahan. 1992. "Empirical Methods of Identifying and Measuring Market Power." *Antitrust Law Journal.* 61, no. 1: 3–16.

———. 2008. "Economic Evidence in Antitrust: Defining Markets and Measuring Market Power." In *Handbook of Antitrust Economics,* edited by Paolo Buccirossi, 1–42. Cambridge, MA: MIT Press.

Baker, Jonathan B., Mark Bykowsky, Patrick DeGraba, Paul LaFontaine, Eric Ralph, and William Sharkey. 2011. "The Year in Economics at the FCC, 2010–11: Protecting Competition Online." *Review of Industrial Organization.* 39, no. 4: 297–309.

Baker, Jonathan B., and Judith A. Chevalier. 2013. "The Competitive Consequences of Most-Favored-Nation Provisions." *Antitrust.* 27, no. 2: 20–26.

Baker, Jonathan B., Joseph Farrell and Carl Shapiro. 2008. "Merger to Monopoly to Serve a Single Buyer: Comment." *Antitrust Law Journal.* 75, no. 2: 637–646.

Baker, Jonathan B., and Steven C. Salop. 2001. "Should Concentration Be Dropped from the Merger Guidelines?" In American Bar Association Section of Antitrust Law, *Task Force Report: Perspectives on Fundamental Antitrust Theory,* 339–354. Chicago, IL: American Bar Association.

———. 2015. "Antitrust, Competition Policy and Inequality." *Georgetown Law Journal Online.* 104: 1–28.

Baker, Jonathan B., and Fiona Scott Morton. 2018. "Antitrust Enforcement Against Platform MFNs." *Yale Law Journal.* 127, no. 7: 2176–2202.

Baker, Jonathan B., and Carl Shapiro. 2008a. "Detecting and Reversing the Decline in Horizontal Merger Enforcement." *Antitrust.* 22, no. 3: 29–36.

———. 2008b. "Reinvigorating Horizontal Merger Enforcement." In *How the Chicago School Overshot the Mark: The Effect of Conservative Economic Analysis on U.S. Antitrust,* edited by Robert Pitofsky, 235–288. New York: Oxford University Press.

Baker, Laurence C., M. Kate Bundorf, and Daniel P. Kessler. 2017. "Does Multispecialty Practice Enhance Physician Market Power?" NBER Working Paper No. 23871. http://www.nber.org/papers/w23871.

Balkin, Jack M., and Sanford Levinson. 2006. "The Process of Constitutional Change: From Partisan Entrenchment to the National Security State" *Fordham Law Review.* 75, no. 2: 489–535.

Balmer, Thomas A. and Gregory J. Werden. 1981. "Antitrust Review of Proposed Administrative Actions." *Boston University Law Review.* 61, no. 1: 90–131.

Bamberger, Kenneth A. and Orly Lobel. 2017. "Platform Market Power." *Berkeley Technology Law Journal.* 32, no. 3: 1051–1092.

Barkai, Simcha. 2016. "Declining Labor and Capital Shares." University of Chicago Stigler Center New Working Paper No. 2. http://home.uchicago.edu/~barkai/doc/BarkaiDecliningLaborCapital.pdf.

Bartels, Larry M. 2008. *Unequal Democracy: The Political Economy of the New Gilded Age.* Princeton: Princeton University Press.

Baumol, William J. 2002. *The Free-Market Innovation Machine. Analyzing the Growth Miracle of Capitalism.* Princeton: Princeton University Press.

Baumol, William J., John C. Panzar, and Robert D. Willig. 1988. *Contestable Markets and the Theory of Industry Structure.* Rev. ed. San Diego: Harcourt Brace Jovanovich.

Baumol, William J., and Robert D. Willig. 1986. "Contestability: Developments Since the Book." *Oxford Economic Papers.* 38, Supp.: 9–36.

Beckner III, C. Frederick, and Steven C. Salop. 1999. "Decision Theory and Antitrust Rules." *Antitrust Law Journal.* 67, no. 1: 41–76.

Behrens, Peter. 2015. "The Ordoliberal Concept of 'Abuse' of a Dominant Position and its Impact on Article 102 TFEU." Paper presented at the 10th Annual ASCOLA Conference, Tokyo, Japan, September 9, https://ssrn.com/abstract=2658045.

Behrman, Bradley. 1980. "Civil Aeronautics Board." In *The Politics of Regulation,* edited by James Q. Wilson, 75–120. New York: Basic Books.

Belleflamme, Paul, Wing Man Wynne Lam, and Wouter Vergote. 2017. "Price Discrimination and Dispersion Under Asymmetric Profiling of Consumers." Aix-Marseille School of Economics Working Paper No. 2017-13. https://hal.archives-ouvertes.fr/halshs-01502452.

Benjamin, Stuart Minor, Howard A. Shelanski, James B. Speta, and Philip J. Weiser. 2012. *Telecommunications Law and Policy.* Durham: Carolina Academic Press.

Benmelech, Efraim, Nittai Bergman, and Hyunseob Kim. 2018. "Strong Employers and Weak Employees: How Does Employer Concentration Affect Wages?" NBER Working Paper No. 24307. http://www.nber.org/papers/w24307.pdf.

Bernheim, B. Douglas, and Michael D. Whinston. 1990. "Multimarket Contact and Collusive Behavior." *RAND Journal of Economics.* 21, no. 1: 1–26.

Bernheim, B. Douglas, and Erik Madsen. 2017. "Price Cutting and Business Stealing in Imperfect Cartels." *American Economic Review.* 107, no. 2: 387–424.

Bessen, James. 2016. "Accounting for Rising Corporate Profits: Intangibles or Regulatory Rents?" CATO Institute, September 21, 2016. https://www.cato.org/publications/research-briefs-economic-policy/accounting-rising-corporate-profits-intangibles.

Bessen, James. 2017. "Information Technology and Industry Concentration." Boston University Law and Economics Research Paper No. 17–41. https://papers.ssrn.com/sol3/papers.cfm?abstract_id=3044730.

Bivens, Josh, Lawrence Mishel, and John Schmitt. 2018. *It's Not Just Monopoly and Monopsony: How Market Power Has Affected American Wages.* Economic Policy Institute Report. https://www.epi.org/publication/its-not-just-monopoly-and-monopsony-how-market-power-has-affected-american-wages/.

Blake, Harlan M., and William K Jones. 1965. "In Defense of Antitrust." *Columbia Law Review.* 65, no. 3: 377–400.

Blinder, Alan S., and Jeremy B. Rudd. 2013. "The Supply-Shock Explanation of the Great Stagflation Revisited." In *The Great Inflation: The Rebirth of Modern Central Banking,* edited by Michael D. Bordo and Athanasios Orphanidees, 119–180. Chicago, IL: University of Chicago Press.

Bliss, Jeff. 2016. *Disconnected: How AT&T's Bid for T-Mobile USA Failed and Exposed the Limits of Corporate Power.* Washington: MLex Market Insight.

Blonigen, Bruce A., and Justin R. Pierce. 2016. "Evidence for the Effects of Mergers on Market Power and Efficiency." NBER Working Paper No. 22750. http://www.nber.org/papers/w22750.

Bloom, Nicholas, Brian Lucking, and John Van Reenen. 2018. "Have R&D Spillovers Changed?" NBER Working Paper 24622. http://www.nber.org/papers/w24622.

Bloom, Nicholas, and John Van Reenen. 2010. "Why Do Management Practices Differ Across Firms and Countries?" *Journal of Economic Perspectives*. 24, no. 1: 203–224.

Blume, Marshall E., and Donald B. Keim. 2014. "The Changing Nature of Institutional Stock Investing." Working Paper. https://fnce.wharton.upenn.edu/profile/948/research.

Boik, Andre. 2018. "Prediction and Identification in Two-Sided Markets." CESifo Working Paper No. 6857. https://papers.ssrn.com/sol3/papers.cfm?abstract_id=3104846.

Bolton, Patrick, Joseph F. Brodley, and Michael H. Riordan. 2000. "Predatory Pricing: Strategic Theory and Legal Policy." *Georgetown Law Journal*. 88, no. 8: 2239–2330.

Bone, Robert G. 2003. *Civil Procedure: The Economics of Civil Procedure*. New York: Foundation Press.

Borenstein, Severin, and Nancy L. Rose. 2014. "How Airline Markets Work . . . Or Do They? Regulatory Reform in the Airline Industry." In *Economic Regulation and Its Reform: What Have We Learned?* edited by Nancy L. Rose, 63–135. Chicago, IL: University of Chicago Press.

Bork, Robert. 1978. *The Antitrust Paradox: A Policy at War with Itself*. New York: Basic Books.

Bork, Robert H., and Ward S. Bowman, Jr. 1965. "The Crisis in Antitrust." *Columbia Law Review*. 65, no. 3: 363–376.

Boudreaux, Donald J., Thomas J. DiLorenzo, and Stephen Parker. 1995. "Antitrust Before the Sherman Act." In *The Causes and Consequences of Antitrust: The Public Choice Perspective*, edited by Fred S.McChesney and William F. Shugart II, 255–270. Chicago, IL: University of Chicago Press.

Bourreau, Marc, and Bruno Jullien. 2017. "Mergers, Investments and Demand Expansion." Toulouse School of Economics Working Paper No. 17–880. https://www.tse-fr.eu/sites/default/files/TSE/documents/doc/wp/2017/wp_tse_880.pdf.

Braghieri, Luca. 2017. "Targeted Advertising and Price Discrimination in Intermediated Online Markets." Working Paper. https://papers.ssrn.com/sol3/papers.cfm?abstract_id=3072692.

Brand, Donald. 1988. *Corporatism and the Rule of Law: A Study of the National Recovery Administration*. Ithaca: Cornell University Press.

Branham, J. Alexander, Stuart N. Soroka, and Christoper Wlezien. 2017. "When Do the Rich Win?" *Political Science Quarterly*. 132: 43–62.

Bresnahan, Timothy F. 1989. "Empirical Studies of Industries with Market Power." In *Handbook of Industrial Organization,* edited by Richard Schmalensee and Robert D. Willig, vol. 2, 1011–1057. New York: Elsevier.

———. 1992. "Sutton's Sunk Costs and Market Structure: Price Competition, Advertising, and the Evolution of Concentration." *RAND Journal of Economics.* 23, no. 1: 137–152.

———. 2010. "Monopolization and the Fading Dominant Firm." In *Competition Law and Economics: Advances in Competition Policy Enforcement in the EU and North America,* edited by Abel M. Mateus and Teresa Moreira, 264–290. Cheltenham, UK: Edward Elgar.

Bresnahan, Timothy F., and Shane Greenstein. 1999. "Technological Competition and the Structure of the Computer Industry." *Journal of Industrial Economics.* 47, no. 1: 1–40.

Bresnahan, Timothy F., and Valerie Y. Suslow. 1989. "Oligopoly Pricing with Capacity Constraints." *Annales D'Economie et de Statistique.* 15 / 16: 267–289.

Brinkley, Joel, and Steve Lohr. 2000. *U.S. v. Microsoft: The Inside Story of the Landmark Case.* New York: McGraw-Hill.

Bristol, Nellie. 2012. "Republican Presidential Candidates United on Healthcare." *Lancet.* 379, no. 9811: 107.

Brodley, Joseph F. 1987. "The Economic Goals of Antitrust: Efficiency, Consumer Welfare, and Technological Progress." *New York University Law Review.* 62, no. 5: 1020–1053.

Bryant, Peter G., and E. Woodrow Eckard. 1991. "Price Fixing: The Probability of Getting Caught." *Review of Economics and Statistics.* 73, no. 3: 531–536.

Brynjolfsson, Erik, Daniel Rock, and Chad Syverson. 2017. "Artificial Intelligence and the Modern Productivity Paradox: A Clash of Expectations and Statistics." NBER Working Paper No. 24001. http://www.nber.org/papers/w24001.pdf.

Burns, Malcolm. 1986. "Predatory Pricing and the Acquisition Costs of Competitors." *Journal of Political Economy.* 94, no. 2: 266–296.

Byrne Edsall, Thomas. 1984. *The New Politics of Inequality.* New York: Norton.

Caballero, Ricardo J., Emmanuel Farhi, and Pierre-Olivier Gourinchas. 2017. "Rents, Technical Change, and Risk Premia: Accounting for Secular Trends in Interest Rates, Returns on Capital, Earnings Yields, and Factor Shares." *American Economic Review.* 107, no. 5: 614–620.

Calkins, Stephen. 1986. "Summary Judgment, Motions to Dismiss, and Other Examples of Equilibrating Tendencies in the Antitrust System." *Georgetown Law Journal.* 74, no. 4: 1065–1162.

Calvano, Emilio, Giacomo Calzolari, Vincenzo Denicolò, and Sergio Pastorello. 2018. "Algorithmic Pricing: What Implications for Competition Policy?" Working Paper. https://ssrn.com/abstract=3209781.

Calzolari, Giacomo, and Vincenzo Denicolò. 2015. "Exclusive Contracts and Market Dominance." *American Economic Review.* 105, no. 11: 3321–3351.

Carlton, Dennis W., and Michael Waldman. 2002. "The Strategic Use of Tying to Preserve and Create Market Power in Evolving Industries." *RAND Journal of Economics*. 33, no. 2: 194–220.

Carlton, Dennis, Mark Israel, Ian MacSwain, and Eugene Orlov. 2017. "Are Legacy Airline Mergers Pro- or Anti-Competitive? Evidence from Recent U.S. Airline Mergers." Working Paper. https://ssrn.com/abstract =2851954.

Caro, Robert A. 2012. *The Years of Lyndon Johnson, The Passage of Power*. London, UK: The Bodley Head.

Carpenter, Daniel. 2014. "Detecting and Measuring Regulatory Capture." In *Preventing Regulatory Capture*, edited by Daniel Carpenter and David A. Moss, 57–68. New York: Cambridge University Press.

Carrier, Michael A. 1999. "The Rule of Reason: Bridging the Disconnect." *Brigham Young University Law Review*. 1999: 1265–1366.

———. 2012. "Why the 'Scope of the Patent' Test Cannot Solve the Drug Patent Settlement Problem." *Stanford Technology Law Review*. 16, no. 1: 1–8.

Carrier, Michael A., and Carl Minniti. 2016. "Citizens Petitions: Long, Late-Filed, and At-Last Denied." *American University Law Review*. 66, no. 2: 305–352.

Carstensen, Peter C. 2015. "The Philadelphia National Bank Presumption: Merger Analysis in an Unpredictable World." *Antitrust Law Journal*. 80, no. 2: 219–268.

Chace, James. 2004. *1912: Wilson, Roosevelt, Taft and Debs—The Election That Changed the Country*. New York: Simon & Schuster.

Chamberlin, Edward. 1933. *The Theory of Monopolistic Competition*. Cambridge, MA: Harvard University Press.

Christiansen, Matthew R., and William N. Eskridge Jr. 2014. "Congressional Overrides of Supreme Court Statutory Interpretation Decisions, 1967–2011." *Texas Law Review*. 92, no. 6: 1317–1515.

Ciliberto, Federico, and Jonathan W. Williams. 2014. "Does Multimarket Contact Facilitate Tacit Collusion? Inference on Conduct Parameters in the Airline Industry." *RAND Journal of Economics*. 45, no. 4: 764–791.

Cohen, Wesley M. 2010. "Fifty Years of Empirical Studies of Innovative Activities and Performance." In *Handbook of the Economics of Innovation*, edited by Bronwyn H. Hall and Nathan Rosenberg, vol. 1, 129–213. New York: Elsevier.

Collard-Wexler, Allan, and Jan De Loecker. 2015. "Reallocation and Technology: Evidence from the US Steel Industry." *American Economic Review*. 105, no. 1: 131–171.

Collection. 2018. "Unlocking Antitrust Enforcement." *Yale Law Journal*. 127, no. 7: 1742–2203.

Competition and Markets Authority. 2017. *The Deterrent Effect of Competition Authorities' Work: Literature Review*. September 7. https://assets.publishing .service.gov.uk/government/uploads/system/uploads/attachment_data/file /642801/deterrent-effect-of-competition-authorities-work-lit-review.pdf.

The Conference Board. 2010. *The 2010 Institutional Investment Report.* http://ssrn
.com/abstract=1707512.

Connor, John M. 2007. *Global Price Fixing: Our Customers Are Our Enemy.* New
York: Springer.

Connor, John M., and Robert H. Lande. 2012. "Cartels as Rational Business
Strategy: Crime Pays." *Cardozo Law Review.* 34, no. 2: 427–489.

Cooper, James C., Luke M. Froeb, Dan O'Brien, and Michael G. Vita. 2005a.
"Vertical Antitrust Policy as a Problem of Inference." *International Journal of
Industrial Organization.* 23, no. 7–8: 639–664.

Cooper, James C., Luke Froeb, Daniel P. O'Brien, and Steven Tschantz. 2005b.
"Does Price Discrimination Intensify Competition? Implications for Antitrust." *Antitrust Law Journal.* 72, no. 2: 327–373.

Cooper, James C., and William E. Kovacic. 2010. "U.S. Convergence with
International Competition Norms: Antitrust Law and Public Restraints on
Competition." *Boston University Law Review.* 90, no. 4: 1555–1610.

Corts, Kenneth S. 1998. "Third-Degree Price Discrimination in Oligopoly:
All-Out Competition and Strategic Commitment." *RAND Journal of
Economics.* 29, no. 2: 306–323.

Cosman, Jacob, and Luis Quintero. 2018. "Market Concentration in Home-
building." Working Paper. jacobcosman.ca/research/.

Counsel of Economic Advisers. 2016a. *Labor Market Monopsony: Trends, Consequences, and Policy Responses.* Issue Brief. https://obamawhitehouse.archives
.gov/sites/default/files/page/files/20161025_monopsony_labor_mrkt_cea.pdf.

———. 2016b. *Benefits of Competition and Indicators of Market Power.* Issue Brief.
https://obamawhitehouse.archives.gov/sites/default/files/page/files/20160414
_cea_competition_issue_brief.pdf.

Cowling, Keith, and Michael Waterson. 1976. "Price-Cost Margins and Market
Structure." *Economica.* 43, no. 171: 267–274.

Crane, Daniel A. 2011. *The Institutional Structure of Antitrust Enforcement.*
Oxford: Oxford University Press.

———. 2015. "Balancing Effects Across Markets." *Antitrust Law Journal.* 80,
no. 2: 391–411.

———. 2018a. "Antitrust and Democracy: A Case Study from German Fascism."
University Michigan Law & Economics Research Paper No. 18–009.
https://papers.ssrn.com/sol3/papers.cfm?abstract_id=3164467.

———. 2018b. "Antitrust's Unconventional Politics." *University of Virginia Law
Review Online.*

Crane, Daniel A., and Joshua D. Wright. 2009. "Can Bundled Discounting
Increase Consumer Prices Without Excluding Rivals?" *Competition Policy
International.* 5, no. 2: 209–220.

Crawford, Gregory S. 2000. "The Impact of the 1992 Cable Act on Household
Demand and Welfare." *RAND Journal of Economics.* 31, no. 3: 422–449.

Crawford, Gregory S., Robin S. Lee, Michael D. Whinston, and Ali Yurukoglu.
2018. "The Welfare Effects of Vertical Integration in Multichannel Television
Markets." *Econometrica.* 86, no. 3: 891–954.

Crawford, Susan. 2013. *Captive Audience: The Telecom Industry and Monopoly Power in the New Gilded Age.* New Haven: Yale University Press.

Creighton, Susan A., D. Bruce Hoffman, Thomas G. Krattenmaker, and Ernest A. Nagata. 2005. "Cheap Exclusion." *Antitrust Law Journal.* 72, no. 3: 975–995.

Crouzet, Nicolas, and Janice Eberly. 2018. "Understanding Weak Capital Investment: The Role of Market Concentration and Intangibles." Working Paper. https://www.kansascityfed.org/publications/research/escp/symposiums /escp-2018.

Cunningham, Colleen, Florian Ederer, and Song Ma. 2018. "Killer Acquisitions." Working Paper. http://faculty.som.yale.edu/songma/files/cem _killeracquisitions.pdf.

Cutler, David M., and Fiona Scott Morton. 2013. "Hospitals, Market Share, and Consolidation." *Journal of the American Medical Association.* 310, no. 18: 1964–1970.

Dafny, Leemore, Kate Ho, and Robin S. Lee. 2016. "The Price Effects of Cross-Market Hospital Mergers." NBER Working Paper No. 22106. http://www.nber.org/papers/w22106.

Dal Bó, Ernesto. 2006. "Regulatory Capture: A Review." *Oxford Review of Economic Policy.* 22, no. 2: 203–225.

Dansby, Robert E., and Robert D. Willig. 1979. "Industry Performance Gradient Indexes." *American Economic Review.* 69, no. 3: 249–260.

David, Paul. 1990. "The Dynamo and the Computer: A Historical Perspective on the Modern Productivity Paradox." *American Economic Review.* 80, no. 2: 355–361.

Davies, Stephen W., and Peter L. Ormosi. 2013. "The Impact of Competition Policy: What Are the Known Unknowns?" Center for Competition Policy Working Paper No. 13–7. http://competitionpolicy.ac.uk/documents/107435// -7+complete.pdf/fd9c-e6e-40fd-80aa-dbd147af8275.

Davis, Joshua P., and Robert H. Lande. 2013. "Toward an Empirical and Theoretical Assessment of Private Antitrust Enforcement." *Seattle University Law Review.* 36, no. 3: 1269–1335.

DeBow, Michael E. 1988. "What's Wrong with Price Fixing: Responding to the New Critics of Antitrust." *Regulation.* 12, no. 2: 44–50.

Deck, Cary A., and Bart J. Wilson. 2003. "Automated Pricing Rules in Electronic Posted Offer Markets." *Economic Inquiry.* 41, no. 2: 208–223.

Decker, Ryan A., John Haltiwanger, Ron S. Jarmin, and Javier Miranda. 2016. "Where Has All the Skewness Gone? The Decline in High-Growth (Young) Firms in the U.S." *European Economic Review.* 86: 4–23.

———. 2017. "Declining Dynamism, Allocative Efficiency, and the Productivity Slowdown." *American Economic Review.* 107, no. 5: 322–326.

———. 2018. "Changing Business Dynamism and Productivity: Shocks v. Responsiveness." NBER Working Paper No. 24236. http://www.nber.org /papers/w24236.pdf.

de Figueiredo, John M. 2004. "The Timing, Intensity, and Composition of Interest Group Lobbying: An Analysis of Structural Policy Windows in the

States." NBER Working Paper No. 10588. http://www.nber.org/papers /w10588.pdf.

De Loecker, Jan, and Jan Eeckhout. 2017. "The Rise of Market Power and the Macroeconomic Implications." NBER Working Paper No. 23687. http://www .nber.org/papers/w23687.pdf.

DeLong, J. Bradford. 2000. "Cornucopia: The Pace of Economic Growth in the Twentieth Century." NBER Working Paper No. 7602. http://www.nber.org /papers/w7602.pdf.

Delrahim, Makan. 2017. Remarks at the USC Gould School of Law's Center for Transnational Law and Business Conference. https://www.justice.gov/opa /speech/assistant-attorney-general-makan-delrahim-delivers-remarks-usc -gould-school-laws-center.

Demsetz, Harold. 1974. "Two Systems of Belief About Monopoly." In *Industrial Concentration: The New Learning,* edited by H. J. Goldschmid, H. M. Mann and J. F. Weston, 164–184. Boston: Little, Brown & Co.

Deng, Ai. 2017. "When Machines Learn to Collude: Lessons from a Recent Research Study on Artificial Intelligence." Working Paper. https://ssrn.com /abstract=3029662.

———. 2018. "What Do We Know About Algorithmic Tacit Collusion." Working Paper. https://ssrn.com/abstract=3171315.

Denicolò, Vincenzo, and Michele Polo. 2018. "The Innovation Theory of Harm: An Appraisal." Working Paper. https://ssrn.com/abstract=3146731.

Derthick, Martha, and Paul J. Quirk. 1985. *The Politics of Deregulation.* Washington, D.C.: Brookings Institute.

Devlin, Alan, and Michael Jacobs. 2010. "Antitrust Error." *William and Mary Law Review.* 52, no. 1: 75–132.

Dick, Andrew R. 1996. "When are Cartels Stable Contracts?" *Journal of Law and Economics.* 39, no. 1: 241–83.

Díez, Federico J., Daniel Leigh, and Suchanan Tambunlertchai. 2018. "Global Market Power and Its Macroeconomic Implications." IMF Working Paper No. WP/18/137. https://www.imf.org/en/Publications/WP/Issues/2018/06 /15/Global-Market-Power-and-its-Macroeconomic-Implications-45975.

DiLorenzo, Thomas J. 2004. *How Capitalism Saved America.* New York: Crown Forum.

Dobbs, Richard, Tim Koller, Sree Ramaswamy, Jonathan Woetzel, James Manyika, Rohit Krishnan, and Nicolo Andreula. 2015. "The New Global Competition for Corporate Profits." McKinsey Global Institute. https://www .mckinsey.com/business-functions/strategy-and-corporate-finance/our -insights/the-new-global-competition-for-corporate-profits.

Dube, Arindrajit, Jeff Jacobs, Suresh Naidu, and Siddharth Suri. 2018. "Monopsony in Online Labor Markets." NBER Working Paper No. 24416. http://www.nber.org/papers/w24416.pdf.

Easterbrook, Frank H. 1981. "Predatory Strategies and Counterstrategies." *University of Chicago Law Review.* 48, no. 2: 263–337.

———. 1984. "The Limits of Antitrust." *Texas Law Review.* 63, no. 1: 1–40.

Easterly, William. 2001. *The Elusive Quest for Growth.* Cambridge, MA: MIT Press.

Edlin, Aaron S. 1997. "Do Guaranteed-Low-Price Policies Guarantee High Prices, and Can Antitrust Rise to the Challenge." *Harvard Law Review.* 111, no. 2: 528–575.

———. 2002. "Stopping Above-Cost Predatory Pricing." *Yale Law Journal.* 111, no. 4: 941–991.

Edlin, Aaron, and Rebecca Haw. 2014. "Cartels by Another Name: Should Licensed Occupations Face Antitrust Scrutiny?" *University of Pennsylvania Law Review.* 162, no. 5: 1093–1164.

Edlin, Aaron, Catherine Roux, Armin Schmutzler, and Christian Thöni. 2017. "Hiding Unicorns? Experimental Evidence on Predatory Pricing Policies." University of Zurich Department of Economics Working Paper No. 258. https://ssrn.com/abstract=2997073.

Eggertsson, Gauti B., Jacob A. Robbins, and Ella Getz Wold. 2018. "Kaldor and Piketty's Facts: The Rise of Monopoly Power in the United States." NBER Working Paper No. 24287. http://www.nber.org/papers/w24287.pdf.

Ehrlich, Isaac, and Richard A. Posner. 1974. "An Economic Analysis of Legal Rulemaking." *Journal of Legal Studies.* 3, no. 1: 257–286.

Eichenwald, Kurt. 2001. *The Informant: A True Story.* New York: Random House.

Ellickson, Paul B. 2007. "Does Sutton Apply to Supermarkets?" *RAND Journal of Economics.* 38, no. 1: 43–59.

Ellison, Glenn. 1994. "Theories of Cartel Stability and the Joint Executive Committee." *RAND Journal of Economics.* 25, no. 1: 37–57.

Elzinga, Kenneth G., and David E. Mills. 2009. "Predatory Pricing in the Airline Industry: Spirit Airlines v. Northwest Airlines (2005)." In *The Antitrust Revolution: Economics, Competition, and Policy,* edited by John E. Kwoka Jr. and Lawrence J. White, 219–247. 5th ed. New York: Oxford University Press.

Emery, Fred. 1994. *Watergate: The Corruption of American Politics and the Fall of Richard Nixon.* New York: Times Books.

Engstrom, David Freeman. 2013. "Agencies as Litigation Gatekeepers." *Yale Law Journal.* 123, no. 3: 616–712.

Ennis, Sean, Pedro Gonzaga, and Chris Pike. 2017. "Inequality: A Hidden Source of Market Power." OECD. http://www.oecd.org/competition /inequality-a-hidden-cost-of-market-power.htm.

Ennis, Sean F., and Yunhee Kim. 2017. "Market Power and Wealth Distribution." In OECD and World Bank Group, *A Step Ahead: Competition Policy for Shared Prosperity and Inclusive Growth,* 133–154. http://dx.doi.org/10.1596/978 -1-4648-0945-3.

Eskridge Jr., William N., and John Ferejohn. 2010. *A Republic of Statutes: The New American Constitution.* New Haven: Yale University Press.

Evans, David S. 2006. "Tying: The Poster Child for Antitrust Modernization." In *Antitrust Policy and Vertical Restraints*, edited by Robert W. Hahn, 65–88. Washington, D.C.: Brookings Institution.

Evans, David S., and Keith N. Hylton. 2008. "The Lawful Acquisition and Exercise of Monopoly Power and Its Implications for the Objectives of Antitrust." *Competition Policy International*. 4, no. 2: 220–241.

Evans, David S., and Michael D. Noel. 2005. "Defining Antitrust Markets When Firms Operate Two-Sided Platforms." *Columbia Business Law Review*. 2005 no. 3: 667–702.

———. 2008. "The Analysis of Mergers That Involve Multisided Platform Businesses." *Journal of Competition Law and Economics*. 4, no. 3: 663–695.

Evans, David S., and A. Jorge Padilla. 2005. "Designing Antitrust Rules for Assessing Unilateral Practices: A Neo-Chicago Approach." *University of Chicago Law Review*. 72, no. 1: 73–98.

Evans, William N., Luke M. Froeb, and Gregory J. Werden. 1993. "Endogeneity in the Concentration—Price Relationship: Causes, Consequences, and Cures." *The Journal of Industrial Economics*. 41, no. 4: 431–438.

Evans, William N., and Ioannis N. Kessides. 1994. "Living by the 'Golden Rule': Multimarket Contact in the U.S. Airline Industry." *Quarterly Journal of Economics*. 109, no. 2: 341–366.

Ezrachi, Ariel, and David Gilo. 2009. "Are Excessive Prices Really Self-Correcting?" *Journal of Competition Law and Economics*. 5, no. 2: 249–268.

Ezrachi, Ariel, and Maurice Stucke. 2016. *Virtual Competition*. Cambridge, MA: Harvard University Press.

Fahri, Emmanuel, and François Gourio. 2018 (Forthcoming). "Accounting for Macro-Finance Trends: Market Power, Intangibles, and Risk Premia." *Brookings Papers on Economic Activity*. 2018, Fall.

Farrell, Joseph, Janis K. Pappalardo, and Howard Shelanski. 2010. "Economics at the FTC: Mergers, Dominant-Firm Conduct, and Consumer Behavior." *Review of Industrial Organization*. 37, no. 4: 263–277.

Farnsworth, Ward. 2007. *The Legal Analyst: A Toolkit for Thinking About the Law*. Chicago, IL: University of Chicago Press.

Faull, Jonathan, and Ali Nikpay, eds. 2014. *The EU Law of Competition*. Oxford: Oxford University Press.

Federal Trade Commission. 2003. *To Promote Innovation: The Proper Balance of Competition and Patent Law and Policy*. https://www.ftc.gov/reports/promote -innovation-proper-balance-competition-patent-law-policy.

———. 2010. *Pay-for-Delay: How Drug Company Pay-Offs Cost Consumers Billions: A Federal Trade Commission Staff Study*. https://www.ftc.gov/reports /pay-delay-how-drug-company-pay-offs-cost-consumers-billions-federal-trade -commission-staff.

Federal Trade Commission, Bureau of Competition. 2017. *Agreements Filed with the Federal Trade Commission Under the Medicare Prescription Drug, Improvement, and Modernization Act of 2003*. https://www.ftc.gov/reports/agreements

-filed-federal-trade-commission-under-medicare-prescription-drug
-improvement-9.

Federico, Giulio, Gregor Langus, and Tommaso Valletti. 2017. "A Simple Model of Mergers and Innovation." *Economics Letters.* 157, August: 136–140.

———. 2018. "Horizontal Mergers and Product Innovation." *International Journal of Industrial Organization.* 59: 1–23.

Feldman, Robin, Evan Frondorf, Andrew K. Cordova, and Connie Wang. 2017. "Empirical Evidence of Drug Pricing Games—A Citizen's Pathway Gone Astray." *Stanford Technology Law Review.* 20, no. 1: 39–91.

Feldman, Robin, John Gray, and Giora Ashkenazi. 2018. "Empirical Evidence of Drug Companies Using Citizen Petitions to Hold Off Competition." University of California Hastings Research Paper No. 269. https://ssrn.com/abstract =3116986.

Fichtner, Jan, Eelke M. Heemskerk, and Javier Garcia-Bernardo. 2017. "Hidden Power of the Big Three? Passive Index Funds, Re-Concentration of Corporate Ownership, and New Financial Risk." Working Paper. https://ssrn.com /abstract=2798653.

Fidrmuc, Jana P., Peter Roosenboom, and Eden Quixian Zhang. 2017. "Antitrust Merger Review Costs and Acquirer Lobbying." Working Paper. https://ssrn .com/abstract=3083503.

Field, Alexander J. 2017. "Ideology, Economic Policy, and Economic History: Cohen and DeLong's *Concrete Economics.*" *Journal of Economic Literature.* 55, no. 4: 1526–1555.

First, Harry, and Eleanor M. Fox. 2015. "Philadelphia National Bank, Globalization, and the Public Interest." *Antitrust Law Journal.* 80, no. 2: 307–351.

First, Harry, and Spencer Weber Waller. 2013. "Antitrust's Democracy Deficit." *Fordham Law Review.* 81, no. 5: 2543–2574.

Fisher, Franklin M. 1985. "The Social Costs of Monopoly and Regulation: Posner Reconsidered." *Journal of Political Economy.* 93, no. 2: 410–416.

Foer, Franklin. 2017. *World Without Mind: The Existential Threat of Big Tech.* London, UK: Jonathan Cape.

Fudenberg, Drew, Richard Gilbert, Joseph Stiglitz and Jean Tirole. 1983. "Preemption, Leapfrogging, and Competition in Patent Races." *European Economic Review.* 33, no. 1: 3–31.

Fumagalli Chiara, and Massimo Motta. 2013. "A Simple Theory of Predation." *Journal of Law and Economics.* 56, no. 3: 595–631.

Furman, Jason, and Peter Orszag. 2015. "A Firm-Level Perspective on the Role of Rents in the Rise of Inequality." Working Paper. https://obamawhitehouse .archives.gov/sites/default/files/page/files/20151016_firm_level_perspective _on_role_of_rents_in_inequality.pdf.

———. 2018. "Slower Productivity and Higher Inequality: Are They Related?" Peterson Institute for International Economics Working Paper 18–4. https:// piie.com/publications/working-papers/slower-productivity-and-higher -inequality-are-they-related.

Gal, Michal S. 2018. "Algorithms as Illegal Agreements." *Berkeley Technology Law Journal.* https:ssrn.com/abstract-3171977.

Gal, Michal, and Niva Elkin-Koren. 2017. "Algorithmic Consumers." *Harvard Journal of Law & Technology.* 30, no. 2: 309–353.

Ganapati, Sharat. 2017. "Oligopolies, Prices, Output, and Productivity." Working Paper. https://ssrn.com/abstract=3030966.

Gans, Joshua. 2018. "Enhancing Competition with Data and Identity Portability." Hamilton Project Policy Brief 2018–10. www.hamiltonproject.org /assets/files/Gans_20180611.pdf.

Garcés, Eliana. 2018. "Data Collection in Online Platform Businesses: A Perspective for Antitrust Assessment." *Competition Policy International.* https://www.competitionpolicyinternational.com/data-collection-in-online -platform-businesses-a-perspective-for-antitrust-assessment/.

Garcia-Macia, Daniel, Chang-Tai Hsieh, and Peter J. Klenow. 2016. "How Destructive is Innovation?" NBER Working Paper No. 22953. http://www .nber.org/papers/w22953.pdf.

Gavil, Andrew I. 2002. "A First Look at the Powell Papers: *Sylvania* and the Process of Change in the Supreme Court." *Antitrust.* 17, no. 1: 8–13.

———. 2007. "Antitrust Bookends: The 2006 Supreme Court Term in Historical Context." *Antitrust.* 22, no. 1: 21–26.

Gavil, Andrew I., and Harry First. 2014. *The Microsoft Antitrust Cases: Competition Policy for the Twenty-First Century.* Cambridge, MA: MIT Press.

Gavil, Andrew I., William E. Kovacic, Jonathan B. Baker, and Joshua D. Wright. 2017. *Antitrust Law in Perspective.* 3rd ed. St. Paul: West Academic Publishing.

Gaynor, Martin, and Robert Town. 2012. "The Impact of Hospital Consolidation—Update." *Robert Wood Johnson Foundation.* http://www.rwjf .org/en/library/research/2012/06/the-impact-of-hospital-consolidation.html.

Gehrig, Thomas, Oz Shy, and Rune Stenbacka. 2011. "History-Based Price Discrimination and Entry in Markets with Switching Costs: A Welfare Analysis." *European Economic Review* 55, no. 5: 732–739.

Genesove, David, and Wallace P. Mullin. 2006. "Predation and Its Rate of Return: The Sugar Industry, 1887–1914." *RAND Journal of Economics.* 37, no. 1: 47–69.

Ghosal, Vivek, and D. Daniel Sokol. 2018. "The Rise and (Potential) Fall of U.S. Cartel Enforcement." Working Paper. https://ssrn.com/abstract=3162867.

Gibson, James L., and Michael J. Nelson. 2017. "Reconsidering Positivity Theory: What Roles Do Politicization, Ideological Disagreement, and Legal Realism Play in Shaping U.S. Supreme Court Legitimacy?" *Journal of Empirical Legal Studies.* 14, no. 3: 592–617.

Gilbert, Richard J. 2015. "E-books: A Tale of Digital Disruption." *Journal of Economic Perspectives.* 29, no. 3: 165–184.

———. 2018. "Mergers and R&D Diversity: How Much Competition is Enough?" Working Paper. https://ssrn.com/abstract=3190478.

————. 2019 (Forthcoming). "U.S. Federal Trade Commission Investigation of Google Search (2013)." In *The Antitrust Revolution,* edited by John E. Kwoka Jr. and Lawrence J. White. 7th ed. New York: Oxford University Press.

Gilbert, Richard J., and Hillary Greene. 2015. "Merging Innovation into Antitrust Agency Enforcement of the Clayton Act." *George Washington Law Review.* 83, no. 6: 1919–1947.

Gilbert, Richard, and Carl Shapiro. 1997. "Antitrust Issues in the Licensing of Intellectual Property: The Nine No-No's Meet the Nineties." *Brookings Papers: Microeconomics.* 1997, Microeconomics: 283–349.

Gilens, Martin. 2012. *Affluence & Influence: Economic Inequality and Political Power in America.* Princeton, NJ: Princeton University Press.

Gilens, Martin, and Benjamin I. Page. 2014. "Testing Theories of American Politics: Elites, Interest Groups, and Average Citizens." *Perspectives on Policy.* 12, no. 3: 564–581.

Ginsburg, Douglas H. 1991a. "Vertical Restraints: De Facto Legality Under the Rule of Reason." *Antitrust Law Journal.* 60, no. 1: 67–81.

————. 1991b. "Antitrust as Antimonopoly." *Regulation.* 14, no. 3: 91–100.

Ginsburg, Douglas H., and Joshua D. Wright. 2015. "Philadelphia National Bank: Bad Economics, Bad Law, Good Riddance." *Antitrust Law Journal.* 80, no. 2: 201–219.

Global Antitrust Institute. 2017. "Comment of the Global Antitrust Institute, Antonin Scalia Law School, George Mason University, on the Canadian Competition Bureau's White Paper, 'Big Data and Innovation: Implications for Competition Policy in Canada.'" George Mason University Law and Economics Research Paper No. 17-44. https://gai.gmu.edu/wp-content/uploads/sites/27/2017/11/GAI-Comment-for-Canada-on-Big-Data-2.pdf.

Goolsbee, Austan, and Amil Petrin. 2004. "The Consumer Gains from Direct Broadcast Satellites and the Competition with Cable TV." *Econometrica.* 72, no. 2: 351–381.

Gorton, Gary, and Andrew Metrick. 2012. "Getting up to Speed on the Financial Crisis: A One-Weekend-Reader's Guide." *Journal of Economic Literature.* 50, no. 1: 128–150.

Gramlich, Jacob, and Serafin Grundl. 2017. "Testing for Competitive Effects of Common Ownership." Federal Reserve Board Finance and Economics Discussion Series No. 2017-029.

Granitz, Elizabeth, and Benjamin Klein. 1996. "Monopolization by 'Raising Rivals' Costs': The Standard Oil Case." *Journal of Law and Economics.* 39, no. 1: 1–47.

Green, Edward J., and Robert H. Porter. 1984. "Noncooperative Collusion Under Imperfect Price Information." *Econometrica.* 52, no. 1: 87–100.

Green, Mark. 1972. *The Closed Enterprise System: Ralph Nader's Study Group Report on Antitrust Enforcement.* New York: Bantam.

Greenwald, Bruce, and Judd Kahn. 2005. *Competition Demystified: A Radically Simplified Approach to Business Strategy.* New York: Penguin Random House.

Groll, Thomas, and Christopher J. Ellis. 2016. "Repeated Lobbying by Commercial Lobbyists and Special Interests." CESifo Working Paper No. 5809. https://papers.ssrn.com/sol3/papers.cfm?abstract_id=2764804.

Grullon, Gustavo, Yelena Larkin, and Roni Michaely. 2016. "Are U.S. Industries Becoming More Concentrated?" Working Paper. https://finance.eller.arizona.edu/sites/finance/files/grullon_11.4.16.pdf.

Gutiérrez, Germán, and Thomas Philippon. 2017a. "Declining Competition and Investment in the U.S." NBER Working Paper No. 23583. http://www.nber.org/papers/w23583.pdf.

———. 2017b. "Investment-Less Growth: An Empirical Investigation." NBER Working Paper No. 22897. http://www.nber.org/papers/w22897.pdf.

———. 2018. "How EU Markets Became More Competitive than US Markets: A Study of Institutional Drift." NBER Working Paper 24700. http://www.nber.org/papers/w24700.

Guzma, Jorge, and Scott Stern. 2016. "The State of American Entrepreneurship: New Estimates of the Quantity and Quality of Entrepreneurship for 15 US States, 1999–2014." NBER Working Paper No. 22095. http://www.nber.org/papers/w22095.pdf.

Hacker, Jacob S., and Paul Pierson. 2005. *Off Center: The Republican Revolution and the Erosion of American Democracy.* New Haven: Yale University Press.

Hale, G. E., and Rosemary D. Hale. 1958. *Market Power: Size and Shape Under the Sherman Act.* Boston, MA: Little, Brown.

Hall, Andrew B., and Daniel M. Thompson. 2018. "Who Punishes Extremist Nominees? Candidate Ideology and Turning Out the Base in U.S. Elections." *American Political Science Review.* 112, no. 3: 509–524. https://doi.org/10.1017/S0003055418000023.

Hall, Robert E. 2018. "New Evidence on the Markup of Prices Over Marginal Costs and the Role of Mega-Firms in the US Economy." NBER Working Paper No. 24574. http://www.nber.org/papers/w24574.pdf.

Hamilton, Alexander. 1824. *Report of the Secretary of the Treasury on The Subject of Manufactures, made the fifth of December, 1791.* Philadelphia, PA: J. R. A. Skerrett.

Harrington Jr., Joseph E. 2018. "Developing Competition Law for Collusion by Autonomous Artificial Agents." Working Paper. https://www.competitionpolicyinternational.com/developing-competition-law-for-collusion-by-autonomous-price-setting-agents/.

Harrington Jr., Joseph E., and Yanhao Wei. 2017. "What Can the Duration of Discovered Cartels Tell Us About the Duration of All Cartels?" *Economics Journal.* 127, September: 1977–2005.

Hastings, Justine S., and Richard Gilbert. 2005. "Market Power, Vertical Integration and the Wholesale Price of Gasoline." *Journal of Industrial Economics.* 53, no. 4: 469–492.

Hathaway, Ian, and Robert E. Litan. 2014. "Declining Business Dynamism in the United States: A Look at States and Metros." Brookings Economic Study. https://www.brookings.edu/search/?s=Hathaway+Litan.

Hatzitaskos, Kostis, Nicholas Hill, and Brad T. Howells. 2017. "Aetna-Humana and Algorithmic Market Definition in the Guidelines." *Antitrust Source.* 2017, October: 1–6.

Haw, Rebecca. 2012. "Adversarial Economics in Antitrust Litigation: Losing Academic Consensus in the Battle of the Experts." *Northwestern Law Review.* 106, no. 3: 1261–1306.

Hawley, Ellis W. 1966. *The New Deal and the Problem of Monopoly.* New York: Fordham University Press.

Heilemann, John. 2001. *Pride Before the Fall: The Trials of Bill Gates and the End of the Microsoft Era.* New York: Harper Collins.

Hemphill, C. Scott. 2013. "Higher Profits as a Merger Defense: Innovation, Appropriability, and the Horizontal Merger Guidelines." In *European Competition Law Annual: 2010,* edited by Philip Lowe and Mel Marquis, 43–52. Oxford, UK: Hart Publishing.

Hemphill, C. Scott, and Marcel Kahan. 2018. "The Strategies of Anticompetitive Common Ownership." NYU Law and Economics Research Paper No. 18-29. https://ssrn.com/abstract=3210373.

Hemphill, C. Scott, and Nancy Rose. 2018. "Mergers that Harm Sellers." *Yale Law Journal.* 127, no. 7: 2078–2109.

Hemphill, C. Scott, and Philip J. Weiser. 2018. "Beyond *Brooke Group:* Bringing Reality to the Law of Predatory Pricing." *Yale Law Journal.* 127, no. 7, 2048–2077.

Hemphill, C. Scott, and Tim Wu. 2013. "Parallel Exclusion." *Yale Law Journal.* 122, no. 5: 1182–1253.

Hill, Nicholas, Nancy L. Rose and Tor Winston. 2015. "Economics at the Antitrust Division 2014–15: Comcast / Time Warner Cable and Applied Materials / Tokyo Electron." *Review of Industrial Organization.* 47, no. 4: 425–435.

Hofstadter, Richard. 1955. *The Age of Reform.* New York: Knopf.

———. 1964. "Whatever Happened to the Antitrust Movement?" In *The Paranoid Style In American Politics,* 188–237. New York: Knopf.

Holmes, Thomas J., and James A. Schmitz Jr. 2010. "Competition and Productivity: A Review of Evidence." *Annual Review of Economics.* 2: 619–642.

Hortaçsu, Ali, and Chad Syverson. 2007. "Cementing Relationships: Vertical Integration, Foreclosure, Productivity, and Prices." *Journal of Political Economy.* 115, no. 2: 250–301.

Horton, Thomas J. 2018. "Rediscovering Antitrust's Lost Values." *University of New Hampshire Law Review.* 16, no. 2: 179–242.

Houde, Jean-François. 2012. "Spatial Differentiation and Vertical Mergers in Retail Markets for Gasoline." *American Economic Review.* 102, no. 5: 2147–2182.

Hovenkamp, Herbert J. 2005. *The Antitrust Enterprise: Principle and Execution.* Cambridge, MA: Harvard University Press.

———. 2010. "The Obama Administration and § 2 of the Sherman Act." *Boston University Law Review.* 90, no. 4: 1611–1665.

———. 2013. "Implementing Antitrust's Welfare Goals." University of Iowa Legal Studies Research Paper No. 12–39. http://ssrn.com/abstract=2154499.

———. 2016. *Federal Antitrust Policy: The Law of Competition and Its Practice.* 5th ed. St. Paul, MN: West Academic.

———. 2018a. "Progressive Antitrust." *University of Illinois Law Review.* 2018, no. 1: 71–114.

———. 2018b. "Prophylactic Merger Policy." University of Pennsylvania Law School Research Paper No. 18–3. https://scholarship.law.upenn.edu/cgi /viewcontent.cgi?referer=https://www.google.com/&httpsredir=1&article =2957&context=faculty_scholarship.

———. 2018c. "Whatever *Did* Happen to the Antitrust Movement?" University of Pennsylvania Law School Research Paper No. 18–7. https://ssrn.com /abstract=3097452.

Hovenkamp, Herbert J., and Carl Shapiro. 2018. "Horizontal Mergers, Market Structure, and Burdens of Proof." *Yale Law Journal.* 127, no. 7: 1742–2203.

Hudson, Henry. 1890. "The Southern Railway & Steamship Association." *Quarterly Journal of Economics.* 5, no. 1: 70–94.

Hylton, Keith N., and Haizhen Lin. 2010. "Optimal Antitrust Enforcement, Dynamic Competition, and Changing Economic Conditions." *Antitrust Law Journal.* 77, no. 1: 247–276.

Hylton, Keith N., and Michael Salinger. 2001. "Tying Law and Policy: A Decision-Theoretic Approach." *Antitrust Law Journal.* 69, no. 2: 469–526.

Hyytinen, Ari, Frode Steen, and Otto Toivanen. Forthcoming. "Cartels Uncovered." *American Economic Journal: Macroeconomics.*

Ippolito, Pauline M. 1991. "Resale Price Maintenance: Empirical Evidence from Litigation." *Journal of Law and Economics.* 34, no. 2: 263–294.

Irons, Peter. 1982. *The New Deal Lawyers.* Princeton, NJ: Princeton University Press.

Ittoo, Ashwin, and Nicolas Petit. 2017. "Algorithmic Pricing Agents and Tacit Collusion: A Technological Perspective." Working Paper. http://ssrn.com /abstract=3046405.

Iyigun, Murat. 2012. "Are We There Yet? Time for Checks and Balances on New Institutionalism." IZA Discussion Paper No. 6934. https://ssrn.com/abstract =2164663.

Jackson, Robert H. 1937a. "Should the Antitrust Laws Be Revised?" *United States Law Review.* 71, no. 10: 575–582.

———. 1937b. "The Struggle Against Monopoly." *Georgia Bar Association Reports.* 1937: 203–214.

Jaffe, Adam B., and Josh Lerner. 2004. *Innovation and Its Discontents: How Our Broken Patent System Is Endangering Innovation and Progress, and What to Do About It.* Princeton, NJ: Princeton University Press.

James, Charles. 2002. "Interview with Charles James, Assistant Attorney General for Antitrust, U.S. Department of Justice." *Antitrust.* 16, no. 2: 12–18.

Joskow, Paul W., and Alvin K. Klevorick. 1979. "A Framework for Analyzing Predatory Pricing Policy." *Yale Law Journal*. 89, no. 2: 213–270.

Jullien, Bruno, and Yassine Lefouili. 2018. "Horizontal Mergers and Innovation." Working Paper. https://ssrn.com/abstract=3135177.

Kalman, Laura. 2010. *Right Star Rising: A New Politics, 1974–1980*. New York: W.W. Norton.

Kaplow, Louis. 1985. "Extension of Monopoly Power Through Leverage." *Columbia Law Review*. 85, no. 3: 515–556.

———. 2010. "Why (Ever) Define Markets?" *Harvard Law Review*. 124, no. 2: 437–517.

———. 2012. "Burden of Proof." *Yale Law Journal*. 121, no. 4: 738–859.

———. 2013. *Competition Policy and Price Fixing*. Princeton, NJ: Princeton University Press.

———. 2018a (In press). "Price-Fixing Policy." *International Journal of Industrial Organization*. https://doi.org/10.1016/j.ijindorg.2017.12.008.

———. 2018b. "Recoupment, Market Power, and Predatory Pricing." *Antitrust Law Journal*. 82, no.1: 167–219.

Kaplow, Louis, and Carl Shapiro. 2007. "Antitrust." In *Handbook of Law and Economics*, edited by A. Mitchell Polinsky and Steven Shavell, 1073–1225. 2nd ed. Amsterdam: Elsevier, North-Holland.

Karabarbounis, Loukas, and Brett Neiman. 2018. "Accounting for Factorless Income." NBER Working Paper No. 24404. http://www.nber.org/papers /w24404.pdf.

Katz, Michael L. 2018. "Exclusionary Conduct in Multi-sided Markets." In OECD, *Rethinking Antitrust Tools for Multi-Sided Platforms*. http://www.oecd .org/competition/rethinking-antitrust-tools-for-multi-sided-platforms.htm.

Katz, Michael L., and Carl Shapiro. 1999. "Antitrust in Software Markets." In *Competition, Innovation and the Microsoft Monopoly: Antitrust in the Digital Marketplace*, edited by Jeffrey A. Eisenach and Thomas M. Lenard, 29–81. Boston, MA: Kluwer Academic.

Katz, Michael L., and Howard A. Shelanski. 2007. "Mergers and Innovation." *Antitrust Law Journal*. 74, no. 1: 1–85.

Katznelson, Ira. 2013. *Fear Itself: The New Deal and the Origins of Our Time*. New York: Liveright Publishing.

Kauper, Thomas E. 2008. "Influence of Conservative Economic Analysis on the Development of the Law of Antitrust." In *How the Chicago School Overshot the Mark: The Effect of Conservative Economic Analysis on U.S. Antitrust*, edited by Robert Pitofsky, 40–50. New York: Oxford University Press.

Kaysen, Carl, and Donald F. Turner. 1959. *Antitrust Policy: An Economic and Legal Analysis*. Cambridge, MA: Harvard University Press.

Kearns Goodwin, Doris. 2013. *The Bully Pulpit*. New York: Simon & Schuster.

Keil, Jan. 2016. "The Trouble with Approximating Industry Concentration from Compustat." University of the West Indies Department of Economics Working Paper. https://ssrn.com/abstract=2879035.

Kessler, Daniel P., and Daniel L. Rubinfeld. 2007. "Empirical Study of the Civil Justice System." In *Handbook of Law and Economics,* edited by A. Mitchell Polinsky and Steven Shavell, vol. 1, 343–401. Amsterdam: Elsevier, North-Holland.

Khan, Lina. 2017. "Amazon's Antitrust Paradox." *Yale Law Journal.* 126, no. 3: 710–805.

Khan, Lina, and Sandeep Vaheesan. 2017. "Market Power and Inequality: The Antitrust Counterrevolution and Its Discontents." *Harvard Law & Policy Review.* 11: 235–294.

Kirkwood, John B. 2014. "Collusion to Control a Powerful Customer: Amazon, E-Books, and Antitrust Policy." *University of Miami Law Review.* 69, no. 1: 1–63.

Kleiner, Morris M., and Alan B. Krueger. 2013. "Analyzing the Extent and Influence of Occupational Licensing on the Labor Market." *Journal of Labor Economics.* 31, no. 2: S173–S202.

Klick, Jonathan and Joshua D. Wright. 2008. *The Effects of Vertical Restraints on Output: Evidence from the Beer Industry.* Working Paper. http://.utexas.edu/law/wp/wp-content/uploads/centers/clbe/wright_effects_of_vertical-restraints.pdf.

Knee, Jonathan A., Bruce C. Greenwald, and Ava Seave. 2009. *The Curse of the Mogul: What's Wrong with the World's Leading Media Companies.* New York: Penguin Random House.

Kobayashi, Bruce H. 2010. "The Law and Economics of Predatory Pricing." In *Antitrust Law and Economics,* edited by Keith N. Hylton, 116–156. 2nd ed. Cheltenham, UK: Edward Elgar.

Kobayashi, Bruce H., and Timothy J. Muris. 2012. "Chicago, Post-Chicago, and Beyond: Time to Let Go of the 20th Century." *Antitrust Law Journal.* 78, no. 1: 147–172.

Kolasky, William J. 2001. "Lessons from Baby Food: The Role of Efficiencies in Merger Review." *Antitrust.* 16, no. 1: 82–87.

———. 2002a. "United States and European Competition Policy: Are There More Differences Than We Care to Admit?" Remarks at the European Policy Center, Brussels, Belgium, April 10. https://www.justice.gov/atr/speech/united-states-and-european-competition-policy-are-there-more-differences-we-care-admit.

———. 2002b. "U.S. and EU Competition Policy: Cartels, Mergers, and Beyond." Remarks at the Council for the United States and Italy Bi-Annual Conference, New York, NY, January 25. https://www.justice.gov/atr/speech/us-and-eu-competition-policy-cartels-mergers-and-beyond.

———. 2011a. "The Election of 1912: A Pivotal Moment in Antitrust History." *Antitrust.* 25, no. 3: 82–88.

———. 2011b. "Theodore Roosevelt and William Howard Taft: Marching Toward Armageddon." *Antitrust.* 25, no. 1: 97–104.

Kovacic, William E. 1982. "The Federal Trade Commission and Congressional Oversight of Antitrust Enforcement." *Tulsa Law Journal.* 17, no. 4: 587–671.

———. 1989. "Failed Expectations: The Troubled Past and Uncertain Future of the Sherman Act as a Tool for Deconcentration." *Iowa Law Review.* 74, no. 5: 1105–1150.

———. 1999. "Designing Antitrust Remedies for Dominant Firm Misconduct." *Connecticut Law Review.* 31, no. 4: 1285–1319.

———. 2003. "The Modern Evolution of US Competition Policy Enforcement Norms." *Antitrust Law Journal.* 71, No. 2: 377–478.

———. 2007. "The Intellectual DNA of Modern US Competition Law for Dominant Firm Conduct: The Chicago / Harvard Double Helix." *Columbia Business Law Review.* 1, no. 1: 1–80.

———. 2009. "Assessing the Quality of Competition Policy: The Case of Horizontal Merger Enforcement." *Competition Policy International.* 5, no. 1: 129–150.

———. 2014. "Politics and Partisanship in U.S. Federal Antitrust Enforcement." *Antitrust Law Journal.* 79, no. 2: 687–711.

Kovacic, William E., Robert C. Marshall, Leslie M. Marx, and Halbert L. White. 2011. "Plus Factors and Agreement in Antitrust Law." *Michigan Law Review.* 110, no. 3: 393–436.

Kovacic, William E., Robert C. Marshall, and Michael J. Meurer. 2018. "Serial Collusion by Multi-Product Firms." Boston University School of Law, Law and Economics Research Paper No. 18-18. https://ssrn.com/abstract =3235398.

Kovacic, William E., and Marc Winerman. 2015. "The Federal Trade Commission as an Independent Agency: Autonomy, Legitimacy, and Effectiveness." *Iowa Law Review.* 100, no. 5: 2085–2113.

Kreps, David M., and Jose A. Scheinkman. 1983. "Quantity Precommitment and Bertrand Competition Yield Cournot Outcomes." *The Bell Journal of Economics* 14, no. 2: 326–337.

Kühn, Kai-Uwe. 2015. "The Coordinated Effects of Mergers in Differentiated Products Markets." CEPR Discussion Paper No. 4769. https://cepr.org/active /publications/discussion_papers/dp.php?dpno=4769.

Kulick, Robert. 2017. "Ready-to-Mix: Horizontal Mergers, Prices, and Productivity." Center for Economic Studies Working Paper No. 17–38. https://www2 .census.gov/ces/wp/2017/CES-WP-17-38.pdf.

Kurz, Mordecai. 2017. "On the Formation of Capital and Wealth." SIEPR Working Paper No. 17–016. https://siepr.stanford.edu/research/publications /formation-capital-and-wealth-it-monopoly-power-and-rising-inequality.

Kutler, Stanley I. 1971. *Privilege and Create Destruction: The Charles River Bridge Case.* Philadelphia, PA: Lippincott.

Kutsoati, Edward, and George Norman. n.d. "Mutual Forbearance in a Differentiated Duopoly." Unpublished manuscript.

Kwoka, John. 1989. "The Private Profitability of Horizontal Mergers with Non-Cournot and Maverick Behavior." *International Journal of Industrial Organization.* 7, no. 3: 403–411.

———. 2015. *Mergers, Merger Control, and Remedies: A Retrospective Analysis of U.S. Policy.* Cambridge, MA: MIT Press.

———. 2017a. "Mergers, Merger Control, and Remedies: A Response to the FTC Critique." Working Paper. http://www.ios.neu.edu/j.kwoka/A%20 Response%20to%20the%20FTC%20Critique%20of%20MMCR.pdf.

———. 2017b. "The Structural Presumption and the Safe Harbor in Merger Review: False Positives or Unwarranted Concerns?" *Antitrust Law Journal.* 81, no. 3: 837–872.

Kwoka, John, Kevin Hearle, and Phillipe Alepin. 2016. "From the Fringe to the Forefront: Low Cost Carriers and Airline Price Determination." *Review of Industrial Organization.* 48, no. 3: 247–268.

Lamoreaux, Naomi R. 1985. *The Great Merger Movement in American Business, 1895–1904.* Cambridge: Cambridge University Press.

Lambert, Thomas A., and Michael Sykuta. 2013. "Why the New Evidence on Minimum Resale Price Maintenance Does Not Justify a Per Se or 'Quick Look' Approach." *CPI Antitrust Chronicle.* 11, no. 1: 2–10.

Lande, Robert H. 1982. "Wealth Transfers as the Original and Primary Concern of Antitrust: The Efficiency Interpretation Challenged." *Hastings Law Journal.* 34, no. 1: 65–151.

———. 1989. "Chicago's False Foundation: Wealth Transfers (Not Just Efficiency) Should Guide Antitrust." *Antitrust Law Journal.* 58, no. 3: 631–644.

Lande, Robert H., and Joshua P. Davis. 2008. "Benefits from Private Antitrust Enforcement: An Analysis of Forty Cases." *University of San Francisco Law Review.* 42, no. 4: 879–918.

Landes, William M., and Richard A. Posner. 1980. "Market Power in Antitrust Cases." *Harvard Law Review.* 94, no. 5: 937–996.

Lando, Hendrik. 2006. "Does Wrongful Conviction Lower Deterrence?" *Journal of Legal Studies.* 35, no. 2: 327–337.

Lao, Marina. 2014. "Ideology Matters in the Antirust Debate." *Antitrust Law Journal.* 79, no. 2: 649–685.

———. 2018. "Erring on the Side of Antitrust Enforcement When in Doubt in Data-Driven Mergers." In *Douglas H. Ginsburg—Liber Amercorum: An Antitrust Professor on the Bench,* edited by Nicolas Charbit, Carolina Malhado and Ellie Yang, vol. 1, 497–530. New York: Institute of Competition Law.

Leary, Thomas B. 2002. "The Essential Stability of Merger Policy in the United States." *Antitrust Law Journal.* 70, no. 1: 105–142.

Lerner, Josh. 1995. "Pricing and Financial Resources: An Analysis of the Disk Drive Industry, 1980–88." *Review of Economics and Statistics.* 77, no. 4: 585–598.

Lehman, Ari. 2005. "Eliminating the Below-Cost Pricing Requirement from Predatory Pricing Claims." *Cardozo Law Review.* 27, no. 1: 343–386.

Levenstein, Margaret C. 1996. "Do Price Wars Facilitate Collusion? A Study of the Bromine Cartel Before World War I." *Explorations in Economic History.* 33, no. 1: 107–137.

———. 1997. "Price Wars and the Stability of Collusion: A Study of the Pre-World War I Bromine Industry." *Journal of Industrial Economics.* 45, no. 2: 117–137.

Levenstein, Margaret C., and Valerie Y. Suslow. 2006. "What Determines Cartel Success?" *Journal of Economic Literature.* 44, no. 1: 43–95.

———. 2011. "Breaking Up is Hard to Do: Determinants of Cartel Duration." *Journal of Law and Economics.* 54, no. 2: 455–492.

———. 2014. "How Do Cartels Use Vertical Restraints? Reflections on Bork's The Antitrust Paradox." *Journal of Law and Economics.* 57, no. 3: S33–S50.

Lewis, William W. 2004. *The Power of Productivity: Wealth, Poverty, and the Threat to Global Stability.* Chicago, IL: University of Chicago Press.

Lieber, James B. 2000. *Rats in the Grain: The Dirty Tricks and Trials of Archer Daniels Midland, the Supermarket to the World.* New York: Four Walls Eight Windows.

Lindsay, Michael, Jaime Stilson, and Rebecca Bernhard. 2016. "Employers Beware: The DOJ and FTC Confirm that Naked Wage-Fixing and 'No-Poaching' Agreements are Per Se Antitrust Violations." *Antitrust Source.* 2016, December: 1–12.

Liscow, Zachary D. 2018 (Forthcoming). "Is Efficiency Biased?" *University of Chicago Law Review.* https://papers.ssrn.com/sol3/papers.cfm?abstract_id =3018796.

Lo, Andrew W. 2012. "Reading About the Financial Crisis: A Twenty-One Book Review." *Journal of Economic Literature.* 50, no. 1: 151–178.

Lopatka, John E., and William H. Page. 2002. "'Obvious' Consumer Harm in Antitrust Policy: The Chicago School, the Post–Chicago School and the Courts." In *Post-Chicago Developments in Antitrust Analysis,* edited by Roger van den Bergh, Roberto Pardolesi, and Antonio Cucinotta, 129–160. Northampton, UK: Edward Elgar.

Luco, Fernando, and Guillermo Marshall. 2018. "Vertical Integration with Multiproduct Firms: When Eliminating Double Marginalization May Hurt Consumers." Working Paper. https://ssrn.com/abstract =3110038.

Lynn, Barry C. 2010. *Cornered: The New Monopoly Capitalism and the Economics of Destruction.* Hoboken, NJ: John Wiley.

Lyon, Leverett S., Paul T. Homan, Lewis L. Lorwin, George Terborgh, Charles L. Dearing, and Leon C. Marshall. 1935. *The National Recovery Administration: An Analysis and Appraisal.* Washington, D.C.: Brookings Institution.

MacKay, Alexander, and David Aron Smith. 2014. "The Empirical Effects of Minimum Resale Price Maintenance on Prices and Output." Working Paper. https://ssrn.com/abstract=2513533.

Mahoney, Neale, Andre Veiga, and E. Glen Weyl, 2014. "Competition Policy in Selection Markets." *CPI Antitrust Chronicle.* 2014, no. 1: 2–9.

Makkai, Toni, and John Braithwaite. 1992. "In and Out of the Revolving Door: Making Sense of Regulatory Capture." *Journal of Public Policy*. 12, no. 1: 61–78.

Malmendier, Ulrike, Enrico Moretti, and Florian S. Peters. 2018. "Winning by Losing: Evidence on the Long-Run Effects of Mergers." *Review of Financial Studies*. 31, no. 8: 3212–3264. https://doi.org/10.1093/rfs/hhy009.

Mankiw, N. Gregory, and Michael D. Whinston. 1986. "Free Entry and Social Inefficiency." *RAND Journal of Economics*. 17, no. 1: 48–58.

Manne, Geoffrey A., and Joshua D. Wright. 2010. "Innovation and the Limits of Antitrust." *Journal of Competition Law and Economics*. 6, no. 1: 153–202.

Marinescu, Ioana, and Herbert Hovenkamp. 2018. "Anticompetitive Mergers in Labor Markets." University of Pennsylvania Faculty Scholarship 1965. https://scholarship.law.upenn.edu/faculty_scholarship/1965/.

Marshall, Robert C. 2017. "Unobserved Collusion: Warning Signs and Concerns." *Journal of Antitrust Enforcement*. 5, no. 3: 329–340.

Mas-Colell, Andreu, Michael D. Whinston, and Jerry R. Green. 1995. *Microeconomic Theory*. New York: Oxford University Press.

Maskin, Eric, and Jean Tirole. 1987. "A Theory of Dynamic Oligopoly III: Cournot Competition." *European Economic Review*. 31, no. 4: 847–868.

Mason, Lilliana. 2018. "Ideologues Without Issues: The Polarizing Consequences of Ideological Identities." *Public Opinion Quarterly*. 82, no. 1: 280–301.

Masur, Jonathan. 2011. "Patent Inflation." *Yale Law Journal*. 121, no. 3: 470–532.

May, James. 1989. "Antitrust in the Formative Era: Political and Economic Theory in Constitutional and Antitrust Analysis, 1880–1918." *Ohio State Law Journal*. 50, no. 2: 257–395.

———. 2007. "The Story of *Standard Oil Co. v. United States*." In *Antitrust Stories*, edited by Eleanor M. Fox and Daniel A. Crane, 7–59. New York: Foundation Press.

McAfee, R. Preston. 2002. *Competitive Solutions: The Strategist's Toolkit*. Princeton, NJ: Princeton University Press.

McChesney, Fred S. 2004. "Talking 'Bout My Antitrust Generation." *Regulation*. 27, no. 3: 48–55.

McClellan, James. 1971. *Joseph Story and the American Constitution*. Norman: University of Oklahoma Press.

McGahan, Anita M. 1995. "Cooperation in Prices and Capacities: Trade Associations in Brewing After Repeal." *Journal of Law and Economics*. 38, no. 2: 521–559.

McGee, John. 1958. "Predatory Price-Cutting: The Standard Oil (N.J.) Case." *Journal of Law and Economics*. 1: 137–169.

McMurray, James. 2017. "Ideology as Opinion: A Spatial Model of Common-Value Elections." *American Economic Journal: Microeconomics* 9, no. 4: 108–149.

McSweeney, Terrell, and Brian O'Dea. 2017. "The Implications of Algorithmic Pricing for Coordinated Effects Analysis and Price Discrimination Markets in Antitrust Enforcement." *Antitrust*. 32, no. 1: 75–81.

Meese, Alan J. 2012. "Standard Oil *as* Lochner's *Trojan Horse.*" *Southern California Law Review.* 85, no. 3: 783–813.

Mehata, Mihir N., Suraj Srinivasan, and Wanli Zhao. 2017. "Political Influence and Merger Antitrust Reviews." Working Paper. https://ssrn.com/abstract=2945020.

Mehra, Salil K. 2016. "Antitrust and the Robo-Seller: Competition in the Time of Algorithms." *Minnesota Law Review.* 100, no. 4: 1323–1375.

———. 2017. "Robo-Seller Prosecutions and Antitrust's Error-Cost Framework." *CPI Antitrust Chronicle.* 2017, no. 2: 36–39.

Melamed, A. Douglas, and Carl Shapiro. 2018. "How Antitrust Law Can Make FRAND Commitments More Effective." *Yale Law Journal.* 127, no. 7: 2110–2141.

Mendonça, Sandro. 2013. "The 'Sailing Ship Effect': Reassessing History as a Source of Insight on Technical Change." *Research Policy.* 42, no. 10: 1724–1738.

Mikians, Jakub, László Gyarmati, Vijay Erramilli, and Nikolaos Laoutaris. 2012. "Detecting Price and Search Discrimination on the Internet." Proceedings of the 11th ACM Workshop on Hot Topics in Networks (HotNets'12), Redmond, WA. 2012: 79–84.

———. 2013. "Crowd-assisted Search for Price Discrimination in E-Commerce: First Results." Proceedings of the 9th International Conference on emerging Networking Experiments and Technologies (CoNEXT'13), Santa Barbara, CA. http://dx.doi.org/10.1145/2535372.2535415.

Miller, Nathan H., and Matthew C. Weinberg. 2017. "Understanding the Price Effects of the MillerCoors Joint Venture." *Econometrica.* 85, no. 6: 1763–1791.

Moeller, Sara P., Frederik P. Schilingemann, and René M. Stulz. 2006. "Wealth Destruction on a Massive Scale? A Study of Acquiring-Firm Returns in the Recent Merger Wave." *Journal of Finance.* 60, no. 2: 757–782.

Mokyr, Joel. 1990. *The Lever of Riches: Technological Creativity and Economic Progress.* New York: Oxford University Press.

———. 2002. *The Gifts of Athena: Historical Origins of the Knowledge Economy.* Princeton, NJ: Princeton University Press.

Motta, Massimo. 2004. *Competition Policy: Theory and Practice.* Cambridge: Cambridge University Press.

Motta, Massimo, and Helder Vasconcelos. 2012. "Exclusionary Pricing in a Two-Sided Market." Centre for Economic Policy Research, Discussion Paper No. 9164. https://cepr.org/active/publications/discussion_papers/dp.php?dpno=9164.

Naidu, Suresh, Eric A. Posner, and E. Glen Weyl. 2018. "Antitrust Remedies for Labor Market Power." *Harvard Law Review.*

Nalebuff, Barry J. 2004. "Bundling as a Way to Leverage Monopoly." Yale School of Management Working Paper No. ES-36. http://ssrn.com/abstract=586648.

Neuchterlein, Jonathan E., and Philip J. Weiser. 2005. *Digital Crossroads: American Telecommunications Policy in the Internet Age.* Cambridge, MA: MIT Press.

Nevo, Aviv. 2014. "Mergers that Increase Bargaining Leverage." Remarks at the Stanford Institute for Economic Policy Research and Cornerstone Research Conference on Antitrust in Highly Innovative Industries. https://www.justice .gov/atr/speech/mergers-increase-bargaining-leverage.

Newham, Melissa, Jo Seldeslachts, and Albert Banal-Estanol. 2018. "Common Ownership and Market Entry: Evidence from the Pharmaceutical Industry." DIW Berlin Discussion Paper No. 1738. https://www.diw.de/documents /publikationen/73/diw_01.c.591375.de/dp1738.pdf.

Noel, Hans. 2013. *Political Ideologies and Political Parties in America.* New York: Cambridge University Press.

Noll, Roger G. 2005. "'Buyer Power' and Economic Policy." *Antitrust Law Journal.* 72, no. 2: 589–624.

North, Douglass C., John Joseph Wallis, and Barry R. Weingast. 2009. *Violence and Social Orders: A Conceptual Framework for Interpreting Recorded Human History.* Cambridge: Cambridge University Press.

Nourse, Victoria F. 2013. "Overrides: The Super-Study." *Texas Law Review See Also.* 92: 205–216.

Oberlander, Jonathan. 2003. "The Politics of Medicare Reform." *Washington and Lee Law Review.* 60, no. 4: 1095–1136.

O'Brien, Daniel P. 2008. "The Antitrust Treatment of Vertical Restraints: Beyond the Possibility Theorems." In *The Pros and Cons of Vertical Restraints,* edited by Swedish Competition Authority, 40–101. http://www.konkurrensverket.se/en /research/seminars/the-pros-and-cons-vertical-restraints/.

O'Brien, Daniel P., and Keith Waehrer. 2017. "The Competitive Effects of Common Ownership: We Know Less Than We Think." *Antitrust Law Journal.* 81, no. 3: 729–777.

Olson, Mancur. 1982. *The Rise and Decline of Nations.* New Haven, CT: Yale University Press.

Orbach, Barak Y. 2010. "The Antitrust Consumer Welfare Paradox." *Journal of Competition Law and Economics.* 7, no. 1: 133–164.

———. 2017. "Antitrust Populism." *New York University Journal of Law and Business.* 14, no. 1: 1–25.

Padilla, Jorge, Douglas Ginsburg, and Koren Wong-Ervin. 2018. "Antitrust Analysis Involving Intellectual Property and Standards: Implications from Economics." Working Paper. https://ssrn.com/abstract=3119034.

Page, William H. 1995. "Legal Realism and the Shaping of Modern Antitrust." *Emory Law Journal.* 44, no. 1: 1–70.

———. 2008. "The Ideological Origins and Evolution of U.S. Antitrust Law." In *Issues in Competition Law and Policy,* edited by Wayne Dale Collins, vol. 1, no. 1: 1–17. Chicago, IL: ABA Section of Antitrust Law.

———. 2010. "Microsoft and the Limits of Antitrust." *Journal of Competition Law and Economics.* 6, no. 1: 33–50.

———. 2013. "Objective and Subjective Theories of Concerted Action." *Antitrust Law Journal.* 79, no. 1: 215–272.

———. 2015. "Signaling and Agreement in Antitrust Law." Working Paper, http://ssrn.com/abstract=2620786.

Page, William H., and John E. Lopatka. 2007. *The Microsoft Case: Antitrust, High Technology, and Consumer Welfare.* Chicago, IL: University of Chicago Press.

Parente, Stephen L., and Edward C. Prescott. 2000. *Barriers to Riches.* Cambridge, MA: MIT Press.

Pate, R. Hewitt. 2004. "Antitrust in a Transatlantic Context—From a Cicada's Perspective." Remarks at the "Antitrust in a Transatlantic Context" Conference, Belgium, Brussels, June 7. https://www.justice.gov/atr/speech/antitrust-transatlantic-context-cicadas-perspective.

Patel, Menesh S. 2018. "Common Ownership, Institutional Investors, and Antitrust." *Antitrust Law Journal.* 82, no. 1: 279–334.

Patterson, Mark R. 2017. *Antitrust Law in the New Economy.* Cambridge, MA: Harvard University Press.

Peltzman, Sam. 2014. "Industrial Concentration Under the Rule of Reason." *Journal of Law and Economics.* 57, no. 3: S101–S120.

Peters, Craig T. 2003. "Evaluating the Performance of Merger Simulation: Evidence from the U.S. Airline Industry." Department of Justice Economic Analysis Group Discussion Paper No. 03–1. https://ssrn.com/abstract=399941.

Philippon, Thomas. 2018. "A Primer on Competition, Investment, and Growth." Working Paper. https://www.kansascityfed.org/publications/research/escp/symposiums/escp-2018.

Phillips-Fein, Kim. 2009. *Invisible Hands: The Making of the Conservative Movement from the New Deal to Reagan.* New York: Norton.

Piketty, Thomas. 2014. *Capital in the Twenty-First Century.* Cambridge, MA: Harvard University Press.

Pitofsky, Robert. 1979. "The Political Content of Antitrust." *University of Pennsylvania Law Review.* 127, no. 4: 1051–1075.

———. 1987. "Does Antitrust Have a Future?" *Georgetown Law Journal.* 76, no. 2: 321–337.

———, ed. 2008. *How the Chicago School Overshot the Mark: The Effect of Conservative Economic Analysis on U.S. Antitrust.* New York: Oxford University Press.

Porter, Michael E. 1980. *Competitive Strategy: Techniques for Analyzing Industries and Competitors.* New York: Simon & Schuster.

Porter, Robert H. 1993. "A Study of Cartel Stability: The Joint Executive Committee, 1880–1886." *Bell Journal of Economics.* 14, no. 2: 301–314.

Posner, Richard A. 1973. "An Economic Approach to Legal Procedure and Judicial Administration." *Journal of Legal Studies.* 2, no. 2: 399–458.

———. 1975a. "Antitrust Policy and the Supreme Court: An Analysis of the Restricted Distribution, Horizontal Merger and Potential Competition Decisions." *Columbia Law Review.* 75, no. 2: 282–327.

———. 1975b. "The Social Costs of Monopoly and Regulation." *Journal of Political Economy.* 83, no. 4: 807–827.

———. 1976. *Antitrust Law.* 1st ed. Chicago, IL: University of Chicago Press.

———. 1979. "The Chicago School of Antitrust Analysis." *University of Pennsylvania Law Review.* 127, no. 4: 925–948.

———. 1981. "The Next Step in the Antitrust Treatment of Restricted Distribution: Per Se Legality." *University of Chicago Law Review.* 48, no. 1: 6–26.

———. 1999. "An Economic Approach to the Law of Evidence." *Stanford Law Review.* 51, no. 6: 1477–1546.

———. 2001. *Antitrust Law.* 2nd ed. Chicago, IL: University of Chicago Press.

Prasad, Monica. 2006. *The Politics of Free Markets: The Rise of Neoliberal Economic Policies in Britain, France, Germany, & the United States.* Chicago, IL: University of Chicago Press.

Priest, George L. 2010. "The Limits of Antitrust and the Chicago School Tradition." *Journal of Competition Law and Economics.* 6, no. 1: 1–9.

Rahman, K. Sabheel. 2018. "The New Utilities: Private Power, Social Infrastructure, and the Revival of the Public Utility Concept." *Cardozo Law Review.* 39, no. 5: 101–171.

Ramseyer, J. Mark, and Eric B. Rasmusen. 2014. "Exclusive Dealing: Before Bork, and Beyond." *Journal of Law and Economics.* 57, no. S3: S145–S160.

Reimers, Imke, and Joel Waldfogel. 2017. "Throwing the Books at Them: Amazon's Puzzling Long Run Pricing Strategy." *Southern Economic Journal.* 83, no. 4: 869–885.

Rhee, Ki-Eun. 2017. "Price and Output Effects of Oligopoly Price Discrimination Under Best-Response Asymmetry." Kaist College of Business Working Paper No. KCB-WP-2017-013. https://papers.ssrn.com/sol3/papers.cfm?abstract_id=3005029.

Rill, James F., and Stacy L. Turner. 2014. "Presidents Practicing Antitrust: Where to Draw the Line." *Antitrust Law Journal.* 79, no. 2: 577–599.

Riordan, Michael H., and Steven C. Salop. 1995. "Evaluating Vertical Mergers: A Post-Chicago Approach." *Antitrust Law Journal.* 63, no. 2: 513–568.

Roback, Herbert. 1946. "Monopoly or Competition Through Surplus Plant Disposal? The Aluminum Case." *Cornell Law Quarterly.* 31 no. 3: 302–326.

Rodrik, Dani. 1998. "Why Do More Open Economies Have Bigger Governments?" *Journal of Political Economy.* 106, no. 5: 997–1032.

———. 2018. "Populism and the Economics of Globalization." *Journal of International Business Policy.* 1, no 1–2: 12–33.

Röller, Lars-Hendrik, Johan Stennek, and Frank Verboven. 2006. "Efficiency Gains from Mergers." In *European Merger Control: Do We Need an Efficiency Defence,* edited by Fabienne Ilzkovitz and Roderick Meiklejohn. Cheltenham, UK: Edward Elgar.

Rosenberg, Nathan, and L. E. Birdzell Jr. 1986. *How the West Grew Rich: The Economic Transformation of the Industrial World.* New York: Basic Books.

Rossi-Hansberg, Esteban, Pierre-Daniel Sarte, and Nicholas Trachter. 2018. "Divergent Trends in National and Local Competition." NBER Working Paper No. 25066. http://www.nber.org/papers/w25066.

Rubinovitz, Robert N. 1993. "Market Power and Price Increases for Basic Cable Service Since Deregulation." *RAND Journal of Economics*. 24, no. 1: 1–18.

Rule, Charles F. 1986. "The Administration's Views: Antitrust Analysis after the Nine No-No's." *Antitrust Law Journal*. 55, no. 2: 365–372.

Rybincek, Jan M., and Joshua D. Wright. 2014. "Outside In or Inside Out? Counting Merger Efficiencies Inside and Out of the Relevant Market." In *William E. Kovacic—Liber Amicorum: An Antitrust Tribute*, edited by Nicolas Charbit and Elisa Ramundo, vol. 2. New York: Institute of Competition Law.

Sagers, Chris. 2019 (Forthcoming). *Apple, Antitrust, and Irony*. Cambridge, MA: Harvard University Press.

Salant, Stephen. 1987. "Treble Damage Awards in Private Litigation for Price Fixing." *Journal of Political Economy*. 95, no. 6: 1326–1236.

Salcedo, Bruno. 2015. "Pricing Algorithms and Tacit Collusion." Working Paper. http://brunosalcedo.com/docs/collusion.pdf.

Salop, Steven C. 1986. "Practices That (Credibly) Facilitate Oligopoly Co-ordination." In *New Developments in the Analysis of Market Structure*, edited by Joseph E. Stiglitz and G. Frank Mathewson, 265–290. London, UK: MacMillan.

———. 2008. "Economic Analysis of Exclusionary Vertical Conduct: Where Chicago Has Overshot the Mark." In *How the Chicago School Overshot the Mark: The Effect of Conservative Economic Analysis on U.S. Antitrust*, edited by Robert Pitofsky, 141–155. New York: Oxford University Press.

———. 2010. "Question: What Is the Real and Proper Antitrust Welfare Standard? Answer: The True Consumer Welfare Standard." *Loyola Consumer Law Review*. 22, no. 3: 336–353.

———. 2013. "Merger Settlements and Enforcement Policy for Optimal Deterrence and Maximum Welfare." *Fordham Law Review*. 81, no. 5: 2647–2681.

———. 2014. "What Consensus? Ideology, Politics and Elections Still Matter." *Antitrust Law Journal*. 79, no. 2: 601–648.

———. 2015. "The Evolution and Vitality of Merger Presumptions: A Decision-Theoretic Approach." *Antitrust Law Journal*. 80, no. 2: 269–306.

———. 2017. "An Enquiry Meet for the Case: Decision Theory, Presumptions, and Evidentiary Burdens in Formulating Antitrust Legal Standards." Georgetown Law Faculty Publications and Other Works. https://scholarship.law.georgetown.edu/cgi/viewcontent.cgi?article=3025&context=facpub.

———. 2018. "Invigorating Vertical Merger Enforcement." *Yale Law Journal*. 127, no. 7: 1962–1994.

Salop, Steven C., and Daniel P. Culley. 2016. "Revising the U.S. Vertical Merger Guidelines: Policy Issues and an Interim Guide for Practitioners." *Journal of Antitrust Enforcement*. 4, no. 1: 1–41.

Salop, Steven C., and R. Craig Romaine. 1999. "Preserving Monopoly: Economic Analysis, Legal Standards, and *Microsoft*." *George Mason Law Review*. 7, no. 3: 617–664.

Salop, Steven C., and Carl Shapiro. 2017. "Whither Antitrust Enforcement in the Trump Administration?" *The Antitrust Source.* 2017, February: 1–20.

Sanders, Elizabeth. 1999. *Roots of Reform: Farmers, Workers, and the American State, 1977–1917.* Chicago, IL: University of Chicago Press.

Sass, Tim R. 2005. "The Competitive Effects of Exclusive Dealing: Evidence from the U.S. Beer Industry." *International Journal of Industrial Organization.* 23, no. 3–4: 203–225.

Scherer, F. M. 1996. *Industry Structure, Strategy, and Public Policy.* New York: Pearson.

Schmalensee, Richard. 1989. "Inter-Industry Studies of Structure and Performance." In *Handbook of Industrial Organization,* edited by Richard Schmalensee and Robert D. Willig, vol. 2, 951–1009. New York: Elsevier.

Schmalz, Martin C. 2018. "Common Ownership, Concentration, and Corporate Conduct." *Annual Review of Financial Economics.*

Schwartz, Warren F. 2000. "Legal Error." In *Encyclopedia of Law and Economics,* edited by Boudewijn Bouckaert and Gerrit De Geest, vol. 1, 1029–1040. Cheltenham, UK: Edward Elgar.

Scott Morton, Fiona. 1997. "Entry and Predation: British Shipping Cartels 1879–1929." *Journal of Economics and Management Strategy.* 6, no. 4: 679–724.

Segal, Ilya R., and Michael D. Whinston. 2000. "Exclusive Contracts and Protection of Investments." *RAND Journal of Economics.* 31, no. 4: 603–633.

———. 2006. "Public vs. Private Enforcement of Antitrust Law: A Survey." Stanford Law and Economics Olin Working Paper No. 335. https://ssrn.com /abstract=952067.

Sertsios, Giorgo, Daniel Ferrés, Gaizka Ormazabal, and Paul Povel. 2016. "Capital Structure Under Collusion." Working Paper. https://ssrn.com /abstract=2877374.

Shapiro, Carl. 1989. "Theories of Oligopoly Behavior." In *Handbook of Industrial Organization,* edited by Richard Schmalensee and Robert D. Willig, vol. 1, 329–414. Amsterdam: Elsevier, North-Holland.

———. 1999. "Exclusivity in Network Industries." *George Mason Law Review.* 7, no. 3: 673–683.

———. 2012. "Competition and Innovation: Did Arrow Hit the Bull's Eye?" In *The Rate and Direction of Inventive Activity Revisited,* edited by Josh Lerner and Scott Stern, 361–410. Chicago, IL: University of Chicago Press.

———. 2018 (In press). "Antitrust in a Time of Populism." *International Journal of Industrial Organization.* https://doi.org/10.1016/j.ijindorg.2018.01.001.

Shapiro, Carl, and Hal R. Varian. 1999. *Information Rules: A Strategic Guide to the Network Economy.* Boston, MA: Harvard Business School Press.

Shelanski, Howard A. 2011. "The Case for Rebalancing Antitrust and Regulation." *Michigan Law Review.* 109, no. 5: 683–732.

———. 2013. "Information, Innovation, and Competition Policy for the Internet." *University of Pennsylvania Law Review.* 161, no. 6: 1663–1705.

Shelanski, Howard, Samantha Knox, and Arif Dhilla. 2018. "Network Effects and Efficiencies in Multi-Sided Markets." In OECD, *Rethinking Antitrust Tools for Multi-Sided Platforms*. http://www.oecd.org/competition/rethinking -antitrust-tools-for-multi-sided-platforms.htm.

Shleifer, Andrei, and Robert W. Vishny. 1998. *The Grabbing Hand: Government Pathologies and Their Cures*. Cambridge, MA: Harvard University Press.

Singh, Vishal, and Ting Zhu. 2008. "Pricing and Market Concentration in Oligopoly Markets." *Marketing Science*. 27, no. 6: 1020–1035.

Snyder, Edward A., and Thomas E. Kauper. 1991. "Misuse of the Antitrust Laws: The Competitor Plaintiff." *Michigan Law Review*. 90, no. 3: 551–598.

Sokol, D. Daniel. 2014. "The Transformation of Vertical Restraints: Per Se Illegality, the Rule of Reason and Per Se Legality." *Antitrust Law Journal*. 79, no. 3: 1003–1016.

Sowell, Thomas. 1987. *A Conflict of Visions: Ideological Origins of Political Struggles*. New York: Basic Books.

Srinivasan, Sridhar. 2018. "Patents v. Innovation: Evidence from Public Firms." Working Paper. https://ssrn.com/abstract=3185148.

Stigler, George J. 1964. "A Theory of Oligopoly." *Journal of Political Economy*. 72, no. 1: 44–61.

Stiglitz, Joseph E. 1987. "Technological Change, Sunk Costs, and Competition." *Brookings Papers on Economic Activity*. 1987, no. 3: 883–937.

———. 2012. *The Price of Inequality: How Today's Divided Society Endangers Our Future*. New York: W. W. Norton.

Stimson, James A. 2015. *Tides of Consent: How Public Opinion Shapes American Politics*. New York: Cambridge University Press.

Stole, Lars A. 2007. "Price Discrimination and Competition." In *Handbook of Industrial Organization*, edited by Mark Armstrong and Robert Porter, vol. 3, 2221–2299. Amsterdam: Elsevier, North-Holland.

Stucke, Maurice E. 2013. "Looking at the Monopsony in the Mirror." *Emory Law Journal*. 62, no. 6: 1509–1562.

Stucke, Maurice E., and Ariel Ezrachi. 2015. "Artificial Intelligence and Collusion: When Computers Inhibit Competition." Oxford Legal Studies Research Paper No. 18/2015. https://ssrn.com/abstract=2591874.

Stucke, Maurice E., and Allen P. Grunes. 2016. *Big Data and Competition Policy*. Oxford. Oxford University Press.

Sullivan, Lawrence A., Warren S. Grimes, and Christopher L. Sagers. 2000. *The Law of Antitrust: An Integrated Handbook*. St. Paul, MN: West Academic.

Sutton, John. 1991. *Sunk Costs and Market Structure: Price Competition, Advertising and the Evolution of Concentration*. Cambridge, MA: MIT Press.

———. 1998. *Technology and Market Structure: Theory and History*. Cambridge, MA: MIT Press.

Svolik, Milan W. 2017. "When Polarization Trumps Civic Virtue: Partisan Conflict and the Subversion of Democracy by Incumbents." Unpublished

Paper, Yale University. https://campuspress.yale.edu/svolik/files/2017/09
/polarization3-15ap6tb.pdf.

Tabakovic, Haris, and Thomas Wollmann. 2018. "From Revolving Doors to
Regulatory Capture? Evidence from Patent Examiners." NBER Working
Paper No. w24638. https://ssrn.com/abstract=3185893.

Taplin, Jonathan. 2017. *Move Fast and Break Things: How Facebook, Google, and
Amazon Cornered Culture and Undermined Democracy.* New York: Little, Brown.

Tarbell, Ida M. 1904. *The History of the Standard Oil Company.* New York:
McClure, Phillips.

Teles, Steven M. 2008. *The Rise of the Conservative Legal Movement.* Princeton,
NJ: Princeton University Press.

Telser, Lester G. 1960. "Why Should Manufacturers Want Fair Trade?" *Journal of
Law and Economics.* 3: 86–105.

Traina, James. 2018. "Is Aggregate Market Power Increasing? Production Trends
Using Financial Statements." Chicago Booth Stigler Center New Working
Paper No. 17. https://papers.ssrn.com/sol3/papers.cfm?abstract_id=3120849.

Transportation Research Board, National Research Council. 1991. *Winds of
Change: Domestic Air Transport Since Deregulation—Special Report 230.*
Washington, D.C.: The National Academies Press.

Tucker, Catherine. 2018. "What Have We Learned in the Last Decade? Network
Effects and Market Power." *Antitrust.* 32, no. 2: 77–81.

Turner, Donald F. 1969. "The Scope of Antitrust and Other Economic Regulatory Policies." *Harvard Law Review.* 82, no. 6: 1207–1244.

Tushnet, Mark. 2003. *The New Constitutional Order.* Princeton. NJ: Princeton
University Press.

Ulfelder, Jay. 2010. *Dilemmas of Democratic Consolidation: A Game-Theory Approach.* Boulder, CO: FirstForumPress.

U.S. Department of Justice and Federal Trade Commission. 2010. *Horizontal
Merger Guidelines.* https://www.justice.gov/sites/default/files/atr/legacy/2010
/08/19/hmg-2010.pdf.

Vaheesan, Sandeep, and Frank A. Pasquale. Forthcoming. "The Politics of
Professionalism: Reappraising Occupational Licensure and Competition
Policy." *Annual Review of Law and Social Science.* https://papers.ssrn.com/sol3
/papers.cfm?abstract_id=2881732.

Van Reenen, John. 2018. "Increasing Differences Between Firms: Market Power
and the Macro-Economy." Working Paper. https://www.kansascityfed.org
/publications/research/escp/symposiums/escp-2018.

Vance, Sarah S. 2006. "A Primer on the Class Action Fairness Act of 2005."
Tulane Law Review. 80, no. 5–6: 1617–1644.

Vickers, John. 2010. "Competition Policy and Property Rights." *The Economic
Journal.* 120, No. 554 (Conference Papers): 375–392.

Vita, Michael, and F. David Osinski. 2018. "John Kwoka's Mergers, Merger
Control, and Remedies: A Critical Review." *Antitrust Law Journal.* 82, no. 1:
361–388.

Wald, Douglas L., and Deborah L. Feinstein. 2004. "Merger Enforcement in Innovation Markets: The Latest Chapter—Genzyme/Novazyme." *Antitrust Source.* 2004, July: 1–11.

Waller, Spencer Weber. 2004. "The Antitrust Legacy of Thurman Arnold." *St. John's Law Review.* 78, no. 3: 569–613.

———. 2019 (Forthcoming). "Antitrust and Democracy." *Florida State University Law Review.* 45.

Walzer, Michael. 1983. *Spheres of Justice.* Oxford: Blackwell.

Ward, Patrick R. 2017. "Testing for Multi-Sided Platform Effects in Market Definition." *University of Chicago Law Review.* 84, no. 4: 2059–2102.

Wells, Wyatt. 2002. *Antitrust & the Formation of the Postwar World.* New York: Columbia University Press.

Weiman, David F., and Richard C. Levin. 1994. "Preying for Monopoly? The Case of Southern Bell Telephone Company, 1894–1912." *Journal of Political Economy.* 102, no. 1: 103–126.

Weiss, Leonard W. 1989. "Conclusions." In *Concentration and Price,* edited by Leonard W. Weiss, 266–284. Cambridge, MA: MIT Press.

Wen, Wen, and Feng Zhu. 2017. "Threat of Platform-Owner Entry and Complementor Responses: Evidence from the Mobile App Market." NET Institute Working Paper No. 16–10. https://ssrn.com/abstract=2848533.

Werden, Gregory J. 1988. "The Divergence of SIC Industries from Antitrust Markets: Some Evidence from Price Fixing Cases." *Economics Letters.* 28, no. 2: 193–197.

———. 2004. "Economic Evidence on the Existence of Collusion: Reconciling Antitrust Law with Oligopoly Theory." *Antitrust Law Journal.* 71, no. 3: 719–800.

———. 2017. "Cross-Market Balancing of Competitive Effects: What is the Law, and What Should it Be?" *Journal of Corporation Law.* 43, no. 1: 119–142.

Werden, Gregory J., and Luke Froeb. 2018. "Don't Panic: A Guide to Claims of Increasing Concentration." *Antitrust Magazine.* https://papers.ssrn.com/sol3/papers.cfm?abstract_id=3156912.

Werden, Gregory J., Scott D. Hammond, and Belinda A. Barnett. 2011. "Deterrence and Detection of Cartels: Using All the Tools and Sanctions." *Antitrust Bulletin.* 56, no. 2: 207–234.

White, Lawrence J. 1988. "Litigation and Economic Incentives." *Research in Law and Economics.* 11: 73–90.

———. 1991. *The S&L Debacle: Public Policy Lessons for Bank and Thrift Regulation.* New York: Oxford University Press.

White, Lawrence J., and Jasper Yang. 2017. "What Has Been Happening to Aggregate Concentration in the U.S. Economy in the 21st Century?" Working Paper. https://ssrn.com/abstract=2953984.

Wickelgren, Abraham L. 2012. "Determining the Optimal Antitrust Standard: How to Think About Per Se Versus Rule of Reason." *Southern California Law Review.* 85, no. 3, Postscript: 52–59.

Widiss, Deborah A. 2014. "Identifying Congressional Overrides Should Not Be This Hard." *Texas Law Review See Also.* 92: 145–169.

Wiebe, Robert H. 1959. "The House of Morgan and the Executive, 1905–1913." *The American History Review.* 65: 49–60.

———. 1967. *The Search for Order, 1877–1920.* New York: Hill and Wang.

Williamson, Oliver E. 1968. "Economies as an Antitrust Defense: The Welfare Tradeoffs." *American Economic Review.* 58, no. 1: 18–36.

Wilson, James Q. 1980. *The Politics of Regulation.* New York: Basic Books.

Winerman, Marc. 2003. "The Origins of the F.T.C.: Concentration, Cooperation, Control, and Competition." *Antitrust Law Journal.* 71, no. 1: 1–97.

Winston, Clifford. 1993. "Economic Deregulation: Days of Reckoning for Microeconomists." *Journal of Economic Literature.* 31, no. 3: 1263–1289.

Winters, Jeffrey A. 2011. *Oligarchy.* Cambridge: Cambridge University Press.

Wolff, Edward, N. 2014. "Household Wealth Trends in the United States, 1962–2013." NBER Working Paper No. 20733. http://www.nber.org/papers /w20733.pdf.

Wollmann, Thomas. 2018. "Stealth Consolidation: Evidence From an Amendment to the Hart-Scott-Rodino Act." Working Paper. http://faculty .chicagobooth.edu/thomas.wollmann/docs/Stealth_Consolidation_Wollmann .pdf.

Wright, Joshua D. 2009. "Overshot the Mark? A Simple Explanation of the Chicago School's Influence on Antitrust." *Competition Policy International.* 5, no. 1: 1–34.

———. 2012a. "Abandoning Antitrust's Chicago Obsession: The Case for Evidence-Based Antitrust." *Antitrust Law Journal.* 78, no. 1: 241–271.

———. 2012b. "Moving Beyond Naïve Foreclosure Analysis." *George Mason Law Review.* 19, no. 5: 1163–1198.

Xie, Jin, and Joseph Gerakos. 2018. "Institutional Cross-holdings and Generic Entry in the Pharmaceutical Industry." Working Paper. http://abfer.org/media /abfer-events-2018/annual-conference/accounting/AC18P5001_Institutional _Cross-holdings_and_Generic_Entry.pdf.

Zaller, John R. 1992. *The Nature and Origins of Mass Opinion.* Cambridge: Cambridge University Press.

Zhu, Feng, and Qihong Liu. 2018. "Competing With Complementors. An Empirical Look at Amazon.com." *Strategic Management Journal.* 39, no. 10: 2618–2642.

Zingales, Luigi. 2012. *A Capitalism for the People: Recapturing the Lost Genius of American Prosperity.* New York: Basic Books.

Zitzewitz, Eric W. 2003. "Competition and Long-Run Productivity Growth in the U.K. and U.S. Tobacco Industries, 1879–1939." *Journal of Industrial Economics.* 51, no. 1: 1–33.

Acknowledgments

My high school routinely fielded a top team on a citywide quiz show. Teams had three members, each of whom specialized in a different area: math and science, current events and history, and literature and humanities. In the tryouts, I ranked second in all three areas and so became first alternate. I suspect I was thwarted by my wide-ranging interests.

Like the quiz show, this book covers many academic fields. But unlike the show, the book synthesizes fields, so exposure to multiple disciplines is an advantage. In the course of writing, I have also been fortunate to benefit from the knowledge and insights of many first-teamers in those disciplines.

My greatest debt is to Andy Gavil and Steve Salop, who were exceptionally generous with their time and expertise. From the inception of this project, they discussed issues with me, commented on work in progress, and provided innumerable and invaluable suggestions. I also want to thank Dan Crane, Paul de Sa, Rich Gilbert, and Jon Sallet for reviewing and commenting on a draft. In addition, I am grateful to Tim Bresnahan, Carl Shapiro, and Robert Tsai for helpful discussions; to American University Washington College of Law for supporting this project through course releases and a sabbatical; to Sarah Pugh and Jonathan Wright for research assistance; to Simon Waxman for sharpening my exposition; and to Thomas LeBien for unwavering, timely, and knowledgeable editorial support. Chapter 5 was originally published as "Taking the Error Out of 'Error Cost' Analysis: What's Wrong with Antitrust's Right," *Antitrust Law Journal* 80, no. 1 (2015) and is reprinted here with minor edits by permission of the American Bar Association. Portions of Chapter 1 were originally published in March 2017 by The Washington Center for Equitable Growth in "Market Power in the U.S. Economy Today" and are reprinted here with permission.

Finally, I am grateful to many teachers and mentors, formal and informal, including Tim Bresnahan, Dick Bower, Gary Chamberlain, Bruce Lewis, Bob Pitofsky, Mitch Polinsky, Steve Salop, Joe Stiglitz, and Bobby Willig. Bobby may not remember it, but he came up with my title, *The Antitrust Paradigm*, two decades ago.

Index

Page numbers followed by n or nn indicate notes.